John Lodge

The Peerage of Ireland or a Genealogical History Of The Present Nobility of that Kingdom

Vol. IV

John Lodge

The Peerage of Ireland or a Genealogical History Of The Present Nobility of that Kingdom
Vol. IV

ISBN/EAN: 9783337271077

Printed in Europe, USA, Canada, Australia, Japan

Cover: Foto ©ninafisch / pixelio.de

More available books at **www.hansebooks.com**

THE
PEERAGE OF IRELAND:

OR,

A GENEALOGICAL HISTORY

OF THE

PRESENT NOBILITY

OF THAT

KINGDOM.

WITH ENGRAVINGS OF THEIR PATERNAL COATS OF ARMS.

Collected from Public Records, authentic Manuscripts, approved Historians, well-attested Pedigrees, and personal Information.

By JOHN LODGE, Esq.

Deputy Keeper of the Records in Birmingham Tower, Deputy Clerk and Keeper of the Rolls, and Deputy Register of the Court of Prerogative.

REVISED, ENLARGED AND CONTINUED TO THE PRESENT TIME;

By MERVYN ARCHDALL, A. M.

RECTOR OF SLANE IN THE DIOCESS OF MEATH, MEMBER OF THE ROYAL IRISH ACADEMY, AND AUTHOR OF THE MONASTICON HIBERNICUM.

VOL. IV.

DUBLIN:

JAMES MOORE, 45, COLLEGE-GREEN.

M DCC LXXXIX.

TO

THE RIGHT HONOURABLE

JAMES CAULFEILD,

EARL AND VISCOUNT OF CHARLEMOUNT,

BARON CAULFEILD,

KNIGHT OF THE MOST ILLUSTRIOUS ORDER OF ST. PATRICK,

ONE OF HIS MAJESTY's MOST HONORABLE PRIVY COUNCIL,

AND

PRESIDENT OF THE ROYAL IRISH ACADEMY,

THE FOURTH VOLUME OF

THE PEERAGE OF IRELAND,

IS RESPECTFULLY INSCRIBED BY

MERVYN ARCHDALL.

Butler, Visc.t Mountgarret

Villiers, Visc.t Grandison.

Annesley, Visc.^t Valentia.

Dillon-Lee, Visc.^t Dillon.

Netterville, Visct. Netterville

Needham, Visct. Kilmorey

Bourk, Visc.t Mayo.

Lumley Saunderson, Visc.t Lumley.

Smythe, Visc.t Strangford.

Wenman, Visc.t Wenman.

Taaffe, Visc.t Taaffe

Jones, Visc.t Ranelagh.

Fitz William, Visct. Fitz William.

Cockaine, Visct. Cullen.

THE
PEERAGE
OF
IRELAND.

VISCOUNTS.

BUTLER, Viscount MOUNTGARRET.

THE original descent of this illustrious family is diversely deduced by genealogists*, but we shall begin with Herveius, who is unquestionably proved by Sir James Ware, and William Roberts, Esq. Ulster King of Arms in the reign of K. Charles I. and by the indisputable authority of ancient records, to be the true and direct ancestor of the family.

I.

He

---

* Some writers assert, that their descent is derived from Godefroy or Geoffrey, Regent of Brionis, in Normandy, son of Richard, first duke of Normandy (grandson of Rollo) who was the father of Gislebert, surnamed Crispin, Earl of Brion, guardian to the Conqueror of England during his minority, whose son Richard, accompanied the Norman Duke in his expedition to England (his name being in the roll of Battel Abbey, amongst the Conqueror's attendants), and for his great services and propinquity of blood, was dignified with the Earldom of Clare.—He married Adeliza sister to Randolph Mcschines, Earl of Chester, and had five sons, viz. Gilbert, surnamed de Tonbridge, from whom descended the Earls of Clare, Gloucester, and Hertford, which ended in Gilbert, Earl of Clare, killed in the battle of Bannockburn, 8 July 1314 (8 Edward II.); Roger, and Walter, both died childless; Robert, and

BUTLER, Viscount MOUNTGARRET.

He accompanied the Conqueror in his expedition to England, and obtained large possessions in the counties of Norfolk, Suffolk, and Lancaster; in which he was succeeded by Herveius Walter, his son, having also a daughter Alicia, who became wife of Ormus Magnus.

Herveius and Richard, who both (their father being cup-bearer to the King) used in his life-time to execute that office for him and thence assumed the surname of Boutcillers.—Robert, at his father's death, had the office conferred upon him, and was cup-bearer to K. Henry I. in which he was succeeded by his eldest son Walter, whose son Herveius was father of Theobald the first *Butler* of Ireland. Mr. Carte, in his History of James, Duke of Ormond, disapproves of this pedigree (which was drawn by Mr John Butler a beneficed clergyman in the county of Northampton and cotemporary with Sir William Dugdale) for which he there assigns his reasons. Others [1] affirm that the first of this family was Gilbert, surnamed Becket, a native of London, not inferior to any of his fellow citizens, for kindred and riches, and superior to most of them in a singular good carriage, and holy conversation and who, in the flower of his youth, voluntarily received the Holy Cross to serve against the Infidels, and travelled into the Holy land; on his return, being taken prisoner and made an infidel Admiral's captive, he so continued for a year and a half during which time the Admiral's only daughter, (Mahold or Maud) was so taken with his good qualities and weighty reasoning, in matters concerning the Christian religion that obtaining his liberty by flight she forsook all and secretly followed him into England, where (after instruction in the Christian Religion and being baptised by the Bishop of London, in St Paul's Church in the presence of six prelates) she was married to him, and had two sons and two daughters viz. Thomas Becket Archbishop of Canterbury; Walter Fitz-Gilbert; Agnes, wife to Thomas Fitz-Theobald de Kelly; and Mary a nun, made (19 Henry II.) Abbess of Barking; [2] Walter married Matilda de Manfeo, and had a son Theobald Fitz-Walter (as appeareth by an ancient deed without date) of whom by Hooker, [3] in his Chronicle of the Conquest and Antiquities of Ireland it is thus written: " Theobald " Fitz-Walter who, by his nation was made Becket, but, by his wife, *Butler*, " was the son of Gilbert, and was the first *Butler* that came into Ireland, who " being a wife and expert man; was first sent thither with William Fitz-Adelm, " when he came over, Governor of the kingdom, upon the death of the Earl " of Chepstow, (who died 23 Henry II.) [4] and after with K. John 31 " Henry III. to view and search the country, and in the end, grew to such great " credit, that he was enfeoffed with great livings there, and also advanced, (and " his posterity after him) to great honours and promotions." And finding by several pedigrees made in England for Thomas, Earl of Ormond, and allowed and approved by the heralds there, and also by certain old books and pedigrees made in this kingdom, that the said Walter, father to the said Theobald, was the son of the said Gilbert Becket, and brother to the said holy martyr, Thomas Becket, Archbishop of Canterbury (says Robert Rothe, Esq. one of the counsel to Thomas Earl of Ormond and Ossory, in his Registry, collected in 1616, containing the pedigree, offices, and services, &c. out of the several Chronicles, pedigrees, records, and evidences of this family both in England and Ireland) But Mr. Richard Laurence signifies to the Duke of Ormond, (in a note before a copy of Mr. Rothe's registry) that having examined and compared this R. with Roberts's MS. genealogy, he found no material difference, but in the 3 first descents and the little paper annexed to Mr. Roberts's arguments carried so much truth and strength, and his authority quoted was so authentic and full for *Walter* rather than Becket, that it was not to be answered.

[1] Rothe's Registry. [2] Idem. [3] Hooker. p. 40. 54. [4] Idem.

BUTLER Viscount MOUNTGARRET.

Herveius Walter (which continued the furname until dif- Hervey Walter. ufed by Edmond, Earl of Carrick, when (according to the cuftom) the Chriftian name only was to be ufed with the title) married Maud, eldeft daughter of Theobald de Valoines, and had iffue five fons, Theobald, the firft Butler of Ireland, Hubert, Walter, Roger and Hamon.—Hubert, the fecond fon, was born at Weft-Derham in Norfolk, where he built a Monaftery; and encompaffed the tower of London with a ftrong wall and deep moat: He was brought up, with his brother Theobald, under Ranulph de Glanville, Juftice of England, his Uncle by the mother's fide; and in Henry IId's reign was one of the Barons of the Exchequer, and Dean of York; whence K. Richard I. advanced him (1 November 1189) to the fee of Salifbury; and being taken prifoner in the Holy Land, where he commanded the Englifh forces at the fiege of Acon, was tranflated (while there) in 1193 to the fee of Canterbury; and on his return, made Chancellor, Chief Juftice, and Treafurer of England; which laft great truft he managed fo well, that in two years, (befides defraying the public expences) he faved the King of his own revenue 110,000 marcs. He died of a fever, in July 1205, at his manor of Tenham, and was buried 13 at Canterbury.

Theobald, the eldeft fon, attended K. Henry II. into Theobald France, when that Prince came to an agreement with the Butler of French King on the behalf of Thomas Becket, Archbifhop Ireland. of Canterbury, murdered 28 December 1171; and the next year accompanied him into Ireland, where he ferved in the reduction of the kingdom, and being rewarded with very large poffeffions, made it the place of his refidence [1] having alfo conferred upon him the Butlerfhip of Ireland in the year 1177, whereby he and his fucceffors were to attend the Kings of England at their coronation, and that day prefent them with the firft cup of wine; for which they were to have certain pieces of the King's plate.—Some time after, that King granted him the prifage of wines, to enable him, and his heirs, the better to fupport the dignity of that office.* In 1185 he was witnefs to a charter of K. John, then Earl of Morton, to the canons of Lanthony, of the lands of Ballybemmer and other eftates. In 1 Richard

B 2

---

* By this grant, he had two tons of wine out of every fhip, which broke bulk in any trading port of Ireland, and was loaden with 20 tons of that commodity, and one ton from 9 to 20; fee a decree dated 12 February 1584, 27° D. and proportionably for a lefs quantity, if it amounted to nine tons.

[1] Rothe's Regiftry.

BUTLER, Viscount MOUNTGARRET.

Richard I. he accompted to the pipe-roll in the Exchequer 72l. 6s. 8d. of the suitage of the Knights of the honour of Lancaster.—In 1194, he was appointed by his brother Hubert, collector of the fees to be paid to the King by those, who should perform tournaments or feats of arms in England, viz. from an Earl 20 marcs; from a Baron 10; a Knight, who had lands, 4; and a Knight who had no lands, 2 marcs. In that reign he was a benefactor to the Abbey of Furnes in Lancashire; was a person of large possessions † in England and Ireland, being a Baron of both kingdoms; and, 6 Richard I, was appointed sheriff of the county of Lancaster, in which office he continued to the first of K. John inclusive, and founded a monastery therein at Cockersands, as he also did at Arklow for Cistertian Monks, [1] endowing it with his lands on the south side of the river, the Salt Pits, and the island of Arklow to found the Abbey on. He likewise in 1205 founded and endowed with all the lands of Wodeney O'Flinn, the impropriate rectories of Thurles and Arklow [2] the Abbey of Wotheney, or Woney (Abington) in the county of Limerick, having in the year 1200 founded and liberally endowed that of Nenagh in the county of Tipperary, being a priory or hospital of St. John Baptist, for the maintenance of Augustine canons, with a provision, that at least 13 sick persons should be maintained in the house, with the daily allowance of a loaf, drink, and a dish of meat, and as their possessions should encrease so the number of canons were to be augmented [3].

In 1204 he gave two Palfreys for licenfe to go into England, and dying in 1206 [4] was buried in a tomb, made for him in Wotheney Abbey. [5] He married Maud, daughter and heir to Robert de Vavafor, a great Baron of Yorkshire,

---

† Amongst which, was the Lordship of Preston in Amunderness in Lancashire, which was confirmed to him and his heirs by the charter of K. Richard, 22 April 1194; to be held by the service of three knights fees, and containing almost half that county. He had also a grant of the lands of Inchemeholmer, Kilsach, Kylnewy, Strehmoyl, Vothehan, Kylearnewy, and divers others, with the Advowson of the churches, and all liberties, from Richard, Archbishop of Dublin yielding to the Bishops of that see two marcs of silver yearly, and to each of the Cathedral churches two pounds of wax at Easter. And John, Earl of Morton, gave and confirmed to him the castle and town of Arklow, with the appurtenances, to hold by the service of one Knight's fee.

[1] Mon. Angl. V. 2. p. 1015. [2] Rothe's Register. [3] Mon. Angl. V. 2. p. 1044. [4] Rothe's Register. [5] Ibm. [6] Rothe.

BUTLER, Viscount MOUNTGARRET.

Yorkshire, (with whom he had the manors of Edlington and Newborough, and the lands of Bolton) and by her, who was afterwards married to Fulk Fitz-Warine [1] had one son Theobald, and a daughter Beatrix, to whom he gave a large estate in marriage with Thomas de Hereford, after whose death she remarried with Sir Hugh Purcell, Knight.

Theobald, the second, was about six years of age at his father's death and attaining his full age 5 Henry III. had a livery of his estate 18 July, 6th of that reign, and thereupon assumed the surname of Butler from the said office of Chief Butler of Ireland. He gave a considerable part of his lands at Sleiwn, with the tithes that lay near the church, to the priory of All-Saints in Dublin, [2] and in 1247 was L. J. of Ireland. He married Joan, eldest sister and co-heir to John de Marreis (de Marisco) (father of Herbert, father of Sir Stephen de Marreis, who died issueless 14 Richard II.) a considerable Baron in Ireland, to whose estates, both in this kingdom and in England, his posterity succeeded; and departing this life in 1248 (33 Hen. 3) was buried in the Abbey of Arklow; and left Theobald, the third, who was then also six years of age [3] and adhered to the King in his wars with the Barons. He married Margery, eldest daughter of Richard de Burgo, (ancestor to the Earl of Clanrickard) with whom he had, besides other lands, the manors of Ardmaile and Killmorarkill [4] and being buried by his father at Arklow, left Theobald, the fourth Butler of Ireland, who assisted K. Edward I. in his wars with Scotland, and married Joan fourth and youngest daughter of John Fitz-Geoffrey-Fitz-Peter de Barronis lord of Kirtling, and L. J. of Ireland, youngest son of the famous Geoffrey Fitz-Piers, Lord Justiciary of England; and co-heir with her three sisters to her brothers John and Richard. (She brought him the manor of Faubridge in Essex, the hamlet of Shippeley in Hants, the manor of Shire in Surrey, the Hamlet, called the Vacherie, and the manor of Ailesbury in Bucks) [5] and dying 26 September 1285 in the Castle of

Theobald, 2

Theobald, 3

Theobald, 4

---
[1] Idem. [2] Idem. [3] Idem, and Inq. post mortem taken in 1249, which found that he died seized of the manors of Bellagh and other lands in Staffordshire, the minor of Whichton in Lancashire, and Tiberley in Yorkshire. [4] Roths. [5] Mf. Annals. in Trin. Coll.

of Arklow, was buried in the monastery there, leaving issue by her, who died about 1303 (31 Edw. I.) two daughters, Maud and Joan, and eight sons, Theobald; Edmond created Earl of Carrick; Thomas, ancestor to the Baron of Dunboyne; John; Richard; Gilbert; Nicholas, elected Archbishop of Dublin by the Prior and Convent of the Holy Trinity in January 1306, but was never consecrated; and James.

Theobald, 5

Theobald, the fifth honorary Butler of Ireland, was present in the Irish Parliament of 1295, and stands the fifth on the Roll. In the spring of 1296 he attended the King in his invasion of Scotland, and accompanied him in all those expeditions, wherein Edinburgh, with the loss of 25,000 Scots, and all the fortresses of that kingdom, were reduced; and gained a great reputation by his valour.—In 1297 he * purchased from Philip de Rupella the manor of Bree in the county of Dublin, with all the lands of the Brinns; and also the cantred of Omany in Conaught, the lands in Cronn, and divers others. [1] He died unmarried at his manor of Turvey, 14 May 1290, and was buried 27 in Wotheney-Abbey, being succeeded in estate, and the Butlership of Ireland by his brother, [2].

Edmond, Earl of Carrick.

Edmond, who in 1302 sat in Parliament as a Baron, by the name of Edmond le Botiller, and about the feast of St. Hillary that year, recovered the manor of Hollywood near Ballymore from Richard, Archbishop of Dublin, (except the advowson of the church) reserving to the see two pounds of wax, and half an ounce of gold yearly, and releasing all his right to one messuage and five acres of land, with their appurtenances, in Luske.—He was knighted in London by K. Edward II. in 1309, and that year, with John, after Earl of Kildare, dispersed the rebellion in Conaught and Offaley; and in 1312, being L. D. he repressed the excursions of the Byrnes and Tooles, numerous and potent clans, forced them to submit; and being a great encourager of servitors, made a noble feast at Dublin on Sunday 29 of September 1313, when he created 30 Knights, [3] by patent, dated at Langley 4 January 1314, he was L. J. of Ireland, with the fee of 500l. a year, and 9 Edward II, held a Parliament at Kilkenny, to raise a subsidy for defence of the realm, against Edward Bruce and the Scots;

---

* Rothe says the deeds of purchase are in Birmingham Tower, 26 E. I.

[1] Rothe's Registry. [2] Id. [3] Mss. Ann.

Scots; for his services against whom, and the rebellious Irish, he was created Earl of Carrick-Mac Griffyne in the county of Tipperary, by patent, dated at Lincoln 1 September that year, 1315; and by a record of the same [1] date, had given him the return of all the King's writs in the cantreds of Oreman, Elyogerth, and Elyocarroll in Tipperary; to which was added, 12 November 1320, all the lands of William de Carran in Finagh and Faymolin in the county of Waterford; in which year (after many services against the O Mores, O Tooles, O Byrnes, O Murroughs, and other Irish septs) going on pilgrimage into Spain to the shrine of St. James of Compostella, he died after his return to London 13 September 1321, and was buried on St. Martin's eve at Gowran in the county of Kilkenny.

In 1302 he married Joan, daughter of John, the first Earl of Kildare, and by her had three sons and two daughters;

James, his successor in the Earldom and Butlership of Ireland. (1)

John, who died in 1330, from whom the present Earl of Carrick derives his descent. (2)

Laurence, who on the vigil of St. Cecilia the Virgin, in 1329, with Sir Henry Trahern, were taken prisoners by O Nolan, in Sir Henry's house of Kilbegg, in revenge of which, his brother James wasted their country. (3)

His daughter Joan was married 1321 to Roger Mortimer, second son of Roger, brother to Edward, Earl of March. (1)

—— to Sir Thomas Dillon of Drumrany, ancestor to the Viscount Dillon. (2)

James, who succeeded, was under age at his father's death, but notwithstanding his nonage, had a licence, 3 December 1325, for the fine of 2000 marcs, to marry whom he pleased; and 1 March 1326, had a grant and confirmation of the prize-wines; and was created Earl of Ormond (the north part of the county of Tipperary) by patent, bearing date 2 November 1328 at Salisbury, the K. then holding a Parliament there, with the creation-fee of 10l. a year out of the fee-farm of Waterford; and by patent, dated at Wallingford seven days after, in consideration of his services, and the better to enable him to support the honour, had given to him the regalities, liberties, knights fees, and other royal privileges of the county of Tipperary, and the rights of a palatine in that county for life; which being re-assumed by that King were restored to him again 23

James 1 Earl of Ormond.

April

[1] Enrolled. A°. 10°. Eliz. D.

April 1337, and with the prize-wines (which were also re-assumed by the King 17 November 1343) were granted in fee to his son James, and his heirs male, 5 June 1372 (46 Edw. III.) in virtue of which grant they were enjoyed by the family until the year 1716.

In 1336 he founded the friary of Carrick-Begg, on the river Suir in the county of Waterford for Franciscan Friars; to whom, 3 June that year, [2] he gave his castle and estate of Carrick, of which they took possession on Sunday the feast of St. Peter and Paul [3]. He is characterised by Clynn, the Annalist to be a liberal, amicable, facetious, and comely person, and dying in the flower of his youth, 6 January 1337, was buried at Gowran; having, in 1327, married Elenor, second daughter of Humphrey Bohun, the fourth Earl of Hereford and Essex, High Constable of England, (by Elizabeth his wife, seventh daughter of K. Edward I) and by her, who after married Sir Thomas Dagworth * had two sons and one daughter, viz. John, born at Ardee on St. Leonard's day 1330, died an infant; James his successor; and Petronilla, the first wife of Gilbert, Lord Talbot, ancestor to the Earl of Shrewsbury.

James, 2 Earl.
James, the second Earl of Ormond, was born at Kilkenny 4 October 1331, and given in ward, 1 September 1344, to Maurice, Earl of Desmond, for the fine of 2300 marcs; and afterwards to Sir John Darcy L. J. of Ireland, who married him to his daughter Elizabeth. He was usually called the noble Earl, on account of his descent from the Royal Family; and by the Irish, James the Chaste, an appellation procured by his modesty and virtue. Through his extraction, and in recompence of his services, he obtained several grants of lands and other favours from K. Edward III. and Richard II. 18 April 1359, he was appointed L. J. of the kingdom, as he was again, 15 March 1360, in which year he published proclamations, and made divers regulations, for the advancement of the English interest in Ireland; and did great service against the rebellious Irish in the provinces of Ulster, Leinster, and Munster. 8 September 1361, Lionel, Duke of Clarence, third son of K.

---

* A commission, dated at Dublin 18 October 1344, 18 Edward III. was granted to this Thomas de Dagworth, and Alianore his wife, of the custody of the castles of Nenagh and Moialiny with the appurtenances, and the manors of Karkenliff, Bretage, and Carriemacgriffin in Munster; which, by reason of the minority of James, Earl of Ormond, were in the King's hands, to hold till he accomplished his full age, rendering yearly into the Exchequer the full extent hereof.

[1] Rot. A°. 17°. Edw. III. D. R. 8. [2] Ms. Annals in Trin Col. [3] Id.

K. Edward III, being made L. L. he attended him from England with many other great men, having an allowance for himself of 4 s. a day and for his retinue; 2 s. a-piece for two Knights; 12 d. for 17 Esquires; 6 d. for 20 hobellars armed; and 4 d. for as many unarmed. In 1362, he slew 600 of Mac Murrough's followers at Teigstaffen in the county of Kilkenny; and 2 April 1364, was appointed L. D. to the said Duke of Clarence; as he was L. J. 24 July 1376, with the usual salary of 500l. a year, in which office he was continued by K. Richard II. On 2 April 1372, he was made constable of the Castle of Dublin, with the fee of 18l. 5s. a year; was summoned to the Parliaments held by K. Richard II; and 16 January 1381, had a commission dated at Cork, during pleasure, to treat with all rebels, English and Irish, though indicted and outlawed, and to grant them safe conducts, in order to reform them to peace, and preserve the tranquillity of the country; so as such treating should not tend to the prejudice of the King's faithful subjects. He died 18 October 1382 (or 1383) in his castle of Knocktopher (near which he had, in 1356, founded a Friary for Carmelite friars) and was buried in the Cathedral of St. Canice in Kilkenny.

By his said wife, (who re married with Sir Robert Herford, and by her deed, 5 Rich. II, surrendered to her son all her dower in Ireland, except that of the prize wines) he had two sons, James, his heir, then under age; Thomas who by commission, dated at Kilkenny 25 May 1380, was constituted, with Nicholas White of Clonmell, the King's Justices in the county of Cork, during pleasure, to inquire upon oath, of all seditions, transgressions, felonies, oppressions, conspiracies, confederacies, and other crimes whatsoever, committed against the K. or his liege people, and to administer justice throughout that county, &c. and two daughters, Ellen married to Gerald, Earl of Desmond, and died in 1404; and Joan to Teige O Carrol, Prince of Elye, and died of the plague in 1383.

James, the third Earl of Ormond, by building and making the castle of Gowran his usual residence, was commonly called Earl of Gowran; but, 12 September 1391, he concluded the purchase of the castle of Kilkenny † which became

James 3 Earl.

† This castle was built by William, Earl Marshal, the elder, who came into Ireland in 1207; and also founded the House of the Black Friars there; and his son William succeeding him in 1220, granted a charter to the town 6 April 1223, with privileges, which they enjoy to this day. The Earl of Ormond

became the chief seat of the family. He also built the castle of Dunsert, (commonly called Danes-Fort) and in 1386 founded a Friary of minorites at Ailesbury in Bucks. In 1384 he was deputy of the kingdom to Philip de Courtenay, the King's cousin; and, 25 July 1392, again made L. J. as he was in 1401; and 26 October 1404, on the departure of Sir Stephen Scrope to England. By commission, dated at Carlow, 12 February 1388-9, he was appointed (by reason of the excessive losses and damages, sustained by the King's liege subjects in the counties of Kilkenny and Tipperary, by the Irish and English rebels) keeper of the peace and governor of those counties and the people thereof, as well within liberties as without, with full power to treat with, to execute, to protect, and to give safe conduct to any rebels, &c. In 1397 he assisted Edmond Earl of March, L. L. against O Brien, and in 1399 took prisoner Teige O Carrol, Prince of Elye, who escaping the year after from Gowran, was slain in 1407 by the L. D. Scrope. By commission dated at Kilkenny 9 May 1400, he, Sir Edward Perers, and others, were appointed Commissioners of Oyer and Terminer in the counties of Kilkenny, Wexford, Waterford, Tipperary, Cork, and Limerick; and, 30 May 1401, a writ, dated at Trim, by Thomas, Earl of Lancaster, L. L. was directed to him and John Lumbard, appointing them justices or commissioners of Oyer and Terminer in the county of Kilkenny, to adjourn the Parliament summoned to meet at Kilkenny; and on the anniversary of St Vitalis the martyr in 1404 [1] he held a Parliament in Dublin, which confirmed the statutes of Dublin and Kilkenny, and the charter of Ireland. Being a mighty strong man, he is stiled in some annals, the head of the chivalry of Ireland, which kingdom he governed to the content of the King and his good subjects [2]. He married Anne, daughter of John Lord Welles, and dying 7 September on the vigil of the Blessed Virgin [3] 1405 at Gowran, greatly regretted, after his return from invading O Connor's country, was there buried, leaving two sons, James his heir; and Sir Richard Butler, whose god-father was K. Richard II, of whom mention will be made hereafter.

James,

Ormond purchased the castle, with divers manors and lordships, from the heirs of Sir Hugh le Despenser, Earl of Gloucester and Isabel his wife, daughter and coheir to Gilbert de Clare, Earl of Gloucester.

[1] MS. Annals T. Coll. [2] Lodge. [3] Annals.

James, the fourth Earl of Ormond, commonly called the White Earl, was a man of good parts, and master of a great share of learning, (which at that time was very rare in noblemen) and before he attained his full age, was, on Whitsunday, 4 Henry VI, together with the King, knighted by John, Duke of Bedford, the King's uncle and regent; after which, returning into Ireland, he accompanied the deputy Scrope in his invasion of Mac-Murrough's territory, when that sept was routed, and O Nolan, with his son and many others, made prisoners [1] and being informed that Walter de Burgo and O Carrol had ravaged the county of Kilkenny, they marched to Callan with such expedition, that they surprized and defeated the rebels with the slaughter of at least 800. [2] On his return to Dublin, not yet being of age (for that year his wardship was granted to Thomas, Duke of Lancaster, son of K. Henry IV) he was left L. D. of the kingdom, his commission bearing date 18 December 1407; 9 Henry IV. and held a Parliament there, which again confirmed the statutes of Dublin and Kilkenny, and the charter granted under the Great Seal of England [3]. Richard Plantagenet, Duke of York, having a son born in Dublin, well known afterwards by the name of George Duke of Clarence, his Lordship and the Earl of Desmond, were god-fathers. In harvest, 1412, he accompanied Thomas of Lancaster, Duke of Clarence, into France, in which year Henry V. mounting the Throne, he was in great favour with that victorious Monarch †; by whom he was appointed L. L. by a very large commission, bearing date 10, February 1419, and landing at Waterford 10 April, held a Parliament 7 June on St. Laurences day [3] which granted the King two subsidies, and to himself 70 marcs; after which he made great preys upon O Reily, [4] Mac-Murrough, (who at that time made all Leinster tremble) Mac-Mahon, and others; for his services against whom the Parliament granted him a further sum of 300 marcs after the feast of St. Andrew [5]. On the nones of

James,
4
Earl.

---

† At his motion his Majesty first created a King of arms in Ireland, appointing John K teley, herald in England, to that office, by the title of Ireland King of Arms; which continued as long as the Kings of England were stiled Lords of Ireland, when it was altered by Henry VIII. to that of Ulster King of Arms, Bartholomew Butler, York Herald, being the first so appointed: And his son Philip Butler was the first pursuivant at arms in Ireland, being so created 16 June 1552, by the title of Athlone pursuivant, by John, Duke of Northumberland, Earl Marshal of England.

[1] Id.   [2] Id.   [3] Id.   [4] Mf. Annals in T. Coll.   [5] Id.

of May 1421, a slaughter was committed on the family of the Earl, whilst L. L. near the monastery of Leys, where 27 English were slain, the chief of whom were Purcel and Grant, noblemen, ten were taken prisoners and 200 saved themselves by flight, in the castle; and 7 June the Earl invaded Leys, and obliged the Irish to sue for peace [1].

K. Henry V deceasing 31 August 1422, his Lordship was continued in the government until the arrival of Edmond Mortimer, Earl of March, to whom, 9 May 1424, he was made deputy, as he was the next year to John, Lord Furnival, and again 15 April 1426; and 13 September following, he sent James Cornwalsh, chief baron of the Exchequer, to lay before the King and council the state of affairs, and to prosecute several matters relating to the benefit and preservation of the kingdom, for which he was allowed 6 s. 8 d. a day. Also, 28 August 1427, he declared to the council, that he had expended 40 marcs in resisting Gerald O Cavenagh, an Irish enemy, who had lately assembled a multitude of Kerns, to destroy the king's subjects; for which sum he had a liberate 11 October following; and the day after, another for 50 marcs, for maintaining and keeping in safe custody, divers Irish hostages, for the good conduct of Bernard Mac-Mahon and Neylan O Donnel, captains of their nations, Owen O Neile and Meiler Birmingham.

In 1440 he was twice again made chief governor, first as L. L. and after as L. D. and that year had the temporalties of the fee of Cashel granted to him for ten years, after the death of the Archbishop, Richard O Hedian.—In 1443 he was again made L. L. and 24 June 1444, he assembled at Drogheda many of the privy council, nobility, and gentry of the English Pale, and declared, that he had now held the place of chief governor of the kingdom for the space of three years and more, and that it had pleased the King by his letter and writ under the privy seal, sent by Robert Mansfield, Esq; groom of his bedchamber, to command him over to his presence, without delay or excuse, notwithstanding the commotions then subsisting in Ireland; wherefore he required of them, that they would declare before the said messenger, if he had committed, during his government, any extortion contrary to the laws, or had been remiss in executing the laws. Whereupon, after some time spent in consideration of his conduct, Sir James Allen declared, that there was not one there that could in any matter

---

[1] Mf. Annals in Trin. Coll.

ter complain of him, but were all fully thankful to him for his good and gracious government; for the pains he had taken in defence of the land, having undergone great and continual labours; and had also, besides the allowance of the government, been at great expence for the honour of the King and defence of the kingdom; and added, that if at that time he should leave the kingdom, it would be exposed to great danger; and desired that Richard Wogan Chancellor, father Hugh Mideleton, or Robert Mansfield, would repair to the King, and procure a safe passage for him; and declare, that there was then great confederacy to destroy his liege subjects, and that if it pleased his highness to give the L. L. leave to stay till Michaelmas, so that his subjects might gather in their harvest, it would be a great comfort to them, and confusion to their enemies. Upon this representation, the King dispensed with his attendance in England: But two years after (1446) some of the Lords and Commons petitioned his Majesty for his removal, setting forth, " That he was old and feeble, and had lost " many of his old castles for want of defence, and there- " fore was not likely to maintain, much less enlarge, the " King's possessions in Ireland." Upon this he was dismissed, though the bishop and chapter of Cork, the corporations of Cork and Youghall, the Lords Barry, Roche, and others, gave a full testimonial of his great services; which however had this good effect, that the next year, when the Earl of Shrewsbury L. L. accused him of high treason before the Duke of Bedford, Constable of England, in the Marshal's court, the King quashed the accusation; and examining the cause himself, was so fully convinced of its being founded in malice, that he ordered all the proceedings to be cancelled, and declared by patent, 20 September 1448, " That the Earl of Ormond was faithful in " his allegiance, meritorious in his services, and untainted " in his fame; that no one should dare, on pain of his in- " dignation, to revive the accusation, or reproach his con- " duct; and that his accusers were men of no credit, nor " should their testimony be admitted in any case." And a writ reciting all this, dated 21 November, attested by his mortal enemy, Richard, Archbishop of Dublin, deputy to his brother Shrewsbury, was sent to the Magistrates of Limerick and other towns, to cause proclamation thereof to be made throughout the kingdom.

His Lordship was a great lover of history and antiquities, and gave lands for ever to the College of Heralds, for which,
until

until the reformation of religion, he was prayed for in all their public meetings, and constantly after remembered as a special benefactor. He built the castles of Tulcophelim, Nenagh, Roscrea, and Templemore; and gave the manor and advowson of Huckcote in Bucks to the Hospital of St. Thomas D'Acres in London, which was confirmed by Parliament 3° Hen. VI. at the suit of his son. He married first Johan, daughter of Gerald, the fifth Earl of Kildare, who dying 3 August 1430, was buried in the said hospital; and secondly in 1432, Elizabeth, daughter of William Beauchamp, Lord Bergavenny, and widow of John, Lord Grey of Wilton; but by her, who died 6 August 1452, a few days before him, he had no issue; having by the first three sons, James, John, and Thomas, successive Earls of Ormond; and two daughters, Elizabeth, the second wife of John, the second Earl of Shrewsbury, and died on the Saturday after the nativity of the Virgin Mary [1] in 1473; and Anne, who died unmarried, and lies buried in the church of Shene in Surrey, under a marble gravestone, on the north side of the High Altar, with this memorial;

  Hic jacet Anna filia Comitis d'ORMOND, quæ
  Obiit IV. die Januar. Anno Dni MCCCCXXXV.

He died at Ardee 23 August 1452, on his return from an expedition against Connor O Mulrian, and was buried in St. Mary's Abbey near Dublin; being succeeded by his eldest son

James 5 Earl.
James, the fifth Earl of Ormond, who was born 24 November 1420, and knighted when very young by K. Henry VI. with whom he was in great esteem. He attended Richard, Duke of York, Regent of France into that kingdom; and, in consideration of his adherence and fidelity to the Lancastrian interest against the House of York, was created a Peer of England 8 July 1449, by the title of Earl of Wiltshire, to him and the heirs male of his body; and in 1450 constituted one of the commissioners, to whom the custody of Calais, the tower of Risebank and Marches of Picardy were committed for the term of five years.—In 1451 he was made L. D. of Ireland, the next year succeeding his father in the title of Ormond, was appointed L. L. 12 May 1453 for ten years; and that year going to England, he undertook, with the Earl of Salisbury, and other Lords,

[1] MS. Annals in Trin. Coll.

Lords, the guarding of the seas for three years, receiving the tonage and poundage to support the charge thereof ¹ also 15 March 1455, was appointed Lord High Treasurer of England; and shortly after attended the King at the battle of St. Albans, where the Yorkists prevailing, he fled, casting his armour into a ditch; yet, on a turn of affairs, was restored to his post of Treasurer 37 Henry VI. and the next year created a Knight of the Garter, and made keeper of the forest or park of Pederton in Somersetshire, and of Cranbourn Chace in the counties of Wilts and Dorset.—He soon after fitted out five great ships of Genoa, to fight the Earl of Warwick's fleet, with which he sailed to the Netherlands; but returning before the battle of Wakefield, fought 31 December 1460, he commanded one wing of the army, which inclosed and slew the Duke of York, father of K. Edward, IV; but 29 March 1461, being at the bloody battle of Towton-Field, he was taken prisoner by Richard Salkeld; beheaded at Newcastle 1 May, and in the ensuing Parliament, which met 4 November, attainted.

He married three wives; first Avicia, only daughter of John Fitz-Alan, Earl of Arundel, Duke of Touraine in France, and heir to her brother Humphry, who died 16 Henry VI; to his second, Avicia, daughter of Sir Richard Stafford, a great heiress; and to his third, Elenor, eldest daughter of Edmond Beaufort, Duke of Somerset, and Earl of Mortaigne in Normandy, and coheir to her brother, Edmond Duke of Somerset, beheaded 5 May 1471, two days after the battle of Tewksbury for his adherence to the Lancastrian line; ² but having no issue, was succeeded by his brother

John, the sixth Earl of Ormond, who was knighted at Leicester by the Duke of Bedford, the King's uncle, ³ for his faithful adherence to K. Henry VI. for which he was also attainted; yet by K. Edward IV. was restored in blood, and to all his estates, except the manor and hundred of Rochford, and other lands in Essex.—That King was used to say of him, "That he was the goodliest Knight he "ever beheld, and the finest gentleman in Christendom; "and that if good breeding, nurture, and liberal qualities "were lost in the world, they might all be found in John, "Earl of Ormond." He was a perfect master of all the languages of Europe; and there was scarce a Court in it,

John, 6 Earl.

¹ Lodge. ² Id. ³ Id.

to which that Prince did not send him as Ambassador; but, in a fit of devotion, making a journey to Jerusalem, he died in the Holy Land, 1478, unmarried, and was succeeded by his only brother

Thomas, 7, Earl.

Sir Thomas Butler, the seventh Earl of Ormond, who was also attainted; but in November 1485 restored by Henry VIIth's first Parliament; and the statutes made at Westminster, 1 Edward IV. which declared him and his brothers traitors, were utterly abrogated. He was soon after sworn of the Privy Council of England; in 1491 accompanied the King with a powerful army, in aid of Maximilian the Emperor against the French; in 1492 was appointed Chamberlain to the Queen; and in September that year, sent with Thomas Goldston, Prior of Canterbury, Ambassadors to Charles VIII. K. of France, to transact a treaty between the two crowns. In 1494 he accompanied the L. D. into Ulster, when the territories of O Hanlon and Magennis were wasted; and 14 October 1495, was summoned as a Baron to the English Parliament, by the title of Thomas Ormond de Rochford; and in 1497 sent Ambassador to the Duke of Burgundy.

He departed this life * 8 August 1515, and was buried in the church of St. Thomas D'Acres, London, now called Mercer's Chapel in Cheapside, with this epitaph to his memory, as preserved by Weever: hic jacet Thomas filius Jac. 6. Ormandiæ, ac frater Jac. 6 Wilts et Orm: qui quidem Thomas ob. 2 die Aug. 1515, et Anno regni Regis Henrici. 8. 7. cujus—¹ leaving issue by Anne, daughter and heir to Sir Richard Hankford by Anne, eldest daughter of John Montacute, the third Earl of Salisbury, ² two daughters, heirs to his estate in England, containing 72 manors, with divers other lands, and to several lands in Ireland; whereof Anne was married to Sir James St. Leger, ancestor

---

* This appears by inquisition taken that year in the county of Dublin, finding that he died seized of the manors of Luske, Turvy, Rushe and Ballscaddan. He left 40,000l. in money, besides jewels, and as much land in England, as at this day would yield 30,000l. a year, so that he was said to be the richest subject of that time; on 31 July before he made his will, and therein left to his grandson Sir Thomas Bulleyne, and his issue male, remainder to Sir George St. Leger and his issue male, remainder to the next issue male of his grandfather James, Earl of Ormond, " a white horn of Ivory, garnished " at both the ends with gold, and corse thereunto of white silk, barred with " bars of gold. Lodge.

¹ Weever p. 400. ² Lodge.

Ancestor to the family of Eggesford in Devonshire; and Margaret, to Sir William Bullen, Knight of the Bath, by whom she had Sir Thomas Bullen, created 18 June 1525, Baron and Viscount Rochford, and 29 November 1527 Earl of Wiltshire and Ormond; who dying in 1538, had issue by Elizabeth, daughter of Thomas, Duke of Norfolk, George, Lord Rochford, beheaded 17 May 1536; and two daughters, the Ladies Anne and Mary; the younger of whom was married to William Carey, father by her of Henry, Lord Hunsdon; and the elder, 25 January 1532, to K. Henry VIII, and after living his wife three years, three months, and 25 days, was beheaded 19 May 1536, and buried in the chapel of the Tower, leaving one daughter, the Lady Elizabeth, born at Greenwich on Sunday 7 September 1533, who succeeded to the Crown of England and Ireland on Thursday 17 November 1558.

To Thomas, Earl of Ormond, succeeded his next heir male Sir Pierce Butler, descended from Sir Richard, younger son of James, the third Earl of Ormond. Which Sir Richard was seated at Poolestown in the county of Kilkenny, and married Catharine, daughter of Gildas O Reily, Lord of the county of Cavan; by whom he had Sir Edmond Butler Mac Richard, who built the castle of Potletsrath, and the castle and bridge of Carrick, and dying 13 June 1464, was buried in the Grey Friars, Kilkenny, leaving issue by Catharine, (who died in 1506) daughter of Moelrony O'Carroll, *Burbutus*, three sons, Sir James, Walter, and John who had two sons, Pierce (the father of Richard Butler Fitz Pierce, who died childless) and John-oge, whose son [1] William Butler Fitz-John-oge, was attainted of felony at Kilkenny, and executed in Queen Elizabeth's Reign.

Walter, the second son, had issue Edmond of Poolestown, who had four sons, Walter, Peter, Theobald, and Richard. Peter, the second Son, was of Roscrea, and by his wife Catharine de Burgo, had three sons, who all died without issue, and were, Edmond; Walter, who being a commander under the Emperor, had given him the Lordship of Hesberg in Germany, which descended to the House of Poolestown; and Theobald, who died in Poland in 1634. Walter Fitz-Edmond, the eldest son, who succeeded at Poolestown,

Family of Poolestown Baronets.

[1] Lodge's Collect.

Pooleſtown, had iſſue Sir Richard his heir; Thomas of Clonmore in the county of Carlow, and a daughter Joan, *

Sir Richard of Pooleſtown died 20 Auguſt 1619, leaving Edmond, Richard, Peter, and Walter. Edmond was then 24 years age, and 20 November 1618, had a ſpecial livery of his eſtate. He [1] married Ellice, daughter of Nicholas Shortall of Claragh in the county of Kilkenny, and dying 21 April 1636, was buried in Kilkenny, according to directions in his will, bearing date the 13th, becauſe his anceſtors were uſed to be buried there; having had iſſue Walter, Theobald, Pierce, Richard, Thomas; Ellice, married to Murtogh Cavenagh, of Garryhill in the county of Carlow, Eſq; Margaret, Anne, Elizabeth, and Ellen. Sir Walter, the eldeſt ſon, was created a Baronet by privy ſeal, dated at Oxford 19 April 1643, and by patent at Dublin 8 July 1645, and marrying Elizabeth, eldeſt daughter of Richard, the third Viſcount Mountgarret, left iſſue by her, who died 21 Auguſt 1636, Sir Richard Butler of Pooleſtown, the ſecond Baronet, who died in 1686, leaving one ſon (by his wife Elizabeth, who re-married with Theobald Denn Eſq;) [2] Sir Walter; and three daughters, whereof ―――― was married to Pierce Aylward of Shankill in the county of Kilkenny, Eſq; and had a ſon Nicholas, the father of John Aylward Eſq; late of ſame place; [3] and Heſter, in May 1698, to James Butler of Cournellane in the county of Carlow, Gent.―Sir Walter Butler, the third Baronet, was born in 1679, and died 8 October 1723, having been for ſome time lunatick.―He married in April 1697 Lucy, daughter of Walter Butler of Garryricken, Eſq; and by her who died in 1703, had one ſon Richard, who died before him, and a daughter Mary, who after the deceaſe of her mother was taken into the care of her uncle, Thomas Butler of Kilcaſh, Eſq; by whom ſhe was ſent abroad to a Convent, where [4] ſhe became a profeſſed Nun.

Sir James Butler (eldeſt ſon of Sir Edmond Mac Richard) ſided with the Houſe of Lancaſter againſt K. Edward IV. for which he was attainted; but when that King was ſettled on the Throne, he overlooked this miſtake in his conduct, and

---

* It was agreed upon by bond dated 10 January 1573, that Richard ſhould marry Ellen, daughter of Gerald and grand-daughter of Edmond Blanchvield, and that the ſaid Gerald's eldeſt ſon Leonard, ſhould marry the ſaid Walter Butler's daughter Joan 5.

[1] Chan. decree, dated 12 Feb. 1596.   [2] Id.   [3] Id.   [4] Id.   [5] Id.

and an Act of Parliament passed in Ireland, repealing all attainders, judgments, and outlawries, against him the said James Butler Fitz-Edmond Fitz-Richard; and the King, in consideration of his faithful services from that time, granted him, 11 April 1468, among other things) the manor and advowson of Callan for life: And 12 October 1477, he was constituted by John, Earl of Ormond, his attorney and deputy, to manage his lands and jurisdictions in Ireland; by virtue whereof he laid down a certain order for the reformation and good government of the town of Carrick. He was well beloved in his country, being a promoter of peace; was knighted, and built the castle of Nehom near Gowran; but dying 16 April 1487, was buried in the priory of Augustine eremites at Callan, of which priory he was the founder.—He married Sawe (Sabina) daughter of Donnell Reogh Mac Murrough Cavenagh, Prince of his sept, and by her, who died in 1508, left issue two sons and two daughters.

    Pierce, who became Earl of Ormond. (1)

    John Fitz James Butler, Esq; whose only daughter and heir, Margaret, was married to Edmond Blanchville of Blanchville's-Town in the county of Kilkenny, Esq; (2)

    Daughter Margaret was the second wife of Sir Alexander Plunket of Rathmore, Chancellor of Ireland in the reign of K. Henry VII. (1)

    Ellice, the first wife of Sir George Fleming of Stephen's-town, second son of James Lord Slane, and was mother of James, who by Ismay, daughter of Sir Bartholomew Dillon of Riverstown, Chief Justice of the King's Bench, had Thomas who succeeded to the title of Slane,[1] and was ancestor to the Lord Slane. (2)

    Sir Pierce Butler, the eighth Earl of Ormond, in 1516 accompanied the Deputy into Imaly against O Toole, O Carrol, and other rebels; and 6 March 1521 was appointed L. D. to Thomas, Earl of Surrey, his intimate friend, who consulted him during his Administration, in all matters of moment; and he did very great service in suppressing rebellions, and distributing justice to all good subjects. 13 May 1524, he was made Lord Treasurer of Ireland; and the King conferring the title of Ormond on Thomas Bullen, Viscount *Sir Pierce 8 Earl.*

---

[1] Lodge's Collect.

BUTLER, Viscount MOUNTGARRET.

Viscount Rochford, at his earnest suit, did in lieu * thereof create Sir Pierce (who to satisfy the King's pleasure, had been contented to resign his ancient and rightful title of Ormond) Earl of Ossory by patent, dated at Westminster 23 February 1527, with the creation annuity of 20l. out of the manor of Newcastle of Lyons in the county of Dublin.

Soon after this, he returned to Ireland, where, 13 May 1528, he was chosen L. D. by the Council, and proceeding through the city on horseback to St. Mary's Abbey, was there sworn into that office †.—And Thomas Bullen, Earl of Ormond, dying without issue male, the King, 22 February 1537, restored him to the title of Ormond, which was confirmed to the family at the suit of his son James, Earl of Ormond, by Act of Parliament 6 November 1541; and in consideration of the eminent services of himself and son, performed in the wars of Ireland, he had a grant and confirmation, dated at Westminster 23 October 1537, to them respectively for life, and to the heirs male of his body, of all their estates ‡ in the counties of Kilkenny, Tipperary, Carlow, Dublin, Kildare, Meath, Wexford, Waterford, and Wicklow, to hold by the service of one Knight's fee.

He was a man of unshaken honour and integrity; familiar and liberal to his friends; an enemy and severe scourge to rebels and malefactors; was very religious through the course of his life; and every year, in the last fortnight of Lent, retired from all business, and lay during that time in a chamber

---

* The King also 5 November 1526. granted to him and his Heir Male, the manors, castles, and hereditaments of Callan, Ballycallan, Darmagh, Kylmanagh, in the county of Kilkenny; Lissronagh, and Kylmo re O Cushing, &c. in Tipperary.

† By patent, dated at Westminster 26 February 1534, the King granted to him and his Heirs Male, all such lands, as he should conquer or recover from the Irish rebels in his dominion of Ossory, to hold in Capite; and made him Seneschal, Constable and Governor of the manor and castle of Dungarvan, with the fee of 100l. a year for life; remainder to his son and heir James for life; remainder to the son and heir of the said James for life; remainder to the King and his heirs for ever. ᵃ And 31 May 1535 being, with his son, made Governor of the counties of Kilkenny, Tipperary, and Waterford, and the territories of Ossory and Ormond, they engaged to use their utmost endeavours to recover the said castle of Dungarvan from the forcible intrusion of the Earl of Desmond; and to resist the usurpations of the Bishop of Rome; which Sir R. Cox observes, is the first engagement he had met with of that kind.

‡ Consisting (among other hereditaments of the manors of Gowran, Dunfert, Knocktopher, Kilkenny, Glashare, Rosbareon, Catrick, Killandule, Thures, Knockgraffan, Nenph, Referes, Rathvile, Clonmore, Leighlin, Rushe and Ballesaddan. (Lodge)

ᵃ Rot. Pat Annis 19° 25°. H. n. 8. f.

a chamber near St. Canice Church, called Paradise; where, by prayers and alms, he prepared himself for the reception of the sacrament on the approaching festival of Easter. He and his Lady, with whom he lived many years in great honour and prosperity, planted great civility in the counties of Kilkenny and Tipperary; and, to give that people an example of industry, brought from Flanders and elsewhere, artificers, whom they employed in their castle of Kilkenny, to work diaper, tapestry, Turkey-carpets, cushions, and other like works, some whereof remained there till of late years. He married in 1485 Margaret, † second daughter of Gerald the eighth Earl of Kildare, and dying in the favour of his Prince, and the love of his friends, 21 or 26 August 1539, was buried under a monument in the chancel of St. Canice's Church, leaving issue three sons and six daughters viz.

James his successor, commonly called the Lame. * (1)
Richard, created Viscount of Mountgarret. (2)
Thomas, slain by Dermoid Mac Shane, Mac Gill-Patrick of Ossory, and left an only daughter Margaret, first married to Rory O More of Leix, and lastly to Sir Maurice Fitzgerald of Lackagh. (3)

Daughter, Lady Margaret, first married to Thomas, second son of the Earl of Desmond, and secondly, to Barnaby the first Lord of Upper-Ossory. (1)

Lady Catherine, first married to Richard Lord Poer, secondly to James Earl of Desmond, and died in 1552. (2)

Lady Joan, to James Butler Lord Dunboyne. (3)
Lady Ellice, first to Mac Morrish; and secondly to Gerald Fitz-John Fitzgerald, of Dromana, Lord of Decies. (4)
Lady Eleanor to Thomas Butler Lord Cahier. (5)
Lady Ellen, to Donogh O'Brien, Earl of Thomond. (6)

Richard

* We shall here pursue the descent of this noble family, in the eldest branch, to its failure in the person of Charles Earl of Arran, and shall add thereto the line of its present Representative.

James

† She survived him a few years, and led a most exemplary life for charity and devotion; she built a school near the Church-Yard of St. Canice; rebuilt the castle of Gowran, and was called the *great Countess of Ormond*. Stanihurst thus writes of her: "The Earl was of himself a plain and simple " gentleman, saving in feats of arms; and yet nevertheless he bare out his ho- " nour and charge of his government very worthily, through the singular wis- " dom of his Countess; a Lady of such port, that all estates of the realm, " crouched unto her, so politic, that nothing was thought substantially de- " bated

Richard 1. Viscount.

Richard, the second son is described to have been a Knight of goodly personage, and as comely a man as could be seen; he was a very honourable and worthy gentleman, and performed many great services to the Crown of England;

James 9 Earl.

James, the ninth Earl of Ormond, was a most honourable and worthy nobleman, and in great esteem with K. Henry VIII. In the last Session of whose Parliament held 13 June, an Act passed for confirming the title of Ormond, of the following tenor viz. " Whereas sithence the 9th year of the reign of the noble Prince of famous memory K. Edward III. unto 6 Hen. VIII. James, James, James, James, James, John and Thomas Butler, Earls of Ormond, have had and enjoyed, the one after the other, the name, honour, degree, style, title, and dignity of Earl of Ormond with a yearly annuity of 10l Irish, in of and upon the fee farm of the city of Waterford for the better maintenance of the said name of Earl of Ormond; and from the decease of the said Thomas, which died the said 6 Hen. VIII. unto the 19 year of his Grace's Reign, for that the said Thomas late Earl of Ormond died without issue male of his body, Peter Butler Knight, as cousin and next heir male to the said Thomas, that is the son to James, son to Edmund, son to Richard, brother to James, father to the said Thomas, late Earl of Ormond, as well by our Sovereign Lord the King that now is, Grace's sundry letters patents, and many his letters missives and otherwise, as also by all others has been named, reputed, accepted and taken as Earl of Ormond and had and yearly received the said annuity of 10l. Irish; and after again our said most dread Sovereign Lord by his letters patents the 29 year of his reign made to the said Peter, did name the said Peter Earl of Ormond, sithence which time the said Peter till his death, and James his son and heir, father unto these present, has by our said Sovereign Lord and all others, been named, called, accepted, and taken, as Earl of Ormond aforesaid. In consideration whereof, and for the right faithful and laudable service which the said Peter and James, his said son and heir ever have done the King, our said Sovereign Lord's Majesty, his Highness of his most bounteousness and goodness extended to the said James, son to the said Peter, to the intent that all desires, ambiguities, arguments, reasons, and questions for the title that hereafter *mought chaunce* to *sourde* rise, or be made to the said James, or any other the heir male of the body of the said Peter, concerning the same name of honour

---

" bated, without her advice; she was manlike and tall of stature; very liberal
" and bountiful; a secure friend; a bitter enemy; hardly disliking, where she
" fancied, not easily fancying, where she disliked."

land; as a recompence for which, the Lords of the council, in their letter to the L. D. St. Leger, dated at Windfor 5 Auguſt 1550, tranſmitted [1] the directions of K. Edward VI. to create him Viſcount Mountgarret * which was accordingly done by patent, bearing date at Dublin 23 October following ‡.—In the Reigns of that King and Queen Mary, he was keeper of the caſtle of Fernes; and 20 March 1558 (1 Eliz.)

nour of Earl of Ormond, and the annuity aforeſaid of 10l. Iriſh; is contented and pleaſed that it be enacted and eſtabliſhed by this preſent Parliament, that the ſaid James, and the heirs male of the body of the ſaid Peter his ſaid father, have, hold, inherit and enjoy the ſaid name, honour, degree, ſtyle, title and dignity of Earl of Ormond, and the ſaid annuity of 10l. Iriſh, to be provided off the ſaid fee farm, of the ſaid city of Waterford, for the better maintenance of the ſaid name of honour of Earl of Ormond in as ample manner and form, and with the like preheminences and *auncientie* as any the above named Earls of Ormond at any time has had, uſed, or enjoyed," which act of parliament was exemplified by an inſpeximus at the inſtance of Thomas Earl of Ormond and Oſſory, Lord High Treaſurer of Ireland, 10 April 1573. 15 Elizabeth. On 5 July 1532, [2] he was made Lord High Treaſurer of Ireland for life; after which he had a ſpecial livery (without date) of his eſtate, granted to him as ſon and heir of Earl Pierce deceaſed; [3] and 11 May 1535, was appointed Admiral of the kingdom, with the cuſtody of all the ports thereof.—In 1534 he not only refuſed to join with his kinſman Thomas, Lord Offaley, in his rebellion, who earneſtly ſolicited his concurrence by letter; but in his anſwer told him, he had rather in that quarrel die his enemy, than live his partner; and when that Lord thought to force him to a compliance, by invading his lands, he reſolutely oppoſed him, and in an engagement at Jerpoint near Thomaſtown, ſlew many of his followers; but being himſelf ſore wounded, was carried to his houſe at Dunmore; and

---

* In the Records, this name is variouſly written, as Monkegarret, Montegarrete, and in the patent of creation Montegarret. (Lodge.)

‡ The preamble. Rex, &c. Omnibus ad quos, &c. Salutem. Sciatis quod, nos grata et laudabilia obſequia, quæ dilectus & fidelis noſter Richardus Butler, Miles, filius ſecundo genitus Petri Butler Militis, nuper Comitis Ormond et Oſſory defuncti, nobis antehac multipliciter impendit, indieſque impendere non deſiſtit: Necnon Circumſpectionem, Strenuitatem, et Fidelitatem ipſius Richardi mature conſiderantes, de Gratia noſtra ſpeciali, &c. (Lodge.)

[1] Rot. Can. 4º Edward, 6. d. [2] Enrolled. 15º Jac. 1. 1º. p. D. R 7.
[3] Rot. pat. de Aº. 28, 29, 30, 31, Hen. 8. f.

(1 Eliz) joined in a commission of martial law with Sir Nicholas Devereux for the territories of Fassaghbentry and LeMoroe's country: Also, 13 April 1559 was in two several commissions for the preservation of the peace in the counties of Kilkenny, Tipperary and Wexford, during the absence of the L. D. Sussex in the North, upon his expedition against and the enemy apprehending another battle with fresh forces, retired out of the country, and were soon after subdued.—He was created Viscount Thurles by patent 2 January 1535, the Privy Seal, for which, runs thus:

".By the K I N G,

"Trusty and right well beloved, we greet you well, and will and command you, that with convenient speed ye, under our Great Seal, of that our land of Ireland, being in your custody, ye address out in due form, our letters patents for the creation to the honor, name, style, and dignity, of our right trusty and well beloved counsellors, the Lords James Butler, High Treasurer of that our land of Ireland, to the name of Viscount Durles, and the Lord Leonard Grey, Marshal and Lieutenant of our Army within the same, to the name of Viscount Grane, in like form and manner as was used in the creation of Viscount Gormanston. And these our letters shall be your sufficient discharge in this behalf. Yeven under our signe at the town of Southamptone, the thirde day of October, the 27 year of our Reign.

"To our Right Trustie and well beloved counsellor of Trymletlon, Lord Chancellor of our land of Ireland, or to any other having the custody of our great Seal." [1]

31 May 1535, he was made joint Governor, with his father, of the counties of Kilkenny, Tipperary and Waterford.—In 1536, he timely opposed the disturbances in Munster, begun by James Earl of Desmond; and the L. L. Grey going to England with the Fitz-Geralds, he marched to Clonmell, to extinguish the remains of their rebellion, which he did by reducing Dungarvan, Youghall, Cork, and other places of strength; and restored peace and quiet to the whole country.

In consideration of his services to the Crown, he had a grant 4 January 1539, of the priory and rectory of Kenlis, &c. in the county of Kilkenny; the manors of Rathvillie, Clonmore, and other lands of the ancient possessions of the Earls of Kildare. Also 5 May 1542, the King conveyed to him and his heirs the moiety of the monastery of the friars minor of Clonmell, with all the lands thereto belonging, to hold by the eighth part of a Knight's fee.

He was commissioned 8 August 1539, to pursue and take into protection the rebels of Conaught, and such as were in arms in the South parts of Munster: And 10 April 1543, was, by special

[1] Rot. As 27. 28. 29, 30. Hen. 8. f.

against Shane O Neile; and 12 January following was present in the Parliament, then opened by the said L. D. He departed this life in 1571, and was buried in the Cathedral Church of St. Canice, Kilkenny, in a tomb, whereon is engraven his effigies in armour, with his feet resting against a dog,

cial commission, authorized to levy and lead men, through the counties of Tipperary, Waterford, Cork, Kerry, Ormond, and Desmond,; to imprison as he saw fit; to pursue and give protections for suppressing rebels, and quieting the country; and the next year was, with others, sent by the L. D. and council into Clanrickard, to pacify a tumult raised there, after the death of Ulick, chief of that country, which he soon performed. In 1545, at the King's instance, he went General of the Irish forces into Scotland, in aid of the Earl of Lenox, with 28 ships, to recover that Earldom to Matthew Steuart, of which he had been dispossessed; but without success; for when he came upon the Scotch coast, (where the Hamiltons had promised to deliver the castle of Dunbritton to Lenox) he perceived a vast army gathered to oppose him, whereupon, by common assent, he returned into England; and 17 October 1546, himself and 35 of his servants were poisoned at a supper at Ely-House in Holbourn, of whom James White, Steward of his houshold, and 18 more died, and he languishing until the 28, then deceased. His body was interred in St. Thomas D'Acres, according to the orders he had given in a codicil to his will, but his heart was brought into Ireland, and reposited in the Cathedral of Kilkenny. His Will whereby he disposes of his estate, bears date 10 March 37 Hen. VIII; and the codicil 18 October of that King; in which, after directing his burial, he says, " Item, That my sonne and heyre
" being in the Prince Grace's Court, shall have me bason and
" ewer, which I have here, a silver pott, a salte, a nywe boll, a
" trencher and a spone of silver. Item, my wyfe to have me
" best bracelet of golde sent her for a token. Iem, to me Lord
" Chancellor of England me nywe gilded goblet, with the cover,
" for a token. Item, Mayster Fitz-Williams to have a
" of them that were made of late, for a token. Item,
" Houthe to have his pension of twenty nobles yearly during his
" lyfe. Item, Lewes Bryane to have White's-Wall during his
" lyfe free, as he hath it before;" with several other legacies.

He married Joan, daughter and heir to James, 11 Earl of Desmond, with whom he had the manors of Clonmell, Kilsheelane, and Killfeacle in Tipperary, and had a special livery of his estate (no date granted by K. Henry VIII.) and by her, (who after married first Sir Francis Bryan, Knight Marshal of Ireland, and, secondly, Gerald, Earl of Desmond, and died in 1564) had seven sons, viz.

Thomas,

[1] Rot. pat. A. 28, 29, 30, 31 Hen. 8.

a dog, and a circumfcription now defaced; what remains legible being

Richardus Butler, Vicecomes Montgarret,
Qui obiit 20. Dece⁻bris 1571.

He married to his firſt wife Eleanor, daughter of Theobald Butler of Nechum in the county of Kilkenny, Efq; by whom he had Edmund, his fucceſſor; fecondly, Catharine, daughter and heir to Peter Barnewall of Stackallan in Meath, Efq; and by her he had a fon Barnewall, who died

(1) Thomas, Vifcount Thurles, his fucceſſor.
(2) Sir Edmond Butler of Rofcrea and Cloughgrenan, who, in 1562, was in commiſſion for prefervation of the peace in the county of Carlow, during the D puty's abfence in the North againſt Shane O Neile; and in 1567 was knighted, and had a grant for the return of all Writs in the cantreds of Oremon, Elyogerth, and Flyecarrol in Tipperary: But after this, with his brothers Edward and Pierce, he went into rebellion, raifed great commotions in Munſter, and was declared a traitor; yet, on his fubmiſſion, being pardoned, and with his brother Pierce, furrendering his eſtate to the Queen, 10 October 1570, had a pardon, (together with their brother Edward) dated at Gorhambury 12 March 1573, of all their treafons [2] after which he did great fervice in Leix againſt the O Mores.—He married Eleanor, fecond daughter of Sir Rowland Euſtace, Vifcount Baltinglaſs, fiſter to James, Vifcount Baltinglaſs, (who was in rebellion againſt Q. Elizabeth, and died without iſſue); and dying at Enniſteige, was buried in the Cathedral of St. Canice, leaving iſſue four fons and two daughters, viz. Pierce the eldeſt, to whom by indenture 14 October 1593, the Queen granted a leafe in reverſion for 40 years, of Ballylax in the county of Kildare, parcel of the poſſeſſions of the late Duke of Norfolk and the Lord Berkeley, who were coheirs, and then in leafe for 21 years to Robert Nangle, Gent. After the death of Thomas Earl of Ormond, earneſt pretences were made to K. James I. by the faid Pierce Butler, who proved with much confidence, that he was the fon and heir of Pierce Butler deceafed, who was nephew to the faid Earl, and had he lived would have been the next heir male inheritable to that honour; and to himfelf, the right of the Earldom, would now of right appertain if he could prove himfelf to be the true and lawful fon and heir of the faid Pierce, by Mary his wife, now wife of one Mulloy, the King, by letters from Newmarket,

---

[1] Rot. pat. Aᵒ 15°. 16°. Eliz. f.

died unmarried; thirdly, in 1541 Anne, daughter of John Plunket, Lord Killeen, from whom he was divorced in the first year of their marriage: Having issue in all five sons and four daughters, viz. Edmund and Barnewall aforesaid; Pierce, ancestor to the family of Caher, otherwise Clounegeragh *; John and Thomas, who both left issue; Ellice or Cicely married

Market 5 February 1623, directed a Commission to issue, that this pretence in respect of the violation it had to a great family, should be duly examined, for discovery and manifestation of the truth, and accordingly 12 May 1624, the L. D. Falkland, Donogh, Earl of Thomond, Francis, Lord Aungier, master of the Rolls, and Laurence, Lord Esmond, Privy Counselors, were commissioned to examine the said Mary Molloy, and all other witnesses, as should be nominated by the said Pierce Butler, as they should think fit, for finding out the truth of the premises. 1 He left an only daughter Ellen, married to John O Carroll, chief of his name, and she died in December 1620, leaving issue, John, Elizabeth, and Joan [2]; James, John, and Theobald, who all died without children; the last of whom had by patent, dated at Westminster 13 July 1603, the titles of Ormond and Ossory entailed and secured to him, after the death of Thomas, then Earl of Ormond, without issue male; remainder to the heirs male of his great-grandfather Pierce, Earl of Ormond and Ossory. —He was also created, 4 August following by patent at Westminster (or at Hampton-Court) Viscount Butler of Tulleophelim in the county of Carlow; of which county, 18 June 1605, he was made Governor and L. L—He married his cousin-german the Lady Elizabeth Butler [3] only daughter of the said Thomas, Earl of Ormond; but dying soon after in January 1613, [4] was buried in St. Canice Church.—The two daughters were Joan, (married to Teige, Lord Upper Ossory, died in 1631, and was buried at St. Canice's); Catharine, the fourth wife of William Fitz-John Eustace of Castlemartin in the county of Kildare, Esq; (father of

Theobald, Viscount Tulleophelim.

---

* By deed, dated 2 June 1563, his father enfeoffed John Devereux, Dean of Fernes, and others, in the manor and lands of Caher, alias Clounegeragh, &c. to the use (in part) of his said son Pierce and Margaret Devereux his wife, for life, and the remainder, in which Caher was included, to his heirs male. And he deceasing 30 June 1599, had three sons, Edward, James and Thomas, besides daughters.——Edward, who succeeded, was twenty-two years old at his father's death; built the house of Caher; married Catherine, daughter of Sr Richard Masterson of Fernes; died 9 September 1628, and left two sons and two daughters, Pierce, Richard, Mary and Joan.

1 Rot. pat A°22° Jac. 1. 1 a p. D. R. 5.   2 Ulster Office.   3 Ulster Office.   4 Id.

married to Walter Walſh of Caſtlehoel in the county of Kilkenny, Eſq; (and by him, who died 19 May 1619, had five ſons, Robert, whoſe eldeſt ſon Walter, when eighteen years old, ſucceeded his grandfather; Edmund, James, William, and

of Sir Maurice Euſtace, Chancellor of Ireland) and by him who died 25 June 1615 ſhe had no iſſue.[1]

(3) John Butler of Kilcaſh, Eſq; who married Catharine, daughter of Cormac Mac Carthy Reagh, and dying at his ſeat 10 May 1570, was buried in Kilkenny, leaving Sir Walter Butler of Kilcaſh, who became Earl of Ormond; and two daughters, Joan, married firſt to Nicholas Shortall of Upper Claragh in the county of Kilkenny, Eſq; and by him who died there 14 September 1600, had ſeven daughters, coheirs, viz. Catharine, Mary married to Patrick Denn of Grennan in ſaid county, Eſq; Joan, Eilin, Ellinor, Ellice, and Anne; her ſecond huſband was Sir Oliver Shortall, Knt. Eleanor, the ſecond daughter, married Thomas Prendergaſt of Newcaſtle in Tipperary, Eſq.

(4) Family of Nodſtown. Walter Butler of Ballynenoddagh, Nodſtown, or Moyaliffe, Eſq; who married Anne, daughter of Mac Brien O Gonagh, and dying in 1560, was buried at Kilkenny; leaving one ſon Pierce, and two daughters, viz. Joan (married to John O Dwyer of Dundromy in Tipperary, and by him, who died in January 1627, had Philip their heir, who married Gyles, daughter of Meiler Magrath, Archbiſhop of Caſhell; Connor, Dorogh, Margaret, and Winifred;) and Ellice firſt married to John Sherlock of Mothe in the county of Waterford, Eſq; by whom ſhe had Patrick, and other children; ſecondly, to Sir Edward Gough, by whom ſhe had a ſon and a daughter; and thirdly, to Sir Laurence Eſmond, a wife and worthy man, who did great ſervice to the Crown, in Ireland and other countries; repreſented the county of Wicklow in Parliament in 1613, was Governor of the Fort of Duncannon, Major General of all the King's forces in Ireland and [2] created Baron of Lymbrick in the county of Wexford, 20 May 1622, he died 26 March 1645, and ſhe deceaſing 16 January before him, was buried at Ardkavan in the ſaid county. Pierce Butler, Eſq; of Nodſtown, was only two years old at his father's death; he married Ellen, daughter of Thomas Purcell, Baron of Loughmoe, and dying 21 February 1627, was buried in the Abbey of Holy-Croſs, having iſſue James his heir; Richard of Rorane, (who married firſt Fynola, daughter of Carroll O Carroll of Beaghagh; and ſecondly, Ellen, daughter of Gerald Wale of Coolenemucky in the county of Waterford, Eſq; by whom he had Pierce, his ſucceſſor at Rorane)

[1] Ledge. [2] Id.

and John) Margaret to Sir Nicholas Devereux, the younger, of Ballymagin in the county of Wexford, Knt. and had no issue; Elinor, first to Thomas Tobin of Cumpshinagh in Tipperary, Esq; secondly to Gerald Blanchville of Blanchvillestown in the

Rorane) Ellen, Joan, Ellenor, married 9 November 1618 to [1] Nicholas Meyler, Gent. with whom her uncle Laurence, Lord Esmond gave 300l. English, half of which his Lordship bestowed upon her, and the other half was to be repaid him [2], Margaret and Mary.—James, the eldest son, had a special livery of his estate 9 December 1628. married Ellinor, second daughter of Sir John Fitz Gerald of Dromana, [3] and dying 5 February 1633, had issue ten sons and three daughters, Walter, Thomas, Edmond, John, Pierce, James, Edward, Theobald, Gilbert, Richard; Ellen, Ellane, and Ellice.—Walter, who succeeded at Noditown, was then 21 years old; had a special livery 26 November 1634; and 20 February 1637, in virtue of the commission for remedy of defective titles, and for the fine of 133l. 6s. 8d. Irish [4] had a confirmation of his estate by patent; but engaging in the rebellion of 1641, went about New-Year's Day that year to the city of Cashell, and with others, rifled that place, with the murder of 14 of the inhabitants.—This branch of the family ceased in the time of King Charles II.

James, who 26 Jan. 1560, had a lease for 21 years of the mo- (5) nastery and lands of Duiske in the counties of Wexford and Carlow, at the rent of 15l during the life of Charles Cavanagh, the late Abbot, and after his death 25l. a year, maintaining two able horsemen for the defence of Ireland, and reserving three couples of tithe corn; [5] which, with other hereditaments, on the recommendation of the L. D. Sidney, were granted 10 August 1567, in fee-farm to his son James.—He married Margaret, daughter of James Tobin of Cumpsenagh, Esq; by his wife Catharine, daughter of the Lord Dunboyne, [6] and had the said James, his only son, who left no children.

Edward Butler of Cloghinche in Tipperary, Esq; who mar- (6) ried Margaret, eldest daughter of Richard, the fourth Earl of Clanrickard, and had one son James, who died childless.

Pierce Butler of Grantstown in Tipperary, and of Leix-Abbey, (7) of which place he was nominated, when he was pardoned 12 Family of March 1573 for his rebellion against the Queen.—[7] On him, his Killinoylcr. wife and children, his brother Thomas, Earl of Ormond, 14 May 1595, settled Ballygurteen, and other lands in Tipperary, to be holden of the manor of Donowghill, by the 40th part of a Knight's fee, and 4l. rent.—He married Catharine, daughter of

---

[1] Decree in Chancery 1617. [2] Rot. de An 15°. 16°. Eliz. f. [3] Decree ut antea. [4] Lodge. [5] Idem. [6] Collect. [7] Rot. ut antea.

BUTLER, Viscount MOUNTGARRET.

the county of Kilkenny Esq; and thirdly to Thomas, Lord Cahier; and Ellen was the first wife of Sir Oliver Shortall of Ballylarkan in the said county, Knt. by whom she had James, his successor there.

Edmund,

of John, Lord Poer, by whom he had six sons, James his heir, William, Thomas, Edward, (who by Ellen Blanchville his wife who re-married with James Walsh of Greaghlaghbegg in Tipperary, Esq; left an only daughter and heir. Elynor, about a year old at his decease, who became the wife of Richard Butler of Killenaule, Gent.) Richard of Killenaule, Edmond, and several daughters, whereof Catharine was married to John Tobin, of Killahay.—James, the eldest son, was of Killmoyleagher, or Killveleigher, married Anne, daughter of Meiler Magrath, Archbishop of Cashell, and left one son James Butler Oge, living in the reign of K. James I who married first, Ellen, daughter of the Earl of Ormond; and secondly, Mary, third daughter of Thomas, Lord Kerry; by the former he had two sons, Pierce and Theobald.—Pierce of Killmoyler, and of Bellacarren, married Catharine, elder daughter and coheir to William Bowen of Ballyadams in the Queen's county, Esq; by his first wife Bridget, daughter of Sir Robert Tynte, Knt and had issue three sons and one daughter Hellen, married to —— Creagh, of Conge in the county of Mayo, Esq; by whom she had Stephen Creagh Butler, of Brittas in the county of Limerick, Esq; Hellen, married in September 1740, to George Macnamara of Conge Esq; by whom she left Mary, Hellen and Phœbe [1]; and Mary unmarried. The sons were James Butler, of Killveleigher, and of Ballyadams, Esq; Page of honour to K. Charles II. who 10 March 1602, married first, Margaret, daughter of Caryll, Lord Viscount Molyneux, widow of Jenico, the seventh Viscount Gormanston, and secondly, Mary Dennis, in England, and died 3 January 1738, Æt 94; Thomas, Counsellor at Law, who died 18 May 1746, unmarried, and was buried at Killardriff near Killmoyler, in the tomb of his ancestors; he bequeathed his Tipperary estate to his nephew aforesaid, Stephen Creagh, now Stephen Creagh Butler, and his Queen's county estate to his natural son, William Butler [2]; Captain John Butler, who went into Spain with his regiment, and having married Frances, daughter of Theobald Matthew of Thomastown, Esq; left one son James, who died unmarried; and two daughters, Elizabeth married to Thomas Arthur, of Ballyquin in the county of Clare, Esq; who left her a widow 23 December 1755, with one son, and one daughter, since deceased, she re-married with Mr.

Luke

---

[1] Bill in Chan. filed 27 April 1757. [2] Id.

BUTLER, Viscount MOUNTGARRET.

Edmund, the second Viscount Mountgarret, did great service against the rebels of Leix, Upper Ossory, and other countries bordering upon the Pale, being a stout and valiant man; and was well beloved in his country, especially in the county of Kilkenny, where he made his general abode, having

Edmund
2
Viscount

Luke Wall, [3] and [4] Catherine, to Mr. Benjamin Ellard of Cork, who died in 1750.

Thomas, the tenth Earl of Ormond, being at his father's death only 14 years old, it was ordered by the state, that the L. J. with the army, should draw into those parts of the country, to preserve the peace and his inheritance; and that the rule of the counties of Kilkenny and Tipperary, should be committed to his mother, his uncle Richard, and other friends.—He was brought up from his infancy in the Court of England, where he was instructed with K. Edward VI. who took great delight in his company, at whose coronation 20 February 1546, he was made a Knight of the Bath; and was a youth of such hopes, that the King 8 September 1548, directed the L. D. Sir Edward Bellingham, to allow him 200 marcs a year during his minority; and 17 October 1551, ordered a year's release of his wardship.—He served as a volunteer under the Duke of Somerset in his Scots expedition, and behaved with great bravery in the battle of Musselburgh.—In Queen Mary's reign he commanded a troop of horse, and gave extraordinary proofs of his fidelity and courage, as a Lieutenant of the horsemen, in suppressing Wyat's rebellion in 1554; after which, in November, he came to Ireland, and in July 1556, accompanied the L. L. with a body of 200 horse and 500 foot, which he maintained at his own charge, against the Scots Islanders, who made a descent into Ulster and besieged Carrickfergus, when he distinguished himself in the battle, fought 18 of that month, in which the Scots were entirely routed: 10 August 1557, he served against another body of them, who had invaded Tyrconnel; and soon after relieved the Earl of Thomond, besieged in his castle of Bunratty, and took the castle of Clare; after which, 20 June 1558, attended with many gentlemen, he joined the L. L. in the county of Limerick, on his march against Donald O Brien, the Earl of Thomond's uncle. This zeal and activity in the service of the Crown, induced Q. Mary to confirm his patent for the regalities and liberties of Tipperary, and the prize wines 11 March 1555; and 13 December 1557, to grant the religious houses of Athassil, Jerpoint, Callan, Thurles, Carick, Kilcowle, and Tulleophelim, with all their hereditaments in the counties of Tipperary, Kilkenny, and Waterford; the manor

Thomas
10
Earl

[3] Lodge. [4] Bill in Chancery.

ing a particular esteem for the inhabitants thereof, in whose quarrel and defence he was ever ready to spend his blood.— In the Parliament, held at Dublin 12 January 1559, he represented the county of Carlow; and in August 1579 accompanied the L. D. in his Munster expedition against the Spaniards,

manor of Kilrush in the county of Kildare, &c. the monastery of Athasiil to him, his heirs and assigns; and the rest of the premisses to his heirs male, to hold by the service of the 20th part of a Knight's fee, and the yearly rent of 49l. 3s. 9d. Irish.— Which reserved rent Q. Elizabeth remitted, and confirmed the said grant 8 March 1562; having 27 January 1560, given him a discharge of all such sums, as he stood indebted to the Crown, for arrears of rent in the Exchequer or any other Court, owing for the Earl his father: And whereas in the time of Edward VI. he was appointed to repair to Ireland for service to be done there, one year before he had sued out his livery, during which time he had the farm of his own lands granted to him, the rents whereof for that year remained unpaid; the Queen, in consideration of his good service, discharged him from the same, as she also did the arrears of rent due upon certain lands, granted to him by Q. Mary: Also, for his services against the traitors of Leix, by patent, dated 28 February 1562, she granted to him and his heirs male, the Abbey of Leix in the Queen's County, with all its lands, estimated at 820l. and 3 October 1563 in feefarm, all the possessions of the Monastery of the Holy Cross, advowsons of churches excepted. By privy seal 30 June 1569, as a reward for suppressing the rebellion of his brothers, who by strength of arms endeavoured to assume their right to a certain territory, claimed by Sir Peter Carew, which they could not maintain by the laws, he was restored to the prize wines of Youghall and Kingsale, which had been sequestered in 1563. on a claim laid to them by Garret, Earl of Desmond; and had his lands exempted from all cesses and impositions, subsidies to the Crown excepted, by reason of the damages he had sustained and the impoverishment of his tenants by the rebels, which exemption was confirmed by K. James, 5 December 1611. He received other considerable grants from Q. Elizabeth, viz. 24 September 1574, the estate of John Burnell of Ballgriffen in county of Dublin Esq; forfeited by treason, and three carucates in Rathnemeddagh, county of Westmeath. And making suit to the Queen that in consideration of his faithful services performed in the affairs of Ireland, she would grant to him in fee-farm 100l. Irish, (in lands) a year, which grant she was pleased to make by privy seal at Greenwich 7 July 1513, containing the manor of Old-Rosse, and other lands. Also 12 December 1578, he had a grant

of

Spaniards, sent over by their King and the Pope, to disturb the Government.——In 1585, he sat in Sir John Perrot's Parliament; and in 1602, being sensible of his decline of life, he made his will, and therein recommends his soul to God of the rectories of Dunmore and Donaghmore, with many others in co's. Kilkenny, Tipperary, Carlow, and Wexford; and at his Lordship's instance, K. James I. by patent 26 November, 1604, granted to him and his heirs, all the premises contained in the patents of Q. Mary, by the 20th part of a Knight's fee; and all contained in the patents of Q. Elizabeth, at the rent of 10l. 5s. Irish [1]. He continued in the esteem of Q. Elizabeth throughout her long reign; she considered him as her relation, and had the highest opinion of his capacity, fidelity, and zeal for her service, which he took all occasions to promote and advance, by suppressing the commotions in Munster and elsewhere, of which our public histories relate many particulars, and shew his services to have been very considerable. The Queen, 26 August 1559, (in the first year of her reign) made him Lord Treasurer of Ireland, in which post he continued to his death, and 30 of that month was sworn of her privy council.—13 April 1563, he was joined with Richard, Lord Mountgarret, and others in commission, to preserve the peace in the counties of Kilkenny and Tipperary, during the deputy's absence, against Shane O'Neile: 6 October that year, he was in commission to make inquiry in order to redress all offences in ecclesiastical matters; also, 21 November 1564, was commissioned to prosecute and subdue, as notorious rebels and traitors, such of the O'More's and their adherents, as before the 28 of April preceding, had not submitted to the observation of such orders as were taken and concluded for them by the Earl of Sussex, L. L. [2] and was generally named in all commissions of public importance. In 1575 the L. D. Sidney appointed him L. L. of the counties of Kilkenny and Tipperary, whom in November that year, he splendidly entertained in his castle of Kilkenny, when on his Leinster progress; and the O'More's having almost ruined the county of Kildare, Rory Oge, their chief, was prevailed on by his Lordship to come and submit to the Lord Deputy in Kilkenny.—By patent dated 6 January, 1578, he was made Governor of the province of Munster, when he subdued O'Sullivan More, took many of that sept prisoners, and delivered them to the L. L. Sussex; he also subdued Pierce Grace, Rory Oge, and the Mac Swiney's, and taking the Earl of Desmond prisoner, destroyed 46 of his Captains, 800 notorious traitors, and 4000 common soldiers [3]. In 1581 the Queen constituted him Lord High Marshal of England, in which office he continued for a time, until (at his earnest suit) he was discharged

[1] Lodge. [2] Id. [3] Id.

BUTLER Viscount MOUNTGARRET.

God his Maker, Saviour and Redeemer, and his body to be buried in his father's tomb, and deceasing 24 November that year, lies there interred.—He married Grany, or Griffel[1], daughter

discharged ; the cause moving him to surrender this honourable employment, was the apprehension that he should be tied to continual attendance in England, and thereby be made a stranger to his own country, a thought he could not endure. He arrived at Waterford about the end of January 1582, with a supply of 400 men, and a commission, appointing him General of Munster. —He obtained also two pence a day in addition to the soldier's pay, which with permitting them to enjoy what spoils they took from the enemy, procured him the general love of the army[2].

He was present in the parliaments of 1559 and 1583, sitting in both as Lord High Treasurer. 15 August 1594, he was appointed Chief Leader (in the Deputy's absence) and commander of the forces in Leinster, and in 1595, the Fort of Blackwater being destroyed by the Earl of Tyrone, his Lordship joined the L. D. at Ardee, in his march to relieve it, attended with 80 horse and 200 foot, furnished and victualled at his own expence ; and the L. D. returning from that service, left him with his men to defend the place, which having done and supplied it in January following with ammunition and victuals for six months, he returned to Dublin ; and[3] was made a Knight Companion of the Order of the Garter 23 May 1596 ; in the next year the rebels growing very formidable, and the deputy 13 September marching into the North, his Lordship was appointed General of Leinster, but without either army or ammunition, which the L. D. took with him ; a want however that he supplied, for he took the field at his own charge ; where he continued all the months of October and November to cover the castles of Leighlin and Carlow ; and in the beginning of December, was ordered to take on him the command of the army at Dundalk, having been 29 October by a particular commission, appointed Captain and Lieutenant-General of all her Majesty's forces in Ireland by sea and land ; and by her letter from Westminster 15 November, had the principal charge of all martial services, with the entertainment of 100 marcs by the month, 30 horsemen, and as many footmen in wages. After which, Tirōen applied to him to procure a commission to treat with him, which being obtained, they met at Dundalk 22 December, and Tirōen making his submission in writing, a cessation of arms for eight weeks was concluded on nine certain articles, and his lordship sending his submission

[1] Decree in Chancery, 4th June, 1592. [2] Lodge. [3] Id.

daughter of Barnaby, the first Lord of Upper-Ossory, and had issue eight sons and as many daughters, viz.

Richard, his successor. (1)

James of Tullahinch, or Tenehensy in the county of Carlow, engaged in the rebellion of 1641; he married Catharine, daughter and co-heir to Thomas Lord Slane, and widow of Pierce Butler, of Grangedoufke, Esq; after which marriage (2)

mission and grievances to England, received authority to make a final conclusion with the rebels; meeting him again at Lundalk, 15 March, he received him and all the inhabitants of Tyrone to mercy, and upon his entering into conditions to renounce the name of O'Neile, to keep the peace, disperse his forces, &c. at his Lordship's instance a general pardon passed [1] to him 11 April 1598; yet, though he received it, being resolved to continue his disloyal courses, he never pleaded it, so that in the year 1600, he was outlawed upon an indictment, brought against him in September 1595.—He continued to prosecute the rebels with great vigour; and held, in 1599, all his castles in the county of Kilkenny, and six in Carlow for the Queen; and the L. D. Mountjoy, arriving 26 February that year, his Lordship advertised him of Tyrone's motions in Munster, in which province he employed his forces so well, that in the beginning of January 1600, he expelled Redmond Bourke and others out of Ormond, with great loss; killed his brother Thomas Bourke, and forced Redmond with his company into the river Nore, where 70 of his men were drowned, and all his baggage lost.—But 10 of April same year [2] going eight miles from Kilkenny to parley with Owny Mac Rory O'More, he was treacherously taken prisoner, and detained by him to 12 June, where he obtained his liberty by delivering hostages for the payment of 3000l. if he should seek revenge for that injury; but the custody of the provinces of Leinster and Munster being committed to him, his Lordship (notwithstanding his hostages were in Owny's hands, who in a little time found means to escape) abated nothing of his wonted activity and severity; and securing those parts by the submission of the rebels, went to defend the Pale, against the incursions of the Irish, whilst the Deputy was in the North, and in 1601 executed twenty-nine rebels in the borders of Kilkenny and Tipperary [3]; 28 May 1603, he had his commission of Lieutenant-General of the army renewed by K. James I.

His Lordship, having lost his sight about 15 years before his death, departed this life at his house in Carrick 22 November 1614 [4]. This shews, says the author, how erroneous is the following

---

[1] Lodge.   [2] Id.   [3] Id.   [4] Id.

marriage he lived at Douſke, and left [1] a ſon Edmund, who married Suſan, daughter of Thomas Luttrel [2] of Luttrellſtown in the county of Dublin, Eſq;

(3) Edward.
(4) Thomas.
(5) Pierce of Killagheen in Tipperary.
(6) Theobald of Tynehinch, who married firſt Lettice, daughter of ——— Fitzgerald of the Queen's county, by whom

lowing account, given by Mr. Anſtis, Garter King of Arms, in his Hiſtory of the Garter. "Thomas Earl of Ormond married Lora, daughter of Sir Edward Barklay of Beverſton, widow of John Lord Mountjoy, and alſo of Sir Thomas Montgomery, Knight of the Garter, which Earl of Ormond in his will made in 1615, (a year after he was dead) mentions Dame Lore, late his wife, by whom he had a daughter that lies buried at Sheffield in Yorkſhire.") in the 82d year of his age, and was buried 17 April, in the choir of St. Canice church, where a monument was erected for him by Sir Walter Butler, his ſucceſſor in the Earldom: the work was executed by Nicholas Stone, of London, ſtatuary, for which he was paid 100l. in hand, and 300l. more when finiſhed and ſet up [3]. He married three wives; firſt Elizabeth, only daughter of Thomas, Lord Berkeley, but by her, who was buried in the chapel of St. Paul in Weſtminſter, he had no iſſue; ſecondly, Elizabeth, only daughter of John, the ſecond Lord Sheffield; and by her, who was buried at St. Canice, Kilkenny 21 April 1601, (or according to Sir G. Carew, her death ſeems to have happened in November or December 1600; for the Earl 26 November, met the Lord Preſident of Munſter, to whom he was of council, at Clonmell, to conſult about the proſecution of the rebels in the borders of Ormond; which he readily undertook, and would have immediately performed, had not the immature death of his moſt virtuous and honourable lady, the lamentable tidings whereof were now brought him to Clonmell, oppreſſing his aged heart with miſerable ſorrow, cauſed the ſame for a time to be deferred [4]). he had two ſons and a daughter; thirdly, Helena, daughter of David Viſcount Buttevant, and widow of John, ſon and heir of Richard, Lord Poer; but by her, who died in 1642, he had no iſſue. His children were John, Viſcount Thurles, born in 1584, who died an infant, and was buried in St. Paul's Chapel, Weſtminſter;

---

[1] Decree 10 March 1603, 2nd Lodge.   [2] Pedig. Earl Carhampton.
[3] Walpole's Anecdotes of Painting, 4to. V. II. p. 24.   [4] Pacata Hiber.

whom he had four sons, Gilbert, who left no issue by his wife Margaret Shee; Edmund, slain at Linch'sknock without issue; Edward; and James, who married Ellen, daughter of ———— Blanchville. His second wife was the daughter

minster; Thomas, buried in the church of Carrick under a flat stone, yet remaining, with this circumscription:

    Here lieth Entombed the Bodie of THOMAS BUTLER Esquier, Son to the Righte Hon[ble] th' Earle of Ormond and Ossory, &c. who dyed being Shirife of the County of Typerary 12 of Janu. Anno Dom. 1605.

So that the only daughter Elizabeth[1] became heir, and was first married to Theobald, Lord Tulleophelim[2], as before observed and secondly, to Sir Richard Preston, created 6 June 1614, Lord Dingwall in Scotland, and Earl of Desmond; and she dying in Wales 10 October 1628, had issue by him, who was drowned in his passage from Dublin to England 28 of the same month and year, an only daughter the Lady Elizabeth Preston, born 25 July 1615, and married to James, Duke of Ormond, as hereafter. He was a man of very great parts, admirable judgment, vast experience, and a prodigious memory; his capacity and talents rendered him equal to the most important and difficult employments, and his loyalty made him fit to be employed in those of the greatest trust, in the most intricate and dangerous situation of affairs. He was a very comely and graceful personage, and of a black complexion, which made the Irish give him the sobriquet of Duffe, and gave occasion to the Queen, to call him her black husband. He was in his time the flower of his country; and all his life kept the greatest house, and used the most hospitality of any person in the kingdom; and for his valour, wisdom, liberality and virtue, was greatly honoured, not only in England and France, but in all other realms where he was known, and was commonly called and taken by them to be the pattern of true honour. He repaired his Castle of Kilkenny, and house of Carrick at great expence; made a Deer-park at the Earl's-Cragg near Kilkenny; built the Castle of Drehednesarney near Holy-Cross, as a strength for the county of Tipperary, against the O'Mulrians, and other Irish borderers; and by his will appointed his nephew Walter, (after Earl of Ormond) to build an hospital in Kilkenny, leaving lands of his own purchase for maintenance thereof, and that he should procure a charter of incorporation, with licence of Mortmain; which he did, bearing date 16 May 1631, by the name of master, brethren, and sisters, of the hospital of our most Holy Saviour Jesus Christ of Kilkenny.

                                                  Sir

---

[1] Rot. Inq. post. mort. Tho. Comit. Ormoniæ 10 Oct. 1631 and Ulster Office.   [2] Id.   [3] Id.

ter of ——— Mac-Cody, and by her he had a daughter Elinor.

(7) Gilbert, and
(8) John, both died young.

Daughter

Walter, 11 Earl.
Sir Walter Butler of Kilcash, for his devotion, ſtiled Walter of the beads and roſaries¹ was ſon of John, third ſon of James the ninth Earl of Ormond; and did good ſervice to the crown in the latter end of Q. Elizabeth's reign, when, with his own company and ſome few gentlemen of the county Tipperary, he purſued the traitor Redmond Bourk, and forced him to fly into Spain, with the ſlaughter of his brother Thomas and many of his followers, taking his brother John priſoner, who was ſoon after executed at Kilkenny; in this action Sir Walter was wounded. He ſucceeded to the honour became the 11 Earl, and thought to have taken poſſeſſion of the eſtate entailed upon him, but was oppoſed therein by Sir Richard Preſton. The King, to ſupport a favourite, took upon him to make award himſelf in the caſe. The Earl refuſing to ſubmit, the King ſeized upon all his eſtate and impriſoned him in the fleet, where he continued for eight years, in a moſt ſhameful want of all things. The behaviour of K. James reflects particular diſgrace on the character of that monarch; for he became convinced that he had made an unjuſt deciſion; he was ſenſible that he ought to unravel what he had done, and yet he perſiſted in depriving the Earl of his right, and in ſuffering him to be kept a priſoner for ſo many years². He married Hellena, eldeſt daughter of Edmond, the ſecond Viſcount Mountgarret, and dying at Carrick 24 February 1632, was buried 18 June 1633, at Kilkenny, having iſſue by her (who died 28 January 1631³, and was buried there 27 March) three ſons and nine daughters, viz.

(1) Thomas, his heir apparent, who died before him.
(2) James, who died young in England.
(3) John, who died in France, without iſſue.
(1) Daughter Margaret was married to Bryan, Lord Upper-Oſſory.
(2) Catharine, to Pierce Power of Monaghalargy in Tipperary, Eſq; ſecond ſon of Richard, Lord Poer.
(3) Ellan, to Sir Bierce Butler, the firſt Viſcount Ikerrin.
(4) Hellena, to James Butler of Grellagh, Eſq; eldeſt ſon of James, the ſecond Lord Dunboyne, by his ſecond wife Margaret, daughter of Connor, Earl of Thomond.

Joan

---

¹ French's Unkind Deſerter, p. 28. ² Biograph. Britan. ³ Ulſter's Office.

BUTLER, Viscount MOUNTGARRET.

Daughter Hellena was married to Walter, Earl of Ormond, and died 28 January 1631. (1)

Ellan,

Joan, to George Bagenal of Dunleckney, in the county Carlow, Esq; ancestor to Beauchamp Bagenal, of that place, Esq; (5)

Mary, died unmarried. (6)

Elizabeth, married first to Sir Edmond Blanchville, of Blanchville's Town, by whom she had Gerald, who dying before them, 21 February 1646, they erected a monument to his memory in the cathedral of Kilkenny [1]; and secondly, to Richard, sixth Earl of Clanrickard. (7)

Eleanor died unmarried, in 1633 [2]. (8)

Alice, married to Terence (or Turlogh) Mac-Ibrien-Arragh. (9)

Thomas, Lord Thurles, the eldest son, was Governor of the counties of Kilkenny, Tipperary and Waterford, and the territories of Ossory and Ormord; but was unfortunately drowned in his passage from England to Ireland, near the Skerries, 15 December 1619; leaving issue by Elizabeth, (who according to Mr. Carte [3], lived a widow near 54 years, and died at Thurles in May 1673, in her 86th year, but " in this particular," says the Author, " as well as in others, Mr. Carte is mistaken, for, she re-married with George Matthew, of Thurles, Esq; [4]) daughter of Sir John Pointz, of Acton, in the county of Gloucester, Bart. three sons and four daughters, viz.

James, successor to his grandfather, created Duke of Ormond, one of the ablest statesmen, and worthiest persons of the age in which he flourished. (1)

John, who died unmarried at Naples, on his travels, in 1626. (2)

Richard, of whom presently. (3)

Daughter Ellen, married to Donogh, Earl of Clancarthy, and dying in April 1682, Æt. 70, was buried 24 in the Chancel of St. Michan's church. (1)

Elizabeth, first married to James Purcell, Esq; titular Baron of Loughmoe, by whom she had one son Nicholas [5], and two daughters; Catharine [6], married to Nicholas Darcy, of Platen in the county of Meath, Esq; and Mary [7] to ——— Cheevers of Mountown, Esq; Nicholas, Baron of Loughmoe, married Rose, daughter (2)

---

[1] Lodge. [2] See Lord Cahier. [3] Hist. Duke of Ormond, V. II. p. 445.
[4] MS. Collect. of Adam Molyneux, N° 12, 23. in Bib. T. Col. Dub. and Council Office. Lib. Ord. N° 1.—See Landaff. [5] Ulster. [6] Id.
[7] Id.

(1) Ellan, to Lucas Shee of Upper-Court, Esq; *
(2) Eleanor, the first wife to Morgan Mac Bryan Cavenagh, Chief of the Sept, called Sleight-Dermot, of Polomonty in the

daughter of Marcus, Viscount Dungannon, and had issue Nicholas his heir, who died 4 March 1722; and by Alice, daughter of Valentine, Lord Kenmare, left only daughters, whereof Helen, married Thomas Coke, of Painstown in the county of Carlow, Esq; and had one son William, and a daughter Anne married in December 1750 to Thomas, Viscount Kenmare —Her second husband was Colonel John Fitz-Patrick, of Castletown, in the Queen's County¹, and she dying 6 December 1675, was buried the 8 in St Patrick's church.

(3) Mary, married to Sir George Hamilton, ancestor by her to the Earl of Abercorn, and died in August 1680.

(4) Eleanor, to Sir Andrew Aylmer, of Donedea in the county of Kildare, Baronet.

Family of Kilcash. Richard Butler of Kilcash, Esq; the youngest son, had a confirmation (by virtue of the commission of grace) 24 June 1639, of the lands of Kilcash, Garryricken, and many others in the counties of Tipperary and Kilkenny; with a limitation thereof to his heirs male; remainder to the respective heirs male of Walter Earl of Ormond; Pierce Butler Fitz-Walter, late of Nodstown;

Pierce

* Sir Richard Shee, of Kilkenny, Knt. died 10 August 1608, leaving two sons, viz. the said Lucas his heir, then thirty years old and married; and Marcus Shee of Sheestown, Esq; great-grandfather to Richard Shee of that place, Esq; who died 10 December 1748, leaving by Daphna, daughter of Robert Lord Trimbleston², Marcus his heir, since deceased.—Lucas, who married as above, was the pious founder of the hospital of Jesus in Kilkenny, by his father's appointment; and 4 November 1608 certain ordinances, statutes and constitutions were agreed upon by the L. D. Chichester and the Privy Council, for the regulation of the master, brethren and sisters, and of their estate.—This hospital was founded for such as were either blind, lame, impotent, diseased, or aged, not able to work or get their living, and such as were poor, and not worth 5l.—He died 27 July 1622, and was buried in St. Mary's church, Kilkenny, leaving by her, who survived him, two sons and six daughters. Robert, his heir; Edmund, who left no issue by his wife Dorothy, daughter of Nicholas Dermer, of Ross, Esq, Robert, the eldest son³, married Margaret, daughter and co-heir to Sir Richard Masterson, of Fernes, and had Richard Shee, Esq; who carried an Irish regiment to Flanders into the Spanish service, during the exile of K. Charles II. most of which was lost at the siege of Arras. He married first Catharine, daughter of Sir Richard Everard, Bart. by whom he had a daughter Margaret, married to Richard, Lord Mountgarret, as will follow; and secondly Bridget, daughter of —— Malone, by whom he had Edmund Shee of Cloghrane, Esq; whose son Richard died there in 1743, leaving an only son.

¹ Ulster's Office.   ² Lodge.   ³ Idem.

BUTLER, Viscount MOUNTGARRET.

the county of Carlow, who died at Borrafs 19 June 1636, and was buried at St. Molafh, having fixteen children, of whom five

Pierce Butler Fitz-James, of Grantftown; Sir Richard Butler Lord Mountgarret; Edmond Butler Fitz-Richard, of Pooleftown; James lord Dunboyne; Theobald Butler, Lord Cahier; remainder to the right heirs[1] of Walter, Earl of Ormond. And the creation of the premiffes into the manors of Killcafh, Ballenla, and Garryricken, with free warren and liberty to impark 1000 acres. In 1641 he joined with the Irifh; by whom he was made Governor of the county of Waterford, and in January fent as one of the commiffioners for the county of Tipperary, to take the city of Waterford, and feize all the goods of the Englifh, for the maintenance (as they termed it) of the holy war of the confederate Catholics; but they were prevented by the mayor and council, until an opportunity of fhipping was got to preferve the goods. He was a reputed Lieutenant-General among the rebels, and acted with great vigour in that ftation, reducing Caperquin and other places

He married the Lady Frances Touchet[2], youngeft daughter of Mervin, Earl of Caftlehaven, and dying in 1701, had iffue three fons and four daughters; Walter, his heir; John; Thomas; Lucia, married to Sir Laurence Efmond, of Clonegall, county of Carlow, fon and heir to Sir Thomas, of Ballytroman, county of Wexford, Bart. and fhe died 7 April 1685, leaving iffue Laurence, Richard, John, Water, Frances, Elizabeth and Lucia[3]; Mary, married to Chriftopher, Lord Delvin, and died 28 March 1737; Frances, to Sir Patrick Barnwall, and was buried 1 February 1709, at St. James's church, Dublin, (being mother of Sir George Barnwall, Bart.); and —— married to Sir Redmond Everard, of Fethard in Tipperary, Bart. who died in 1686, and left iffue Sir John Everard, Bart. James, and Margaret. Colonel John Butler, the fecond fon, married Catharine, daughter of James Aylmer, of Cragbryen in the county of Clare, Efq. widow of Sir Nicholas Plunket; and dying in March 1714, had iffue Richard Butler, of Weftcourt, in the county of Tipperary, Efq; who married Helen, third daughter of Thomas Butler, of Kilcafh, Efq. as hereafter; and a daughter Mary, married to Mr. Galway, of Lota, near Cork.

Walter Butler of Garryricken, Efq; the eldeft fon, married the Lady Mary Plunket, only daughter of Chriftopher the Second Earl of Fingall and dying the year before his father, left three fons and four daughters.

Thomas,

---

[1] Lodge.   [2] Ulfter's Office.   [3] Id.

five sons and four daughters survived and were, Bryan, his successor, who married Ellen, or Eleanor, daughter of Sir Thomas

(1) Thomas, successor to his grandfather.
(2) John Butler of Garryricken, Esq; who married Frances, daughter of George Butler, of Ballyragget, Esq; and had an only son Walter, who succeeded to the estates of the Earl of Arran.
(3) Christopher, titular Archbishop of Cashel.
(1) Daughter ———, married to ——— Tobin, of Cumpshinagh, Esq; by whom she had one daughter, first married to Valentine, youngest brother to Richard Talbot, of Malahide, Esq; and secondly to ——— Powell, Esq.
(2) Frances, to Mr Gould, merchant.
(3) Lucy, to Sir Walter Butler of Poolestown, Bart.
(4) ——— ——— to Maurice Fitzgerald, of Castle Ishin in the county of Cork, Esq; by whom she had two sons and a daughter Mary, married first to Justin, Earl of Fingall; secondly to Valentine, Viscount Kenmare, and thirdly to John Lord Bellew.

Thomas Butler, of Kilcash, Esq, who succeeded his grandfather, was Colonel of a regiment of foot in the army of K. James, II.; and in 1696, married the Lady Margaret Burke, eldest daughter of William Earl of Clanrickard, widow of Bryan Magennis, Viscount of Iveagh, and deceasing 1738, had issue by her, who died at Kilcash 19 July 1744, three sons and five daughters, viz.

(1) Richard, killed by a fall from his horse at Kilcash, in 1711.
(2) Walter, who died, unmarried, of the small-pox, at the Royal Academy at Paris.
(3) John Butler, of Kilcash, Esq; who succeeded to the estates of the Earl of Arran, and married in April 1763, the daughter of ——— Storey, Esq, grand-daughter of General Webb, and niece to Earl Powis; he died 24 June 1766, without issue, and she re-married 24 October, 1771, with Rev. Alleyne Walker, L. L. D. of the Hermitage, county of Surrey [r].

(1) Daughter Mary, married to Bryan Cavenagh, of Borrass in the county of Carlow, Esq; who left her a widow 22 April 1741, with one son Thomas, and six daughters, Margaret, Hellen, Frances, Lucy, Honora, and Mary.
(2) Honora, in November 1720, to Valentine, Lord Kenmare, and died of the small-pox in 1730, having two sons, Valentine, who died young; Thomas, the present lord, born in 1726, and two daughters, Hellen, married in 1738-9 to John, then son and heir of Nicholas

[r] Collect.

BUTLER, Viscount MOUNTGARRET.

Thomas Colclough of Tynterne in the county of Wexford, Knt; Charles, who married Uny, daughter of Sir Bryan Nicholas Wogan, of Rathcoffey in the county of Kildare, Esq; who left her a widow in 1743 [1]; and Catherine.

Hellen, first to Mr Esmond, brother to Sir Laurence and John Esmond, Parts. who died 17 December 1736, by the accidental discharge of his gun, when fowling [2]; and secondly, to Richard Butler of Westcourt, as before observed. (3)

Margaret, to George Mathew of Thurles, afterwards of Thomastown, Esq; and died 30 July 1743, leaving one daughter, who died in 1752. (4)

Catharine, became the third wife of James Mandeville, of Ballydvne in Tipperary, Esq; and had no issue. (5)

James, the eldest son of Thomas, Lord Thurles, and successor to his grandfather Walter, was the twelfth Earl of Ormond, and was born in the year 1607 [3], (according to Mr. Carte, he was born at Clerkenwell, London, 19 October 1610 [4], but it appears from the undoubted authority of an inquisition, taken at Clonmell, 21 April 1622, after his fathers death, before the King's Commissioners, upon the oaths of 12 gentlemen of the county of Tipperary, that he must be born in 1607 The words of the inquisition are these: " Prædictus Thomas Vicecomes " Thurles 15º die Decembris Anno Dom. 1619 obiit & quidam " Jacobus Butler, communiter vocatus Dominus Vicecomes Thur- " les, fuit filius et hares præfati Thomæ Butler, et quod præfatus Ja- " cobus Butler, tempore mortis prædicti Thomæ fuit ætatis duode- " cim annorum, et, non amplius.") He was granted in Ward 26 May 1623, to Richard, Earl of Desmond, and by order of K. James I. educated under the eye of Doctor George Abbot, Archbishop of Canterbury, who took care to have him instructed in the Protestant Religion, as professed in the church of England, to which he adhered with great constancy and steadiness to his death. (James 12 Earl, and 1 Duke)

On 7 February 1626, his Majesty by privy seal directed, that he might receive all the rents of his lands, which were in sequestration on account of the long unhappy differences between his grandfather and the said Earl of Desmond, concerning their respective titles to the estate; to which in 1629, he put as happy a period, by gaining in marriage the Lady Elizabeth Preston, only child of the said Earl of Desmond; who being then very young and in ward to the Earl of Holland, he was forced to pay that Lord 15,000l in lieu of her wardship and marriage: Soon after, which, he retired with her to Acton, in Gloucestershire, ten miles

[1] His will proved 15 December 1743. Prereg. Office.   [2] Lodge.
[3] Carte, V. 1. p. 9.   [4] Hist. J. D Ormond, V. 1. p. 3.

BUTLER, Viscount MOUNTGARRET.

Bryan Mac-Mahon, of the county of Monaghan, widow of Gerald Byrne, of Roscrea, Esq; Arthur, who married Mary,

miles from Bristol, where he employed his time in learning the Latin tongue; and after about a year's stay with his uncle Sir Robert Pointz, came to Ireland in the conclusion of the year 1630; where, 2 June 1632, for the fine of 566l. 13s 4d he sued out a livery of his Lady's estate, as he did of his own 15 August 1633, for the fine of 900l. Irish.

In 1631 he purchased a troop of horse; and in 1634, gave an uncommon instance of his undaunted resolution, in opposing the commands of the Lord D. Wentworth, who calling a parliament to meet 14 July at the Castle of Dublin, publish'd a proclamation, (to prevent any ill effects from their animosity, which was now risen very high) that no member should enter with their swords; all obeyed except this young Lord, who told the Usher of the Black Rod at the door, when he demanded his sword, that he should have no sword of his except in his guts; being the only Peer who sat that day in the house, in defiance of the proclamation; it so fired the deputy, who was not accustomed to have his orders disobeyed that his Lordship was called upon in the evening to answer it; who thereupon produced his Majesty's writ, calling him to Parliament, *Cinctum cum Gladio*, or *Per Cincturam Gladii*. Which answer being unexpected, and finding him likely to prove an untractable companion, it was in deliberation that night between the L. D. and his two friends, Sir George Ratcliffe and Mr. Wandesford, whether to trample under foot, or to oblige so daring a young man, who was now also grown so very popular; when the more benign extreme being resolved on, he was taken into favour [1], and by the deputy, in his letter of 16 December, recommended to the King to call him into his Privy Council, as a person of solid judgment, grave and sober carriage, and good affection to his Majesty's service; who, (added to that testimony) considering both his nobility and worth, thought fit to encourage and enable him for his service; and therefore by his letter from Westminster, 20 January 1634, ordered the Deputy to call him into the Privy Council [2]. In 1633 his troop was taken from him; but he was promoted to the command of a troop of cuirassiers, consisting of a Captain, Lieutenant, Cornet, and 101 horsemen, with the pay of 24s. a day, and 5 spare horsemen, at 2s. 6d each; and 25 May [3] 1639, made C. Rot. Pacis, of the county of Kilkenny; also in 1640 advanced to the command of a regiment of horse, with the pay of 1l. 10s a day; and 16 September appointed Lieutenant-General of the horse at

4l.

[1] Biog. Brit. [2] A°. 11°. Car. 1 do. p. Do. [3] 15° Car. 1 9. p. f.

BUTLER, Viscount MOUNTGARRET.

Mary, daughter of Edmund Fitzgerald of Brownsford, in county of Kilkenny, Esq; Richard; Garret; Elinor; Grany, married

4l. a day, and Commander in Chief of all the forces in Ireland, in the abfence of the L L Strafford, which were then raifed by that Earl, and rendezvoufed at Carrickfergus, to affift the King againft the Scots; but were the fame month (upon the pacification) ordered to be difbanded, which was not executed till June 1641. On 23 October that year, the rebellion broke out, and his Lordfhip being then at his houfe in Carrick, the L J by an exprefs, notified the difcovery of the plot; advifed him to ftand upon his guard; to make the beft provifion he could for the defence of the country about him; and defired him prefently to repair to Dublin with his troop of horfe: And the King referring the whole bufinefs of Ireland to the Parliament of England, they made the Earl of Ormond (that the army might be led by an honourable and promifing perfon) Lieutenant-General; who being approved by the King, as one, who by his relations, integrity, and quality, was pitched on as the fitteft perfon for that employment, his Majefty confirmed him therein by his letter from Edinburgh of the 31 of that month: in which fituation he behaved with indefatigable activity and undaunted refolution; for, as foon as an army could be raifed, he marched from Dublin (31 January), took the Caftle of Lyons; routed the rebels at Kilfaghlan; fecured Naas with a garrifon, and placed in the town a new Sovereign, eight Burgeffes, and fifty families of defpoiled Proteftants; and having loft a trumpeter with four foldiers, by the garrifon of Tipper, he marched thither, and caufed it, with all therein, to be blown up; after which, 15 April 1642, he gained a very fignal victory over the Irifh army under the Lord Mountgarret, at Kilrufh, on his march from Athy to Dublin, killing 700 men, and taking all their ammunition, the General's waggon drawn by eight oxen, and 20 colours. For this great fervice he received (8 Auguft) the following letter of thanks from the Speaker of the Houfe of Commons; accompanied with a jewel of 620l. value;

" My Lord,

" I am commanded by the Houfe of Commons, to let your
" Lordfhip know, that with much contentment they received in-
" formation from Ireland, of the good fervice performed by you,
" againft thofe wicked bloody rebels; and in teftimony of their
" good acceptance and efteem of it, they do prefent you with
" this jewel, to be unto you a remembrance of their affection,
" as

married to John Comerford, of Ballybirr, Esq; Elizabeth, to Edmund Wale, of Ruchlin, in county of Carlow, Esq; and

" as also a pledge of their intentions of taking all occasions to
" acknowledge your merit, continuing in the same zealous en-
" deavours to serve this state and the true religion, by the sup-
" pression of that unnatural rebellion. These lines will further
" assure you, that no misreports or false scandals, which any
" malicious tongue may have raised concerning you, can make
" the least impression on them, who can easily see through such
" empty clouds, and fasten a clear judgment upon true and ho-
" nourable desert;—my Lord, you have here the public ex-
" pression of the sense of the House, made unto you by their
" own command; receive now, I beseech you, the tender of his
" particular service, who heartily prays for the continuance of
" your prosperous success, in so pious a cause, and desires to re-
" main

" Your Lordship's most humble and
" most affectionate servant,
" WILLIAM LENTHALL, Speaker."

15 April 1642.
To the Right Honourable the Earl of
Ormond and Ossory, Lieutenant-
General of his Majesty's Army in
Ireland [1].

And at the same time, the King, on his part, by privy seal, dated at Nottingham 23 August 1642, directed a full discharge to be given him, of what mortgages and debts he stood engaged for to those in actual rebellion, and for which the said mortgages were given; and also by patent, dated at the same place the 30 of that month, created him Marquess of Ormond [2].

In November 1641, he was joined in commission with the Lord Mountgarret, to govern and command such forces as they should raise, and be armed by the state, for the defence of the county of Kilkenny; and by commission dated at Oxford 11 January 1642, he was joined with Ulick, Earl of St. Alban's and Clanrickard, Earl of Roscomnion, Viscount Moore, Sir T. Lucas, Knt. Sir M. Eustace, Knt. and T. Bourke, Esq; to receive the propositions of the Irish confederate recusants.—In March 1642, he took the castles of Castlemartin, Kildare, Tully, and Timolin; whence marching to Ross, he obtained on the 18 a compleat victory, though at a great disadvantage, over General Preston. Soon after which, a proposal being set on foot by the King, for a cessation of arms with the Irish for one whole year; he was appointed to conclude

---

[1] Commons Jour. [2] Rot. pat. An. 19. 20. 21. 22. 23. 24. Car. 1. f. the articles are here enrolled.

and Mary to George Wolverston of Piperstown in the County of Dublin, Esq;

Mary, to Bryan O'Connor, Esq; (4)

Ellice (or Elizabeth) to Walter Dalton, otherwise Daton of Killmodalin in the county of Kilkenny, Esq; (5)

Margaret, to Oliver Grace of Carney in Tipperary, son and heir to Gerald Grace of Liegan, Esq; and he died in 1626. (6)

Anne,

clude it by the King's letters, dated at Oxford 23 April, 3 May, and 31 July 1643, and by commission under the Great Seal, dated at Dublin 31 August, he was authorised to treat and conclude for his Majesty, and in his name, with his said subjects, upon a cessation of arms for one whole year, to begin at such time, as to him should be thought fit, and upon such articles and agreements, as to him should seem necessary for his Majesty's service; or otherwise to break off the treaty, as he should see cause. Accordingly, he concluded the treaty 15 September, by which they were to pay 30,800l. and send succours to the King in England: and 16 November his Lordship sent to England about 2000 men; and 3 December 1300 foot and 140 Horse under the command of Colonel Robert Byron.

The cessation being thus concluded, his influence, fidelity, and diligence, became so conspicuous, that it was thought necessary to confer upon him the government of the kingdom; and accordingly being appointed by the king at Oxford¹, 13 November 1643, L. L. of Ireland, he was sworn 21 January following; and 23 March had a reversionary grant of the government of the fort of Duncannon, after the death of Laurence, Lord Esmond, with an augmentation of the warders from 30 to 100; and that nobleman dying 26 March 1645, he had a grant thereof passed to him, 5 December 1646, for life.—The Irish agents presenting to the King several propositions in order to a firm and settled peace; his Majesty appointed the Marquefs of Ormond, by commission dated at Buckingham 24 June 1644, to treat concerning the establishment of a firm and perfect peace in Ireland, and if he found it not reasonable to consent to such propositions, as should be made for a full peace, then to conclude on a further cessation of arms. By virtue of this commission he concluded a peace, consisting of thirty articles, which were signed and sealed 28 March 1646; whereby the Irish were to furnish a body of 10,000 men for the service of the King against the parliament; and he had a commission 17 August, authorizing him to give out commissions

for

¹ Carte, V. I. p. 475.

(7) Anne, to Edward Butler, Lord Viscount of Galmoy *.
Joan to William O'Farrell, of Ballintober, in county of Longford, Esq; son of ———— O'Farrell (Bane,) of Annally.

Richard,

for raising officers, as well natives of Ireland, as others his Majesty's subjects.

He continued in the government until the year 1647', when, with the King's approbation, he concluded a treaty with the Parliament's

Family of V. Galmoy.
* Pierce or Peter Butler, of the Abbey of Duiske or Dowske, was also called Peter or Piers Butler, of Grange-Douske, Esq; of which Abbey, with all the spiritual and temporal livings thereto belonging or parcel thereof, he was seized by deed indented from Thomas, Earl of Ormond, dated 18 June 1597, to hold to the heirs male of his body, in which he was succeeded by Edward his son [2]; who married Catharine, daughter and co-heir of Thomas Fleming, Lord Slane, who died 9 November 1597, and by her who married James Butler of Dowske, gent. brother to Lord Mountgarret [2] had the said Edward, Viscount Galmoy, and Sir Richard Butler of Knoctopher, whose son Colonel Thomas Butler of that place, was engaged in the wars of 1641.—Sir Edward Butler, 2 April 1618, received a grant of the Abbey of Duiske, with divers other lands in the counties of Kilkenny, Wexford, and Carlow, which were erected into the manor of Graigeduiske, with power to hold there a Thursday market, and two fairs on the feasts of St. Barnabas, and St. Simon and Jude. He resided at the Old-Abbey, and at Lowgrange in the county of Kilkenny, and by Privy Seal, dated at Oxford 31 January 1645, and by patent 16 May 1646, was created Viscount of Galmoy in the said county ; by his said wife he had two sons and two daughters; Pierce, Thomas , ———— married to ———— Masterson of the county of Wexford, Esq; and ———— to Thomas Davells of Killsheen in the Queen's county, Esq; Thomas Butler, the younger son, died in 1667, and by Catharine, daughter of Geoffrey Fanning, of Ballingarry in Tipperary, Esq; who re-married with Charles Mac-Carthy of Rathlin, in county of Carlow, Esq; [3] had an only daughter Anne, born in 1663, and married to William Coke of Painstown, near Carlow, Esq; Governor of that county for K. James II. whose son and heir Thomas Coke, Esq; married Helen, daughter and co-heir to Nicholas Purcell, Esq; titular Baron of Loughmoe in Tipperary, great nephew to James, the first Duke of Ormond, and had issue one son William, and one daughter Anne, married in December 1750 to Thomas, Viscount Kenmare. ———— Pierce Butler of Barrowmount, Esq; the elder son, was a Captain of Horse in the King's army during the troubles and being taken prisoner in the battle of Lampston, was killed (after safe quarter given) by Captain William Bolton in 1650, his father then living, and having married in November 1626 Margaret, second daughter of Nicholas, Viscount Netterville, left twelve children, of whom Edward succeeded his grandfather. Nicholas died in 1653 without issue ; Richard, died in 1684, or 1678, leaving by Anne, daughter of Edward Wolley, Bishop of Clonfert, a daughter married to Mr. Minchin of the county of Tipperary ; James died without issue; Edmund ; and of the daughters four were married, viz. Jane, to

¹ Chan. Decree at Rathfernon, 10 March 1603.   ² Idem.
³ Pedigree of Hay, penes J. L.

BUTLER, Viscount MOUNTGARRET.

Richard, the third Viscount, in 1597 (being then son-in-law to O'Neile, Earl of Tyrone) partook in his rebellion against

Richard, 3 Viscount.

Parliament's Commissioners, 18 June, for delivering into their hands the next day all the garrisons of the kingdom, which he did, together with the city of Dublin; and 28 July the regalia of the government. He then left the kingdom, and landed 2 August at Bristol; about which time the King being delivered by the Scots to the English army, and brought a prisoner to Hampton Court, he attended his Majesty there, who received him with extraordinary grace, as a person, who had served him with great zeal and fidelity, and with the universal testimony of all good men. After some stay, he embarked on board a shallop, in the obscure and unguarded port of Hastings in Sussex, (25 December) which safely transported him to Dieppe in Normandy; whence he waited on the Queen and Prince of Wales at Paris, by whom he was consulted in every transaction, being the person most depended upon to begin to give a turn to their fortune, and recommended to them by the King for that purpose.

Here he held a close correspondence with the Lord Inchiquin, on whose promise to prepare the province of Munster to receive him, as the King's L. L. he ventured over, and arrived at Cork,

to Walter Murray of Rathvilly in co. Carlow, Esq; Mary, first to Mr. Lewis of Ballyogan, and secondly to John Tobin of Cumpshinagh, Esq; Frances to Harvey Morres of Castle-Morres, Esq. created Viscount Mount-Morres; and Ellinor to William Grace of Ballylinch, E.q. —— Edward, the second Viscount Galmoy, married Ellinor daughter of Charles White of Leixlip, Esq. widow of Sir Arthur Alton, Knt. and had issue Pierce his successor; and Richard who married Lucia, daughter of —— Cavenagh, Esq. and had a daughter Sophia, wife to —— Hay, of the county of Wexford [1]; and a son Pierce of Newtown and Urlingford, who married Domvile, younger daughter of Sir Robert Hartpole of Shrule in the Queen's county, Knt. and dying in 1716, had four daughters and three sons, Edmund of Urlingford, after of Newtown, who married, and had issue five sons [2]; William of Bayswell; and Alderman Richard Butler of Kilkenny, who died 28 June 1753. —— Pierce, the third Viscount, was created L. L. D. 6 August 1677, by the Duke of Ormond, Chancellor of the University of Oxford; commanded a troop of guards in K. James's army; was outlawed 11 May 1691; and was one of the Commissioners for agreeing on the Articles of Surrender, on behalf of the Irish inhabitants of the city and county of Limerick, and the counties of Clare, Kerry, Cork, Sligo, and Mayo, which were ratified and confirmed by patent, bearing date at Westminster 24 May 1691 [3]. He married the daughter of Toby Mathew, of Thomastown in Tipperary, Esq. and left Edward his successor, who was Colonel of foot in K. James's army, and retired into France, where he died without issue; hence, had it not been for the attainder, the honour would have devolved on the aforesaid Edmund Butler, of Newtown eldest son of Pierce, son of Richard, youngest son of Edward, the second Viscount Galmoy [4].

[1] Lodge.   [2] Id.   [3] Id.   [4] Id.

against Q. Elizabeth, and with his kindred and followers, to the number of 130 foot and 20 horse, held out the Castles of

Cork [1], 29 September 1648; whence 11 October he went to his house of Carrick, and there treated of peace with the Commissioners of the General Assembly, which (17 January) was solemnly confirmed and proclaimed at Kilkenny; on the 30 of which month the King being beheaded, the Marquess received the news with inexpressible grief, and a suitable resentment; and 17 February K. Charles II. continuing him L L. he caused him to be solemnly proclaimed 19 March, and used his utmost endeavours to recover the kingdom to his obedience; which proving ineffectual, he appointed the Marquess of Clanrickard his Deputy; and again leaving Ireland 6 December 1650, arrived safe in France, where he gave the Queen an account of the condition of the kingdom; and for these his services to his King and country, was excepted from pardon for life or estate, by Cromwell's act of parliament for the settlement of Ireland.

When the King returned to Paris after the defeat at Worcester, he was sworn of the Privy Council; and constantly attending his Majesty, was consulted by him in all his affairs. In 1654, with great steadiness of spirit, he brought the Duke of Gloucester from the Queen at Paris to the King at Cologne, to prevent his being perverted in his religion; and soon after attended the Princess Royal from the Hague to the King; as he did his Majesty in his journey to Frankfort; and was present at the interview with Christina, Queen of Sweden, at Koningstein. In June following he was dispatched to engage the Duke of Neuburg's interest, to dispose the Court of Brussels to espouse the King's cause, and promote a treaty of alliance between their Britannick and Catholic Majesties.—When the King settled at Bruges, and raised four regiments, he gave the command of one, in December 1656, to the Marquess, that the Irish might be tempted to come over and increase his forces; and by the Marquess's interest, the town of St. Ghislain, in which the French had a garrison, was delivered up to the Spaniards in the beginning of 1657. a service of great importance, considering its vicinity to Brussels; and in February after, he was present at the Duke of York's attempt upon Mardike, when he had his horse killed under him.

Having been elected a Knight of the Garter 18 September N.S. 1649, he constantly wore the ensigns, though not installed or invested with the habit till 15 April 1661; and on his Majesty's restoration was appointed, 1 June 1660, Lord Steward of the

---

[1] Carte, II. 39.

BUTLER, Viscount MOUNTGARRET.

of Ballyragget and Colechill or Cullihill.—Being twenty-four years old at his father's death, he had a special livery of his

the houshold; sworn of his Privy Council [1]; made a Lord of his Bedchamber; and soon after L. L. of the county of Somerset; High Steward of the city and liberties of Westminster, Kingston, and Bristol; and was restored to the Chancellorship of the University of Dublin, which he had held before the usurpation, and soon redressed the evils, which had befallen it in that period.— In consideration of his distinguished loyalty, services, and sufferings, he was created a Peer of England 20 July 1660, by the titles of Baron Butler of Llanthony, and Earl of Brecknock.—30 November 1660, the King, by his declaration from Whitehall, appointed the Duke of Albemarle, and the Marquess, Trustees for the several towns of Ireland, and other the securities for the satisfaction of the arrears of the 49 officers.—7 February 1660, he was made Colonel of a regiment of horse, and Captain of a foot company; 30 March 1661, created Lord High Steward of England to assist at the coronation on the 23 April, in which solemn procession he walked immediate'y before the King, and carried St. Edward's crown, wherewith his Majesty was crowned: that very day (30 March) he was created Duke of Ormond [2] in Ireland, with the creation fee of 40l. payable out of the Exchequer: And the county of Tipperary, which had been seized by K. James I. was restored to him by patent 2 April 1662. *The preamble:* Cum summè dilectus et fidelissimus Consanguineus noster Jacobus Marchio Ormondiæ et Ossoriæ, Vicecomes Thurles, Dominus Baro de Arclo, Dominus Regalitatum et Libertatum Comitatus Palatini Tipperariæ. Cancellarius Universitatis Dubliensis Baro Butler de Lanthony in Comitatu nostro Monmouth in regno nostro Angliæ, Comes de Brecknocke in Dominio nostro Walliæ, unus à Sanctioribus nostris Consiliis tam Angliæ quam Hiberniæ, Dominus Senefchallus Hospicii nostri, unus Nobilium a Cubiculo nostro, et nobilissimi Ordinis Garterii Miles, Comes ex Comitibus prædictæ Ormondiæ per cerciter quatercentum annos semper intactæ fidei semper aut bello aut pace conspicuis, merita Majorum tot et tantorum propriis superaverit, nec dum satisfactum judicemus duorum Regum debito, et utriusque nostrum singulari benevolentiæ congestis in eum hactenus Honoribus quum et ipsum in statum gradum stilum titulum, dignitatem, nomen et honorem Ducis Ormondiæ in Regno nostro Hiberniæ prædicto sublimari censuimus. Sciatis igitur quod nos ex uberiori gratia, mero motu et certa scientia, nostris propter servicia satis per se nota alibi etiam succinctim

---

[1] Carte, II. 200. [2] Id. p. 220.

his estate 22 February 1605*; and sat in the Parliaments of 1613, 1615, and 1634; and after the rebellion of 1641 commenced,

succinctim repertita et ab ipsæ indies renova, præsatum Jacobum in honorem Ducis Ormondiæ in regno nostro Hiberniæ prædicto ereximus, &c.¹ to this the King added the county-cross of Tipperary; which grants were confirmed by act of parliament; and by the acts of settlement he was restored to his whole estate.

4 November 1661, he was declared L. L. of Ireland, which gave universal satisfaction; and arriving at Dublin 27 July ², 1662, after a dangerous passage, (being the day of the same month, on which 15 years before he had been compelled to deliver up the government to the English parliament) he continued in the administration until 14 February 1668, when he was succeeded by John, Lord Robartes, and the parliament of Ireland, as a testimony of their gratitude and affection, presented him with a gift of 30,000l. but his removal (accomplished by the Duke of Buckingham, and other enemies) prevented his receipt of 98,256l. due to him, which made him all his life struggle with many difficulties, and at his death leave debts of 89,324l. 13s. 10d. after having lost for his loyalty, beyond all profits received, 868,590l. 16s. 9d—His Majesty by patent, dated at Westminster 23 April 1662, having thought fit to raise in England a regiment of 1200 foot, to be his regiment of guards in Ireland, authorised his Grace to raise and transport them into this kingdom, and to give commissions to such, as he should think fit to be officers.—20 February 1663. he was made commander of the port of Passage in the county of Waterford, pursuant to Privy Seal at Whitehall 19 January preceding, in which the King writes, "Whereas
" we understand that our Fort at Passage in our county of Wa-
" terford, on the other side of the water from our Port of Dun-
" cannon in our county of Wexford, is of great importance, and
" that it may tend very much to our service, and the safety
" of

---

* Which he afterwards surrendered to K. James, and in consideration of his faithful and acceptable services, had a confirmation thereof 9 January 1619, with the creation of the several manors of Ballaragged (Ballyragget) alias Donaghmore, Cowlechill, Kenlis, Ballin, otherwise Ballyeyen, Hillingford, and Mountgarret, with power to hold Courts; to impark 2000 acres, with free warren and chace; liberty of tanning leather; and to hold a Thursday market, and two fairs on the feasts of St. Barnabas and Bartholomew, and the day after each at Ballyragget. Also, 9 January 1621 he had a further confirmation thereof by two patents; and by virtue of the commission of grace, K. Charles I. for the fine of 270l. 9 February 1638, released to him all his lands in the counties of Kilkenny and Wexford, confirming the aforesaid privileges.

¹ Rot. p. A°. 15°. Car. II. 1ˢ. p. f. R. 16.   ² Carte. II. 257.

commenced, his Lordship, being a man of years and experience, was joined in commission with the Earl of Ormond by

" of that harbour, and of the parts of the country thereabouts;
" that good correspondency and intelligence be held between
" those our forts; and our Royal Father having by his let-
" ters patent, granted the command of the said Fort of Duncan-
" non unto you, during your life; we think fit that for the ends
" and purposes aforesaid, you have the command also of our
" said Fort of Passage, and the town of Passage East and West,
" during your natural life, with power to appoint a Deputy [1]."
And 24 July 1669, he was empowered to hold Court of Sessions and Gaol Delivery in the county Palatine of Tipperary

4 August 1669, he was chosen Chancellor of the University of Oxford, on the resignation of Doctor Gilbert Sheldon, Archbishop of Canterbury, who earnestly recommended him to be his successor, having a great and just opinion of his integrity and honour; and to shew the higher esteem of him, he did this at a juncture, when his Grace was out of favour at Court. 17 January 1672, he was joined in commission with Prince Rupert and others, to inspect the affairs of Ireland, viz. the execution of the acts of settlement; the disposition of forfeited lands, the state of the revenue [2], &c. and 24 August 1677, he was a third [3] time sworn L. L. of Ireland, in which station he continued till 1682, when with great difficulty he procured leave to go to England; and 9 November following was created an English Duke [4], retaining the title of Ormond, with the creation fee of 40l. a year, in consideration of his faithful services, and particularly for his keeping the kingdom of Ireland quiet all the time of the Popish plot, whilst England was in the utmost distraction. He was commissioned with others, 14 March 1683, for the remedy of defective titles; and whilst he continued in England, attempted to have a parliament called in Ireland, but ineffectually, and upon the disappointment thereof, returned in August 1684, with a heavy heart, as he declared to many in Ireland [5].

15 February 1684, he was continued by K. James II. Lord Steward of his houshold, and constituted Lord High Steward of England for his coronation [6], at which, 23 April 1685, he assisted by carrying the same crown, as before at the coronation of K Charles II This solemnity performed, he returned to Ireland; but in March following was recalled, and on his arrival at Court, found himself in displeasure with the King; had his regiment taken from him; and perceiving the measures, which the

---

[1] Carte, II. 381. [2] Carte and Lodge. [3] Carte. p. 463.
[4] Id. p. 524. [5] Carte and Lodge. [6] Carte. p. 543.

by the L. J. to govern the county of Kilkenny, and provide for the peace and security thereof; upon that Earl's removal

the King was pursuing, would carry him to the most violent actions, he entertained dismal apprehensions of what might ensue, which are thought to have hastened his death, that happened 21 July 1688 [1], at his seat of Kingston-Hall in the county of Dorset; and 4 August he was interred in Westminster-Abbey. During his administration of affairs in Ireland, he procured many favours from the crown, for the public benefit of the kingdom. In Aug. 1660, he prevailed with the King to fill the 4 archiepiscopal, and 12 episcopal sees, with the most eminent men to be found among the Irish clergy; at which time great endeavours being used to prevent the admission of episcopacy, and the constitution of the church of England, the clergy of Ireland addressed themselves to him for protection, and soon felt the good effects of his interposition: and the grants he procured for them, drew from all the Bishops then in Dublin an address of thanks, in the name of all the orthodox clergy of Ireland. And that the kingdom might never want an able and learned clergy, he had a body of statutes drawn up for the government of the University of Dublin, to whom he was an eminent and singular benefactor in many respects. At a considerable expence and labour he revived the linen manufacture, the foundation of which was laid by the Earl of Strafford, to which is owing its now flourishing state. He obtained the allowance of a free trade to all foreign nations, either in war or peace with England. He procured the King's letter for incorporating a College of Physicians in Dublin, to improve the science and reform the practice of physick in Ireland (which society had the grant of a new charter 29 Sept. 1692.) He accomplished the foundation of the hospital near Dublin, for ancient and maimed officers and soldiers of Ireland; which 19 Feb. 1683, was incorporated a body politic of governors, to have perpetual succession, &c. He founded a publick school called the College of Kilkenny, and endowed it with lands to the amount of 140l. a year. He set up and encouraged, at a great expence, both the woollen and linen manufactures. And lived to see four Kings, three of whom he served for 57 years, with an unshaken zeal and untainted loyalty, as all his ancestors had done before him. He had seen three generations above him, his father, grandfather, and great-great uncle Thomas, Earl of Ormond; and as many below him, his son, his grandson, and his great-grandson Thomas, who was playing in the room but a few hours before

---

[1] Carte, II. 549.

BUTLER, Viscount MOUNTGARRET.

moval to Dublin, to take upon him the command of the army, he was folely invefted with the fupreme authority of ordering

before his death, being about two years old. Thus he paffed through a long life, and variety of fortunes, with honour and reputation ; being beloved and efteemed by the good men of all parties ; and died as much regretted, as it was poffible for man to be, without courting popular applaufe, or purfuing any other rule in his conduct, than doing what, in his own judgment, was right.

By his aforefaid lady, (who was godmother with the Duchefs of Buckingham, to Q. Mary, died of a fever 21 July 1684, in the 69 year of her age, and was buried in Weftminfter Abbey) his Grace had iffue eight fons and two daughters, viz.

Thomas, born in 1632, who died before he was two days old, and was buried at Kilkenny. (1)

Thomas, Earl of Offory, of whom hereafter, (2)

James, born in 1635, who did not live above two days, and was buried at Kilkenny. (3)

James, born 24 March 1636, and dying 3 April 1655, was buried in Chrift Church, Dublin. (4)

Richard, born 15 June 1639, was created 13 May, 1662, Baron Butler of Cloughgrenan, Vifcount of Tullogh, and Earl of Arran, with limitation of the honours to the iffue male of his brother John ; was fworn of the Privy Council 26 Auguft 1663 ; and purchafing the ifles of Arran from Erafmus Smith, Efq; had a confirmation thereof, and of divers other lands, by feveral patents under the acts of fettlement.—The King having 13 November 1665, ordered certain Light-Houfes to be built in or near the ports of Dublin, Carrickfergus, Waterford, and Kingfale, for the prefervation of his fhips, which were to pay a certain duty for the charge and maintenance thereof; his Majefty, 29 March 1667, granted thofe that were then built (viz. two upon the Hill of Howth, one in the Ifle of Magee, two near Kingfale, and one at the Tower of Hooke, otherwife the Tower of Roffe) to his Lordfhip for 61 years, at the rent of 40s. 1 September 1666, he was made Alnager of Ireland ; and 15 May 1671, had a warrant to receive the pay of two common foldiers out of each field company, and of one foldier out of every other company in his Majefty's Regiment of Guards in Ireland: Of which regiment having the command, he did good fervice in reducing the mutineers of Carrickfergus ; and alfo behaved with diftinguifhed valour in the fea-fight of 1673 with the Dutch ; for which he was created 27 Auguft that year, a Peer of England by the

(5) Richard, Earl of Arran.

dering the forces raifed by the county, and fecuring it. But being alarmed by the defigns, which (as was confidently faid, and

the title of Baron Butler of Wefton. 21 October 1675 [1], he was made C. Rotulorum of the county of Carlow ; and 2 May 1682, fworn deputy to his father in the government of the kingdom ; being alfo 10 September 1684, made Marfhal of the army, with the fee of 52l. 17s. 8d. per month, which was renewed to him 16 July 1685.

He firft married in September 1664, the Lady Mary Steuart, only furviving child of James, Duke of Richmond and Lenox, who died 30 March 1655, and heir to her brother Efme, who died in 1666, Æt. 10 ; but by her, (who died 4 July 1688, at the age of 18 years, and was buried 19 Auguft at St. Canice's Cathedral in Kilkenny [2], with all the pomp that her quality and the memory of her virtues deferved, the like folemnity having never been feen in Ireland), he had no iffue ; he married fecondly, in June 1673, Dorothy, daughter of John Ferrers of Tamworth-Caftle in Warwickfhire, Efq; and by her, who deceafed 30 April 1715, had feveral children, whereof his eldeft fon Thomas, was buried in the choir of Chrift Church 7 June 1681 ; two others died in 1685 ; Elizabeth born in 1677, who died before him, and only one daughter furvived him (he died 26 January 1685, and was buried in Weftminfter Abbey) which was the Lady Charlotte, born 30 November 1678, and married 1 June 1699 to Charles, Lord Cornwallis, whofe widow fhe died 8 Auguft 1725, and was mother of Charles, Lord Cornwallis, and grandmother of Charles the prefent Earl.

(6) Walter, born 6 September 1641, died in March 1643, and was buried in Chrift Church.

(7) John, Earl of Gowran.
John, born in 1643, was Captain of the Troop of Horfe Guards in Ireland ; and 13 April 1676, created Baron of Agherim, Vifcount of Clonmore, and Earl of Gowran, *with this preamble* ; Nos regia mente noftra recolentes eximiam fidelitatem et immaculatam Ligeantiam prædilecti et perquam fidelis confanguinei et conciliarii noftri Jacobi, Ducis Ormondiæ, Senefchalli Hofpitii noftri regii, ac etiam quamplurima egregia et perquam acceptabilia fervicia tam nobis quam regali patri noftro, beatæ memoriæ, per præfatum Jacobum, Ducem Ormondiæ, tam in feperalibus regni noftris, quam in partibus tranfmarinis præftita ; confiderantes etiam merita, et Virtutes Domini Johannis Butler, tertii filii præfati Jacobi, Ducis Ormondiæ, ac fervicia per eum nobis hactenus impenfa, quæ nobis abunda innotuerint, hinc eft quod nos præfatum Dominum Johannem Butler —— perpetuo regii favoris noftri

---

[1] Rot. Can. 27° Car. 2. 4ᵃ p. D.   [2] Ulfter's Office.

BUTLER Viscount MOUNTGARRET.

and then generally believed by the Roman Catholics) had been formed against the Lords of the Pale, for extirpating

noftri monumento Pofteris fuis tranfmittando ornare et decorare decrevimus, ac eum ad ftatus et dignitates—Baronis, Vicecomitis, et Comitis regni noftri Hiberniæ promovendum ce: fum . Sciatis igitur &c.' purfuant to privy fignet, at Whitehall 10 February in the preceding year².---In January 1676, he married the Lady Anne Chichefter, only daughter of Arthur, Earl of Donegal; but his Lordfhip travelling to Paris for the recovery of his health, died there in Auguft 1677, leaving no iffue, whereby the titles ceafed.

James, born in 1645, who being carried to take the air, and the horfes running away with the coachman down the Phœnix-Hill near Dublin, the woman, who had the care of him, in her fright threw him out of the window, and he was killed by the fall 20 May 1646, being fix months old.

Daughter Lady Elizabeth was born 29 June 1640, married in 1656 to Philip Stanhope, the fecond Earl of Chefterfield, to whom fhe was fecond wife, and died in July 1665.

Lady Mary, born in 1646, was married at Kilkenny 27 October 1662, to William Cavendifh, the fourth Earl (after Duke) of Devonfhire, and was grandmother of William, Duke of Devonfhire, L. L of Ireland: dying 31 July 1710, fhe was buried in Weftminfter Abbey.

Thomas, Earl of Offery, the eldeft fon, born at Kilkenny 8 July 1634, by the time he was 21 years of age, gave fuch proofs of his genius, prudence, good difpofition and virtue, that Sir Robert Southwell then drew his character, and fhewed him to the world in very lively colours. "He is," fays he, "a young " man with a very handfome face; a good head of hair; well-" fet; very good-natured; rides the great horfe very well; is " a very good tennis-player, fencer and dancer; underftands " mufic, and plays on the guitar and lute; fpeaks French ele-" gantly; reads Italian fluently; is a good hiftorian; and fo " well verfed in romances, that if a gallery be full of pictures " and hangings, he will tell the ftories of all that are there de-" fcribed. He fhuts up his door at eight o'clock in the evening, " and ftudies till midnight; he is temperate, courteous, and " excellent in all his behaviour."

8 February 1660, he was made colonel of a regiment of foot in Ireland; 13 June 1661, Colonel of the next regiment of horfe that fhould become void; and on the Earl of Mountrath's

---

¹ Rot. 28°. Car. 2 1°. p. f. R. 19.   ² Idem D. R. 19. ?

BUTLER, Viscount MOUNTGARRET.

ting their religion, with its profeffors, out of the nation, he came to a refolution of taking up arms, and to embark himfelf

Mountrath's death, fucceeded to his troop of horfe and regiment of foot; was appointed the 19 Lieutenant-General of the horfe; fworn of the Privy Council 16 April 1661; and his Majefty judging it of importance to his fervice, that he fhould be qualified to fit in the Houfe of Lords in Ireland, thought fit to direct the L. L. by writ or otherwife, as had been accuftomed, to call him to fit in the faid Houfe of Lords by Privy Seal at Hampton Court 22 June 1662 [1], at which time he reprefented the city of Briftol and the Univerfity of Dublin; and 8 Auguft being brought by the Commons to the bar of the Houfe of Lords, an order was made, that by the confent of the Earl's Bench, the Earl of Offory fhould be placed above all of that degree. By patent 16 September 1665, he was [2] conftituted Lieutenant-General of the army in Ireland; and the next year a Lord of the King's bedchamber; was fworn in June of the Privy Council of England; and 14 September fummoned by writ to the Englifh parliament, by the title of Lord Butler of More-Park.

In the years 1664 and 1668, he was deputy to his father; and 24 April 1669, had full power granted him to give licenfes for the tranfporting of wool. In January 1671, he received a commiffion to command the Refolution, a third-rate ship, and another in April 1672, to command the Victory, a fecond-rate, and 3 June behaved with great valour and conduct in Southwould-Bay fight with the Dutch, endeavouring to lay Admiral de Ruyter's fhip aboard, but he fheering off avoided the engagement: The Earl of Offory however gained fo much reputation, that when he returned to Court, he was 30 September, elected a Knight of the Garter, and 29 October inftalled at Windfor. In November he was fent Envoy Extraordinary to the Court of France, with compliments of condolence on the death of Louis-Francis, Duke of Anjou, and at his parting was prefented with a jewel of 2000l. value. 17 May 1673, the King gave him the command of the St. Michael, a firft-rate fhip, then newly built, and made him Rear Admiral of the Blue fquadron, in order to that great fea-fight againft the Dutch, which happened fhortly after, wherein, as Anthony à Wood fays, he gallantly acted beyond the fiction of a romance. After the fight, he was made Rear Admiral of the Red Squadron; and 10 September difplayed the Union Flag, as Commander in Chief of the whole fleet, in the abfence of Prince Rupert, by the King's fpecial command. 10 November 1674, he embarked for Holland, to treat with the

Prince

---

[1] Rot. 14°. Car. 2. 3. p. f.   [2] Idem 17°. Car. 2. 1. p. D. R. 34.

himself and family in opposing a step, which appeared so destructive to his religion and interest.——That this was his design

Prince of Orange concerning a marriage with the Lady Mary, eldest daughter of James, Duke of York; was appointed in August 1675, a Commissioner of the Admiralty; had a pension 13 March following, granted for three years of 2666l. 13s. 4d. a year; and 18 November 1676, was sworn Lord Chamberlain to Queen Catharine.

In July 1677, he joined the Prince of Orange at the siege of Charleroy; and in February following going over to command the English forces in the pay of the States, had a commission from them to be Colonel and Captain of one of their six regiments, being also made Major-General and Commander in Chief of the English Brigade, by the Prince of Orange's patent; and in the campaign of 1678, was fought the famous battle of Mons, in which the Mareschal de Luxemburgh was forced to retreat, and the Earl of Ossory gained so much glory; the States of Holland, the Duke de Villa Hermosa, governor of the Low Countries, and the King of Spain himself, in a letter under his own hand, acknowledging his great services in that campaign. But this excellent nobleman (of whom enough cannot be said) was snatched away by a fever at Whitehall 30 July 1680, to the universal regret of England, and the general grief of great part of Europe, and his body was conveyed to the family vault in the Cathedral of Kilkenny.

He married 17 November 1659, N. S. the Lady Amelia Nassau, eldest daughter of Louis, Lord of Beverweart, La Leeke, Odyke, and Averquerque, Governor of Sluys, natural son of Maurice, Prince of Orange, by Madame de Beverweart, Countess of Mecklin, and had issue by her, who was naturalized by act of Parliament 13 September 1660, and buried in Christ Church 25¹ January 1684, six sons and as many daughters, who all died young or unmarried, except two sons and three daughters, viz. James, Duke of Ormond; Charles, Earl of Arran; Lady Elizabeth, married in July 1673, to William-Richard-George, the ninth Earl of Derby, died 28 June 1717, and was buried 12 July in Westminster Abbey; Lady Emilia, born 29 May 1660, and died 30 March 1760, unmarried ²; and Lady Henrietta married in 1696 to Henry D'Auverquerque, Earl of Grantham, her first cousin, and died 11 October 1724.

James, the second Duke of Ormond, was born 29 April 1665, in the Castle of Dublin, when his father was deputy to his grandfather; was educated in Christ Church, Oxford, till his father's

James
2
Duke

¹ Ulster's Office.   ² Lodge.

design is manifest from his letter * to the Earl of Ormond, with the declaration and grievances inclosed; and this he was

ther's decease, when he was complimented with the degree of Master of Arts, after which (by his grandfather's order) he returned to Ireland¹, and went a volunteer in April 1684 to the siege of Luxembourg, then invested by the French, whence he returned

* The letter runs thus: " My Lord, since I have been forced into this general cause by the example of some, as innocent and free from infringing of his Majesty's laws as myself, who have been used in the nature of traitors, I forebore, for avoiding your displeasure, to acquaint you with my proceedings and other motives therein: But now, for fear of being mistaken by the state, concerning my loyalty, and presuming of your Lordship's favour and good meaning towards me, I make bold to send you, here inclosed, an exact remonstrance of those principal grievances, that have procured this general commotion in this kingdom; wherewith I shall humbly desire your Lordship to acquaint the L. J. and Council, to the end they may, by a fair redress of them, prevent the fearful calamities, that doubtless shall ensue for want thereof. It is not my case alone, it is the case of the whole kingdom; and it hath been a principal observation of the best historians, that a whole nation, how contemptible soever, should not be so incensed by any Prince or State, how powerful soever, as to be driven to take desperate courses, the event whereof is uncertain, and rests only in the all-guiding power of the Omnipotent. This has been most lively represented by the French Chronicler Philip de Comines, in the passages between the Duke of Burgundy and the Switzers. I need not press this matter further, (a word is enough to the intelligent) and I cannot harbour any thought of your Lordship, but that you are sensible of the miseries of this kingdom, whereof you are a native, and do wish the quiet and tranquility thereof. I do, for a further expression of my own sincerity in this cause, send to your Lordship here inclosed my declaration and oath, joined with others, which I conceive to be tolerable, and no way inclining to the violation of his Majesty's laws, whereof I am and always will be very observant, as becomes a loyal subject, and

" My Lord,
" 25 March 1641. Your Lordship's humble servant,
MOUNTGARRET."

———— In confirmation hereof, it appears from the deposition of William Parkinson of Castlecomer, Esq; that so little were his lordship's inclinations to take up arms against his Majesty, that Walter Butler of Poolestown, Walter Bagenal of Dunleckney, and Robert Shee of Kilkenny, Esqrs. were the chief instruments that made him do so; and so high was the insolence of those rebels grown, that the deponent had read a petition of one Richard Archdeacne, Captain of the Irish-Town of Kilkenny, and the Aldermen of the city, directed to the Lord Mountgarret and his Council, desiring (among other things) that Philip Purcell of Ballyfoile, Esq; his Lordship's son-in-law, might be punished for relieving the Protestants.—Also, the titular Bishop of Cashel, Turlogh

¹ Lodge.

was the better enabled to do, by reason of his alliance to most of the gentlemen of the county of Kilkenny; who being returned to London in July, and was made Colonel of a regiment of horse in Ireland. In May 1685, he was appointed a Lord of his Majesty's Bedchamber, and serving in the army, was sent down into the West against the Duke of Monmouth, and had a share in the victory over that unfortunate Nobleman 6 July, at Sedgemore near Bridgewater. He was elected Chancellor of the University of Oxford 25 July 1688, in the room of his grandfather, and installed 23 August at his house in St. James's-square. In his power he opposed the despotick measures of K. James's Court, and 17 November 1688, joined with several Lords and Bishops, in a petition to the King, to prevent, by calling a free Parliament, the miseries his person and kingdoms were exposed to; but meeting with a sharp answer, his Grace left the Court, along with Prince George of Denmark; and declaring for the laws and liberties of his country, was one of the first of the English nobility that went over to the Prince of Orange; for which K. James seized his estate in Ireland, to the value of 25,000 l. a year, and 20 April 1692, excepted him out of his general pardon; his Parliament at Dublin having attainted him 7 May 1689.

On K. William's advancement to the throne, his Grace 14 February 1688 (the day after the King and Queen were proclaimed) was made a Gentleman of his Bedchamber, and Colonel of the Second Troop of Guards; installed a Knight of the Garter 5 April 1689, and 11, constituted High Constable of England for their Majesties Coronation. In 1690 he attended his Majesty into Ireland; was at the Battle of the Boyne, and two days after detached with his uncle Henry, Lord Auverquerque, and nine troops of horse to secure and take possession of the city of Dublin; and the King afterwards advancing towards Kilkenny, his Grace was dispatched from Castledermot, to secure that city and the adjacent country from plunder; when his Majesty came there 19 July, he splendidly entertained him in his Castle, attended him into England and Holland; and 29 July 1693, was at the battle of Landen, wherein he charged the enemy at the head of one of Lumley's squadrons, received several wounds, and having his horse shot under him, was rescued by a gentleman of the

---

logh Oge O'Neile, brother to the arch rebel Sir Phelim, and the Popish citizens of Kilkenny, petitioned the rest of the Council of Kilkenny, that all the English Protestants there should be put to death; whereunto Alderman Richard Lawless in excuse answered, that they were all robbed before, and he saw no cause that they should lose their lives; and at divers other times, when it was pressed that the English should be put to death, the Lord Mountgarret, with his son Edmund, and his son-in-law Purcell, by their strength, means, and persuasions, prevented it.

BUTLER, Viscount MOUNTGARRET:

being generally of his religion, readily joined with him, and attended him with a numerous train to the city of Kilkenny, into

the French guards from the hands of a villain, about to stab him; being thus taken prisoner, he was carried to Namure, where he signalized his charity, by distributing a great part of his revenues to his fellow prisoners, by the hands of Count Guifcard, the Governor [1]; but was after exchanged for the Duke of Berwick, made prisoner by Brigadier Churchill, and when at liberty, attended his post in the army, where, the grandeur of his table and retinue, were an honour to the English nation, as his valour had been an example to the nobility [2].

By Q. Anne he was appointed 20 April 1702, Commander in Chief of the land forces, set against France and Spain, when he destroyed the French fleet, sunk the Spanish galleons in the harbour of Vigo, and took the Fort of Redondella, for which he received the thanks of both houses of Parliament. 24 June 1702, he was made L. L. of the county of Somerset; and 4 February following, her Majesty declared him L. L. of Ireland, where he was received with every demonstration of joy; and during his stay till the year 1706 in this high post, governed with more affection from the people, and kept his Court in greater splendor, than ever was known in this kingdom.

In 1707, he was appointed Colonel of the third troop of horse guards; 19 October 1710, again declared L. L. of Ireland; and 1 January 1711, made Colonel of the first regiment of Foot Guards, and declared Captain General and Commander in Chief of the land forces in Great Britain, or which were or should be employed abroad, in conjunction with the troops of the allies; which post (his commission being signed 26 February [3]) he held till the treaty of Utrecht in 1713. 26 June that year he was made Warden and Admiral of the Cinque Ports, and Constable of Dover Castle; and on the Queen's death was one of the Privy Council, who signed the proclamation, declaring K. George I. to be the only lawful and rightful King of Great Britain; on whose arrival, he was graciously received by his Majesty; appointed 9 October 1714 of his Privy Council in Ireland; and L L of the county of Somerset; from which he was removed a few days after, as he had been 18 September before from being Captain-General of the army, the Lord Viscount Townshend then acquainting him, that his Majesty had no longer occasion for his service in that quality, but would be glad to see him at Court.

The Parliament meeting 17 March 1714, his Grace was impeached 21 June 1715, by Mr. Secretary Stanhope, of High Treason,

---

[1] Lodge. [2] Idem. [3] Idem.

BUTLER, Viscount MOUNTGARRET.

into which he was admitted, and there declared the reasons of his taking possession of it, and entering into arms; and by Treason, and the House of Commons voted that he should be impeached accordingly; whereupon being advised to avoid the impending storm of a Parliamentary prosecution, although it is presumed by many, had he waited to stand his trial, that his innocent and good intentions in all his actions would have cleared him from the imputed guilt[1]; He retired 8 August into France, and was 20 of that month attainted, his estate forfeited, and honours extinguished; and the Parliament of this kingdom, 26 June 1716, passed an act, for extinguishing the regalities and liberties of the county palatine of Tipperary; for vesting his estate in the crown; and for giving a reward of 10,000l for his apprehension, should he attempt to land in Ireland. But the same English parliament passed an act 24 June 1721, to enable his brother the Earl of Arran to purchase his estate, which he accordingly did.

This great, but unfortunate Nobleman, married to his first wife, 15 July 1682, Anne, eldest daughter of Laurence, Earl of Rochester, who dying 25 January 1684[2] of a miscarriage in Dublin, aged 17 years and 3 days, was buried in the family vault in Christ Church; he married secondly, 3 August 1685, Mary, eldest surviving daughter of Henry, first Duke of Beaufort, and by her, who died 19 November 1733, in the 69th year of her age, and was buried in Westminster Abbey, he had one son Thomas, born 26 September 1686, who died 27 February 1689, and was there buried; and five daughters, whereof the Ladies Mary, Emilia, and Henrietta died in their infancy; Lady Elizabeth died unmarried 20 April 1750, and was buried with her father; and Lady Mary was married 21 October 1710, to John, Lord Ashburnham, and dying 2 January 1712, æt. 23, was buried at Ashburnham. His Grace resided chiefly at Avignon; had a pension from the Court of Spain of 2000 pistoles; and departing this life 16 November 1745, N. S.; his corpse was brought into England, and deposited 22 May 1746, in the family vault, in K. Henry VII. Chapel, Westminster Abbey.

Charles, the younger son of Thomas, Earl of Ossory, was born 4 September 1671, and by K. William made a Lord of his Bedchamber; Colonel of a regiment of horse; and, by Privy Seal, dated at Whitehall 15 January 1693, and patent 8 March following, created Baron of Cloughgrenan, Viscount of Tullogh, and

Charles Earl of Arran.

---

[1] See his conduct in the campaign of 1712 vindicated in a pamphlet, published in 1715. [2] Ulster's Office.

BUTLER, Viscount MOUNTGARRET.

by public proclamation strictly enjoined all his followers, not to pillage or hurt the English inhabitants, either in body or

and Earl of Arran; and also a Baron of England, by the title of Lord Butler of Weston. *The preamble.* Nos regia mente recolentes eximia merita et virtutes præ dilecti et fidelis subditi nostri Caroli Butler, filii secundo geniti egregii viri Thomæ nuper Comitis de Ossory, necnon fidelitatem erga Nos illustrem, ac res per illum contra inimicos nostros fortissime gestas, in magnum rerum nostrarum emolumentum, quæ omnia simul cum partûs ejus nobilitate et hæreditario ejus erga coronam nostram Angliæ studio, nobis amplissime innotuerint. Hinc est quod nos præfatum Carolum Butler pro talibus meritis perpetuo regii favoris nostri monumento posteris suis transmittendo ornare et decorare decrevimus. Sciatis igitur, &c.

His Lordship, 14 January 1702, was made a Brigadier-General of her Majesty's armies, and 22 April 1708 a Lieutenant-General By patent, 6 June 1712, he was constituted Master of the Ordnance, in the room of Lieutenant-General Ingoldsby deceased, but this he resigned on the Queen's demise. In July 1713 he was made Governor of Dover Castle, and Deputy Warden of the Cinque Ports, which he also resigned at the same time. On 10 September 1715 he was elected Chancellor of the University of Oxford; and 28 February following Lord High Steward of the city and liberties of Westminster.

He married Elizabeth, fourth and youngest daughter of Thomas, Lord Crew, of Stene, but by her, who became co-heir to her uncle Nathaniel, Lord Crew, Bishop of Durham, (who died without issue 18 September 1721) and died 21 May 1756, his Lordship had no issue, and deceasing 17 December 1758, æt. 88, the titles became extinct, but the estates devolved pursuant to the settlement made by his Lordship, first, on his sister Lady Emilia Butler, and on her death, to John Butler of Kilcash, Esq; who dying 24 June 1766, without issue,

Walter Butler, only son of John, second son of Walter of Garryricken, eldest son of Richard of Kilcash, the youngest son of Thomas Lord Thurles, son of Walter, the eleventh Earl of Ormond succeeded—he married Eleanor, eldest daughter of Nicholas Morris of the Court in county of Dublin, Esq; (son of Sir John, and great uncle to the late Sir Redmond Morris, Barts.) and by her had two daughters, the elder married to ———— Cavanagh, of Borris, in county of Carlow, Esq; the younger to ———— Cavanagh, Esq; of the same family, and an only son John, elected to Parliament for the county of Kilkenny, and married 26 February 1769, to Lady Anne Wandesford, only daughter

BUTLER, Viscount MOUNTGARRET.

or goods; in which design he so far succeeded, that there was not the least act of bloodshed committed.

Kilkenny being thus seized by his Lordship, he detached parties to secure other adjacent towns, which was done with such success, that in the space of a week, almost all the towns and forts in the counties of Kilkenny, Waterford and Tipperary were in the power of these Irish forces; after which, being chosen by those who prosecuted the same cause, General of all the forces raised by the gentlemen of the country, he marched into Munster, and took Dodd's Castle, with the castles of Knockordane, Ballahey and Mallow; but the county of Cork insisting upon making a General in their own province, he looked on himself to be principally levelled at, and retired with his forces into Leinster, where he met the Earl of Ormond with a powerful army, and gave him battle at Killrush in the county of Kildare 10 April 1642; but being entirely defeated, he returned to Kilkenny, and was chosen President of the Supreme Council, formed there in the summer of 1642.

18 March following he was at the battle of Rosse, fought by General Preston against the Marquess of Ormond; and in 1643, with his son Edmund (Roe) was at the taking of the Castle of Borrass in the Queen's county; and with the Lords Netterville, Ikerrin, Upper Ossory, and Castlehaven, at the siege of Ballynakill, which surrendered 5 May, after a siege first begun 26 November 1641, during which time about 900 men, women and children, endured much want and misery, receiving very little relief from the state, and no arms at all; so that upon the surrender, 753 were alive, the rest being slain, and dead by sickness.—He continued to act in this war, but with as great moderation and care of the distressed Protestants, as the violence of the times would permit him to exercise; and dying in 1651 was excepted

daughter and heir of John, Earl of Wandesford, who deceasing in 1784, his titles became extinct, but his estates devolved on Mr. Butler, (in right of Lady Anne) who, on the death of his father, succeeded also to the estates of the Earl of Arran, and at present represents the several families of Ormond, Kilcash, and Garryricken.

BUTLER, Viscount MOUNTGARRET.

cepted (though dead) from pardon for life or estate by Cromwell's act of parliament for the settlement of Ireland, passed 12 August 1652, having been outlawed before.—He lies buried under a handsome monument in the chancel of St. Canice church, with this inscription:

D. O. M.
Sacrum
Ill.^{mus} ac Nob.^{mus} D'nus Richardus
Butler, Vicecomes de Mount:
:garet, Baro de Kells, &c.
Ex antiquissimis primariæ in Hiberniâ Nobi:
:litatis Familiis oriundus, utpote Petri Butler Or:
:moniæ et Ossoriæ Comitis, ac Margaretæ Fitz:
Gerald Filiæ Comitis de Kildare, Pronepos. Vir
Religione in Deum, Pietate in Patriam, Fidelita:
:te in Regem, Pace Belloque conspicuus ; de Rege,
Regno, Ecclesiâ Dei, pro quibus fortiter periculo:
:sis et maxime turbatis Temporibus stetit, optime
Meritus ; felicis ac fœcundæ Prolis Parens, sibi,
Majoribus ac Posteris, hoc Monumentum pie posuit;
Memoriam sui nunquam moriturim reliquit. Obiit
Ille An'o 16—
Defunctis et Nobilissimæ Vice-Comitum
De Mountgaret Familiæ bene precare
Viator.

He married first Margaret, eldest daughter of Hugh O'Neile, Earl of Tyrone, by whom he had three sons and five daughters ; and secondly Thomasine (who at her confirmation took the name of Elizabeth[1], and was so called in 1619) daughter of Sir William Andrews of Newport Pagnel in the county of Bucks, who dying without issue in 1625, he married thirdly in July[2] 1631 Margaret, daughter of Richard Branthwaite, Esq; Serjeant at Law, and widow of Sir Thomas Spencer of Yarnton in Oxfordshire, Bart. where she was buried in 1655, having no issue by him. His children by the first wife were,

Edmund (Roe) his successor; he resided at Ballyroe, county of Kilkenny in the life-time of his father[3].

Edward

---

[1] Ulster's Office. [2] Articles dated 23 July 1631. [3] Lodge.

Edward of Urlingford, who married Mary, daughter of Edmund Fitz-Patrick, and being engaged in the rebellion, was apprehended in 1652 by Colonel Daniel Axtell * governor of Kilkenny, when several informations were taken against him, and he was examined personally 16 February before Colonel Thomas Herbert and Robert Doily, Members of the High Court of Justice (as it was called) sitting at Dublin, when he declared, that he had lived at Urlingford for 20 years past or thereabouts; that in 1641, or the year after, he had the command of a foot-company, which he laid down in 1642, and was not in arms since, but continued at his said dwelling-house, and from that time meddled not with any military employment; and denied that he had been engaged in any acts of rebellion: but the contrary being fully proved by the depositions of Captain Abel Warren and others, he was executed at Kilkenny. (2)

Captain Richard Butler. (3)

Daughter Elizabeth was marrried to Sir Walter Butler of Poolestown, Bart. and died 21 August 1636. (1)

Ellice, to Andrew Fitz-Patrick of the Queen's County, Esq. (2)

Margaret, in July 1631 to Sir Richard Bealing † of Tirrelston in the county of Dublin, Knt. and died 6 August 1635[1]. (3)

———, to

---

* Colonel Axtell (who, like many more of Cromwell's officers, knew better how to use the sword than the pen) gives the following account of his apprehension, in his letter to the President of the High Court of Justice in Dublin: "My Lord, I have sent your Lordship the inclosed examination against Mr. Edward Butler, secount Son to the late Lord Mount Garrott, and I shall only give your Lordship my nowledge concerning him; when I had receiv'd Orders from the Com' of Parlimt. to apprehend all such Persons in these Parts that had bin guilty of sheedinge the English innoscent Blood in the first Year of the Rebellion, I send a Party in the Night to ceafe the said Butler, but he was not at bombe, and he hearing that thaire was a Cesuer of blood-guilty Persons, he fleed into the Bogs and Pastnesses (out of the Parliment Quarters) for his Saity, and thaire contenewed until he was going (in a disguise Habitt) to Spaine with some Irish Officers, and proudencially taken betwext Thomas-Town and Waterford by some Soldiers (that knew him) of Cpt. Ffrankes Troop. I shall not ad, but remayne, my Lord,

"Kilkeney, 9   Your Lordpp humble Servant
"Ffebb. 1652."   D. Axtell"

† He was son [2] and heir to Sir Henry Bealing of Killeffin or Killessy in the county of Kildare by his wife Maud, and was some time a member of the Supreme

---

[1] Articles. 16 Aug. 1625. Rot. Claus de As. 7°. 8°. Car. 1. D.
[2] Harris's Ware, 165.

(4) ———, to Philip Purcell of Ballyfoile, Efq; a captain in the rebellion of 1641.

(5) Joan, firft to Sir Richard Mafterfon of Fernes, Knt. to whom fhe was fecond wife, and he dying in 1627, fhe re-married with Sir Philip Paulet of Garrylough in the county of Wexford, (fourth fon of Sir Anthony Paulet, governor of Jerfey, and Captain of the Guard to Q. Elizabeth, fon and heir to Sir Amias Paulet) and dying in 1633, had iffue by him, who died 16 May, 1636, and was buried at Fernes, Jofeph, who died unmarried, and Mary.

Edmund, 4 Vifcount.

Edmund (Roe) the fourth Vifcount Mountgarret, in January 1641 was one of the Commiffioners, deputed by the counties of Kilkenny, Tipperary, Waterford, and Wexford, to take the city of Waterford into their government, and to feize all the goods of the Englifh, for the maintenance of their war, which they called the Holy War of the Confederate Catholics; but the Mayor and Council of the city prevented that attempt, and about the middle of March following procured fhips for the efcape of the Proteftants. —He acted in concert with his father during the progrefs of the rebellion; whofe example he followed in protecting the Englifh, and endeavouring to reftore peace to the kingdom: " of which K. Charles II. was abundantly fatisfied, " and particularly by certificate of the Marquefs of Ormond, " and other good teftimonies, that he was very active and
" earneft

Supreme Council at Kilkenny; and died in September 1677, having feven fons, Sir Richard, Henry, James, Francis, Chriftopher, Marrion, and Alfon[1]; and a daughter Helen, the firft wife of Sir John Hales of Woodchurch in Kent, Bart —Sir Richard, the eldeft fon, was Secretary and Treafurer of the Houfhold to K. Charles the IId's Queen, and marrying in December 1670 Frances, daughter and heir to Sir John Arundel of Langherne in Cornwall, his children by her (who died 6 December 1713, Æt. 62) were obliged to take the name of Arundel, to enable them to inherit her eftate; whereof Mary (or Catharine) was married to Sir John Fleming of Staholmuck (fon of James, third fon of William Lord Slane) and the eldeft fon Richard Arundel Bealing of Langherne, Efq. married Anne, fifter of Thomas, Vifcount Gage, and dying in February 1724. left two daughters his coheirs, Frances, married 21 June 1733 to Sir John Giffard of Burftall in Leicefterfhire, Barr. who died in June 1736, and was there buried; and Mary 27 January 1738 to Henry, then eldeft fon of Henry, Lord Arundel of Wardour, whom he fucceeded in 1746, and had two fons, Henry, born 11 April 1740; and Thomas 4 October 1741; his Lordfhip dying 12 September 1756, was fucceeded by Henry, who, 31 May 1762, married Maria-Chriftina, only daughter and heir to Benedict Conqueft of Iraham in county of Lincoln, by whom his Lordfhip has iffue[2].

[1] Lodge Collect.   [2] Collin. V. 7. p. 54.

BUTLER, Viscount MOUNTGARRET.

"earnest to incline the Irish to a submission to K. Charles I.
"in 1646, and did then solemnly publish the peace in the
"city of Kilkenny, whereof he was governor, for which he
"was committed by the opposers thereof, who kept him
"in durance for the space of three months; yet, after the
"interruption of that peace, he used his utmost endeavours
"to restore it; corresponded with the Marquess, then
"L. L.; offered to come to him to Dublin; and followed
"him to France, where he tendered his service to the
"King; attended the Marquess to Ireland in 1648, and
"constantly adhered to his Majesty's authority, employing
"both his person and purse in his service; acting as Co-
"lonel of a foot regiment and Captain of horse in his army,
"until the Marquess's recesse from Ireland; with whom
"he went again into France, and attended his Majesty's
"fortunes abroad, serving as a Captain of Foot in his ar-
"my. The King therefore being sensible of the many
"hardships his Lordship had suffered for him, both at
"home and abroad, conceived himself bound in honour
"and justice, to re-establish him in the possession of his
"estate, whereof he had been deprived by or under colour
"of any actings of any usurped power in Ireland; and
"accordingly in his public declaration touching Ireland,
"provided for him by name, as meriting a particular re-
"ward and favour; and to render that intended grace the
"more speedy and effectual, his Majesty, by letter from
"Whitehall [1] 1 March 1660, required that special care
"might be taken for his immediate restoration and esta-
"blishment in his estate," which was performed accordingly by the acts of settlement; his Lordship having received a
pardon, dated at Westminster 12 December before, for all
treasons, levying of war, rebellions, insurrections, &c.
committed before 10 June 1659, and 12 July 1670, had an
abatement of the quit-rents, imposed on his estate, by the
acts of settlement [2].

He married to his first wife the Lady Dorothy Touchet,
second daughter of Mervyn, Earl of Castlehaven, and by
her, who died at Park's-Grove, near Ballyragget, 10 February (being Shrove-Tuesday) 1634, and was buried
the 11 in the Cathedral of St. Canice, Kilkenny [3], had
two

[1] Rot. Cap. 13°. Car. II. 3. p. f. R. 6.   [2] Lodge.   [3] Idem.

two sons and two daughters; Richard, his successor; James, who died young; Margaret, who died unmarried; and Elizabeth, married to ——— Sutton of the county of Wexford. He married, secondly, in 1637 Elizabeth, daughter of Sir George Simeons of Brightwell in the county of Oxford, Knt. by his first wife Mary, daughter of Edward, Lord Vaux, of Harrowden, and dying in 1679 *, (oppressed with age and infirmities, having been for some time bedrid) had issue by his second wife, who died 18 February 1673 [1], and was buried at St. Michan's, Dublin, a daughter Elizabeth, and a son

Family of Ballyragget. Edward Butler of Ballyragget, Esq. for whose restoration to his estate of Ballyragget, Ballymartin, Knockroe, Damerstown, &c. (settled on him by a fine, levied 13 December 1670) chargeable with 1000l. for the fortune of his sister Elizabeth [2], which had been possessed by Colonel Daniel Axtell, the King sent his directions 4 December 1660, in pursuance whereof he was confirmed therein by the acts of settlement.—He married Elizabeth, daughter of George Mathew of Thomastown in Tipperary, Esq; by whom he had three sons; Edmund, who 13 October 1694 married Rose, daughter of ——— O'Neile, of Dublin Esq. and died without issue; George; Pierce, who died childless; and a daughter Anne, married to Dudley Bagenal of Dunleckney in the county of Carlow, Esq; and was mother of Walter Bagenal, Esq; who died in 1745, leaving Beauchamp his heir, and other children.

George Butler of Ballyragget, Esq; 20 May 1700 [3] married Catharine, eldest daughter of John, Lord Kingston, he died 19 September † 1752, having had issue by her who died in April 1762, three sons and two daughters; James, Edmund, born in 1721; Gerald-Alexander in 1725; Mary, married to Ralph Standish-Howard, Esq. only son to Ralph Standish, of Standish-Hall in Lancashire, Esq; (and by him, who died of the small-pox at Kilkenny in April 1735, had

---

* By his will dated 13 October 1673, he bequeathed to his son Edward, all his goods and chattels, rents, debts and credits, and appointed him executor; and by a codicil dated 28 June 1678 (proved 24 June 1679) gave to his son Richard, a horse of 10l. price or 10l. to buy one; to his daughter Sutton 10l. to his sister Elizabeth Butler of Paulstown, 10l. to his sister Ellis Fitz-Patrick 10l. and to his uncle Theobald Butler of Tynehinch 10l. [4]

† He made his will 2 August 1750 and left her sole executrix and heir. [5]

[1] Ulster's Office.   [2] Lodge.   [3] Marriage Articles 14 February 1699 (whereby she had 2,500l. fortune, and a jointure of 500l. per ann. [4] Prerog. Office.   [5] Idem.

had one son, born 22 October following) and Frances, married 15 November 1740 to Sir James Stanley of Nether-Alderley in Cheshire, Bart. whose great-grand-father Thomas 25 June 1660 was advanced to that dignity.———— James Butler, Esq. the eldest son, born in March 1711, married on 18 May 1734 Frances, daughter and heir to Robert Dillon of King-street, Dublin, Esq. Counsellor at Law, (who died 6 March 1735, and lies buried under a table monument in St. James's Church-yard) by his first wife Mary, and she died in childbirth of the said Frances, being the first child [1], eldest daughter of Sir Richard Talbot, of Malahide, Esq; (who died in August 1703) by his wife Frances, daughter of Sir Robert Talbot, of Cartown, Bart. and deceasing at Ballyragget 20 March 1746, had issue by her, who died 17 November 1749, George, who died 10 March 1735, and was buried with his grandfather at St. James's; Robert, who married first the daughter of Lord Bellew, secondly, 7 September 1779, Elizabeth daughter of Marmaduke, late Lord Langdale, and dying in June 1788, was succeeded in his estates by his next surviving brother James, titular archbishop of Cashel; Edward, James, George and Mary.

Richard, the fifth Viscount Mountgarret, in the reign of Charles II. served abroad as Captain in the French army, but, after K. James's accession to the throne, returned to Ireland, was made a Captain of Horse, and 4 June 1689, led on the Forlorn Hope against the city of Londonderry, when he was taken prisoner, for which and his other services, he was outlawed and forfeited his estate; 29 October 1692 he laid claim to his seat in Parliament, and took the oath of fidelity; but being required to take the oath of supremacy, and make and subscribe the declaration according to act of Parliament, he refused so to do, declaring it was not agreeable to his conscience [2]; whereupon the Lord Chancellor acquainted him, that he knew the consequence of his refusal was, he could not sit in that House; and 19 October 1698 the Lords came to this resolution: That those Lords, whose ancestors stand outlawed, shall not sit in this House, nor their names be continued in the roll of this House in right of such ancestors. And, that such Lords, who stand outlawed on record, shall not have privilege

Richard,
5
Viscount.

[1] Lodge. Collect.   [2] Lord's Jour. I. 466.

vilege to fit in this House, but ought to be struck out of the roll of this House¹. From which privileges (though the outlawry was reversed) this noble family was excluded, on account of their religion, except Richard the seventh, and Edmund the ninth Lord, who conformed to the established Protestant religion, in which persuasion he educated his son.

His Lordship married first Emilia, daughter of William Blundel of Crosby in the county of Lancaster, Esq; by whom he had three sons, Edmund his heir; Richard, and John, whose posterity reside abroad, and two sons and a daughter, who died young. His second wife was Margaret, only daughter of Richard Shee of Shee's-Court, Esq; and widow of Gilbert Butler, by whom he had no issue, and dying in February 1706, was succeeded by his eldest son*

Edmund

---

* 15 November 1715, he complained to the House of Peers of a breach of privilege committed against him, when their Lordships appointed a committee to enquire whether his father Richard or any of his ancestors, under whom he derived his honour, is or were outlawed of high treason, and whether such outlawry or outlawries remain of force: And upon the report from the said Lords committees, it appeared to the House, that the outlawry of Richard, Lord Viscount Mountgarret, for the rebellion of 1641, was not reversed. Whereupon, they ordered his Lordship's name to be expunged out of the list of Peers——But his Lordship at that time, not being able to offer sufficient proofs of the reversal of the said outlawries, deferred doing so, until 5 October 1721, when, by petition, he prayed the aforesaid premises to be taken into consideration, and to grant him a re-hearing. The petition was referred to a select committee of all the Lords present; and the Lord Viscount Strabane reported from the said Lords committees, that, on examination of the matter to them referred, and from the testimony of Mr. Thady Dunn, it appeared, that Philip Savage, Esq. in the year 1687, was Clerk of the Crown of the Court of King's Bench, and the said Dunn produced an affidavit, sworn by the said Philip Savage, before Godfrey Boate, Esq. one of the Judges of the said Court, 24 Nov. 1716, which the Lords committees thought proper to lay before the House, and is as follows:

Philip Savage, Esq; late Clerk of the Crown and Prothonotary of his Majesty's Court of King's Bench, Ireland, came this day before me, and made oath on the Holy Evangelists, that he being in Trinity Term, 1687, and for several years before and after, and until the month of August 1715, Clerk of the Crown and Prothonotary of the said Court of King's Bench, did, pursuant to the annexed rules of the said Court of King's Bench, 10 June 1687, cause records of judgment of reversal of two several outlawries, grounded on indictments of high treason, viz. one in the county Cork, and the other in the county Kildare, alledged to be committed by Richard, (heretofore) Lord Viscount Mountgarret, in the rebellion, which broke out in this kingdom, 23 October 1641, to be made up and enrolled, for which this deponent did about that time, receive the fees due to him for making up and enrolling the same; and this deponent is very sure the same were made and enrolled accordingly, he having perused and often seen the said roll in the said office, and did, by order of the House of Peers of Ireland, cause certificates of the said reversal to be made out

¹ Lord's Jour. I. 690.

BUTLER, Viscount MOUNTGARRET.

Edmund, the sixth Viscount, who by petition to the House of Lords 5 October 1721, claimed his privilege of Parliament; which (upon full proof that the outlawry of Richard,

Edmund, 6 Viscount.

out and certified to the House of Peers, and to the King at Arms of the said kingdom, the first time the Parliament sat in this kingdom after the rebellion, which was in the year 1688; and this deponent further deposeth, that though there were several writs of error brought to reverse the outlawries against several other Lords of the said kingdom, for the said rebellion of 1641, whose heirs brought such writs of error as aforesaid, and obtained the like rules for their reversal, yet they were not reversed, nor the records of their reversal made up and enrolled, by reason none of them required the same to be done, except the said Lord Viscount Mountgarret, and Pierce, heretofore Lord Viscount Ikerrine, whose records of reversal were made up and enrolled, as aforesaid. And this deponent further deposeth, that several records of his said office, being in the late troubles in this kingdom, removed to several places, to be for safe custody kept, and likewise being to this deponent's certain knowledge, several times carried by this deponent's deputy to the House of Peers, and to the late trustees of forfeitures in this kingdom, pursuant to an act of Parliament made in England, the said records of the reversal of the said Lord Mountgarret's said outlawries, are, by that means, as this deponent verily believes, mislaid.

Jur. cor me 24° Die
Novembri 1716.
P. SAVAGE.   GODFREY BOATE.

Said Dunn further deposed, that a motion was made in the Court of King's Bench, upon the said Savage's affidavit, in Michaelmas term, 1716, as he believed, but no rule was made thereon.—And Richard Butler, Esq; deposed, that he was in the Court of King's Bench, when the said Court was moved by Sir Richard Levinge, then a Council at the Bar, upon the said Savage's affidavit, to have the record made up of the reversal of the outlawry of Richard, late Lord Viscount Mountgarret, in the year 1641; but that Lord Ch. J. Whitshead, upon inquiry whether the Attorney General had been attended, and being informed that he was not, the Court thought proper not to make any rule thereupon. All which the Lords committees thought fit to lay before the House, and is submitted to your Lordships.

The resolution of this House of 16 December 1715, was then read.

Resolved, that upon reading the journals of this House, and consideration had of the report made by the Lords committees, to whom the consideration of the petition of Edmund Butler, late upon the roll of Peers of this House, by the name of Edmund, Lord Viscount Mountgarret, was referred, it appears to this House, that the two outlawries of Richard, Lord Viscount Mountgarret, for the rebellion, which began in this kingdom on 23 October 1641, are reversed.

The order for expunging the name of Edmund Lord Viscount Mountgarret out of the list of Peers of the House, 16 December 1715, being then read, it is ordered by the Lords in Parliament assembled, that Ulster King of Arms do forthwith insert into the list of Peers of this House, the name of said Edmund Lord Viscount Mountgarret.

Pursuant to these resolutions of the Lords in his favour, he delivered his writ of summons in the usual manner 9 October, and took the oath of allegiance; but the declaration and oath of abjuration being read to him, he refused to take the one, or make the other, but desired leave to consider thereof, and then withdrew. (Lord's Jour. II. 461. 462. 700. 701. 702.)

BUTLER, Viscount MOUNTGARRET.

Richard, Lord Mountgarret, for the rebellion of 1641, had been reversed in the year 1687) being alowed by a resolution of the House, he delivered his writ of summons the 9 of that month, and took the oath of allegiance.—He married first Mary, daughter of ——— Buchanan of Londonderry, Esq. and secondly Elizabeth, widow of Oliver Grace of Shanganagh in the Queen's County, Esq. which Oliver died 8 June 170 , and his Lady dying in London 13 June 1736, was buried in the church of St. Giles in the fields ; and his Lordship departing this life in Dublin 25 July 1735, was buried in St. Canice, Kilkenny, having issue three sons, successive Lords of Mountgarret, and one surviving daughter Emilia, married in 1712, to Hugh Reilly of Ballinlough in county of Meath, Esq. who dying without issue, he re-married Elinor, only daughter of Sir Daniel O'Neile, Bart. and dying 8 August 1761, æt. 77 left a son of that place [1].

Richard, 7 Viscount.

Richard, the eldest son and seventh Viscount, took his seat in Parliament 7 October 1735 [2], but did not long enjoy the honour; deceasing in Dublin 14 May 1736, he was buried at St. George's Church. 19 October 1711 he married [3] Catharine, sister to Charles O'Neile of Edenduffecarrick or Shane's Castle in the County of Antrim, Esq. and leaving no issue by her, who died 15 April 1739, and was buried at St. Michan's, Dublin, the honour devolved on his brother

James, 8 Viscount.

James, the eighth Viscount, who served many years in the Emperor's army ; and in the campaign on the Rhine against the French in 1735, signalized himself.—In January 1735 he married Margaret, second daughter of John, Lord Trimleston, but dying suddenly without issue 13 May 174 , was succeeded by his only brother

Edmund, 9 Viscount.

Edmund, the ninth Viscount Mountgarret, who conformed to the established church 7 November 1736, and 10 October 1749 took his seat in Parliament [4]. He married Anne, eldest daughter of Major Toby Purcell of Ballymartin and Cloghpooke in the county of Kilkenny, and died 6 March 1750, leaving by her who died in June 1764, an only son

Edmund, 10 Viscount.

Edmund, the tenth Viscount, sworn a Barrister at Law 25 November 1749 ; took his seat in the House of Peers 11 November

[1] Lodge. [2] Lord's Jour. III. 301. [3] Articles of that date.
[4] Lord's Journal. III. 719.

BUTLER, Viscount MOUNTGARRET.

11 November 1751 [1]. In 1744 he married Charlotte, second daughter of Simon Bradstreet, Esq;* Counsellor at Law, and by her who died at Paris 27 March 1778, and was interred at Barony Church, near Ballyconra, had issue three sons and two daughters, viz.

Edmund, his successor. (1)

Richard [2], entered into holy orders and was presented to the rectory and vicarage of Tullophelim in county of Carlow. (2)

Simon [3], Counsellor at Law. (3)

Daughter, Elinor [4] died 28 April 1762, æt. 15 unmarried; and was buried at Barony Church. (1)

Anne-Emilia [5], unmarried. (2)

His Lordship deceasing 9 February 1779, was interred with his Lady in Barony Church near Ballyconra in county of Kilkenny, and was succeeded by his eldest son

Edmund, the eleventh and present Viscount, who was born 27 July 1745, took his seat in Parliament 26 November 1779 [6], and married 7 October 1768 to Lady Henrietta Butler [7], (born 15 August 1750) youngest daughter of Somerset Hamilton the eighth Earl of Carrick, and by her who deceased in 1785, his Lordship has issue four sons and one daughter, viz.

Edmund, 11 Viscount.

Edmund, born 6 January 1771 [8]. (1)

Somerset-Richard, born in December 1771 [9]. (2)

Henry, born in February 1773 [10]. (3)

Pierce, born 6 May 1774 [11]. (4)

Daughter, Charlotte-Juliana, born 6 August 1778 [12]. (1)

TITLES.]

---

* Simon Bradstreet, Esq; Counsellor at Law, was created a Baronet 14 July 1759; he married the daughter of ——— Bradstreet, of Kilkenny, Esq. and died 26 April 1762, leaving issue by his relict, who deceased 25 December 1779, Sir Simon the second Bart. who married 9 October 1755, Anne, daughter of the late and sister to the present Right Hon. Sir Henry Cavendish, Bart. and dying without issue, was succeeded by his only brother Sir Samuel, Barrister at Law, chosen Recorder of Dublin, which city he represented in Parliament, till 13 January 1784, when he was constituted a Justice of the Court of King's Bench. The daughters were, Emilia, married to Colonel Zobell, deceased; and Charlotte, married as before. (Collections)

[1] Lord's Jour. III. 790.   [2] Ulster's Office.   [3] Id.   [4] Id.
[5] Id.   [6] Lord's Jour. V. 141.   [7] Ulster's Office.   [8] Id.
[9] Id.   [10] Id.   [11] Id.   [12] Id.

TITLES.] Edmund Butler, Viscount of Mountgarret, and Baron of Kells.

CREATION.] V. of Mountgarret in the county of Wexford, 23 October 1550, 5 Edw. VI.

ARMS.] Topaz, a Chief indented, Saphire, a Crescent for difference; or within a Border, Gules, at pleasure.

CREST.] In a ducal coronet, topaz, a plume of five Ostrich feathers, and thence a Falcon arising, all pearl.

SUPPORTERS.] The dexter, a Falcon with wings expanded, pearl beaked and membered topaz. The sinister, a male Gryphon, pearl, with beak, rays, plain collar and chain, gold.

MOTTO.] DEPRESSUS EXTOLLOR.

SEAT.] Ballyconra in county of Kilkenny, 8 miles from Kilkenny, and 58 from Dublin.

VILLIERS, VISCOUNT GRANDISON.

Paganus.

THAT this illustrious family hath been seated in the county of Leicester, and possessed a fair inheritance there for many ages, is evident from Burton's history of that county, under the title of Brookesby, their chief seat; and they derived their origin from the noble house of Villiers, Lords of Lisle-Adam in the Dutchy of Normandy, of which House were many eminent persons in France; but the founder of this noble branch of the family was Paganus de Villers, Villiers, Vileres, Villars, Vylars, Esq; (for so the name, like others of long duration, was variously written, and, as Dr. Fuller observes, fourteen several ways in their own evidences) who came into England at the time of the conquest, and soon after was Lord of Crosby in the county of Lancaster, and of Kinaton and Newbold in the county of Nottingham, which he held of the Butlers of Werrington, and which his posterity enjoyed until the reign of K. Edward III. but Crosby went off to the family of Molyneux, by

Beatrix,

VILLIERS, Viscount GRANDISON.

Beatrix, daughter and heir to Robert de Villers, son of Alan, son of the said Pagan.

Which Pagan, was a witness to the Foundation Charter of Roger of Poictou to the monastery of Lancaster; and to him (says Sir William Dugdale) succeeded Gilbert de Villiers, probably his son, after whom, till the reign of K. Edward I. are enumerated by that author and others, without any direct chain of succession, the names of another Gilbert, Roger, or Robert, who had issue Robert, the father of William; and another William the son of Alexander, and Benedict de Vylar; but Dr. Thoroton, in his history of Nottinghamshire, sets the original of the family in a clearer light, so long as it subsisted at Newbold, and other places in that country.

Paganus de Villiers before mentioned, who was first enfeoffed in Newbold, gave to Alan his son five carucates of land, in Knight's service; and to the hospital of Jerusalem, one carucate in Bekaneshou, in Alms. He likewise gave to his son William de Vylers, the lands of Newbold, to hold by Knight's service. Alan, the younger son, had issue Robert, whose daughter and heir Beatrix was married to Robert Molyneux, of Sephton, in Lancashire, as already observed; and William the elder, was the father of Paganus de Vylers, a man of great note, who in Henry II. reign granted to Roger, Archbishop of York, and his successors, for the use of hospitality, and that no other person should be instituted into the church of Kyneldestowe, the whole garden, as well belonging to the church, as not, four bovats of land and one toft; and also twelve acres of his own gift, with common of pasture through the whole territory of the town; to which grant were above sixty witnesses. And the said King confirmed the gift of this Pagan, and his father William, to the abbey of Swinshed in Lincolnshire, of divers lands, and the whole Brouse which belonged to Newbold.

He had issue several children, viz. William his heir; Sir Matthew of Crophill, who had an only daughter Beatrix; Alan (father of Sir Robert Vylers of Outhorpe) Thomas; and Richard; who were all benefactors to the priory of Fiscarton upon Trent, the church of St. Peter and monastery of Thurgarton, the canons of Hokesworth, the priory of St. Cuthbert of Radford, &c.

William,

John.   John, the eldest son, died before his father, and having married Elizabeth, daughter of John Southkill, of Everingham in the county of York, Esq. had issue a daughter Elizabeth, and four sons, viz. John, successor to his grandfather; Thomas, a citizen of London, who died without issue in the reign of Henry VII. Christopher, seated at Burstall, was sheriff of the counties of Leicester and Warwick, 22 Henry VIII. and died without children 5 August 1537; and William Villiers, Clerk, LL. B. Master of the Chantry in the Church of Manton in Rutlandshire *.

John.   John, who succeeded his grandfather in the lordship of Brookesby 20 Henry VI. was sheriff that year of the counties of Leicester and Warwick, as he also was 6, 10, and 15 years of Henry VII. and of the county of Lincoln 14 Edward IV. On 14 November 1501 he was made a Knight at the marriage of Prince Arthur, with Catharine, daughter of Ferdinando King of Spain, in the cathedral church of St. Paul, London; and at the marriage of Margaret, eldest daughter of K. Henry VII. to James IV. King of Scots, 25 January 1502, he was that day Sewer to her Highness at dinner. He departed this life 2 December 1507, leaving by Agnes, daughter of John Digby, of Cole's-Hill, in the county of Warwick, Esq; a daughter Winifred, to whom he assigned lands for life, and eight sons, viz. John; George; Thomas; William; successive possessors of Brookesby; Edward, (who died possessed of lands at Flower and Howthorp, in the county of Northampton, 26 June 1513, whose grandson Edward Villiers, of Howthorpe, Esq; was the last heir male of that place, leaving only daughters, whereof Elizabeth was married in 1610 to George Bathurst, in her right, of Howthorpe, Esq. and by him had four daughters and twelve sons, several of whom died in the service of K. Charles I. and of those that survived, Benjamin the

---

* In which church is this memorandum cut on a brass plate fixed in the north wall :

Orate pro Animabus Magistror. W^t Villers in Legibus Baccallarii quondam Magistri hujus Cantariæ, Thome Vellers fratris ejusdem, Civis et Pannarii Civitatis London. ac Robt. Newton in Decretis Baccellarii, quondam Arprehenticii dicti Thome, posteaque Magistri hujus Cantarie, qui multa Bona eidem Cantarie contulit, ac, Ædificia reparavit, parentum et Benefactor. subr. Quor. An'mabus propitietur Deus. Amen. (Wright's Rutland. p. 86.)

the youngest was ancestor to Earl Bathurst, and Mary was the wife of Calcot Chambre, of Carnew, in the county of Wicklow, Esq. who died 20 October 1635, and was there buried); Leonard; Bartholomew; and Anthony of Cotness, in Yorkshire, of which he died possessed in 1547.

Sir John Villiers of Brookesby, the eldest son, was Sheriff of the counties of Leicester and Warwick, 23 and 29 Hen. VIII. in whose 6 year he died, æt. 56, and was buried in the chancel of the church of Brookesby; leaving issue by his wife Elizabeth, daughter of John Wingar, an only daughter Dorothy, married to Francis Browne, Gent. his brother George succeeded to the manors of Brookesby and Houby, with the advowsons of those churches, which he enjoyed but a short time; dying seized of them, and of the manors of Siwolby and Burstall, 29 August, 38 Henry VIII. leaving issue by Joan, daughter of John Harrington, of Bagworth in the county of Leicester, Richard his heir, aged three years, and a daughter Elizabeth, heir to her brother, who being married to Sir Edward Waterhouse, of Helmstedbury in Hertfordshire, died without issue*.

To George of Brookesby, succeeded his brother Thomas who had before been seated at Wolfby, but leaving only one daughter Dorothy, married to William Smith, of the county of Leicester, Esq. (whose only child and heir, Agnes, was married to James Park of London) the estate devolved on William Villiers, Esq. his next brother; who William. married Colletta, daughter and heir to Richard Clarke, of the county of Huntingdon, Esq. widow of Richard Beaumont, of Coleoverton in Leicestershire, Esq. and, dying 1 November 1558, left George Villiers, of Brookesby, Esq. Sir George.

VOL. IV.   G   his

---

* He removed into Ireland and lived at Drogheda; and she being very young at the time of her marriage, was afterwards at her own request, divorced from him, by Thomas Archbishop of Armagh; from which sentence he appealing 26 March 1578, the Queen issued a commission to George Aldworth, LL. D. Thomas Creiff, Precentor of St. Patrick's, and Thomas Jones, Chancellor of that church; to enquire into that matter and do justice; whereupon they decreed the divorce firm and valid, on the 29 of that month. He was a man of such experience and fidelity in affairs of state, that the L. D. Perrot consulted him on every occasion; by whom he was knighted 22 June 1584, called into the Privy Council, and made Chancellor of the Exchequer: He was very instrumental in modelling the kingdom into counties; and dying at Woodchurch 15 October 1591, without issue, was there buried.

VILLIERS, Viscount GRANDISON.

his heir, aged 14 years or more at his father's death, who was Sheriff of the county of Leicester in 1591, and having received the honour of knighthood, departed this life 4 January 1605-6, and was buried in the chapel of St. Nicholas, Westminster-Abbey, where, in the midst of the floor, is a raised tomb of the finest black and white marble, with the effigies of a Knight, armed with an helmet, and by his side a lady in her robes, with this inscription:

Bonæ Memoriæ
GEORGIO VILLERIO Equiti Aurato, Marito
B. M. juxta fe P. clariffima Conjux,
Maria Comitiffa Buckinghamiæ
S. P. F. F.

He married to his first wife Audrey, daughter and heir to William Saunders, of Harrington in the county of Northampton, Esq. and by her, who died 1 May 1587, had two sons and three daughters, viz.

(1) Sir William Villiers, hereafter mentioned.

(2) Sir Edward Villiers, ancestor to George-Buffy, now Viscount Grandifon.

(1) Daughter Elizabeth, married to Sir John Boteler (or Butler) of Hatfield-Woodhall in the county of Hertford, Knt. and Bart. created in 1625 Lord Butler of Brantfield, by whom she had six sons and as many daughters, five of which sons died unmarried before their father, and William his successor, dying also a batchelor, the daughters became coheirs *, and were Audrey (married first to Sir Francis Anderson, Knt. by whom she was mother of Sir John Anderson, of St. Ives in Huntingdonshire, created a Baronet 3 January 1628, who dying without issue that title ceased; and secondly to Sir Francis Leigh, Bart. created Earl of Chichester, whose three daughters and coheirs were, Audrey, Elizabeth married to Thomas Earl of Southampton. and Mary to Geo. Lord Grandifon); Hellen (married to Sir John Drake, of Ashe in the county of Devon, whose daughter Elizabeth was mother of John Churchill, the illustrious Duke of Marlborough); Jane (first married to James Ley, Earl of Marlborough,

---

* George, Vifcount Grandifon, purchafed their intereft in their father's and brother's inheritance, and became poffeffed of the Manor of Brantfield.

VILLIERS, Viscount GRANDISON.

borough, Lord High Treasurer of England and President of the Council, to whom she was third wife, and had no children; and secondly to Colonel William Ashburnham); Olivia (to Endymion Porter, Esq.); Mary (to Edward Lord Howard of Escrick); and Anne, first to Mountjoy Blount, Earl of Newport, by whom she had three sons, George, Charles, and Henry, successive Earls of Newport; and secondly to Thomas Weston, the late Earl of Portland, by whom no issue.

Anne, married to Sir William Washington, of Packington in the county of Leicester, Bart. (2)

Frances, died unmarried. (3)

The second wife of Sir George Villiers was Mary, daughter of Anthony Beaumont, of Glenfield in Essex, Esq. who surviving him, was created Countess of Buckingham and Baroness Compton, 1 July 1618; She became secondly the wife of Sir William Rayner, and lastly of Sir Thomas Compton, Knight of the Bath, youngest son of Henry Lord Compton. She lies buried under the same tomb with Sir George Villiers, whereon is this memorial:

D. O. M.
Ossa
Mariæ de Bello-Monte, Comitissæ Buc-
kinghamiæ e quinque potentissimorum
Totius Europæ regnorum regibus, id-
que per totidem immediatos
Descensus oriundæ.
Vix. Ann. LXII. M.XI. D.XIX.
Hoc Mon. V. F. C.

Sir George by her had a daughter Susan, married to William Fielding, the first Earl of Denbigh; and three sons, viz.

John, created Baron Villiers of Stoke, and Viscount of Purbeck, 19 July 1619, and had a son Robert, who dying without issue, put an end to that line [1]. (1)

George, the great favourite of K. James and Charles I. created Duke of Buckingham 18 May 1623, which title ceased with his son George, 16 April 1687; for an account of (2)

---

[1] Salmon's Peerage.

VILLIERS, Viscount GRANDISON.

of whom the reader is referred to the English histories and peerages.

(3) Christopher, created 24 September 1620 Baron of Daventry and Earl of Anglesey; he married Elizabeth, daughter of Thomas (or William) Sheldon, of Houby in Leicestershire, Esq. and dying in 1624, left issue by her (who after married Benjamin Weston, of Walton upon Thames in Surrey, Esq.) Charles his heir, and a daughter Anne, married to Thomas Savile, Viscount Savile of Castlebar, and Earl of Sussex; the said Charles, Earl of Anglesey, dying in 1659 without issue by Mary, third daughter of Paul, Viscount Bayning, the titles became extinct, and his sister became sole heir to the estate.

Family of Villiers, Baronets.

Sir William Villiers, the eldest son of Sir George by his first wife, was sheriff of the county of Leicester for the year 1608; was knighted by K. James I. and created a Baronet 19 July 1619 *.—He married three wives; first Anne, youngest daughter of Sir Edward Griffin, of Dingley in Northamptonshire, Knight of the Bath; secondly Anne, daughter of Richard Fienes, Lord Say and Sele, widow of Henry Cave, of Ingarsby in Leicestershire, Esq. and thirdly the daughter of Robert Roper, of Hever in Derbyshire, Esq. and left issue Sir George his heir, and a daughter Audrey, married to Sir St. John Chernocke, of Hulcott in the county of Bedford, and by him, who died in March 1680, was mother of Sir Villiers Chernocke, Bart. father of Sir Pynsent who died in September 1634, father of the present Sir Villiers Chernocke, Bart.[1]

Sir

---

* In 1628 his brother the Duke of Buckingham made him a grant of 6500 acres of arable and pasture land, and 5114 of wood and bogg, in the barony of Dromahere and county of Leitrim, which had been granted to his Grace 5 January 1626, on the resignation thereof to him by Robert, Earl of Nithsdale, and his brother James Maxwell; and the same was confirmed to Sir William by patent, 5 September 1628, to hold in capite by the service of one Knight's fee, and the rent of 83l. 6s. 1d. English; the premisses being erected into the manor of Dromahere, with many large privileges, two weekly markets on Tuesday and Saturday, and two fairs yearly, 10 July and 20 October, at Dromahere; liberty to impark 1000 acres with free warren; to export corn and other commodities growing upon the premisses; to erect two tanhouses; with a licence of absence to him and his heirs (who were to be clerks of the market and say-masters) discharging them of personal residence, on their keeping a sufficient agent upon the premisses; and to build, within four years, a Castle 60 feet in length, 24 in breadth, and 32 in height, with a bawne of 400 feet in circuit, compassed with a stone wall fourteen feet high.

[1] Baronetage III. 480. edit. 1771.

VILLIERS, Viscount GRANDISON.

Sir George Villiers, the second Baronet, married Penelope, daughter and coheir to Sir John Denham, of Blechingley in Oxfordshire, Knt. and dying about the end of K. Charles II. reign, left an only son Sir William, and a daughter Penelope, the second wife of Sir William Jesson, of Coventry and of Newhouse in the county of Warwick, Knt. by whom she had a son Villiers, who dying 14 May 1690, was buried in the church of Chichely, in Bucks; and two daughters, as hereafter. *Sir George, 2 Bart.*

Sir William Villiers, the third Baronet, served in several Parliaments for the county of Leicester, but died without issue 27 February 1711, æt. 67, whereby the title ceased; and he having sold the manor of Brookesby, &c. to Sir Nathan Wright, Lord Keeper of the Great Seal, his sister's daughters became heirs to the remainder of his fortune, and were Penelope (married to George Hewett, of Stretton in the county of Leicester, Esq.); and Anne, to Sir James Robinson, of Cranford in Northamptonshire, Bart. who died 28 August 1731, leaving Sir John Robinson, Bart. and other children. *Sir William, 3 Bart.*

We now proceed with Sir Edward, younger son of Sir George Villiers, and Audrey his first wife, ancestor to the noble Lord of whom we now write. He was knighted at Windsor 7 September 1616; and 3 January 1620 sent ambassador to Bohemia; after his return from whence, by the interest of his brother the Duke of Buckingham, he was appointed by patent, 27 May 1625, to succeed the Earl of Thomond in the Presidentship of Munster; and the next day had a commission for raising forces in that province, and to be chief leader of the army there; where he lived (says Sir Henry Wotton) in singular estimation for his justice and hospitality; and died 7 September 1626 [1], with as much grief of the whole province as ever any Governor did (before his religious lady, who was of a sweet and noble disposition, adding much to his honour) and was buried in the Earl of Cork's chapel at Youghall, where these lines are fixed to his memory: *Sir Edward.*

> Munster may curse the time that Villiers came
> To make us worse, by leaving such a name
> Of noble parts, as none can imitate,
> But those, whose hearts are married to the state:
> But

---

[1] Ulster's Office.

But if they prefs to imitate his fame,
Munster may blefs the time that Villiers came.

He married Barbara, eldeft daughter of Sir John St. John, of Lydiard Tregoze in the county of Wilts, and niece to Sir Oliver St. John, L. D. of Ireland, created Vifcount Grandifon or Grandifone of Limerick, by letters patent [*], bearing date at Weftminfter 3 January 1620, with limitation of the honour to the iffue male of the faid Sir Edward and Barbara [†], and the creation fee of 13l. 6d. 8d. By her Sir Edward had iffue four fons and three daughters, Barbara, Anne, and Ellen; the eldeft whereof was firft married to Richard, only fon and heir to the Lord Wenman; fhe after became the fecond wife of James Howard, the third Earl of Suffolk, and died 13 December 1681, aged 59, leaving a daughter Elizabeth, married to Sir Thomas Felton, of Playford, in Suffolk, Bart. whofe only child Elizabeth was married in 1695 to John Hervey, Earl of Briftol. The fons were William, John, George, fucceffive Lords Grandifon; and Sir Edward Villiers, anceftor to George-Buffy, Earl of Jerfey in England, and Vifcount Grandifon, but of him hereafter.

William, Vifcount Grandifon, of the name of Villiers.

William, the eldeft fon, fucceeding 29 December 1630, to the title of Vifcount Grandifon, was prefent in the parliament of this kingdom 4 November 1634 [1]; and in 1640 was Colonel of a regiment in the army of K. Charles I. raifed againft the Scots; on the breaking out of the civil war, he engaged all his brothers to adhere to his Majefty, and fignalized himfelf on many occafions. In 1641 he commanded a troop of horfe, quartered in the county of Armagh; which being

---

[*] What relates to Sir Edward Villiers in the preamble is as follows: Cumque vera merum nobilitas, dexteritas et prudentia dilecti et fidelis noftri Edwardi Villiers Militis (qui in affinitate et propinquitate cum prædicto Olivero St. John conjunctus eft) necnon ipfius Edwardi erga nos et coronam noftram fidelitas, et generis claritas fatis elucefcit, dictum Edwardum, qui in honore prædicto eundem Oliverum pro defectu hæredum mafculorum de corpore fuo exeuntium fucceffurus fit, dignum cenfuimus. Sciatis igitur, &c.

[†] And by Indenture, dated 26 October 1622, Oliver, Lord Grandifon, fettled in Truftees the Lordfhip and Lands of Limerick, in the county of Leitrim, and the Lordfhip and lands of Endrum in the King's County, with all other his eftates in thofe counties, to the ufe of them, and of the heirs and affignes of Sir Edward, for ever.

[1] Lord's Jour. I. 16.

VILLIERS, Viscount GRANDISON.

being surprised and almost cut to pieces by the rebels on their first rising, who possessed themselves of their arms, he went to England and there served the King, till in December 1642, by the miscarriage of orders, he was exposed at too great a distance from the army, with his own regiment of 300 horse, and another of 200 dragoons, to the unequal encounter of 5000 horse and dragoons; and, after a retreat to Winchester, was taken with all his party; which was the first loss of that kind the King sustained, but without the least fault of the commander, who effected his escape with two or three of his principal officers, and were well received by the King at Oxford.

On 25 July 1634 he commanded the foot at the siege of Bristol, where the next day he led on a division with great resolution; which being beaten off and himself wounded, he was carried to Oxford, and there died, whose loss (says the Lord Clarendon) can never be enough lamented. He was buried in the Cathedral of Christ-Church under a stately monument, erected by his daughter, with this inscription:

H. S. I.
GULIELMUS VILLIERS,
Vice-Comes Grandison
De Limerico
Martis et Gratiarum Certamen;
Qui
Oris venustissimi Decus
Factis pulcherrimis magis honestavit.
Post Res Maximas
In Belgio, Hibernia, demum Anglia gestas,
cum à Partibus Regiis adversus Rebelles
in obsessam Bristoliam legiones duceret,
primas admotis scalis vallum superavit,
Ducisque non uno nomine functus officio,
Militis ita seu Virtutem,
seu Pudorem accendit,
ut Propugnaculis potiretur,
Glande interim femur trajectus,
Cupressum lauro intexuit,
Receptæ Urbis grande nimis pretium
Oxoniam delatus obiit,
Sub finem Mensis Aug. Ann. MDCXLIII.

Ætatis

VILLIERS, Viscount GRANDISON.

Ætatis suæ xxx.
M. H.
Optimo Parenti
Barbara Clevelandiæ Duciſſa
Pietatis ergo
P.

But his eminent virtues have a more laſting remembrance in the character, given him by the aforementioned noble author, in his hiſtory of that war, wherein he fell.

" He was (ſays he) " a young man of ſo virtuous a ha-
" bit of mind, that no temptation or provocation could
" corrupt him; ſo great a lover of juſtice and integrity,
" that no example, neceſſity, or even the barbarity of the
" war, could make him ſwerve from the moſt preciſe rules
" of it; and of that rare piety and devotion, that the court
" or camp could not ſhew a more faultleſs perſon, or to
" whoſe example young men might more reaſonably con-
" form themſelves. His perſonal valour and courage of all
" kinds (for he had ſometimes indulged ſo much to the cor-
" rupt opinion of honour, as to venture himſelf in duels)
" was very eminent, inſomuch as he was accuſed of being
" too prodigal of his perſon; his affection, and zeal, and
" obedience to the king, was ſuch as became a branch of
" that family; and he was wont to ſay, that if he had not
" underſtanding enough to know the uprightneſs of the
" cauſe, nor loyalty enough to inform him of the duty of a
" ſubject, yet the very obligations of gratitude to the King
" on the behalf of his Houſe were ſuch, as his life was but
" a due ſacrifice. And therefore he no ſooner ſaw the war
" unavoidable, than he engaged all his brethren, as well as
" himſelf in the ſervice, and there were then three more
" of them in command in the army, where he was ſo un-
" fortunately cut off."

He married Mary, third daughter of Paul, Viſcount Bayning of Sudbury, and by her (who re-married firſt with Charles, Earl of Angleſey, and ſecondly Arthur Gorges, Eſq.) had an only daughter Barbara, who was married to Roger Palmer, created Earl of Caſtlemaine in 1661, and died in Wales 28 July 1705; and by reaſon of her noble deſcent, her father's death in the ſervice of the crown, and her own perſonal virtues, was created 3 Auguſt 1670, Ducheſs of Cleveland, with remainder to Charles Fitz-Roy her
ſon

VILLIERS, Viscount GRANDISON.

son by K. Charles II. and his heirs male; remainder to George Fitz-Roy, younger brother of the said Charles, and his issue male. She died at her house in Chiswick 9 October 1709, having had issue by King Charles II. three sons and two daughters, viz.

(1) Charles Fitz Roy born at Westminster in June 1662, created Duke of Southampton, and succeeding his mother in the Dutchy of Cleveland, was father of William, Duke of Cleveland and Southampton.

(2) Henry, born 20 September 1663, created Duke of Grafton.

(3) George, born at Oxford in December 1665, created Duke of Northumberland, and constituted Chief Butler of England, which office the Duke of Cleveland enjoys, by his dying childless 27 June 1716.

(1). Daughter Anne-Palmer was married in 1674 to Thomas Lennard, Earl of Sussex.

(2) Charlotte Fitz-Roy to Sir Edward-Henry Lee, created Earl of Litchfield, which title is extinct, but the estate hath devolved on Charles Dillon-Lee, Lord Viscount Dillon of Costello-Gallen in Ireland [1].

To William, Lord Grandison, succeeded his next brother John, the second Viscount; who leaving no issue, the title accrued to his brother George, the third Viscount, who 7 March 1660, was made Captain of a troop of horse [*], and marrying the Lady Mary Leigh, daughter and co-heir to Francis, Earl of Chichester (as before observed) had two sons and two daughters by her, who lies buried in the Chancel of Brantfield Church, in county of Hertford, under a fair monument, with this inscription:

John, 2 Viscount. George, 3 Viscount.

Here lieth the truly Religious
Lady MARY,
Wife to George, Lord Viscount
Grandison;
Who died here the 7th of July
In the year of our Lord,
1671.

His

---

[*] 8 March 1674, his Lordship and his brother Edward had a grant from K. Charles II. of all his Majesty's right and title to the lands of Killien, Rathwiere, Rathgibbin, Lisdoge, Streamstown, Newbegg, and divers others in the King's County, which had been unjustly kept from the crown by Nicholas Herbert, late of Killien, Esq; who forfeited the same by being engaged in the rebellion of 1641. (Lodge.)

[1] See that title.

(1) His children were Edward, his heir,
(2) William, educated in Magdalen College, Cambridge, of which society being a member when K. James II. afcended the throne; he congratulated him with a copy of Latin verfes[1]; afterwards embracing a military life, he became Colonel of a regiment, and died 7 September 1723, having married Catharine, fecond daughter to Sir Edward Villiers, his father's younger brother, and widow of Lewis-James Le Vaflen, Marquefs de Puiflars in France[2].
(1) Daughter Audrey, married to Richard Harrifon of Balls near Hertford, Efq; Member of Parliament for Lancafter, by whom fhe had John Harrifon, Efq. and other children.
(2) —— to Skinner Byde, third fon of Sir George Byde, Knt. by his firft wife Mary, daughter and heir to John Skinner of Hitchin in the county of Hertford, Efq.

Edward Villiers, Efq. the eldeft fon, in 1671 was made a Cornet of Horfe; afterwards firft Lieutenant-Colonel of the firft troop of horfe-guards, whence he was promoted, 31 December 1688, to the Queen's Regiment of Horfe, and to the ftation of a Brigadier-General. In March 1676-7 (being Eafter-eve) he married Catharine, daughter and heir to John Fitz-Gerald of Dromana in the county of Waterford, Efq. and in her right became feized of a large eftate* in that county; and dying in 1693, before his father, left two fons, John and William; and four daughters, Mary, married

---

* K. Charles II. by his warrant from Windfor, 21 Auguft 1680, ordered a confirmation by patent to the faid Edward Fitz-Gerald, otherwife Villiers, and his heirs by the faid Catharine, of all the eftate that belonged to her father, and which he had fettled by deed of feoffment 16 February 1662, limiting the fame, after divers remainders, to his own right heirs. Provided that his faid daughter fhould marry with the confent of his feoffees any worthy perfon of the family of the Fitz-Geralds, or one that fhould affume the name of Fitz-Gerald for himfelf and his heirs by her. Of this eftate, by deed of covenant, bearing date 24 February 1685, he levied a fine in Eafter term that year; and among other things in the faid deed contained, a power was referved to charge the eftate with the fum of 12,000l. for the better provifion of his faid wife, and for raifing portions for his younger children, which he did accordingly by his will, dated 6 June 1691, and proved 15 February 1693, whereby he bequeathed 2000l. a piece to his fon William and to his daughters Mary, Catharine, Harriet, and Elizabeth. (Lodge.)

[1] Lodge Collect.   [2] Decree in Chancery 7 May 1708. N°. 23.

married to Brigadier-General Steuart, and died in January 1763; Catharine died unmarried; Harriet (married to Robert Pitt, Esq. elder brother to Thomas, Earl of Londonderry, which title is now extinct; by him she was mother of the late illustrious William Pitt, created Earl of Chatham in England, and grandmother of the Right Hon. William Pitt, *now* first Lord of the Treasury in Great Britain); and Elizabeth, who died unmarried.

Their mother had a patent from K. William, dated 6 January 1699, granting her the privilege to enjoy the same title and precedence, as if her husband had survived his father, and had been actually possessed of the honour of Viscount Grandison. She re-married with Lieutenant-General William Steuart, appointed in February 1711 Commander in Chief of the army during the Duke of Ormond's absence; Privy-Counsellor and Knight of the Shire for Waterford, who died 3 June 1726, æt. 82; she having deceased before him 24 December 1725.

John, who succeeded his grandfather, and was the fourth Viscount Grandison, took his seat in Parliament 1 July 1707 [1]; and his Majesty K. George I. taking into consideration his personal merits and noble descent, was pleased to advance him to the dignity of Earl Grandison of Limerick by Privy Seal, dated at Kensington 11 August, and by patent 11 [2] September, 1721, with the creation fee of 20l. on 14 of which month he took his seat as such in Parliament [3]; 26 October 1733, he was sworn of the Privy Council; and appointed Governor of the county and city of Waterford [*].

John, Earl Grandison, and 4 Viscount.

His Lordship married Frances [4], daughter of Anthony Carey, Lord Viscount Falkland, Premier Viscount of Scotland, by whom he had two sons and three daughters, viz.

James Fitz-Gerald, Lord Villiers [5], Representative of the county of Waterford in Parliament, who 11 July 1728 married Jane [6], daughter and heir to Richard Butler of London,

(1)

---

[*] 21 March 1750, his Lordship passed patent to hold two markets on Wednesday and Saturday, and two yearly fairs on 15 May and 24 September at Villierstown in county of Waterford. (Lodge.)

[1] Lord's Jour. II. 152.   [2] Rot. Canc. A°. 8°. Geo. I. 1ª. p D.
[3] Lord's Jour. II. 686.   [4] Ulster's Office.   [5] Idem.   [6] Idem.

don, Esq. but dying there 12 December 1732, was interred 29, in a vault belonging to the family in Hertford Church; leaving issue by her, who 16 April 1734 was married to Lucius-Charles, Viscount Falkland, and died in France in December 1751 [1]; one son John, who died 2 February 173', aged nine months and seventeen days; and a daughter Mary, or Frances, who died in May 1738 [2].

(1) William Lord Villiers [3], born 10 January 1715, was educated in Trinity Hall, Cambridge, and was a young nobleman of virtuous principles, amiable qualities, and uncommon improvements in many branches of useful and curious literature, but died at Waterford 173, and was buried at Youghall.

(1) Daughter, Anne, died young and was there buried.

(2) Lady Elizabeth, who married Aland-John Mason of Waterford, Esq. and was created Countess Grandison [4].

(3) Lady Catharine, who died unmarried in May 1738, and was interred at Youghall.

His Lordship died 14 May 1766, at his house in Suffolk-street, in his 85 year, and was interred in the family vault at Youghall, where his lady, who died 17 January 1768, was also interred.—Hence the title of Earl Grandison, ceased, but that of Viscount, devolved on William Villiers, late Earl of Jersey, and the lineal descendant of Sir Edward, fourth son of Sir Edward Villiers, Knt. President of Munster.

Sir Edward. Which Edward Villiers, on the breaking out of the civil wars, engaged himself in the royal cause, and when it was resolved to take the command of the fleet from the Earl of Northumberland, and to send letters to all the Captains, with orders to observe the commands of Sir John Pennington; the whole dispatch to the fleet was committed to the care of Edward Villiers; but though he delivered his letters, and punctually executed his orders, this design, through the ill management of superior officers, put the whole command of the fleet into the hands of the Parliament. He was afterwards a Lieutenant-Colonel in his Majesty's army, and served in many engagements, particularly in the battle of Newbury, 20 September 1643, where he was wounded; having by these and other services recommended himself

---

[1] Lodge. [2] Idem and public prints. [3] Upper's Office. [4] See Earl Grandison.

VILLIERS, Viscount GRANDISON.

self to K. Charles II. he was honoured with knighthood at Whitehall 7 April 1680, and made Knight-Marshall of his houshold on the death of Sir Edmund Wyndham; also Colonel of the Duchess of York's regiment, and Governor of Tinmouth-Castle.

He had likewise a grant from that King, of the Royal House and manor of Richmond, and his Lady was Governess of the Princesses Mary and Anne, afterwards Queens of Great Britain.—He was continued by K. James, in the post of Knight-Marshall, and that King having a mind to nurse the Pretender in the old palace of Richmond, he on a valuable confideration, refigned it.—He lived to fee his eldeſt ſon Maſter of the Horſe to Q. Mary, and dying in 1689, was interred 2 July that year in Weſtminſter-Abbey.

He married Frances, youngeſt daughter of Theophilus, the ſecond Earl of Suffolk, and by her had iſſue, two ſons and ſix daughters, viz.

Edward, his heir, created Earl of Jerſey. (1)

Henry, who ſerved as a Captain under his father in the (1) Duchefs of York's regiment, and afterwards as Colonel of a regiment of foot; 8 July 1702, he was appointed Governor of Tinmouth-Caſtle, and deceaſing 18 Auguſt 1707, æt. 49, was interred at Tinmouth in Northumberland, where a monument was erected to his memory.—He left a ſon Henry, who was Lieutenant-Governor of Tinmouth, and died 29 May 1753; having married, firſt, Arabella, daughter and heir to John Roſſiter of Somerby in county of Lincoln, Eſq. and ſecondly, Mary, daughter of ———— Fowke, and ſiſter to Lieutenant-General Thomas Fowke, but left no iſſue.

Daughter Elizabeth, was maid of honour to Mary, Prin- (1) ceſs of Orange, and married in 1695, to Lord George Hamilton (third ſon of William Duke of Hamilton) afterwards created Earl of Orkney.—In 1709, ſhe founded and endowed an Engliſh ſchool at Middleton in county of Cork [1] and deceaſed in Albemarle-ſtreet, London, 19 April 1733.

Catharine, married firſt, 20 July 1685, in K. Henry VII. Chapel, in Weſtminſter-Abbey, to James-Lewes le Vaſſen, Marqueſs de Puiſſars in France, Colonel of a regiment of foot in the ſervice of K. William, who died in 1703;

---

[1] Of which a particular account is given in Smith's Cork, I. 153. 154. (& n.)

1703[1]; and she married, secondly, William Villiers, second son of George, third Viscount Grandison.

(3) Barbara, married to John Berkeley, Viscount Fitzharding; she died 19 September 1708, and was buried 23 of that month in Westminster-Abbey.

(4) Anne, Maid of Honour to the Princess of Orange, afterwards Q. Mary, and married to William Bentinck, the first Earl of Portland, great-grandfather to William Henry-Cavendish, the present Duke[2].

(5) Henrietta, married 13 May 1695, to John, Earl of Bredalbane, in Scotland, and died 1 February 1719-20.

(6) Mary, to William, third Earl of Inchiquin[3].

Edward, 1 Earl of Jersey.

Edward, the eldest son of Sir Edward, waited on the Princess Mary into Holland, after her marriage with the Prince of Orange, with whom he returned to England in 1688, and on their being proclaimed King and Queen of England, was on the first settlement of their houshold in February 1688-9, made Master of the Horse to the Queen.—27 of May following, being then a Knight, he was chosen by her Majesty to compliment the Dutch Ambassadors on their arrival, who were sent by the States-General, to congratulate their Majesties accession to the throne.—And the death of his father happening soon after, he succeeded him in his place of Knight-Marshall; also, farther advancing in their Majesties favour, he was created 20 March, 3 William and Mary, Viscount Villiers of Dartford, and Baron Villiers of Hoo, both in county of Kent, England.—At the funeral of Q. Mary, 5 March 1694-5, he led a mourning horse, attended by two equerries; but his place of Master of the Horse, determining by her death, he was sent Envoy Extraordinary and Plenipotentiary to the Congress at the Hague, where, 9 September 1695, he had his public audience of the States-General; and April 1697, he was constituted one of the Lords Justices of Ireland, being also about the same time appointed one of the Plenipotentiaries for the treaty of Ryswick; soon after, viz. 13 October, same year, he received the character of his Majesty's Ambassador Extraordinary to the States-General; and to add lustre to his employments, was created Earl of the Island of Jersey, pursuant to letters patent, dated 29 of that month.—Shortly after he had his audience of leave of the States-General; and

---

[1] Lodge. 1 Edit. II. 97.   [2] Collins. II. 28.   [3] See that title.

and returning into England, was sworn of the Privy Council 25 November same year.—In 1698 he succeeded the Earl of Portland, as Ambassador Extraordinary to the Court of France, and made his public entry into Paris 4 January, N. S. 1698-9; he continued at this Court till May 1699, when he returned to England, and 14 of that month, was constituted one of his Majesty's principal Secretaries of State.—31 of that month, his Majesty declaring in Council his intention of going to Holland, Lord Jersey was appointed one of the Lords Justices for the Administration of the government of England.—Being sent for by his Majesty to attend him at Loo, he arrived there 4 October 1699; in same year, he was appointed one of the Plenipotentiaries for the second treaty of partition; and 24 June 1700, he was made Lord Chamberlain of the household.—On the accession of Q. Anne, he was sworn of her Privy Council ; 14 April 1702, was again constituted Chamberlain of the Houshold ; and in August that year, when the Queen was at Oxford, he was created a Doctor of the Civil Law; he continued to fill the post of Lord Chamberlain, till April 1704, after which time he held no public employment.—His Lordship deceased 26 August 1711, in his 56 year, (on which day he was to have been named Lord Privy Seal) and was interred 4 September following in St. Michael's Chapel in Westminster-Abbey.

He married Barbara, daughter of William Chiffinch, Esq. Closet-Keeper to K. Charles II. by whom he left issue two sons, viz. William, his heir ; Henry, who died unmarried; and a daughter Lady Mary, who married in 1709, Thomas Thynne, of Old Windsor, in county of Berks, Esq. and by him (who died of the small-pox 1710) was mother of Thomas, born twenty-seven days after his father's decease, who succeeded his great uncle Sir Thomas Thynne, in the title of Viscount Weymouth [1]. In December 171 , the said Mary, married to her second husband, George Granville, Esq. created Lord Landsdown, by Q. Anne, 31 of that month [2], and by him had several daughters ; she died 17 January 1734-5.

William, the eldest son, succeeded to his father's honours, during whose life, viz. in 1705, he served in the British Parliament for the county of Kent.—He married Judith, only

William, a Earl of Jersey.

[1] Collins, VI. 63,   [2] Idem.

only daughter of Frederick Hern of the city of London, Esq. and deceasing 13 July 1721, was interred at Westerham in Kent, leaving issue by his lady (who was interred in St. Bridget's Church, London, 31 July 1735) two sons and one daughter, viz.

(1) William, who succeeded his father.

(2) Thomas, who during the reign of K. George II. was, several years, Minister at the Courts of Dresden, Vienna, Berlin, and various others in the Empire, and in 1748, was constituted a Commissioner of the Admiralty; at the general election in 1747, he was returned to the British Parliament for Tamworth in county of Stafford, and was re-elected for the same in 1754.—31 May 1756, his late Majesty, pursuant to letters patent, created him Baron Hyde, of Hindon, in county of Wilts, with limitations to his heirs male, by his then wife, and in default of such issue, then the same title to devolve on his said wife, and the heirs male of her body.— 2 September 1763, he was sworn of the British Privy Council, and 10 of same month, was appointed joint Post-Master-General with Robert Viscount Hampden[1], but he resigned this office in July 1765.—14 July 1771, he was appointed Chancellor of the Duchy, and Palatine Courts of Lancaster, and 8 June 1776, was created Earl of Clarendon, in England, with limitations as before.—30 March, 1752, he married Lady Charlotte, third, but eldest surviving daughter of William Capel, third Earl of Essex (by his wife Jane, daughter of Henry Hyde, Earl of Clarendon and Rochester, in whom those titles became extinct, whose wife was Jane, daughter of Sir William Leveson Gower, Bart. great-grandfather to the present Earl Gower[2], and by her Ladyship (who on the decease of her grandfather, the said Earl of Clarendon became intitled to and assumed the name and arms of Hyde.) he hath issue Thomas Lord Hyde, born 26 December 1753; John Charles, born 14 November 1757; George, born 23 November 1759; and Lady Charlotte Barbara, born 27 March 1761[3].

(1) Daughter, Lady Barbara, married in 1725, to Sir William Blacket, of Newcastle upon Tyne, in county of Northumberland, Bart. and he deceasing 27 August 1728; she married secondly 13 March 1728-9, Bussy Mansel, Esq. uncle

---

[1] Collins. VI. 282. [2] Idem. III. 356. V. 142.
[3] Idem. V. p. 480. and 481.

VILLIERS, Viscount GRANDISON.

uncle to Thomas the laſt Lord Manſel; and 16 July 1757, ſhe married, thirdly, George Venables Vernon, Eſq.

William, heir to his father, was a gentleman of the bed- chamber to Frederick Prince of Wales, at whoſe funeral 13 April 1751, he was one of the ſix ſupporters of the pall.— 12 May 1740, he was appointed Chief Juſtice in Eyre of all his Majeſty's foreſts, chaſes, parks, &c. on this ſide Trent; was afterwards ſworn of the Britiſh privy-council; and 14 May 1766, on the deceaſe of John the fourth Viſcount (who was created Earl Grandiſon) without male heirs, he ſucceeded him in the title of Viſcount in right of his great grandfather Sir Edward, youngeſt ſon of Sir Edward Villiers, by his wife Barbara St. John, to whoſe heirs male, the uncle of the ſaid Barbara limited the title.—23 June 1733, his lordſhip married Lady Anne Egerton, daughter of Scroop, Duke of Bridgewater, and relict of Wriotheſley, third Duke of Bedford; by her ladyſhip who died 16 June 1762, he had iſſue Frederick-William, Viſcount Villiers, born 25 March 1734, who died in October 1742, and George-Buſſy; his lordſhip deceaſed 28 Auguſt 1769, and was ſucceeded by his ſaid ſon.

<small>William, 3 Earl of Jerſey, and 5 V. Grandiſon.</small>

George-Buſſy the fourth Earl of Jerſey, and the ſixth and preſent Viſcount Grandiſon, who was born 9 June 1735, and in 1756, was elected to the Britiſh parliament for Tamworth in Staffordſhire; he was re-elected for that borough in 1761, but 21 March that year, he vacated his ſeat on being declared a Lord of the Admiralty, which appointment he reſigned in April 1763; he afterwards ſerved for Aldborough in Yorkſhire, and in 1768, was choſen for Dover in Kent, one of the cinque ports.—6 July 1765, he was appointed chamberlain of the houſhold; which he reſigned 9 September 1769, on being appointed a lord of the bedchamber, whence he was removed in December 1777.—He was appointed maſter of his Majeſty's buck hounds 30 March 1782, and ſworn of the privy-council of Great Britain, in May 1783 (having reſigned this appointment) he was made captain of the band of gentleman penſioners.—26 March 1770, his lordſhip married Frances, daughter and heir to Doctor Philip Twiſden, biſhop of Raphoe, who died 2 November 1752 [1], and by her hath had iſſue two ſons and three daughters, viz.

<small>George-Buſſy, 6 Viſcount.</small>

Vol. IV.   H   George

<small>[1]. Editor's copy of Ware's Bps.</small>

VILLIERS, Viscount GRANDISON.

(1) George, Viscount Villiers, born 19 August 1773.
(2) William-Augustus, born 15 November 1780 [1].
(1) Daughter, Lady Charlotte, born 2 May 1771.
(2) Lady Anne-Barbara-Frances [2], born 22 March 1772, and
(3) Lady Caroline-Elizabeth, born 16 December 1774 [3].
(4) Lady Georgiana, born 24 June 1776 [4]; died same day, and
(5) Lady Sarah, born 17 November 1779 [5].

TITLES.] George-Bussy Villiers, Earl of Jersey, Viscount Villiers, Viscount Grandison, and Baron of Hoo.

CREATIONS.] V. Grandison of Limerick in county of Leitrim, 3 January 1620, 18 James I. B. of Hoo, and V. Villiers of Dartford, both in Kent, 20 March 1690-1, 3 William and Mary, and Earl of the Island of Jersey, 13 October 1697, 9 William III.

ARMS.] Pearl on a cross, ruby, five escallop shells, topaz.

CREST.] On a wreath, a lion rampant. pearl, ducally crowned, topaz.

SUPPORTERS.] Two lions, pearl, crowned with ducal coronets, topaz, each having a plain collar, ruby, charged with three escallop shells of the second.

MOTTO.] FIDEI COTICULA CRUX.

SEAT.] Middleton-Stoney, in county of Oxford, 55 miles from London.

---

[1] Fielding's Peerage. [2] Idem. [3] Collins IV. 191, 192, 193, 194, and 195. [4] Fielding. [5] Idem.

ANNESLEY,

ANNESLEY, Viscount VALENTIA*.

THIS family had its name from the lordship of Annes- 3.
leya, vulgo Anneſlei in the county of Nottingham, which
was probably the place of its refidence before the Norman
conqueſt ; for when the general ſurvey of that kingdom was
taken by the conqueror's appointment, anno 1079, the own-
er thereof was Richard de Anneſlei, to whom ſucceeded his Richard.
ſon Ralph, called Brito, Le Brett, or Britain, who found- Ralph.
ed the priory of Felley in the ſaid county, giving, by the
conſent of his heirs, to God, the Bleſſed Virgin, St. Helen,
and Friar Robert the hermit and his ſucceſſors, the place
of Felley, with the appurtenances, in pure alms ; and with
the approbation of his ſon Reginald, in 1156 he gave to the
priory of St. Cuthbert at Radeford near Workſop, the church
and priory of Felley, which was confirmed by the Bull of
Pope Alexander III. in 1161, the ſecond year of his pontifi-
cate.

He was buried on the north ſide of the altar in the priory
of Felley, leaving by Aubrey his wife two ſons, Reginald Reginald.
and Drogo. Reginald took on him the name De Anneſle-
ga, or Anneſleia, and in 1175 accounted with K. Henry II.
for 100 marcs, the amercement of the foreſt of Shirewood.
At the requeſt of his father, he gave to St. Mary, and the
houſe and brethren of Felley, the right of his patronage of
the church of Anneſley, with the water-courſe and mill at
Bradley, in pure alms, for the health of himſelf, his wife
and his heirs, and the refreſhment of all his parents departed, which gift was confirmed by Geffrey, Archbiſhop
of York ; to which grant was appendant a round ſeal of a
lion paſſant, circumſcribed *Sigilium Reynaldi de Anneſley*.
—He and his ſon were witneſſes to a deed of Reg...l 'e
Inſula, ſon of Geoffrey de Inſula, of Kirkeby-Wodehouſe,
in

---

* This account of the family of Anneſley, to the year 1627, was corrected from a pedigree drawn by Si. William S. gar, Garter King of Arms, and communicated *to the Author* in January 1764, by Lord Viſcount Glerawley.

in 1172, at Easter, whereby he confirmed to the canons of Felley, all they had acquired in the times of his ancestors and his own, saving the foreign service, as much as belonged to one bovat of land, which Arnold Pugil bestowed on that house.

By the counsel and consent of Hawise his wife, he gave likewise to the canons of Felley the whole land, which was Ernulph de Wodehouse's; and dying 25 November, was buried near his father under a stone, adorned with a crucifix; leaving

Ralph. Ralph, or Ranulph de Annesley his son, who, siding with the rebellious Barons, forfeited his estate, but it was restored to him by the King's precept to Philip de Mace, in 1216, sheriff, of the counties of Derby and Nottingham, which he had forfeited when he departed from his allegiance to K. John, father of that king, to whose faith and service he was then returned. He gave to the canons of Felley, common of pasture in all his fields of pasture, with free passage through his demesnes of Annesley, and confirmed the gifts of his ancestors to that priory. In 1217 he was so infirm, that he was excused from serving the office of coroner; and dying 26 March 1218, left Reginald his heir; and Ralph, to whom he gave six bovats of land in Morton, who was knighted, and married Lucia, eldest of the three daughters and coheirs of Adam de Sancta-Maria (son of Paganus, Lord of Roumarsh in Yorkshire, and of Bulcotes and Knyveton in Nottinghamshire) by Albreda, his second wife, daughter of Jordan de Chevercourt, and widow of Robert de St. Quintin, which Albreda paid a fine to K. John 27 November 1213, of three palfreys, for licence to marry this Adam de Sancta-Maria. By the said Lucia he was father of Robert de Annesley, who married Johanna, daughter of Sir Reginald de Annesley his uncle; and had John his heir, whose son John put an end to the line, having only issue by his second wife Isabel, a daughter of her name, married to John Ashwell, to whom by fine she gave the said lands of Morton.

Sir Reginald. Sir Reginald, who succeeded his father Ralph, at Annesley, confirmed to Felley Priory his father's grant of the services of Robert del Broc, his *Villain*; and of the Oxgang of land, which Galfridus, son of Richard del Broc held in the fields of Annesley, to the church of All Saints at Annesley,

ANNESLEY, Viscount VALENTIA.

to find a lamp burning all the hours which were fung in that church. He paid 4l. for two knights fees in Annefley, which he held of Ralph de Freffenville in the time of Hen. III. and deceafing 27 of June, had iffue by the daughter and heir of ———— Honfkerle, a daughter Joan, married to Robert de Annefley her firft coufin; and

Sir John de Annefley, who 4 Auguft, 13 Edward I. had a grant dated at Newfted in Shirewood, of free warren in all his demefnes of Annefley in the lands of Roumarijs, in county of York, fo long as the faid lands were not within the bounds of the King, and that none fhall dare to choofe or take any thing therein under the penalty of 10l.—Witneffes R. bifhop of Bath and Wells; Henry de Lacy, Earl of Lincoln, and others; which grant of free warren was a fpecial favour in thofe days, and being at that time a knight, he was made fheriff, or had the cuftody committed to him during pleafure, of the counties of Nottingham and Derby, 14 Edward I. (to account yearly into the Exchequer) in which office he continued for five or fix years, as appears from the pipe rolls of thofe times.—28 fame reign he was fummoned to attend the King to Scotland, having 40l. a year, and to find horfe and armour, he having lands of that value lying between the rivers Owfe and Derwent. In the 3, 4. and 5 years of K. Edward II. he executed the office of fheriff for the county of Gloucefter; and 8 of fame reign, was in the commiffion of array for that county, and being one of the verdurers of the King's foreft of Shirewood in county of Nottingham, he was removed from thence on account of his infirmities, as appears in a claufe roll 10 Edward II. in the Tower of London. —By a fine, levied the fame year on the morrow after St. John the Baptift's day, the manor of Annefley, with 25 meffuages, 1. mill, 33 oxgangs of land, 57 acres of meadow, 3 of pafture, 12 of wood, 34s. 8d. rent, the third part of a mill, with one pound of cummin, and lands in Gypefmere, Goverton, Blefeby, Morton, Bixton, Bulcote, Lowdham, Kneveton, and Crophill-Butler, were fettled on him and his wife Annora in tail, with the remainder to his right heirs. He died 6 September 1316 (9 Edw. II.) and by her, who was daughter of Sir John de Pierpoint of county of Nottingham, and died 10 May 1356, had five fons, John; Robert or

Sir John.

Roger.

Roger *, rector of Ruddington in Shropshire; Ralph of Kirkeby-Woodhouse (who had a son Roger or Robert, which Robert Fitz-Ralph, by his deed dated 17 Edw. III. granted and confirmed to Sir John de Annesley, Knt. his uncle, his heirs and assigns, all his lands and tenements with their tofts and crofts, which his said father Ralph had received by gift and feoffment, from Sir John de Annesley, in Kirkeby-Woodhouse); Thomas; and Gregory.

Sir John.   Sir John Annesley, the eldest son, was a Knight 2 Edw. III. when he had a grant of the custody of the honour of Peverel in the counties of Nottingham and Derby; and 13 same reign held in the great Eyre, held before William de Herle and his fellow Justice at Nottingham, he pleaded that K. Edw I. by charter, dated at Newsted in Shirewood 4 Aug. 1280 did grant and confirm to his father, whose heir he was, that he and his heirs should have free warren in all their demesne-lands of Annesley; and his plea was allowed.—In 1343 he was a witness to the foundation charter of Nicholas de Cantilupe, Lord of Ilkeston in Derbyshire, dated 0 December, of a monastery in his park of Greseley for a Prior and 12 Monks of the Carthusian order.—His wife was the daughter and heir of Thomas Gregor; and dying 25 June 1357, he was buried near the north door in Annesley Chantry, leaving

Sir John.   Sir John Annesley, Knt. his son and heir, who 23 May 1376 had livery of the manor of Hedyngton, and hundred of Belyndon and Nethyate, or Northgate in Oxfordshire, which Sir Richard Damory (who died in 1375) held for life

---

* With William de Wakebrugge, he founded and endowed a Chantry in the church of Annesley for a secular Priest, to make special mention of them and J hn de A esley in his Mass, whilst they should live, and for their souls, when dead, with the souls of his father and mother, and of their brothers and mother. The presentation of a fit Chaplain to remain to them during their lives; then to devolve to the said John, and his heirs male; remainder to their brothers Thomas and Gregory, and their respective heirs male; remainder to the Prior and Convent of Felley and their successors. The writ of ad quod damnum, issued for this foundation 35 Edw. III. upon which the Jury found it not to the King's loss, if he granted them licence to give 8 messuages and 10 bovates of land, whereof 5 messuages and 6 bovats were in Annesley, Annesley-Woodhouse, and Kirkeby-Woodhouse, and the remainder in Blesebey, Courton and Gypesme, and that their then remained (to the feoffees of Sir John de Annesley) 20 marcs per annum, and lands in Cruch, held of Roger Beler, and in Ruddington, held of John Paveley. The King's licence for this Chantry bears date 10 February 36 Edw. III. and the confirmation of John, Archbishop of York, 27 January 1373.

life in fee-farm, at 81l. per annum.—That same year, and the 8, 9 and 10 of Rich. II. he served in Parliament for the county of Nottingham; and married Isabel, daughter and heir of Margaret, second of the three sisters and coheirs of Sir John Chandos [*], made Knight of the Garter at the first institution of the Order by K. Edward III. Baron [†] of St.
Saviour

---

[*] He was descended from Walter Chandos, the father of Robert, the father of Roger, who married Philippa, daughter of Sir Guy Bryan, Knt. and had Sir Roger Chandos, Knt. which Sir Roger married twice, first Catharine, daughter of Richard Lord Talbot of Goderic-Castle, and by her who died 30 Edw. III. had a daughter Juliana, wife of John Moigne, from whom the Lord Stourton derives. His second wife was Maud, daughter of John Acton, by whom he had Thomas, who married Lucy, and had Sir John Chandos, Knight of the Garter, who died without issue, 35° Edward III. and three daughters Eleanor, Elizabeth and Margaret, coheirs to their brother, of whom Elizabeth was married to Thomas Berkeley of Cubberley, and Margaret, by her husband, was mother of Isabel, who married Sir John Annesley. (MSS. in St. Sepul. Lib. N°. 2. 120.)

[†] Becoming by this marriage interested in a third part of that Barony, he as Appellant, cited Sir Thomas de Haterington, Knt. who had been Governor of the Castle of St. Saviour le Viscount in county of York, into the Court of Chivalry, to appear before the Lord High Constable of England at Westminster, on Wednesday 7 March 1380, 5 Ric. II. to answer his delivering up that Castle to the French (which he did for a sum of money, when he was sufficiently provided for its defence) and Sir John Annesley offering to try the quarrel by combat, Haterington was apprehended and imprisoned, but shortly after set at liberty at the suit of the Lord Latimer, and endeavoured for a time to avoid the challenge by frivolous exceptions: But, it being at length determined by the opinion of true and ancient Knights, that such a foreign controversy, which had no reason within the limits of the realm, was lawful to be tried by battle, if the cause were first notified to the Constable and Mareschall of the realm, and that the combat was accepted by the parties; John, Duke of Lancaster, third son of K. Edward III. (who governed all things at pleasure during his father's last sickness) swore, that if Haterington did not perform what he ought to do therein, according to the law of arms, he should be drawn to the gallows, as a traitor. Thereupon, at a Court of Honor, held on Friday 10 March, they were ordered to engage in duel; and 7 June 1380 all things being provided, the lists railed, and the King, his Nobles, and a prodigious concourse of people assembled in the Palace-Yard of Westminster, Sir John Annesley, armed and mounted on a fair courser, entered first as Appellant, staying till his Adversary, after being thrice summoned by a Herald to defend his cause, should come, who at the third call appeared, in like manner armed and mounted—He was a mighty man of stature, and far overtopped the Knight, who, among those that were of a mean stature, was one of the least. They began first with spears, then with sword, and lastly with daggers; and fought so long, that Sir John bereft his adversary of all his weapons, and manfully overthrew him, so that he fell down in a swoon; on his recovery from which, Sir John called him traitor and false perjured man, asking if he durst try the battle again; but having neither sense nor spirit to answer, proclamation was made that the battle was ended: so that whether justice, or chance, or valour only, decided the business, Sir John prevailed (as Hollinshed, who relates this combat

Saviour le Viscount, in the Isle of Constantine in Normandy, Great Seneschal of Poictou, and High Constable of Aquitaine; and by her had

Thomas.   Thomas Annesley of Annesley, Esq. who, 7 Rich. II. was Knight in Parliament for the county of Nottingham, and in 1413 (1 Hen. V.) required of his freeholders and tenants in Annesley, that he might enclose a certain place called Nicoll-Leys, to his own profit for one year, because of the laying out a certain hedge between Wodehousefields; in consideration whereof he became a benefactor to the fabrick of the church of Annesley, giving before hand 3s. 4d. for that work.—He married the daughter of — Clifton, of Clifton in Nottinghamshire, and had Hugh his heir, and a daughter Isabella*, wife to Sir Gervaise Clifton, of Clifton, Knt. Hugh married a daughter of Sir John Babington † of Chilwell, in county of Derby, Knt. and died 13 September 1429, (2 Henry IV.) leaving one son Hugh, and a daughter Mariana, married to Edmond Willoughby, Esq. ancestor to the Willoughbies of Wollaton.

Sir Hugh.   Sir Hugh Annesley was eight years old at his father's death, and 12 Hen. VI. being then a Knight, was returned one of the gentry of the county of Nottingham, by the King's Commissioners, being the tenth upon the roll; and marrying a daughter of William Fitz-William ‡ had two sons, John and Thomas; the elder of whom John, 14 Hen. VI. enfeoffed John Macworth, Dean of Lincoln, John Curson and Thomas Macworth, Esq; in his manors of Annesley, Bulcoe, and Gyppesmere all his lands in Crophill, and Cossale, in county of Nottingham, and in Rowmersh, and Bolton upon Derne, in county of York, which

bat at large, remarks) to the great rejoicing of the common people, and discouragement of traitors. And Haterington, as Fabian affirms, was drawn to Tyburn, and there hanged for the treason, whereof, being vanquished, he was proved guilty.—The King considering the damage Sir John sustained by the loss of his third part of the Castle, granted 26 May 1385, to him and his wife for their lives, 40l. a year, payable out of the Exchequer.

* Segar makes Isabella the only child of Thomas de Annesley; he does not say that Hugh is his son, the line of descent not being continued from Thomas to him.

† Of a very ancient and knightly family, (says Segar) in county of Derby, and the coat-armour of this Hugh Annesley and his wife, were set up in the chapel of Wiverton, and in divers other places in county of Nottingham.

‡ Their Coat Armour is set up in the Church of Annesley. (Segar.)

ANNESLEY, Viscount VALENTIA.

which descended to him on the death of his grandfather. He died on the Saturday before the feast of St. James the Apostle 1437 (15 Hen. VI.) and left an only child Alice, married first to Sir George Chaworth, third son of Sir Thomas, from whom, by their son Thomas, descended George, Viscount Chaworth of Armagh, so created 4 March 1627, which family (now extinct) made the manor of Annesley their principal residence, and her second husband was Reginald Leigh, Esq.

Thomas, the younger son, was seated at Ruddington, *Thomas.* in the county of Northampton, and had issue two sons, William his heir; and Hugh, who died in 1524, seized of Paveley's and Bugge's manors in Ruddington, &c. leaving Hugh his heir, then upwards of 50 years old, who married Alice, daughter of Randulph Leech, of the county of Derby, and had two sons, Hugh of Ruddington, (father of Gervaise, of the same place, who married the daughter of —— Bleevet, of the county of Lincoln, and was father of Gervaise and John) and James Annesley of Uxbridge, who served Q. Margaret, consort to K. Henry VI. and had one son Henry, not a year old at his father's death; he was educated by John Horne of Sarepden, in county of Oxford, who had married Elizabeth, relict of Richard Blount, which Elizabeth, leased the farm of Maple-Durham to him for sixty years; the said Henry Annesley married Joan, daughter of Robert Lewsam, of Little Rowley, in county of Oxford (by his wife Joan, daughter and heir to John Herbert, of Moreton-Henmarsh, of the noble family of Pembroke) and by her had issue twenty-one children, whereof three sons and eight daughters, arrived at maturity, viz. Edmund (who married Catharine, daughter of Richard Gennour, and had sixteen children, twelve of whom were living in 1627); James (married to Jane, daughter of William Lovelace, of Henley, and had a daughter Elizabeth, married to John Kenne, of Cawsam, in county of Oxford); John, a grocer on London-Bridge, who died without issue at the age of 40 years; daughter Elizabeth (married to Nicholas Tooley, of Burmington, in county of Warwick, and had nineteen children, several of whom were living in 1627); Anne (to Richard Stampe, of Hodcote, in county of Berks, and had fifteen children); Dorothy (to Edmund Busby of Brayler, in county of Warwick, and had seven children);

Grace

Grace (to Thomas or Edmund Snape, of Fowler, in county of Oxford, and had Elizabeth, who, by John Petty, of Stoke-Talmage, had Margaret the first wife of James Ley, Earl of Marlborough); Dionife (to Thomas Freckleton, of Auftrey, in county of Warwick, and had issue); Ellen (to John Bishop of Brayler, in county of Warwick, and had fourteen children); Bridget (to John Stampe of Halton, in county of Oxford); and Anne, to John Turner, of Reading.

William.

William Annesley, Esq; eldeft son of Thomas, of Ruddington, married Mabel, daughter of ———— English, and had issue four daughters and five sons, viz. Cicily, married to John Hall, Esq.; Catharine, to John Langham of London; Isabella; and Johanna: The sons were

(1) Sir Hugh, seated at Maple-Durham, near Reading in county of Oxford, about the time of K. Henry VI. who left three daughters, coheirs, viz. Jane*, (who married William De la Lynde, to whom Maple-Durham was allotted, of whose heir it was purchased by Richard Blount, of Iver, near London, which Richard was brother to William Lord Mountjoy, and from him it descended first to Sir Richard, and next to Sir Michael Blount); ———— to John Norris, Esq.; and Catharine to John Iwareby, Esq.† whose daughter and heir Jane married to Sir John St. John, second son of Sir Oliver, and had issue John, who married Margaret, daughter and coheir to Richard Carew of Bodington, in county of Surry, and had a son Nicholas, who married Elizabeth, daughter of Richard

---

* She was interred in the church of Maple-Durham, in a tomb on the north side of the chancel, with this inscription:

"Here lies Dame Jane, the daughter of Sir Hugh Annesley, and late the wife of William Lynd, Esq. whose souls I pray you hartily remember in your good prayers."

† Upon a grave-stone on the north side of the chancel of Maple-Durham church is this inscription:

Here lies John Iwareby, Esq. who died the 16 August 1470, upon whose foul God have mercy.

And in the north window of the chancel, John Iwareby and Catharine his wife, in their arms, and underscribed, to pray and say, an Ave Maria for their souls, so often as ye shall subjoin the said windows. Their arms are insculped in brass on the grave-stone. Segar.

ANNESLEY, Viscount VALENTIA.

Richard Blount of Maple-Durham, Esq. and was father of Oliver Viscount Grandison in Ireland, and Baron Tregoze in England.

Bryan, second son of William Annesley, lived at Darincourt, near Dartford, in county of Kent, and was servant to K. Henry VIII. he made his will 2 March 27 of that King, and therein bequeathed legacies of rich vestments of velvet to his brothers John and Robert, and to Hugh Annesley his cousin. His son Bryan was father of Bryan, one of the gentlemen pensioners to Q. Elizabeth, and lived at Lewesham and Darent; he married the daughter of ―――― Tyrrell, of county of Essex, warden of the fleet, and had three daughters, viz. Christiana married to William Lord Sandys *of The Vine*, in county of Southampton; Grace (to Sir John Wildgose, of Iredge, in Sussex, Knt. by whom she had Sir Annesley Wildgose, Knt. who married Margaret, daughter of Henry Lennard, Lord Dacre); Cordelia, 5 February 1607, to Sir William Hervey, Lord Hervey of Kidbroke in Kent, (a manor, which came to him by this marriage) and for his signal services against the Spaniards in Ireland, created Baron of Rosse in the county of Wexford 5 August 162 ; to whom she was second wife, and had three sons and three daughters, who all dying unmarried except Elizabeth the youngest, she became heir, and was married to John Hervey of Ickworth in Suffolk, Esq. eldest brother to Thomas Hervey, Knt. whose son John was created Earl of Bristol, and had no issue [1]. (1)

Ralph, whose only daughter and heir Anne, was married to John Perkins of Surry, Esq. by whom she had a daughter Anne, married to William Lennard, of Chevering, county of Kent, (younger son of John Lennard, Esq. ancestor to the Lord Dacre [2]) and his son Sampson, was father of Henry Lennard, Esq. (3)

Robert, of whom presently. And (4)

John, father of Thomas Annesley, of Maidenhead, in county of Berks, Esq. and of Henry of same place, who had a daughter Joan, married to ―――― Atkinson, Esq. and a son Edmund, of Maidenhead, whose son and heir was living in 1627. (5)

Robert

---

[1] Collins, IV. 329. 330.   [2] Idem. VI. 369. 370. and supplement.

Robert.

* Robert Annesley, fourth son of William, from whom Lord Valentia, more immediately derives, was seated at Newport-Pagnel in county of Bucks, and in 1548 appointed Trustee, by William Stokes, to see the sum of 20l. properly applied, which by will he bequeathed to the finishing the steeple of the church at Newport-Pagnel.—He died in 1553 (1 Q. Mary) and by the probate of his will, dated 29 July, desires to be buried in that church before his seat, and gives his son George, his lands in Little-Linford in Bucks. His wife was Joan, daughter of William Clovile of Clod-Hall in Essex, Esq. by whom he had George his heir, and three daughters, Frances married to Thomas Fisher; Anne to Leonard Mount of Newport; and Catherine to John Lamborn of Wodison in Bucks.

George.

George Annesley of Newport-Pagnel, Esq. married Elizabeth, daughter of Robert Dove of Moulsho in county of Bucks, widow of William Stokes, and by her, (who was buried at Newport-Pagnel in 1603, where he was interred near her 17 January 1607) had eight sons and three daughters, viz. James, Matthew, and Thomas, who died young; Robert, who succeeded; James (who by Mary his wife had six sons, viz. George, James, Nicholas, Richard, Anthony, and Bryan); Ralph; George (who 25 April 1625, married Anne, daughter of ———— Saunders, died in the following year, and was buried at Newport Pagnel); Thomas; daughter Judith (married to Ralph Shepherd of Ewelm in county of Oxford); Cicily; and Mary.

Robert.

Robert, the eldest surviving son, was a commander at sea in Q. Elizabeth's time, and also a Captain in her army, raised to suppress the Earl of Desmond's rebellion, after which he became an undertaker in the plantation of Munster; and married Beatrix daughter of John Cornwall of Moore Park in Hertfordshire, Esq. by whom he had two sons and four daughters, Francis, his heir; Robert, a Captain in the army; Elizabeth; Beatrix, married to Richard Saunders of Wawwenden in county of Bedford; Bridget, one of the bedchamber women to Q. Anne, consort to K. James; and Mary,

---

* The descent of Robert is proved by two attestations, one of Oxfordshire, and the other of Buckinghamshire, registered in the library of the College and Office of the King's and Heralds of Arms, directly thus. (Lodge, &c.)

Mary, wife to Matthew Coney of Newport-Pagnel in county of Bucks.

Sir Francis Annesley, the eldest son, made the kingdom of Ireland the scene of his fortune and actions, where he faithfully served K. James and Charles I. near 40 years, in offices and employments of high trust and importance. 3 May 1605 he had a pension granted him of five shillings a day; and whereas there were certain officers established in Ireland, as namely, the clerk of the ordnance, of the victuals, and works, who were from time to time to yield account of their respective disbursements; and that for more assurance of just accompts to be rendered, and for prevention of deceits, there were Comptrollers appointed in the two former offices only, his Majesty erected the office of Comptroller over the Clerk of the Works, by letters patent, dated 16 July 1606, and made choice of Mr. Annesley, as one sufficient for that place, which he conferred upon him for life, with the fee of 20l. a year. Also, 22 May 1607 he was joined with Sir Richard Boyle (after Earl of Cork) in the office of Clerk of the Council, and Keeper of the Signet in the province of Munster, during life.

15 November 1607, he had a pension of 6s. 8d. Irish a day, granted to him pursuant to privy seal, dated at Westminster, upon the surrender of a late pension heretofore granted to Bryan Mac-Geoghagan for life [1]; 21 August he had a reversionary grant of the office of Provost Mareschal in the province of Conaught, also for life: and early in this reign he began to raise a fortune by leases and grants of lands from the crown, which, at his death, amounted to a very considerable one*.

30 April

---

* His acquisitions were chiefly these. On 26 June 1608 he had a lease for 21 years of lands in Ballysax and Callan, with others in the counties of Kildare and Kilkenny; and 31 January 1611 a grant of 480 acres of the escheated lands in the precinct of Mountjoy and county of Tyrone, and of 240 in the precinct of Orier and county of Armagh, at the rent for both of 5l. 5s. 3d. in which last county acquiring certain lands from Patrick O'Hanlon, Gent. to whom the King had granted them in fee-farm 6 October 1609, with a reservation to the crown of the fort of Mountnorris, and 306 acres thereto allotted and adjoining, so long as the King should keep it for a fort, and maintain a ward of soldiers there; he had a lease, dated 12 October 1611, for 21 years, at the rent of 10 shillings per annum, of the said fort and lands,
with

[1] Rot. de A°. 5°. Jac. I. 2ᵈ. p. D.

ANNESLEY, Viscount VALENTIA.

30 April 1612 he was made Constable of the Castle of Mountnorris; and 25 May appointed Muster-Master-General

with the entertaintment of 4 shillings a day, and 8d a piece for 10 soldiers; and in 1618 the King being informed, that the fort was not then, nor ever like to be of such consequent use for his service, as in former times, thought fit, among other abatements of his army, to discharge that ward as a needless burthen; but, in lieu of his said entertainment confirmed to Captain Annesley a pension of five shillings a day for life, which was inserted on the establishment; and for his better encouragement to plant and build there, for the settlement of himself and posterity in that county, where their residence might be of special consequence for his Majesty's service, directed (21 September) that he should have a grant of the said fort and 300 acres, with a confirmation of his other estates; in pursuance whereof he passed patent 9 January 1618 for the said fort, the monasteries of Terrylesartigh and Templebreed in the town of Armagh, and many other lands, towns, tithes, &c. in the counties of Armagh, Tyrone, Wexford and Downe; the premises in Tyrone being erected into the manor of Annesley; those in Armagh into the manor of Mountnorris; those in Downe into the manor of Cloghmaghericatt; and those in Wexford into that of Sampton; with the privileges of Courts leet and baron, waifs, estrays, &c. to hold a Monday market, and a fair on St. John Baptist's day at Ballynegorhagh in Tyrone; a Friday market, and a fair on the same day at Cloghmahericatt; a fair at Mountnorris 5 October (having the grant of a Friday market there 30 April 1612) and two days after each fair; liberty to build tan-houses; to impark 2000 acres for deer, with free warren and other privileges, paying to the crown for all the premises, 50l. 2s. 6d. h. per ann.—In 1615 he purchased from Edward Dowdall of Rathmore in Meath, Gent. the manors of Mullagh and Mullaghmore, with other land, amounting to 2260 acres in the county of Cavan, which being escheated lands, he had them confirmed by patent 25 November, with a grant of Courts, &c. in each manor, paying the crown-rent of 24l. 17s. 9d f.—On 29 January following, as assignee to Edmund Midhoppe, the King granted him the manor, lordship, and castle of Roscomin, with many houses and lands in the town and fields of Roscomon; the site of the monasteries or houses of canons and friars of Roscomon; the rectories and tithes of Kilbegnata, Ballynakilly, Kilcrunie, Dromtempe, Dennaman, Emolashmore, and Clanyne in the county of Roscomon, with the monastery or friary of Loncurt alias Longford in the county of Longford, to hold all the premises at the rent of 32l. 1s. 10d. Irish.—On 17 January 1617 he passed patent for the towns and lands of Ballycastlane, Knockgrenane, Tenecree, and divers others in the county of Wexford, with the creation thereof into the manor of Annesley, at the rent of 5l. 6. 8d. Irish.—As assignee of Thomas, Lord Cromwell, he had four several grants of lands, dated 12 May, and 3 December 1620, 28 July and 22 December 1621, in the counties of Sligo, Mayo, Westmeath, Kerry, Cork, Limerick, Tipperary, Galway, Wicklow, Kildare, Dublin, Louth, Leitrim, and King's County.—On 8 May 1630 (by virtue of the commission dated at Dublin 13 August 1628, for granting anew the escheated lands in Ulster) his Lordship and Sir Robert Dillon had a grant of the small proportion of Latgare in the county of Fermanagh, with the creation thereof into the manor of Latgare, liberty to impark 300 acres, and to set apart 400 for demesne lands, to hold at the rent of 10l. 13s. 4d. English; and 25 November that year a grant of the small proportion of Teemore, &c. containing 1100 acres in the county of Armagh, created into the manor of Mountnorris, with the usual

ANNESLEY, Viscount VALENTIA.

neral and Clerk of the Cheque for life, in reversion after the death of Sir John King; obtaining likewise, 31 July that year, a grant of the office for the writing of tallies, and cutting tallies of all bills to be paid at the receipt of the Exchequer upon all payments and assignations, (that office being then first erected) and also Clerk of the Treasury for entering of tallies, during life, with the fee of 5 shillings a day, which he surrendered 25 May 1625 to Thomas Stockdale, Esq.—In the Parliament of 1613, he was Knight for the county of Armagh, and also Burgess for Lismore; and 1 October 1616 was appointed one of the principal Secretaries for Ireland, and of the Privy Council; but that employment being granted without fee, he had a reversionary patent 8 June 1618 for the office of Secretary of State and Keeper of the Privy Signet, on the avoidance or death of Sir Dudley Norton, whereupon he resigned his reversionary grant of Muster-Master-General: but of this he was for some time deprived by the power of the L. D. Wentworth, who 12 July 1634, conferred it upon Sir Philip Mainwaring.—On 8 August 1619 he was made a Commissioner for the plantation of the county of Longford and the territory of Elye-O'Carrol; and 10 October following the town of Newborough in the county of Wexford being made a corporation, he was one of the first Burgesses.

K. James purposing to institute the order of BARONETS in Ireland, as he had done in England, for the carrying on the more effectually what he had then much at heart, namely, the plantation of Ulster, and reducing it to good order, peace and quiet, acquainted the L. D. with his purpose by letters from Apethorpe 30 July 1619; and therein declares, he intended it as a reward for virtue, and consequently that it should be his care to advance such men only to that dignity, as had well deserved of the crown, either in war or peace; to the end that so fair a title of honour, descending to their posterities might incite them to imitate the

---

usual privileges of holding Courts, impailing a park, &c. at the rent of 11l. 14s. 8d. Of which his Lordship was deprived, after 18 years quiet possession, by the L. D. Wentworth, who, upon a paper petition preferred to him by Richard Rolleston, decreed the said lands of Teemore to the said Rolleston, and by his own warrant removed Lord Mountmorris from the possession thereof.

the worth of their anceſtors, upon whom, for their merits, by his good grace and favour it was conferred. Accordingly by letters patent, bearing date at Dublin, 30 September 1619, his Majeſty erected and eſtabliſhed the degree and order of Baronets in Ireland, then creating Sir Dominick Sarsfield, Chief Juſtice of the Common Pleas, the firſt Baronet: And ſo deſervedly conſpicuous was Sir Francis Anneſley in his Majeſty's eſteem, that he made choice of him to be the ſecond, whom he advanced to that honour; which he did by Privy Seal *, dated at Greenwich 26 June, and by patent 7 Auguſt 1620; and further, by patent † dated at Weſtminſter 11 March 1621, created him Viſcount of Valentia, with the fee of 13l. 6s. 8d. payable out of the cuſtoms of the port of Dublin, in reverſion, after the death of Sir Henry Power, Lord Valentia, without iſſue male; to which honour, at that Lord's death, he ſucceeded.

20 March

* In which the King makes this honourable mention of him. "As we are vigilant to obſerve the courſes of ſuch, as are employed by us in places of conſequence and truſt; ſo we are not weary to heap benefits after benefits upon as many of them, as we find to deſerve them at our hands; which is the cauſe, that as heretofore, upon knowledge of the abilities of our truſty and well-beloved ſervant Sir Francis Anneſley, Knt. to do us ſervice, we firſt conferred many benefits upon him, and afterwards of our own princely election, called him to be one of our principal Secretaries of that kingdom; So, now again taking into conſideration his faithfulneſs, zeal and induſtry in our affairs, we are pleaſed, as a further teſtimony of the good place he holdeth in our favour, and of our gracious acceptance of his endeavours, of our own eſpecial choice freely to beſtow on him the honour of a Baronet of that kingdom. Rot. de A°. 18°. Jac. I. 1ª. p. D.

† The preamble, after expreſſing the creation of Sir Henry Power, by patent dated at Weſtminſter, on 1 March 1620, thus proceeds: Sciatis quod nos nolentes prædictum nomen, ſtatum, titulum et honorem Vicecomitis de Valentia pro defectu Exitus maſculi de corpore prædicti Henrici extingui, ſi contigerit ipſum ſine hærede maſculo de corpore ſuo exeunte obire, ac Virtutes, Mores, et Merita prædilecti et fidelis Conciliarii noſtri in dicto Regno noſtro Hiberniæ Franciſci Anneſley Militis et Baronetti ejuſdem Regni noſtri, ac primarii Secretarii noſtri ejuſdem Regni intuentes, qui cum præfato Henrico, modo Vicecomite de Valentia, Affinitate conjunctus ſit: Necnon ipſius Franciſci Anneſley eximia, gravia et diuturna Concilia, Negotia, et alia quamplurima Servitia nobis et Coronæ noſtræ, non ſine maxima Cura, Diligentia, Dexteritate et Fide antehac præſtita, conſiderantes, in ſignum favoris noſtri regalis, et perpetuam Memoriam Gratiæ noſtræ præfato Franciſco et Familiæ ſuæ, pro hujuſmodi acceptabili ſuo Servitio, quæ idem Franciſcus adhuc nobis impendere non deſiſtit, ipſum Franciſcum et Hæredes ſuos maſculos præfato titulo et honore Vicecomitis de Valentia, poſt mortem prædicti Henrici abſque hærede maſculo de corpore ſuo exeunte ornare decrevimus. Ac idcirco de Gratia, &c. Rot. 15°. Car. II. 1. pª. f.

20 March 1621 he was joined in a most important commission * for the reformation of that kingdom, with the L. D. Chichester and others, to enquire into the state of religion; trade; courts of justice; the army; the covenants, agreements and conditions in the charters, made to undertakers for land in the plantations; the rights and revenues of the crown; what great and notable waste of woods and timber had been made; what offices judicial or ministerial had been granted in reversion; what new offices erected; how the revenue particularly stood; what debts were owing by the King, &c. and to find out how and by what means any abuse in these particulars might with honour, justice, and conveniency be reformed and amended.—15 July 1624, he was appointed one of the Commissioners and Keepers of the Peace in the Provinces of Leinster and Ulster, during the L. D. Falkland's absence on his progress to oversee the plantations; was joined in Commission 19 December 1625 with Sir Thomas Philips and others, to redress the grievances of the army, to take a general muster, to examine their numbers and qualities, to view their arms, and to make perfect rolls thereof; and was joined in several other weighty commissions for the good of the kingdom.—30 May 1625, he was constituted Vice-Treasurer, and General Receiver of his Majesty's Revenues of Ireland; had a Pension of 5s. a day, 3 March following, on the surrender thereof to him by Bryan Mac-Geoghagan; received a warrant 8 July 1627 for the first company of horse or foot that should become void by the death or resignation of any Captain then in

---

* The King introduces this commission with the following reasons for the issuing thereof. "As our great and princely care and desire to advance the flourishing estate of our realm of Ireland, hath many ways appeared; so it is our constant resolution upon all occasions, to express the continuance of the same zeal and affection in perfecting that so glorious a work, whereof God hath pleased to make us (above any our predecessors) a principal instrument: And foreseeing in our royal providence, that as a chief means to produce so good effects, it behoveth us to lay such grounds, and prescribe such ways and courses, as may tend to the advancement of religion and justice, the removing of grievances, increasing of trade, settling of plantations, and securing of that kingdom, we have determined to use all diligence both in the finding out, and following those means; for the better effecting of all which purposes, being matters of great weight and importance, we think it most meet, that some persons of trust, understanding and judgment be employed to discern, discover and find out the whole state of the premises, and all material circumstances touching the same, upon whose information, certificate, and satisfaction given unto us, we may proceed to the effecting thereof, as we shall judge most requisite."

in pay, after such others were first supplied for whom the King had given former particular warrants, it being his pleasure that his several directions in that kind be put into execution, according to the priority of their dates; which the King was induced to confer upon him, having received so many testimonies of his judgment, sufficiency, and forwardness to do him service, that he thought himself obliged to take gracious notice thereof, and to extend his favour towards him upon all fitting occasions, to encourage his faithful continuance therein [1]; and 13 June 1632, he was made Treasurer at War.

By patent[*], dated 8 February 1628 [2], he was created Baron Mountnorris of Mountnorris, and took his seat in the House of Lords 14 July 1634 [3]; and the King having granted a Commission of Grace for the remedy of defective titles, his Lordship, with the Lord-Treasurer, the Lords Fingall, and Lecale, were (1 August) appointed a Committee to view the bill, entitled "An Act for Confirmation of Letters Patent to be passed upon the said Commission:" Upon whose report the same day, the bill was read a third time, put to the vote, and was passed by general assent, and he was nominated one of the Lords, to attend and move the L. D. that he would be pleased to hear with speed, all such as should desire to pass their lands on the Commission of Defective Titles, and to set down easy rates on the same, that his Majesty's grace and favour might be the more welcome to his subjects, and that the subsidies might

---

[*] The preamble. Cum nihil sit quod regiam Majestatem magis deceat, quam eos, qui de seipso et Republicâ sunt bene meritii et laudabilia præstiterant Obsequia, Honoribus augere et promovere; arbitramur enim Coronam nostram regiam quamplurimum honorari et locupletari, cum Viros, illustres Consilio, et Prudentia insignes, et erga nos et Coronam nostram maxime fideles, ad eminentiores Honoris et Dignitatis gradus vocamus et erigimus. Considerantes itaque gratissima et fidelissima Servitia, quæ prædilectus & fidelis Consiliarius noster Regni nostri Hiberniæ Franciscus Annesley, Miles et Baronettus, Vice-thesaurarius et Receptor-Generalis Reddituum et Revencionum nostrorum eodem Regno, ac primarius Secretarius noster dicti Regri nostri, tam præchariffimo nuper Patri nostro beatæ Memoriæ, quam nobis fideliffime et prudentiffime impendit, indiesque impendere non desistit: Necnon considerantes Circumspectionem, Prudentiam, Strenuitatem, Dexteritatem, Integritatem, Providentiam, Curam et Fidelitatem ipsius Francisci erga nos et Coronam nostram, ipsum in Procerum et Magnatum dicti Regni nostri Hiberniæ numerum ascribi decrevimus. Sciatisigitur, &c.

---

[1] Rot de A°. 3°. Car. 1. 3ª. p. D. R. 26. [2] Idem. 4¹º. Car. 1. 5¹º. p. D. R. 45. [3] Lords Jour. I. 2.

might be the better paid. To which the L. D. returned anſwer, it was as great a grace and favour as could be offered to any people, and that as he was the King's ſervant, and muſt tender the King's profit, ſo he would do it with all moderation, and ſatisfaction to the ſubjects [1].

In the year 1629, the King, having by letter called him into England about matters much importing his Majeſty's profit and ſervice, received ſo good ſatisfaction in all things from him, as induced the King to return him to his charge with this teſtimony, " That as he had hitherto
" found him an able and faithful ſervant, for which he
" had extended ſpecial marks of his grace and bounty to-
" wards him, ſo he was confident of his perſeverance
" therein, and accordingly ſhould be ready to enlarge his
" favours to him, as fit occaſion ſhould be offered." And in his letter to the L. J. Elye and Cork, dated at Oatlands 10 Auguſt, writes, " We do let you know, that as
" we do expect from him all due care and induſtry, as
" well for the improvement of our revenues, and ad-
" vancement of our profit, as for the diminution and
" abatement of our preſent charge, by all juſt and honour-
" able means; ſo it is our pleaſure and command, that
" you ſhould take his advice and aſſiſtance, and give him
" all favourable hearing, countenance and ſupportation
" in all matters conducing thereunto, as to a chief Officer
" and well deſerving ſervant of ours, whom we value
" and eſteem; and becauſe we have given him ſome things
" in eſpecial charge for our profit and ſervice, about
" which he may have occaſion to make his repair to our
" Royal Preſence, to give us an account thereof, we do
" will and require you to grant him licence to come unto
" us, when he ſhall deſire it, and give him ſuch allow-
" ance by concordatum, out of the monies allowed for
" extraordinaries, for the time he ſhall attend our ſer-
" vice here, as in like caſes hath been accuſtomed to per-
" ſons of his place and quality."

But, in 1635, during the Government of the L. D. Wentworth, his Lordſhip fell into much trouble, being by him committed to priſon, and 13 [2] December ſentenced to loſe his head by an extraordinary act of power, the deputy cauſing him to be condemned by a Council of War (ſummoned

[1] Lords Jour. l. 19. [2] Rot. Pat. de A°. 12°. Car. 1.ᵗ 4ᵗʰ. p. D.

(summoned by authority of his Majesty's Warrant, dated 31 July) for no other crime, than an unadvised, passionate, mysterious expression, uttered at the Lord Chancellor's table, within three or four days after the Parliament was dissolved; when it being related, that as the L. D. was sitting in the Presence-Chamber, one of his servants, in removing a stool, happened to hurt his foot, then indisposed through an accession of the gout, one of the Company said to the Lord Mountnorris, that it was Annesley, his kinsman, one of the L. Deputy's Gentlemen-Ushers, that had done it: Whereupon his Lordship answered, "Perhaps it was done in revenge of that public affront, which my L. D. had done him formerly, but he hath a brother, that would not take such a revenge." His Lordship, in his defence, protested, that what interpretation soever his words might have put upon them, he intended no hurt or prejudice to the person of the Deputy; affirming, that by these words, "But he hath a brother that would not take such a revenge," he meant only, that the said brother would die, before he would give the Deputy occasion to give him such a rebuke. But notwithstanding, he was adjudged to be imprisoned, deprived of his commands in the army, disarmed, disabled of ever bearing office therein, and lastly, to be shot to death, or lose his head, at the deputy's pleasure.—After this sentence, it appears by the King's letter from Westminster 19 April 1636 [1], that his Majesty had extended some degree of favour towards him; "but being given to understand," says the King, "that his ill carriage hath been such by neglect
" of our Grace, afforded unto him as it hath been held
" fit to cause his study-door to be sealed up by the Commit-
" tee, who have the cognizance of that business; and it
" is likewise conceived that the view and perusal of his
" papers may be of use, for the further discovery of his
" proceedings therein, We do therefore hereby authorise
" and require you to appoint any four of our Privy Coun-
" cil there, whom you shall think fit (in the presence of
" some to be nominated by the said Lord Mountnorris) to
" take a view and sight of his papers, and in case they shall
" find any that may be of use, either in that kind or
" otherwise for our service, to take them into your hands,
" and to dispose of them as you shall see cause, and for so
                                                    " doing.

[1] Rot. Claus. de A°. Car. L. 12°. and 13°. f. R. 7.

"doing, these our letters shall be your sufficient warrant:"
But 6 April 1637 he had a pardon under the great seal[1], (having continued from the time of his sentence, a close prisoner in the Castle of Dublin) upon his humble Petition; which, though he thought absolutely necessary at that time, and his Majesty was pleased in his clemency to grant it, yet he seems to undervalue and despise it in his Petition, which 7 November 1640 he presented to the Commons of England, whereby he relinquished all advantage of defence by the said pardon, and submitted the crimes, to him imputed, to their scrutiny and determination.

He departed this life in 1660, and was buried 23 November in the Chancel of Thorganby Church, Yorkshire; having married to his first wife Dorothea, daughter of Sir John Philips, of Picton-Castle, in the county of Pembroke, the first Baronet of that family[2], by his wife Anne, daughter and coheir to Sir John Perrot of Harrolston, L. D. of Ireland, and by her, who died 3 May 1624, and was buried the next day at St. John's, Dublin, he had five sons and eight daughters, viz.[3]

Sir Arthur, created Earl of Anglesey. (1)

Robert, born 2 August 1615, died at Rome on his travels. (2)

John, born in Dublin, 11 September 1616, was seated at Ballysonan in the county of Kildare; Of whom the King thus writes, (in his Privy Seal from Whitehall 15 December 1660) "Whereas Captain John Annesley, "having the command of a troop of horse in the "service of our late dear father, of blessed memory, "in Ireland, in detestation of that most execrable murder "upon our late most Royal Father, did give up his Com- "mission, and refused to act under that usurped power, "although in those times he had no other subsistence for "himself, his wife, and family, but what he had by his "troop, and hath ever since kept himself out of all em- "ployment under that power, which was a signal proof "of his loyalty to our said father and to us. And for "that we were engaged for the troops and commands now "settled in our realm of Ireland, before application was "made to us in his behalf; we do therefore by these our "letters, (3) Families of Ballysonan, Little-Rath, and Ballysax.

---
[1] Idem. Pat. de A°. 12°. Car. I. 4th. p. D. R. 38.   [2] Ulster't Office.
[3] Mss. Pedigrees penes J. L.

"letters, will and require you to settle upon him the command of Captain of such Troop of Horse, as shall first become void, and be in our gift in our army in Ireland, and thereof you may not fail, but see this our letter served in the first place[1]." Accordingly he had a grant 9 February 1660, of the first troop that should become void; he married Charity, daughter of Henry Warren of Grangebeg, in county of Kildare, Esq and died in 1695, having issue five sons and three daughters, viz. Francis, of Ballysonan; Maurice, of Little-Rath; John, of Ballysax; George, who died unmarried; as did Robert, soon after his father; Dorothea, married (to Maurice, son of Sir John Crosbie, Knt.[2]); Catharine, to Strelly Pegge, of Beauchyeff in Derbyshire, Esq. Counsellor at Law, and deceasing in London, was interred in St. Martin's Church, in the Fields[3]); Elizabeth, (to Jeffrey Paul, of Ballyraggan, Esq. Knight of the Shire for Carlow; he made his will 23 October 1707, in which year he died, and she died in 1741, and was interred with him and her parents, at Ballysonan); and Anne, the youngest daughter married Walter Bourke of Kill, Esq. Francis Annesley, of Ballysonan, Esq. married Deborah, sister of the said Jeffrey Paul, Esq. and died in 1707, leaving by her who died 24 December 1761, four daughters, viz. Charity, born 29 March 1698, and died unmarried in 1741; Deborah, born 15 July 1704, married to Robert Doyne, of Wells, Esq. Member of Parliament for the town of Wexford; Elizabeth, (in June 1720, to Thomas Hughes, of Archerstown, in Tipperary, by whom she had Francis-Annesley Hughes, sworn a Barrister at Law, 9 February 1754 and deceased); and Hannah, the youngest, born 5 October 1706, married 3 December 1703, to Thomas Springe, Esq. Counsellor at Lew, and by him she had one son Thomas, now deceased.

Maurice Annesley, of Little-Rath, in county of Kildare, Esq. in recompence of the many great losses he had suffered by the war, and that a very valuable wood of his in the county of Monaghan, consisting of 30,000 oak trees, which being the only wood in that country, and contiguous to the camp at Dundalk, was cut down and destroyed by K. William's

---

[1] Rot. de de A°. 12°. Car. II. 1ª. p. f.   [2] See Earl of Glandore.
[3] Mrs. Paul's Will.

ANNESLEY, Viscount VALENTIA.

liam; 3 army, for their use in the camp; and also as a reward for his services, eminent affection and forwardness in the King's affairs, had a warrant, dated at Kensington, 26 April 1697, to receive such debts, judgments, mortgages and incumbrances upon such forfeited lands as he should discover, to the amount of 2000l. a year, over and above the fourth part, due to him as a discoverer. He married Sarah, second daughter of Richard, the fourth Lord Blayney, and dying in London 17 February 1718, had issue by her, who died 5 July 1705, two sons Coningsby, and William, who died young[1], and four daughters, viz. Elizabeth, (married to Sir Arthur Gore, of Newtown, Bart. ancestor to Sir Arthur-Saunders, Earl of Arran); Charity[2] (first to Francis Palmer, of Palmerstown, in the county of Mayo, Esq. and secondly, to Henry Blake, of Lehinch, in the same county, Esq. by whom she had Annesley, born in December 1724, who died young; Henry; and Charity-Julia, married 17 March 1743, to Thomas Newburgh of Ballyhayes in Cavan, Esq. died 20 November 1745, and is buried at St. Anne's, Dublin, where a neat monument is erected to her memory by her mother); Sarah, died unmarried; and Dorothea, married to Francis Knox, Esq. and had issue Thomas, James, Francis, and Sarah, who married Francis Blake, Counsellor at Law, and had issue Mary-Anne, Dorothy and Elinor[3]. John Annesley, of Ballysax, Esq. married Eleanor, daughter of —— Bishop of Bishop-Hall, Esq. and died 13 April 1720, leaving issue by her, who died at Killala, in February 1769, aged 96, three daughters, Anne, Jane, and Elizabeth[4], and four sons, viz. Francis, of Ballysax, Esq. born in January 1701, who married[5] Margaret, youngest daughter and coheir to Edward Eyre, of Galway, Esq. who died in November 1739, by his wife Jane, second daughter of Sir William Maynard, of Walthamstow in Essex, Bart. but died 5 March 1750, and was buried at Ballysonan, having no issue by his said Lady, (who re-married with Dominick Burke, of Galway, Esq. son of Dominick Burke, Esq. many years representative in Parliament for that town, and brother to Bingham Burke, late a Captain in his Majesty's service; she deceased

---

[1] Collections in Prerog. Office.   [2] Idem. Will; and see will of said Charity made in 1741   [3] Lodge.   [4] Idem.   [5] Idem.

ANNESLEY, Viscount VALENTIA.

deceased in 1786, leaving no issue by Mr. Burke, who died about a year before her) Rev. Richard Annesley of Kilmore, county of Galway, whose wife was the daughter of Captain Perse of Roxburrow in the county of Galway, by whom he had two sons John ; Charles, an officer in General Adlercron's regiment; and four daughters, Eleanor; Jane, married in February 1770, to James Browne, Esq.; Hannah; and Mary;. he died 3 June 1752, at Kilmore*); John, who died unmarried; and Rev. Maurice Annesley of Water-Park, county of Clare, who married Bridget, daughter of ———— Hawkins, of Carhurley, in same county, and had issue John ; Francis ; Elizabeth, who in February 1764, married William Carden, of Killard, in county of Tipperary, Esq. and other children.

(4)   James, died an infant[1], and was buried in 1621, in the Parish Church, where he was born, viz. in Foster-Lane, London.

(5)   Humphrey, died an infant.

(1)   Daughter, Letitia died unmarried.

(2)   Hesther, married to Sir Richard Lort of Stackpole-Court in the county of Pembroke, Knt.

(3)   Beatrix, first to Sir John Lloyd, Knt. secondly, to Sir Thomas Smyth of Hill-Hall, in Essex, Bart. to whom she was second wife[2], and died 26 March 1688, without issue by him, who died the same year, æt. 67 [3].

(4)   Anne, born in 1620, was first married to Colonel George Cooke, of Pebmarsh, in Essex, to whom she was second wife, and had an only child Anne, who died unmarried ; and secondly, to Sir John Baker, Remembrancer of the Exchequer in England.

(5)   Jane, to ———— Fish, Esq. and died 5 September 1630[4].

(6)   Christian, baptized 15 December 1622, died young.

(7)   Dorothy, born in 1623, and was buried by her mother 6 September 1630.

(8)   Margaret, baptized 5 January 1623-4, died young.

His

---

* All mentioned in his will, dated 2 June 1752, and proved 21 October in the Court of Prerogative, whereby he directed his body to be buried in the vault of his wife's family in the parish church of Tynagh, if he died in the county of Galway, or within ten miles of it. (Prerogative Office.)

[1] Lodge.   [2] Id.   [3] Idem.   [4] Ulster.

ANNESLEY, Viscount VALENTIA.

His Lordship's second wife was Jane, sister to Philip, the first Earl of Chesterfield, widow of Sir Peter Courtene, of Aldington, in Worcestershire, Bart. and by her, who died 12 March 1683, and was buried 15, in St. Mary's Church, Nottingham, he had seven sons and two daughters, viz. Francis, ancestor to Lord Viscount Glerawley; Peter, born in London 3 October 1631, and was buried in Eversley-Church, Hantshire; George (born at Chester, 28 October 1632, drowned in the Thames unmarried, as he was stepping into a Pacquet-boat with letters from his brother Arthur, for K. Charles II.); William, born at Greenwich, 25 April 1636, was buried at Thorganby a child; Peter, born at Woodgate-House, in Hatfield, Hertfordshire, 11 February 1638; and Robert, born 23 November 1643, both died childless; Samuel (born in London, 1 October 1645, married Mary, eldest daughter of the aforementioned Colonel George Cooke, by his first wife, and dying without issue, they were both buried in St. Andrew's church, Dublin, 26 July 1720); Dorothy, born 28 April 1631, died an infant; and Catharine, born 5 January 1634 [1], married in July 1662, to Sir Randal Beresford, Bart. and was buried at St. Michan's, 4 April 1701.

Sir Arthur, the second Viscount Valentia, born in Fishamble-street, Dublin, 10 July 1614, and baptised the 20 in St. John's church, was educated in Magdalen College, Oxford, where having laid a sure foundation of literature, he removed in 1634 to Lincoln's-Inn, to advance his knowledge in the laws and constitution of his country; after which he made the tour of Europe, and came for a time into Ireland.—In the Parliament of 1640, he was returned Knight for the county of Radnor, but his election being questioned, and Charles Price, Esq. voted the legally chosen member, he soon left that Parliament, and followed the King to Oxford, where he sat in That, called by his Majesty in 1643: But returning again to Westminster, and being a man of very considerable parts, and general reputation, he was appointed in May 1645, the first of the three Commissioners to manage the affairs of Ireland; where arriving in October, they brought provision, ammunition, and 20,000l. to be employed against the Irish; whose designs in the provinces of Ulster and Conaught, were thereby frustrated, and many great advantages accrued to the Protestant

Sir Arthur, 2 Viscount.

---

[1] St. Werburgh's Registry.

testant interest: And in 1647 (complying entirely with the Parliament) he was nominated the first of their five Commissioners, to receive the garrisons and ensigns of Government from the Marquefs of Ormond, L. L.—But the Chief Governors of the State running into wild measures, and pursuing confused inconsistent schemes, he foresaw the distractions that must ensue, and wished for nothing more than the restoration of the King, and the re-establishment of the laws and religion of his country: To which end, he was empowered with Sir John Grenvil, Sir Thomas Peyton, Mr. Mordaunt, and Mr. Legge, by a blank commission, dated at Brussels 7 March 1658, to treat with any of his Majesty's subjects in England or Wales, that were, or had been in arms aginst him or his father (except such as were concerned in the murder of his father) and to assure them, if they would join heartily in his restoration, that they should have not only free pardon, but such recompence as their service should merit.—In this trust they proceeded with such caution and activity, that a day in July 1659, was fixed for a general rising, many of the nobility and gentry being engaged by them in the King's service: But though the attempt proved unsuccessful, yet he greatly contributed afterwards to the accomplishment of that work; for, being one of the secluded members, he was restored to his seat 21 February; and being chosen President of the Council of State, appointed to govern in the interval of Parliament, from 16 March to 25 April 1660, he was, as Lord Clarendon writes, very well contented, that the King should receive particular information of his devotion and resolution to do him service, which he manifested in many particulars of importance, had the courage to receive a letter from his Majesty, and returned a dutiful answer to it.

For which faithful services he was sworn of the Privy Council, and 4 June appointed, with Sir William Morris, and others, to tender the oaths of supremacy and allegiance to the House of Commons, which had met 25 April, and was still sitting: Also, 21 August 1660 he was constituted Vice-Treasurer and Receiver-General of Ireland, with the fee of 65l. 13s. 4d. and all other fees, &c. thereunto belonging, together with the office of Treasurer at War [1], and 6 February ensuing, Captain of a troop of horse;

---

[1] Rot. pat. Car. II. A°. 12°. Car. II^{di}. 2°. p. f.

25 of which month the King wrote to the L. J. that he was so employed by him in his councils and services in England, relating unto both kingdoms, that he could not spare him from thence, to follow his own occasions; and more especially his several concernments upon the intended settlement of all the interests of his subjects of Ireland, pursuant to his declaration concerning the same: And whereas for his eminent and many faithful services, performed before and since his restoration, the King was willing to take all opportunities, whereby he might extend his royal bounty and favour to him and his posterity, fully resolving to shew him, in his respective settlement, as much benefit and advantage, as might be consistent with his said declaration, he was pleased to require the L. J. to take effectual and especial care, that all the forfeited lands within the barony of Newcastle in the county of Dublin, and in the islands of Valentia, Bearhaven, &c. should be set out to him for satisfaction of his reprises for such lands, as by the restoration of any persons to their former estates by the aforesaid declaration, should be taken from him.—This letter was followed by another, 16 March, wherein his Majesty shews the sense he had of his services; and being sensible that he had suffered much during the usurpation, and was particularly employed and entrusted by him in the late great and happy work of his restoration, wherein he was very successfully instrumental, and served him with singular prudence and faithfulness, and much to his advantage, without seeking his own, and did still continue indefatigably to render him faithful and acceptable services, for which he had not hitherto received those real marks of his grace and favour, which his Majesty intended, and was resolved to confer upon him, for the honour and advantage of him and his posterity, ordered him a grant of the forfeited estates of L. General Edmund Ludlow, and Colonel John Jones, with all arrears of rent, and the advantage of all the improvements upon the premisses. And by letters patent, dated 20 April 1661, advanced him to the Peerage of England, by the titles of Baron Annesley of Newport-Pagnel and Earl of Anglesey, for the aforesaid reasons, and the services of his father[1].

9 March 1660, he was appointed one of the Commissioners for executing the King's declaration for the settlement

[1] Lodge Collect.

ANNESLEY, Viscount VALENTIA.

ment of Ireland, and sat in the House of Peers by proxy 25 June 1661 [1]. Much injustice and fraud having been used in the procuring of decrees and judgments, given for forfeited lands in the province of Conaught and county of Clare, during the usurpation, his Lordship was empowered 24 October 1662, with others, to enquire and certify how the same had been obtained; being also commissioned 1 December following to enquire into the full yearly value of the lands, that were, or should be set out for the respective adventurers, soldiers, purchasers of transplanted persons, and grantees, as the same were worth in the year 1659.—On 8 March 1665, a pension of 600l. a year was settled on him for life, to commence from the time that any additional (or increase of) pensions had been granted by the King, since his restoration, to any other of his crown-officers in Ireland; and 24 March 1666 he and the Earl of Orrery, and the survivor of them, their heirs, and assignes, by privy-seal dated at Whitehall, received a grant of crown-lands, to the amount of 500l. a year, according to the several rents, ratable for each parcel then remaining on record [2], and 10 October 1667, they had a grant of 5000l. out of forfeited goods *.

In July 1667, he exchanged his office of Vice-Treasurer with Sir George Carteret, for that of Treasurer of the Navy; and 24 Feb. 1670, was appointed by the King in Council, with the Duke of Buckingham, the Lord Holles, Ashley Cooper, and Mr. Secretary Trevor, or any three of them [3] a committee, to revise and take an abstract of all the papers and writings relative to the affairs of Ireland and the settlement

---

* In addition to these favours, he had several grants of lands under the acts of settlement; and 4 Jan. 1666 power to hold a Wednesday market, and three fairs on 29 May, July and Oct. at Camolin. Also 12 July 1671 a reduction was made of the quit-rents on his lands in the Barony of Beare and Bantry to a halfpeony the acre, which had been so reduced by the Commissioners for executing the acts of settlement 12 January 1668, but their commission expiring before they had signed their order for the same; his Majesty's directions were necessary to confirm the decree. And 15 March 1679, he had the lands of Garteen and others in the co. of Cork, erected into the manor of Bantry, and those of Knockmore, &c. into the manor of Altham; with liberty to separate 1000 acres in each for demesne lands, 3000 acres in each for a park, with free warren; and a Wednesday and Saturday market, and three fairs on 19 May, 10 Aug. and 4 Oct. at Ballygobban, otherwise Oldtown, in the former manor. (Lodge.)

[1] Lords Jour. I. 253. [2] Lodge. [3] Idem.

ment thereof, and make a report to his Majesty, which they did at large 12 June 1671; whereupon a new commission was issued 1 August to them, with the addition of Prince Rupert, the Duke of Lauderdale, and Sir Thomas Chichley [1], to inspect the settlement of the kingdom, and all proceedings thereupon; which was followed by a third 17 Jan. 1672, whereunto the Duke of Ormond was added [2], empowering them to inspect the acts of settlement, with their execution and the disposition of forfeited lands, the state of the revenue, &c.

On 22 April 1673, he was appointed on account of his singular prudence and fidelity, to that great office of Lord Privy-Seal; and 26 October 1675, was by commission, appointed one of the Trustees for the (1649) Officers, according to the intents and purposes of his Majesty's gracious declaration, as he had been before 22 May 1662 [3]; 20 April 1679, the King dissolving his Privy Council and constituting a new one, he was made choice of to be one of his Counsellors: But in the year 1682, some apprehensions arising of the King's death and a Popish successor, the Duke of York then professing himself a Papist, his Lordship drew up a paper, entitled "The Account of Arthur, Earl of Anglesey, Lord Privy Seal, to your most Excellent Majesty, of the true State of your Majesty's Government and Kingdoms, April 27, 1682;" and having the year before published another pamphlet, containing "Animadversions upon the Earl of Castlehaven's Memoirs of his Conduct in the Wars of Ireland;" he gave umbrage to the Court, was deprived of that high office, and dismissed from the Council Board 9 August 1682. From which time he lived retired, chiefly at Blechingdon in Oxfordshire, to his death, which happened by a quinsy on Easter-Tuesday, 6 April 1686, at his house in Drury-lane, Westminster*. He married Elizabeth, daughter and coheir to Sir James Altham, of Oxeye, in Hertfordshire, one of the Barons of the Exchequer, in the reign of James I. She lies buried in the North

---

* His Lordship, like other great men, hath fallen under variety of characters; but his just and real one seems to be given by the editors of the Biographia Britannica, Vol. I. p. 192. 2d Edit. and an account of his writings may be found in Mr. Harris's History of the Writers of Ireland, page 102.

[1] Lodge.   [2] Idem.   [3] Idem.

North Chancel of Walton-Church in Surrey, under a blue marble with this inscription:

> Here lyeth Elizabeth,
> Countefs of Anglefey,
> Who died April
> the 12th, 1662.

By her his Lordfhip had iffue feven fons and fix daughters, viz.

(1) James, Lord Annefley, his fucceffor.
(2) Altham, created Lord Altham, of whom hereafter.
(3) Richard, anceftor to the prefent Vifcount Valentia.
(4) Arthur, and
(5) Arthur, both died infants.
(6) Arthur, who died unmarried in January 1703.
(7) Charles, who married Margaret, fifter of Edward Eyre of Galway, Efq.*, and dying in 1702, left an only fon Charles Annefley, Efq fome time Captain of the Battle-Axe Guard, who 9 November 1732 married Mary, widow of Sir Richard Levinge, Bart. and died 23 February 1746, without iffue, by her, who died 2 December 1756 [1].

(1) Daughter Lady Dorothy was married to Richard, Earl of Tyrone.
(2) Lady Elizabeth, firft wife to Alexander, the third Earl of Antrim, but died without iffue before he enjoyed that title.
(3) Lady Frances, firft wife to Sir John Thompfon, Bart. created Lord Haverfham, died in March 1704, and was buried at Haverfham.
(4) Lady Philippa, firft to Charles, Lord Mohun, by whom fhe had Charles, Lord Mohun, killed in a duel by the Duke of Hamilton; and fecondly to William Coward, of county of Somerfet [2], Efq. Serjeant at Law, and died 10 February 1714.

Lady

---

* She was thrice married after his deceafe; firft, before 1709, to Colonel Ambrofe Edgworth, who died in December 1710; fecondly to Andrew Wilfon of Piersfield in Weftmeath, Efq. who died in 1725, and thirdly, 14 May 1726 to John Meares of Meares-Court in the fame county, Efq. where fhe died in Sept. 1742.

[1] Lodge Colleƈt.   [2] Idem.

ANNESLEY, Viscount VALENTIA.

Lady Anne, to Sir Francis Wyngate, of Fellbrigge-Hall, (5) in Norfolk, Knt. who left her a widow, with Arthur, his succeſſor.

Bridget, died young. (6)

Sir James, the third Viſcount Valentia, in his father's Sir James, life-time ſerved in Parliament for the city of Wincheſter; 3 and 17 November 1688, joined with ſeveral Lords and Bi- Viſcount. ſhops in a petition to K. James II. to redreſs the grievances of the nation, and the danger his own perſon was expoſed to, by calling a free Parliament *.—In September 1669, he married ¹ the Lady Elizabeth Manners, fourth daughter of John, the eighth Earl of Rutland, and dying 1 April 1690², had iſſue by her, who died in February 1698, three ſons, James, John, and Arthur, who ſucceſſively enjoyed the honours; and two daughters, Frances, who died an infant; and Elizabeth, married to Robert Gayer, of Stoke-Poges, in Bucks, Eſq. (ſon and heir to Sir Robert Gayer, Knight of the Bath, who died 14 June 1702³), and ſhe died in December 1725, leaving a moſt accompliſhed character.

Sir James, the fourth Viſcount, was left a minor under the Sir James, guardianſhip of James Selby, of the Inner-Temple, Eſq.⁴ 4 but after he came of age, took his ſeat in the Parliament of Viſcount. Ireland 27 Auguſt⁵ 1695, and 8 October following, was made C. Rot. of the county of Wexford⁶. 28 October 1699, he married the Lady Catherine Darnley, natural daughter of K. James II. (by Catherine, only daughter of Sir Charles Sedley, of Ailesford, in Kent, Bart. who 20 January 1685, was created Baroneſs of Darlington, and Counteſs of Dorcheſter for life) and by her, who was born in 1683, and from whom he was ſeparated 12 June 1701 by the unanimous conſent of the King and Parliament, and who 1 March 1705, was married to John Sheffield, Duke of Buckingham, died at her houſe, St. James's Park, 13 March 1742, and was buried 6 April in Weſtminſter Abbey, he had an only daughter Catharine, born 7 January 1700, and

---

* His eſtate of 4000l. a year and his mother's jointure of 1120l. in Ireland, and 160l. in England, were ſequeſtered in that King's Parliament. (Harris, King, &c.)

¹ Articles dated 17 and 18 with 9000l. fortune. ² Decree in Chancery, 18 Dec. 1696, No. 36. ³ Lodge. ⁴ Idem. ⁵ Lords Jour. I. 479. ⁶ Rot. 7°, Gul. III. 4ª. p. f.

and first married in September 1718, to William, son and heir of Constantine Phipps, Lord Chancellor of Ireland, ancestor to Lord Mulgrave. His Lordship deceasing 21 January 1701[1], was buried at Farnborough, in the county of Southampton, and was succeeded by his brother

Sir John, 5 Viscount. Sir John, the fifth Viscount, a Nobleman of great parts and strict honour, who was sworn of the Privy Council 12 July 1710, and constituted 3 August ensuing, Vice-Treasurer, Receiver-General, and Paymaster of the forces in Ireland. 21 May 1706, he married the Lady Henrietta Stanley, eldest daughter and coheir to William-Richard-George, Earl of Derby, and by her, (who remarried 24 July 1714, with John, Earl of Ashburnham, and died 26 June 1718, in the 31 year of her age) had one daughter Elizabeth, born in May 1710, who died an infant; and his Lordship dying of a fever 18 September that year, was buried at Farnborough, and was succeeded by his brother

Sir Arthur, 6 Viscount. Sir Arthur, the sixth Viscount, who was a gentleman of the Privy Chamber to K. William and Q. Anne; and after his succession to the honours, was appointed (11 October) joint Vice-Treasurer of Ireland, and 19, sworn of the Privy Council in England. In 1711, he was one of the Commissioners for building the 50 new churches; and 9 July that year sworn of the Privy Council in Ireland, taking his seat the same day in the House of Peers[2].—On the death of the Queen, he was one of the L. J. of England, to administer affairs, until K. George I. arrived from Hanover; who 1 October 1714, called him into his Privy Council of both kingdoms, and 15 January following again made him joint Vice-Treasurer and Treasurer at War.—On the death of the Duke of Manchester, he was elected in full senate, 16 February 1721, High Steward of the University of Cambridge, where he had his education, and which he had represented in three several Parliaments. On 29 November 1727, he was made L. L. and Governor of the county of Wexford, and sworn a Privy Counsellor to K. George II. on his accession to the crown. He married Mary, third daughter of Sir John Thompson, Lord Haversham, by the Lady Frances Annesley, daughter of Arthur, the first Earl of Anglesey, but by her, who died at Woodstock, in January 1718, and was buried at Farnborough, he had no issue, and deceasing 1 April 1737, was buried

---

[1] Rolls Office, Will, and Lodge Collect.   [2] Lord. Jour. II. 362.

buried with her, being succeeded in his honours by Richard Lord Altham, with which branch of the family we shall now proceed.

Altham, the second son of Arthur, the first Earl of Anglesey, was educated in Magdalen College, Oxford, where 1 February 1670, he took his degree of A. M. and 4 August 1677, addressed James, Duke of Ormond, with a learned speech at his visitation of the said College[1]. By patent dated at Westminster 14 February * 1680, he was created Baron Altham of Altham, with limitation of the honour to the issue male of his younger brethren; but having been attainted by K. James's Parliament, as resident in England, and his estate of 1400l. a year, being sequestered[2], he did not take his seat in the House of Peers, until 2 August 1695 [3]. He married to his first wife in August [4] 1678, Alicia, elder daughter and at length sole heir to Charles Leigh, of Leighton-Buzzard in county of Bedford, Esq. second surviving son of Thomas, the first Lord Leigh; but by her, who died 4 June 1682, æt. 24. having no issue, he married in July [5] 1697 Ursilla, only daughter of Sir Robert Markham, of Sedgebrooke, in Lincolnshire, Ba t. and sister to Sir George, who died unmarried 9 June 1736, and his Lordship deceasing at Bath, in April 1699, had issue by her, (who remarried in 1701 with Samuel Ogle, Esq. Member of Parliament for Berwick, and 2 September 1699, appointed a Commissioner of the Revenue in Ireland †,) an only son

Altham, Lord Altham.

VOL. IV.   K   James-

* The Preamble. Sciatis quod nos Animo recolentes bona et fidel a Servitia, quæ prædilectus et perquam fideli Consanguineu et Consiliarius noster Arthurus, Comes Angliæ, Custos privati Sigilli nostri, nobis summa cum Assiduitate et Integritate diu præstitit et adhuc non desistit; ac ut Filii prædicti Comitis ad eju Exemplum pro sequi magis incitari poterint; accnon in memoria antiquæ illius et fideli Familiæ Althamorum, de Gratia nostra speciali, ac ex certa Scientia & mero motu nostris, dilectum et fidelem nost um Altham Annesley Armigerum, filium natu secundum prædicti Comitis Baronem Altham de Altham in Com tatu nostro Corcag æ in regno nostro Hiberniæ tenore præ entium erigimus, præficimus, et creamus, &c. (Rot. pat. de A°. 33°. Car. II. 1ª. p. f.)

† Mr Ogle died 10 March 1718, having issue three sons and one daughter, viz. George; Robert, baptized 19 May 1706, was a Captain in General Browne's regiment of horse; Thomas, baptized 4 February 1713; and Meliora, married to John, fourth son of Christopher Brought n, of Longdon, in county of Stafford, Esq—George, the eldest son, baptised 18 May 1704, married

[1] Lodge Collect.   [2] Idem.   [3] Lords Jour. I. 479.   [4] Articles dated 29 August.   [5] Articles dated 27 and 28 July.

James-George, the second Lord Altham, who dying in his infancy, the title fell to his uncle Richard, son of Arthur, first Earl of Anglesey.

Which Richard, third Lord Altham, was educated in the same College with his brother, commencing A. M. at the same time; taking Holy Orders, he was Prebendary of Westminster; in 1680, Dean of Exeter[1], and 5 July 1689, created D. D. He married Dorothea, daughter of ———— Davey, of Ruxford, in the county of Devon, and dying 19 November 1701[2], was buried 25 in Westminster-Abbey, leaving issue by her (who 29 December 1720, was married to William Vesey, Esq. and 16 May 1725, buried at St. Peter's, Dublin) two sons and two daughters; Arthur, Richard, Dorothea, married to Mr. John Greene of Nonsuch-Park in Surrey; and Elizabeth; first to that gentleman's brother; secondly, 16 August 1737 to John, Lord Haversham; thirdly, in 1746, to Fitz-William White, Esq. and she died in November 1772[3].

Arthur, the fourth Lord, took his seat in Parliament 9 July 1711[4]; and 22 July 1707, married Mary, natural daughter of John Sheffield, Duke of Buckingham, and deceasing at Inchicore near Dublin 14 November 1727, was buried in Christ-Church; leaving no issue by her, who died 26 October 1729, and was buried in St. Andrew's Church, Holborn. His brother

Sir Richard, born in 1694, became the fifth Lord Altham, and succeeding his cousin Arthur, Earl of Anglesey, in his honours, was the sixth Earl of Anglesey, and seventh Viscount Valentia, by which title 4 October 1737, he sat first in Parliament[5], and was Governor of the county of Wexford. —5 January 1715, he married Anne, daughter of Captain John Prest, of Monckton, near Biddiford, in county of Devon,

married Frances, eldest daughter of Sir Thomas Twysden of East-Peckham, in Kent, Bart. he died in October 1746, leaving issue by her, who died 9 May 1749, an only son George, of Belle-Vue, in county of Wexford, Esq. who was born in 1739, was elected to Parliament for the same county 29 December 1769; appointed a Member of the Privy Council and Public Register of deeds in Ireland in 1784; he married Elizabeth, sister to Lorenzo Moore, Esq. late Colonel of the Battle-Axe-Guards, and M. of P. for the Borough of Dungannon, but by his said Lady (to whom a pension of 800l. a year was granted 16 August 1785) he has no issue. (Lodge Collect. and Pension List.)

[1] Izacke's Exeter, p. 152. [2] Collect. Lodge. [3] Bill in Chancery. [4] Lords Jour. II. 362. [5] Id. III. 363.

ANNESLEY, Viscount VALENTIA.

Devon, which Lady brought him a confiderable fortune, having no iffue by her who died in England 13 Auguſt 1741, and was buried at Monkley[1]. His Lordſhip married ſecondly, 15 September ſame year, Juliana, daughter of Mr. Donovan, of county Wexford[2], and deceaſing at his ſeat of Camolin 14 February 1761[3], left iſſue by his ſaid lady (who remarried with Matthew Talbot, Eſq. and died at Bath 20 November 1776[4]) one ſon and three daughters*, viz.

Sir Arthur, who ſucceeded to the honours.   (1)

K 2   Daughter,

---

* As we find in the following Petition read in the Houſe of Lords, 8 December 1775.

A PETITION of Arthur Viſcount Valentia, Lucy Viſcounteſs Valentia, his wife; George, Juliana-Lucy, Thomas-Littleton, and Charles-Henry Anneſley, Minors, by the ſaid Arthur Viſcount Valentia their father; alſo, of Robert Phaire, Eſq. and Lady Richarda his wife; John Toole, Eſq. and Lady Catharine his wife; Richard Anneſley, E'q.; Juliana Counteſs Dowager of Angleſey; and Conſtantine Lord Mulgrave; ſetting forth, that on the death of Arthur, fifth Earl of Angleſey, his titles of honour did deſcend to Richard then Lord Baron Altham, afterwards Earl of Angleſey, who then was the grandſon and heir-male of Arthur firſt Earl of Angleſey; and ſeveral controverſies did ariſe between the ſaid Richard Earl of Angleſey, and Charles Anneſley, Eſq. who was alſo the grandſon of the ſaid Arthur, firſt Earl of Angleſey, concerning their reſpective titles and claims to the family eſtate, which at length were compromiſed; and by Articles bearing date 16 June, 1737, it was agreed that the ſaid Charles Anneſley ſhould convey all his right to the family eſtate in Great Britain and Wales, and Camolin-Park, and the Woods thereon in co. Wexford, to the ſaid Richard Earl of Angleſey and his heirs; and that lands of the yearly value of 200l. ſhould be ſet out and granted to the ſaid Charles Anneſley and his heirs; that the woods ſhould be equally divided between them; and that two-thirdparts of the remainder of the ſaid eſtate in Ireland, ſhould be ſettled upon theſaid Richard Earl of Angleſey for life, remainder to his firſt and other ſons in tail-male, remainder to the ſaid Charles Anneſley for life, remainder to his firſt and other ſons in tail-male, remainder to the ſaid Richard Earl of Angleſey, and his heirs for ever: And that the remaining third part of the ſaid eſtate in Ireland ſhould be ſettled upon the ſaid Charles Anneſley for life, remainder to his firſt and other ſons in tail-male, remainder to the ſaid Richard Earl of Angleſey for life, remainder to his firſt and other ſons in tail-male, remainder to the ſaid Charles Anneſley and his heirs for ever, with power to the ſaid Richard Earl of Angleſey and Charles Anneſley, reſpectively, to make leaſes, ſettle jointures, and to charge portions for younger children. And it was agreed, that the ſhares of the ſaid Richard Earl of Angleſey, and Charles Anneſley, ſhould ſtand charged proportionably with the jointure of the Ducheſs of Buckingham (who was the widow of James third Earl of Angleſey) alſo with the portion of Lady Catherine, daughter of the ſaid James Earl of Angleſey, and all other incumbrances affecting the ſaid eſtate; and the ſaid agreement was eſtabliſhed by a decree in Chancery about 28 February 1740; and the ſaid decree was, on an appeal, affirmed by the Houſe of Lords of Great Britain, about 10 March, 1741; and about Trinity Term, 17 and 18 K. George

---

[1] Ledge. [2] Inform. Sir F. Flood and Collect. [3] Lords Journals IV. 868—9. [4] Collect. and Sir F. Flood.

(1) Daughter, Lady Richarda, married in July 1761, to Robert Phaire, of Temple-Shannon, in county of Wexford, Esq.

Lady

18 K. George II. several common recoveries were suffered of said estate by the said Richard Earl of Anglesey and Charles Annesley.

That the said Charles Annesley died without issue, about the month of February, 1746; and all his right to the Anglesey estate afterwards became vested in Richard Levinge, of the city of Dublin, Esq. only child and personal representative of Mary Levinge, deceased, who was widow, devisee and sole executrix to the said Charles Annesley: And by deeds of lease and release, bearing date 30 and 31 May, in the year 1758; the said Richard Levinge did grant and convey all his right to the Anglesey estate (such parts thereof as had been granted by the said Richard Earl of Anglesey, to the said Mary Levinge and Richard Levinge respectively, only excepted) unto or in trust for the said Richard Earl of Anglesey, his heirs, executors, administrators and assigns: And the said Richard Earl of Anglesey did agree to indemnify that part of the Anglesey estate, which had been by him granted to the said Mary and Richard Levinge, of, from, and against all demands of the representatives of the said Duchess of Buckingham, and Lady Catherine, her daughter, and all other incumbrances.

That by a decree made on or about 22 November, 1738, in the said Court of Chancery, the sum of 20,413l. 14s. 1d. was decreed to remain due to the Representatives of the said Duchess of Buckingham, and to be and remain a charge on the Anglesey estate, and to be paid with interest.

That the said Richard Earl of Anglesey did duly make and publish his last will, bearing date 7 April 1759, and did thereby bequeath all his personal estate, exempt from the payment of his debts, to the petitioner Juliana Countess Dowager of Anglesey; and did devise all his real estate charged and chargeable with the payment of his debts, daughters portions and legacies, to certain trustees and their heirs, in trust to pay one annuity of 1000l. sterling, to the petitioner Juliana, Countess Dowager of Anglesey for life, and chargeable as aforesaid, to the petitioner Arthur Viscount Valentia for life, remainder to his first and other sons in tail-male, remainder to the second and other sons of the said Richard Earl of Anglesey, in tail-male, remainder to his daughters by the petitioner Juliana, Countess Dowager of Anglesey in tail-general, remainder to the petitioner Richard Annesley, and the heirs male of his body, remainder to the right heirs of the said Richard Earl of Anglesey; and power was thereby given to the petitioner Arthur Viscount Valentia, to charge the said estate with a jointure not exceeding 2000l. per ann. and portions for younger children, not exceeding 20,000l. sterl. And the said Testator did thereby direct, that the woods upon the said estate (Camolin-Park excepted) should be sold, and the money arising by the sale thereof, and also the rents of the said estate during the minority of the Petitioner, Arthur, Viscount Valentia, and after satisfying the annual outgoings, should be applied in case and exoneration of the said estate; and also for any service to be done or performed by any person or persons in the execution of his will; and the said Testator did give and devise 4000l. to the Petitioner Lady Richarda Phaire; 3500l. to his daughter Lady Juliana; and 3500l. to the Petitioner Lady Catherine Toole, for their respective portions; 1000l. sterl. to the Petitioner Arthur Annesley; and some other small legacies, which since his death have been paid; charging the same upon his real estate; and appointed the Petitioner Juliana Countess Dowager of Anglesey sole Executrix of his will.

That

Lady Juliana, to Sir Frederick Flood, of Newtown-Ormond, county of Kilkenny, created a Baronet of Ireland, (1)

That the said Richard Earl of Anglesey died 14 February, 1761, leaving the Petitioner Arthur Viscount Valentia, his only son and heir, and the Petitioners Lady Richarda Phaire, Lady Catharine Toole, and the said Lady Juliana his only daughters, by the Petitioner Juliana Countess Dowager of Anglesey; and the said Lady Juliana inter married with Frederick Flood, Esq. and is since dead, without issue.

That the said decree obtained by the Representatives of the Duchess of Buckingham, against the said Richard Earl of Anglesey, was revived and a suit instituted against him by the Representatives of the said Lady Catharine, the daughter of the said James the third Earl of Anglesey, was also revived; and by a final decree, made by the said Court of Chancery on 10 December 1761, the sum of 21,204l. 17s. 8d. was decreed to the Representatives of the said Duchess of Buckingham, and by another final decree made by the same Court on same day the sum of 37,300l. 17s. 8d. was decreed to the Representatives of the said Lady Catharine, which sums amount together to 58,505l. 3s. 9d. and remain a charge upon the Anglesey estate: And the Petitioner Constantine Lord Mulgrave is now intitled to the same, and is also the heir-general of the first five successive Earls of Anglesey.

That by Articles, bearing date 9 May 1767, made in contemplation of a marriage since had between the Petitioners Lord and Lady Valentia; Arthur Viscount Valentia did charge the said estate with a jointure of 2000l. per ann. for Lucy Viscountess Valentia, and with 20,000l. for portions for younger children; and the Petitioners Lord and Lady Valentia have issue George, Juliana-Lucy, Thomas Littleton, and Charles-Henry Annesley, and no other issue.

That the woods upon the said estate have been sold, and the money arising by the sale thereof and the rents which accrued out of the said estate, during the minority of the Petitioner Arthur Viscount Valentia, have been applied and exhausted in the payment of annuities, interest of charges affecting the said estate, and part of the legacies bequeathed by the said Richard Earl of Anglesey, and the costs and expences of various contests concerning the title of the said Richard Earl of Anglesey: the said charge of 58,505l. 3s. 9d. the portions of the daughters of the said Richard Earl of Anglesey, amounting to 11,000l. and the costs of the said suits still remain unpaid, and are chargeable upon his real estate, and cannot be paid, otherwise than by a sale of a competent part thereof for that purpose; and after the sale of a part of the said estate, to answer the purpose aforesaid, the remainder will be abundantly more than sufficient to answer the jointures of the Petitioners Juliana Countess Dowager of Anglesey and Lucy Viscountess Valentia, the charge of 20,000l. for the younger children of the Petitioners Lord and Lady Valentia, and all other outgoings.

That a doubt hath been conceived, whether by virtue of the said articles of 16 June 1737, the said Richard Earl of Anglesey, was not in equity, tenant for his life only, and disabled to induce any charge upon the said estate for the payment of his debts, or the portions of his daughters, but the Petitioner Arthur Viscount Valentia is desirous, that all the debts of the said Richard Earl of Anglesey, the portions of his daughters, and all other incumbrances, chargeable upon the said estate, shall be paid by mortgage or sale of a part thereof; and that the remainder of the said estate, subject to the jointures of the Petitioners Juliana Countess Dowager of Anglesey, and Lucy Viscountess Valentia; and the portions of the younger children of Lord and Lady Valentia,

land, 3 June 1780; one of his Majesty's Council at Law, and M. P. for the borough of Ardfert, she deceased without issue before the year 1775; and

(3) Lady Catharine, to John Toole, Esq. by whom she hath issue [1].

Sir Arthur, 8 Viscount. Sir Arthur, the eighth and present Viscount Valentia, was born 7 August 1744 [2]; on the death of his father, he succeeded to the honours, and 5 December 1765, he took his seat in Parliament, as he did again 7 November 1771 [3]. His Lordship is a Governor of the county of Wexford, and a Member of his Majesty's most honourable Privy Council.— 10 May 1767, he married Lucy, only daughter of George, the celebrated Lord Lyttleton, and by her Ladyship, who died 20 May 1783, had issue two daughters, Juliana-Lucy; —; and three sons, viz.

(1) George, born at Airly, in county of Worcester, in November 1769.
(2) Thomas-Lyttleton.
(3) Charles-Henry [4].

His Lordship married to his second wife (in December 1783) Sarah [5], second daughter of the Right Hon. Sir Henry Cavendish, Member of the Privy Council in Ireland, (son of Sir Henry Cavendish, of Doveridge, in county of Derby, created a Baronet of England, 3 May 1755 [6],) and hath issue.

TITLES.] Sir Arthur Annesley, Viscount of Valentia, Baron Mountnorris of Mountnorris, Baron Altham, of Altham, and (now) premier Baronet of Ireland.

CREATIONS.] Baronet, 7 August 1620, 18 Jac. I. V. of Valentia, in the county of Kerry 11 March 1621, 19 Jac. I. B. Mountnorris of Mountnorris, in the county of Armagh 8 February 1628, 4 Car. I. and B. Altham, of Altham,

---

lentia, shall enure to the same uses as are appointed, concerning the said estate, by the said last will and testament of the said Richard Earl of Anglesey, which cannot be so effectually done as by the aid of Parliament

And praying their Lordships to give leave, that Heads of a Bill may be introduced for vesting the estate in Ireland, whereof the said Richard Earl of Anglesey died seized, in Trustees, for the purposes aforesaid; which being presented to the House and read,

It was thereupon ordered by the Lords Spiritual and Temporal, in Parliament assembled, that leave be given to bring in Heads of a Bill, according to the prayer of the said Petition. (Lords Jour. IV. 808, 809, 810.)

[1] Vide Petition. [2] Lodge. [3] Lords Jour. IV. 587. [4] Petition. [5] Sir F. Flood. [6] Beatson.

DILLON, Viscount DILLON.

tham, in the county of Cork, 14 February 1680, 33 Car. II.

ARMS.] Pally of Six, Pearl and Saphire, over all a Bend, Ruby.

CREST.] On a Wreath, a Moor's Head in Profile, couped, proper, wreathed about the Temples, Pearl and Saphire.

SUPPORTERS.] The dexter a Roman Knight; the Sinister a Moorish Prince. Both habited and furnished proper.

MOTTO.] VIRTUTIS AMORE.

SEAT.] Camolin-Park, in county of Wexford, 51 miles from Dublin.

DILLON Viscount DILLON[1].

THIS noble family is said to derive its origin from Lochan, or Logan, son to the Monarch O'Neile, which Lochan, in the joint government of Hugh Slane and Colman Riembriech, about the year 595, or 598, happening in some contest to kill the latter, was thereupon called Dilune or Delion, which signifies brave or valiant; but Colman being his father's nephew, Lochan was obliged to fly, to avoid his displeasure; and at that time a war subsisting between the King of France, and the Duke of Aquitaine, he put himself into the Duke's service, and by his conduct and bravery, contributed greatly to support him in his sovereignty; in recompence whereof, (having lost his sons by that war) he gave him his daughter in marriage; in whose right, after his father's death, he became Prince and Sovereign

[1] Chiefly extracted from the MS. Coll. Gieut er Mr. Lodge.

reign of Aquitaine. This principality continued in his posterity, until K. Henry II. married Alienora, daughter and heir to William, Duke of Aquitaine, the fifth of that name, and the ninth in succession from Ranulph, of the House of Burgundy, (which Duke William was descended from the eldest branch) and about the year 1172, by his superior power, obtained Aquitaine. Upon which event, to destroy the popularity of the male descendants of the said Lochan Delion, and prevent any disturbance on their account, he brought Sir Henry Delion, and his brother Thomas, infants, to England, their father and friends being slain in the war he had carried on against them*.

Sir Henry, of Drumrany. The said Henry Delion, (now Dillon) in 1185, was sent into Ireland, first Gentleman and Secretary to John, Earl of Morton, after K. John, who granted to him Mac-Carron's territory, called Corknii, with part of Annaly, now the county of Longford, and a considerable share of Mac-Geoghegan's and O'Melaghlin's territories, &c. extending from the river Shannon to Cloghanenumora, east of Mullingar, to hold *per Baroniam in Capite*, by the service of 60 Knights fees. This large tract was called after its Lord, DILLON'S COUNTRY, and so continued till reduced into shire ground, by K. Henry VIII. when it was divided into the barony of Kilkenny-West, and others. He was then honoured with Knighthood, and by this tenure (attended with a kind of sovereignty) he and his heirs were entitled to have summons to Parliament, like the ancient Barons of England who held their baronies by the same tenure. He built his mansion-house, with a church in Drumrany, pretty much in the centre of his country, in the West of Meath; also a castle in Dunimony; and several abbies (as those of Athlone, Kilkenny-West, Ardnecrany, Holy-Island, Hare-Island, &c.) churches and castles were built and endowed by his descendants, Lords of the said territories. He was progenitor to all who bear the name of Dillon, a name of great note, in the counties of Meath, Westmeath, Longford, Roscomon, Mayo, and other parts of the kingdom, where, and

in

---

* The history of these events may be found in the records of Aquitaine, now in the tower of London, and in ancient MSS. in the Cotton and Lambeth libraries.

in many foreign countries, they have flourished in the highest departments of church and state.

Sir Henry was buried in an abbey of his founding, in Athlone, and left issue three sons, Sir Thomas, his heir, Sir Robert, to whom he gave the seigniory of Dunimony, whose posterity ceased in the reign of Edward IV. John, an ecclesiastic, and a daughter, married to the eldest son of Sir William Pettyt, of Irishton, styled Baron of Mullingar.

Sir Thomas Dillon, of Drumrany, the eldest son, married the daughter of Edmond Butler, created 1 September, 1315, Earl of Carrick, and left Henry, his successor; Dominick, nominated Bishop of Ossory; and James, a Canon regular. Henry, Lord of Drumrany, taking to wife Alivia, daughter of Maurice Fitz-Gerald had also three sons and two daughters; Thomas, a Priest, who built an abbey in Kilkenny-West, where he was buried; Henry, who succeeded; and Maurice, made a Knight Bannaret, who married Letitia, daughter of Sir Richard Tuite, and was killed by the rebels in the north of Ulster; Mary, married to Sir John Dalton, Lord of Dalton's Country; and Bridget, to O'Ferrall, Prince of Annaly.

Sir Henry Dillon, of Drumrany, was living there 1 Edward III. which King committed to him, by patent, the custody of the manor of Kilkenny-West, forfeited by Hugh de Lacie, to hold, with all the appurtenances, during pleasure, rendering 4l. into the Exchequer for the first year, and for every year after the full extent of the manor; which grant, the King, for divers considerations, revoked; and by patent, dated at Dublin 15 May 1343 (17 Edward III.) renewed to him for 12 years, at the rent of 4l. for the first year, and 100 shillings for every year after. Also, by commission of the same date, the King granted him the water-courses and fishings of Athlone, during pleasure, at the rent of 10l. a year; and made him Constable of that Castle, which he surrendered to William, son of Andrew Birmingham, 30 August 1346. He married Bridget, daughter of Meyler de Birmingham, Baron of Athenry, and had four sons, Robert; John, killed in battle, unmarried; William, and Gerald, both religious.

Robert, Lord of Drumrany, married Anne, second daughter of Sir Eustace le Poer, and had issue Henry, who died young; Gerald, who succeeded; John, who resided in England;

DILLON, Viscount DILLON.

England; Thomas, Bishop of Kildare; and Edmund, Abbot of St. Thomas, near Dublin.

Gerald. Gerald, Lord of Drumrany, married Amy or Emilia, a daughter of the illustrious House of Desmond, and by her had issue, four sons and two daughters, viz. Sir Maurice, his heir; Henry, Prior of St. Peter's, of Newtown, near Trim; Sir James, ancestor to the Earls of Roscomon*, which

Sir James, of Proudston. * Sir James Dillon, the third son, was bred in England, honoured with Knighthood, and acquired a large estate about Tarah, in the county of Meath; built his mansion-house of Proudston, and a castle, with a parochial church, in his manor of Skreene; and marrying Honora, daughter of Sir John Darcy,
Sir Robert. L. J. had, besides other children, Sir Robert Dillon, of Proudston and Skreene, who married the daughter of Sir James Birmingham, ancestor to William, Baron of Carbury, which title is now extinct, and had issue five sons, Sir Richard, his successor Gerald; Sir James; Walter; Henry; and two daughters, Anne, married to John, eldest son of Sir James Morris; and Elinor, to O'More, of Leix.

Family of Clonbrock. Gerald, the second son, acquired a good estate in and about Dublin, where he married Elizabeth, daughter of John Lord Barry, and had issue four sons and three daughters, Richard; Gerald; Robert; James, a Canon regular; Ellice, married to Sir Thomas Fitz-Gerald. Mary, to —— Bellew, of Robinstown, and ——, to —— Fitz-Eustace, of Ballymore. Richard, the eldest son, left Thomas Dillon, his heir, who became an eminent lawyer; was a Commissioner in 1576, in the province of Conaught; appointed 2 August, 1577, Chamberlain of the Exchequer, and Clerk of the Crown and Sessions in the counties of Meath, Westmeath, Drogheda, Louth, and Longford, was also made second Justice of the Queen's Bench, and Judge Itinerant of the province of Conaught, where he purchased a large estate, and settled at Clonbrock in the county of Galway. He married the daughter of —— Allen, of Palmerston, and left Thomas of Clonbrock, and of Curraghboy, in the county of Roscomon, who, 6 October 1603, was made Chief Justice of Conaught, and died in Dublin, 24 September 1606, having issue by Elline, sister of Sir James Shaen, Knt. two sons Thomas, killed at an assault of the castle of Curraghboy, by the Burkes and Keoghs, unmarried; and Robert, who succeeded his father, being then twenty nine years old.

He married Catharine, daughter of —— Hussey, of Mulhussey; and dying 18 December 1628 ‡, was buried in the church of Kilclowne, and had issue nine sons and four daughters, viz. Richard, his heir; Lucas; Bartholomew; James; Thomas; Gerald;

‡ Inq. post ejus mortem.

DILLON, Viscount DILLON.

which title is now extinct. John, who is presumed to be Coroner of Meath, in 1407; Daughter Catharine, married to Sir John Nugent, of Brackloon; and Anne, to the Baron Delamar, of Delamar's Country.

Sir Gerald; Edward; Bartholomew; Christopher; Jane, (married to James Dillon, of Canneftown); Mary, (to John Bellew, of Wyliyftown;) Ellice, (to James Darcy, of Cloghenaver, in the county of Galway); Catharine, a nun. Richard, of Clonbrock, the eldeft fon, was 25 years old at his father's death, and married firft a daughter of Alderman Malone, of Dublin, by whom he had Robert, his heir; and three daughters, Bridger, married to ——— Bourk, of the county of Tipperary; Margaret, a nun; and Jeane, the wife of Cornelius O'Kelly. His fecond wife was Jenet, daughter of Sir Dominick Browne; and by her he had Thomas, who died young; and Lucas Dillon, Counfellor at Law, who died in March 1678, unmarried. Robert, who in 1666, fucceeded at Clonbrock, married Mary, only daughter of Geoffrey Browne, Efq; (fon of the faid Sir Dominick) and dying in October 1707, was buried the 11 at St. Audeon's, Dublin, having had iffue two fons and three daughters, Lucas, and Henry; Margaret, married to Colonel Lochlin Donnellan, of Ballydonnellan; Ellice (or Ellen) to William O'Kelly, of Gallagh and Tycooly; and Elizabeth, to Richard Blake, of Ardfry, Efq. Lucas, the elder fon, married firft, in June 1694, Honora, eldeft daughter of Sir John Burke, of Glinfk, Bart. and fhe dying 11 February 1713, he married fecondly, in March [1] 1714, Ellis, widow of Sir Juftin Aylmer, Bart. by whom he had no iffue; and dying 20 March 1716, had by the firft wife, five fons and four daughters, Robert, Richard, John, Luke, Henry, (who made his will 10 July 1734, proved 1 July 1735); Mary, (who with her four younger brothers, died unmarried); as did Bridget, in February 1714; Frances, who left no iffue; and Lettice, married in 1735, to Columb O'Flynn, of Turlagh, in county of Galway, and by him who died 26 February 1753, had Edmund, then under 16 years, who was put under the guardianfhip of Luke Dillon, of Clonbrock, Efq.—Robert Dillon, of Clonbrock, was a Member of Parliament for the borough of Dungarvan, and, in February 1725, married Margaret, daughter of Morgan Magan, of Togherftown, Efq widow of Sir Arthur Shane, Bart. and deceafing 11 June 1746, had iffue three fons, Robert, born in 1729, died young; Lucas, and Thomas.

. We now return to Sir Richard Dillon, eldeft fon of Sir Robert of Proudfton and Skryne, who is faid in the reign of K. Henry VI.

Sir Richard.

---

[1] Articles dated 7 March.

Sir Maurice.

Sir Maurice, the eldest son, was knighted in the life-time of his father, and married two wives; first, Lady Anne Fitzgerald,

VI. to have brought 600 Irish select troops to the battle of Werzell or, Vernevil fought 28 August 1624, and to have arrived so seasonably, and behaved so valiantly, when the Duke of Alenzon was prevailing, that the Duke of Bedford, Regent of France, gained a compleat victory; and rewarded his service with making him a Knight Bannaret, and giving him a *Falcon volant* for his crest, instead of a *Demi Lion*, and adding to his coat armour a *Fess, Azure*, over the *Lion Rampant*, alluding to his command of the said troops; Generals, or chief Commanders, usually wearing belts, or girdles of honour.

The said Sir Richard married Jeane, daughter and heir to —— Wife, of Riverston, by whom that estate came to the family, and had issue a daughter Ismay, married to James Bellew, of Bellewstown; and five sons, viz. James, of Riverston; Robert, of Allenstown, (whose grandson Thomas, marrying Rose, daughter and heir to Thomas Woodlock, of Keppoch, or Kappoch, near Dublin, had Peter, his heir, who by Margaret, daughter of William Moor, of Ath'oy, had Bartholemew Dillon, Esq. who married Catharine, eldest daughter of Sir Bartholomew Dillon, of Riverston, and left Nicholas, his heir, who married Catharine, daughter of Robert Rochfort, of Kilbride, Esq. and dying 3 December 1576, was father of Bartholomew Dillon, of Keppoch, then six years old, who was seized of 8 houses and 120 acres of land in Finglas, Johnstowne, Bodins, Cappocke, &c.[1] shortly after he became a lunatick, and dying 26 March 1643, left by Elizabeth his wife, Robert, his heir, who in January 1618, married Jane, eldest daughter of William Rouls, or Rowles, who died in 1643[2], and deceasing 2 August 1649, left only two daughters, Catharine, married 10 June 1631, to William Herrald, and died without issue, in 1653; and Elizabeth, married 20 May 1652, to Thomas Taylor; she became a lunatick, and left issue two daughters, Mary, who married William Eustace, and Anne, married to —— Betagh[3]); John, of whom presently; Walter, and Nicholas, whose posterity settled in England.

The said John, third son of Sir Richard, of Proudston, was denominated of Skryne, and after of Proudston; he married Juliana, daughter of Patrick Plunket, ancestor to the Baron of Louth, and had issue Sir Bartholomew Dillon, Knt. who married Mary, daughter of Edward Eustace, of Castlemartin, county

of

---

[1] Decrees 23 May and 19 November 1707, No. 1.   [2] Id.   [3] Idem.

DILLON, Viscount DILLON.

Fitzgerald, a daughter of the House of Desmond, by whom he had four sons and two daughters, viz. Thomas, his successor,

of Kildare, Esq. and was father of Sir James, of Proudston, Knt. who by Elizabeth, daughter of —— Dowdall, of Mountown, had Gerald, who by Ellen, daughter and heir to —— Fitz-Rery, was father of Richard, denominated of Proudston and Skryne; he was a Commissioner for the administration of Justice, in the counties of Tipperary, Kilkenny, and Cork, appointed second Justice of the King's Bench, 29 October 1560, and died in or about 1565, leaving by Anne his wife, daughter of —— Cruise, of Meath, Esq. a son Peter, of Proudston, who married Elenor, daughter of Patrick Clynch, of Skryne, Esq. and had Richard, his heir, who made a settlement of his estate, by deed of feoffment 6 December 1598, married first a daughter of —— Finglas, secondly Mary, daughter of Robert Preston, of Ballmadon, in county of Dublin, Esq. and dying 26 October 1619, was succeeded by his second son Gerald or Gerrott, æt 27 years at the death of his father, who sett'ed his estate 5 May 1626, and died 15 of same month, leaving by his wife Margaret, daughter or sister to Christopher St. Laurence, of Crusetown, county of Louth, Esq. a son and successor Francis, æt. 18 years and 7 months at the death of his father; he was a considerable sufferer in the troubles of 1641, and by Mary, daughter of Robert Preston, of Rogerstown, county of Meath, Esq. had William, his heir, the last possessor of Proudston, which William, married thrice, first to Bridget, daughter of Nicholas, Viscount Gormanstown, by whom he had Robert, who died before him; secondly to a daughter of —— Betagh, of Moynalty, and widow of Gerald Cruise, of Brittas, county of Meath, Esq by whom no issue; and thirdly, Mary, daughter of Richard Plunket, Esq. of the house of Dunsoghly, by this lady he had Francis, his heir; Peter; James; Richard (whose house in London was demolished in the riot of 1780, soon after which he died); daughter Catharine; Mary (married to Anthony Delamar of Maynooth, Esq. by whom she had a son William); Bridget. The said William Dillon died about 1730, æt. 104 —Francis, the eldest son, on settling in London, joined with his father, in the sale of his paternal inheritance, and his Imperial Majesty, Joseph II. was pleased to confer on him and his heirs male and female, the dignity and title of a free Baron of the sacred Roman empire, with all the privileges thereunto belonging, as appears from an Imperial diploma, dated Vienna, 2 August 1767, and duly registered in the Supreme Chancery of the empire at Vienna.—The said Francis, Baron Dillon, married in 1731, Mary, daughter and heir to Sir Mervyn Wingfield, Bar.

cessor, and of him hereafter; Christopher, in Holy Orders; Robert and William, both killed near Ballynakill, in the Queen's

(son of Sir Henry, of Easton, county of Suffolk, Bart. by his wife Lady Mary Touchet, daughter of Mervyn, Earl of Castlehaven, and Lord Audley) and deceasing 10 September 1775, was interred at St. Pancras, near London, having had by his Lady, (who died 20 February 1705, and was interred at St. Pancras) a numerous issue, of whom only three sons survived, viz. John-Talbot, his heir; Francis (Lieut. Col. of a regiment of cavalry in the German service, and created a Baron of the empire; he married Elizabeth, daughter of Peter Spendelowe, of Hamburgh, Esq. and has issue Charles, a Lieutenant in the regiment of Falris, in the Imperial service; Mary-Elizabeth; Antonia; and Roselia); and William-Mervin, who married Sophia, daughter of the Chevalier Austin-Parke Goddard, late of Brampton, in Kent, and Knight of the Order of St. Stephen, in Tuscany, (by Anne, his wife, sister of Sir Henry-John Parker, of Honington, in county of Warwick, Bart. and daughter of Hugh Parker, Esq. by Anne, his wife, who after married Michael, tenth Earl of Clanrickarde) by this lady he has a son John-Joseph; and a daughter Henrietta-Sophia.—John-Talbot, the eldest son, Baron of the Empire, hath been enrolled amongst the members of the Royal Irish Academy, and is now resident in London [1].

Family of Riverston. James, the eldest son, became seated at Riverston, in the county of Meath (his mother's inheritance) and marrying Elizabeth, daughter of Bartholomew Bath, of Dullardston, Esq. and widow of —— Kerdiffe, had five sons and two daughters, viz Sir Bartholomew, his heir; Gerald, who left posterity at Skryne and Balgieth; Sir Robert, of Newtown, near Trim, immediate ancestor to the Earl of Roscomon; Thomas, Prior of St. Peter, of Trim; Edmund, Prior of Newtown, and of the abbey of Lusk; Elizabeth, married to —— Cusack, of Portrane; and Thomasin, to John Delafield.

Sir Bartholomew Dillon, of Riverston, being bred to the law, was made Steward, Seneschal, Surveyor, and Receiver of the manors of Rushe, Balscadon, the moiety of Portrane, Woughterade, Castlewarning, Clenton's-Court, and Blackcastle; appointed 1 February 1513, Chief Baron of the Exchequer; and 2 July 1516 (being then in that employment) Deputy-Treasurer of Ireland; after which he was knighted, and, 15 January 1532,

---

[1] Sundry Inq's. in Rolls Office. Clogh. MSS. in Trin. Col. Author's Collect and information, J. Talbot Baron Dillon, and of W. M. Dillon, Esq.

Queen's County; daughter Marian, (married to —— Poer, of Curraghmore, maternal ancestor to the Earl of Tyrone); and

1532, constituted by the King, then at Hoggeston, Chief Justice of the King's Bench, but died the year after. He married first Elizabeth, only daughter of Thomas Barnewall, of Irishton, second son of Robert, Lord Trimleston; and secondly Elinor, only daughter of Edmund, the fourth Lord Killeen (by his first wife) by whom he had one son Patrick, who died childless; and four daughters, Catharine, married to Bartholomew Dillon, of Keppock, Esq; Frances, to Patrick, grandson of Christopher Cusack, of Gerald's-town, Esq. Elizabeth, to Oliver Plunket, of the Clone; and Elinor, the first wife of George Plunket, of Bewley, Esq. By the first wife, Sir Bartholomew had Thomas, his heir; and two daughters, Anne, married to Nicholas Kent, of David's-town, Esq. Ismay, to John Fleming, of Stephen's-town, son of George, second son of James Lord Slane, by whom she had Thomas Lord Slane; secondly to Richard Tath, of Cooke's-town, Esq. and thirdly; to Sir Thomas Barnewall, second son of John Lord Trimleston.

Thomas Dillon, Esq. living in 1541, who succeeded at Riverston, married Anne, daughter of Sir Thomas Luttrell, of Luttrell's-town, Chief Justice of the Common Pleas, and had issue six sons and four daughters, viz.

Sir Robert Dillon, his successor. (1)
Matthew, of Brown's-town, who had an only daughter, Frances. (2)
Gerald, of Balgeith, who married Alison, daughter of Bartholomew Russell, of Seat's-town, and dying 31 May 1619, left James, his heir, then twenty-two years old. who married a daughter of —— Hussey, of Mull-Hussey, and had two sons, the elder of whom Thomas, married a daughter of —— —— Betagh, of Newcastle, Esq. whose wife was sister to Sir Lucas Bath, of Athcarne, in Meath, Knt. and had issue Christopher, who married Anne, daughter of —— Betagh, of Moynalty, and had a son Garret, who, by Jane, his wife, daughter of Peter Nottingham, of Ballyowen, in county of Dublin, by his wife Mary, daughter of Robert Lord Trimleston, had issue three sons, viz. Garrett; Peter, who died unmarried; and John, (who married Alice, daughter of William Gernon, of Clonkeighan, in county of Louth, Esq. and had issue five sons and two daughters, who died young, and two other sons, who arrived at maturity, viz. Garrett, who by Rose, daughter of Bartholomew O'Brien, of Kilmainham-Wood, county of Meath, Esq. had issue Alice, who died young; Jane and Elinor, now living; and Richard, who married (3)

and Bridget, who became first the wife of O'More, and secondly of O'Molloy.—Sir Maurice, married secondly Margaret,

married Margaret, daughter of George Taaffe, of Summer-hill, county of Louth, Efq. by her he had issue, Jane, who died young; Mary, Alice, and a son Garrett, now living.—Garrett, eldest son of Garrett, and grandson of Christopher, married Catharine, daughter of William O'Brien, of Thomas-town, in county of Meath, Esq and by her, had issue two daughters, who died young; and two sons now living, viz. William Dillon, Esq. now of Mananston, and Peter [1].

(4) James, of Hunt's-town, in the county of Dublin, who married Anne, daughter of William Stanley, of Fenore, (by his wife Marian, daughter and heir to Walter Walsh, of Hunt's-town, Esq.) and had Martin, his heir, who, in July 1670, married Alison, sister of Robert Lord Trimleston, and had issue James, who died unmarried; Matthias, of Hunt's-town, Robert, and Jane, married to Mr. Goulding. Matthias, in 1697, married Elinor, daughter of Charles (or Christopher) Geoghegan, of Syonan, in Westmeath, Esq. and dying in 1714, left issue James, his heir; Charles, Alice, Bridget, Margaret, Elinor, Monica. James, the eldest son, was then about thirteen years of age, and died in October 1734; leaving one son, Martin Dillon, Esq. who married Mary, eldest daughter of Gerald Fitz-Gerald, of Rathrone, in county of Meath, and of Killmore, in the county of Kildare, Esq. and one daughter, Charlotta, married to her cousin James Dillon son of her uncle Charles.

(5) Edmond, who by Isabel, daughter of John Williams, left a son, Thomas.
(6) Patrick, the father of Robert Dillon.
(1) Daughter Anne, married to John Allen, of St. Wolstan's, Esq.
(2) Catharine, to Gerald, third son of Robert, Lord Dunsany.
(3) Rose, to Matthew Dowdall, of Drogheda, and
(4) Genet, to Gerald (or George) Stokes, of Mitchel's-town, otherwise Knockengene.

Sir Robert Dillon, of Riverston, became very eminent in his profession of the law, being appointed, 17 January 1553, one of the Justices of the Court of Chief Pleas, as he was again by a new patent, 16 April following. 6 September 1580, he was knighted by the Lord D. Grey; and in 1582, constituted Chief Justice

---

[1] Information of William Dillon, of Mananston, Esq.

DILLON, Viscount DILLON.

Margaret, daughter of Mac-Coghlan, Lord of Coghlan's Country, and by her had three sons and three daughters, viz.

Justice of the said Court, which he surrendered 5 October 1593, to make room for Sir William Wetton, sent from England; but 15 March 1595, he was again preferred to that office, and held it to his death, which happened 27 July 1597, 31 of which month, he was buried in the church of Tarah, with his ancestors. By inquisition, taken at Ratoath, 24 May 1624, it was found that he died seized of Riverstown, Balystown, Condonstown, Morestown, with divers other lands, tenements and hereditaments, of which he made a feoffment to the use of his last will; which he made 6 March 1580, to the following effect: he first bequeaths his soul to Almighty God, merely and undoubtedly hoping to be saved by the merits of his son's passion, and for all other pains, touching salvation, he submitted himself to the direction of the Holy Church, and in every matter did effectually believe, as the church believed. He willed his body to be buried by his ancestors in Taragh, desiring such as he had left in trust, to cause the Parson and Vicar to repair and keep up the chancel, and gave towards the body of the church 20l. Desired his wife and others of his friends, to cause a true inventory to be made of all his goods and chattles, for the payment of his debts, and afterwards the residue to be bestowed as follows, viz. a third part to his wife; another to his children; and another to his executors. Willed that his feoffees and their heirs should stand seized of all his lands and tenements, in Balrathe, with their appurtenances, to the use of his wife, so long as she lived solely, after his death, and the feoffees to stand seized of all the lands and tenements he had within the realm of Ireland, and of the reversion of the same, performing what he had before specified, as hereafter appears, viz. first he leaves to each of his daughters, unpreferred at the time of his death, besides their child's portion, 400l. of the issue and profits of his lands, which being performed, he wills his feoffees to be seized of all the premisses, to the use of his son Bartholomew, and the heirs male of his body begotten; remainder to his son William, and his heirs male; remainder to the heirs male that he should beget upon the body of his wife Cate Sarsfield, or any other wife he should chance to have; remainder to the heirs male of his brethren, as they were of age; his brother Matthew excepted; but he married contrary to his consent; remainder to the heirs male of the body of James Dillon, his great grandfather; remainder to the heirs male of Peter Dillon, father to Bartholomew Dillon, of Cappoche; and for want of such issue, the remainder of Balrathe, Fitz-Leonston; the mill of Ratowtbe and his house there to Michael Dillon and his

viz. Alifon, married to O'Carrol, chief of his name; Jean, to ———— Tuite; and Honora, firft to ———— Fitzpatrick,

his heirs for ever, the tuition and bringing up of his fon Richard, and his daughters with their portions, he left to his father Sir William Sarsfield, and his brothers James and Gerald, defiring them to ufe them as they would have him ufe their children. He appointed his fon Bartholomew fole executor, with the ufe of his plate to him and his heirs male, remainder to him or them that fhould be inheritable by that his will to his lands; and leaves to his wife, (but fhe had no portion of his plate and farms except Mallaghfeene) 20 marcs, iffuing out of all his farms during her life. Wills that his fon Richard, fhould have for his finding yearly, during his life 40l. and if he lived with his brother inheritably by that his will, then he to have the fame, or fo much thereof, as thofe that he had put in truft, fhould think convenient; Willing and requiring his children in general to obey, give honour and pleafe him as their chiefeft and eldeft brother. And adds, I befeech and require all fuch as fhall fee or hear this
" my will, not to think that I have difinherited this my beft beloved
" child, upon any vain or peevifh perfuafion; but that God
" having deprived him of his fight and perfect reafon, whereby
" if he had inherited my faid lands, the utter fpoil and deftruc-
" tion of my houfe might enfue, as I was perfuaded by my beft
" and wifeft friends, whofe advice, contrary to my own affec-
" tion. I was moved to follow, and I do thereunto yield as reafon
" requires." To this he added a codicil, dated 26 May 1593, whereby he willed that his fon William fhould have 100l. towards his maintenance to the *Inne* of court, and revoked the claufe of *Difberifon* of his brother Matthew, willing that he and his heirs male, fhould and might take benefit of the like remainder, as the other brothers in their line fucceffively might take, and in addition to the overfeers and tutors of his children, he appointed his well-beloved Thomas Jones, Lord Bifhop of Meath, whom he defired to take care of his fon William, with his portion [1]. He married firft Elenor, daughter of Thomas Allen, of Kilheel Efq. by whom he had Richard, who died before him unmarried; and Mary, the firft wife to Patrick Sedgrave, of Killeghlan in Meath, Efq. he married fecondly Catharine, daughter of Sir William Sarsfield, of Lucan, Alderman of Dublin, and by her who died 21 December 1615, had five fons and nine daughters, viz. Bartholomew of Riverfton, William, of Fitz-Leonfton, (commonly called Flinfton) in Meath, whofe pofterity have fallen to decay; Thomas, of whom hereafter; Michael, Chriftopher, Eleanor, married to Richard Aylmer,

---

[1] Prerog. Office.

patrick, Baron of Upper-Offory, and secondly to ———
Malone, of Ballynahowna, county of Weftmeath, by both
of whom fhe had iffue. The fons were,

Maurice,
mer, of Dullard's-town, Efq. and died 22 November 1635;
Anne, to ——— Birmingham, of the Carrick; Thomafin, to
Chriftopher Evers, of Rathcain, Efq.; Frances, to ——— Cufack, of Cuffington, Efq.; Genet, to Robert Leicefter, Efq; Margaret, to John Baxter; Amy; Ifmay, to Henry, fecond fon of
Sir John Elliott; and Cicely. Bartholomew, of Riverfton,
was twenty-four years old at his father's death. In confideration
of his fervices to Q. Elizabeth and the ftate, in Tyrone's rebellion,
he had two grants of lands, of 40l a year each, from K. James I.
the one by privy-feal, dated at Weftminfter, 10 December 1615,
and the other at Falkland, 19 July 1617. In 1585, he married
Catharine, daughter of Sir Alexander Fitton, of Gaufeworth,
in Chefhire, of Vany, in the county of Limerick, and of the Bec-
tive, in Meath (by Mary, his wife, daughter and heir to Andrew Wife, of Waterford, Efq.) and dying in Dublin, 6 March,
1633, was buried in the church of Tarah, having iffue Andrew,
his heir; Thomas; James; Francis; Peter; Jane, married in
1620, to Simon Barnewall, of Pinner's-town, fon and heir to Patrick, of Kilbrew, Efq. who died about 1643; and Mary, to
Thomas Barnewall, of Rofskill, in the Queen's County. Andrew, the eldeft fon, was born in 1599 [1], commanded a foot
company at the firft fiege of Drogheda, in 1641, and married the
daughter of Sir Chriftopher Plunket, of Kilfhaghlin, Knt. by
whom he had two fons and two daughters, Edward and Thomas,
who both died young; Catharine, married to Mr. Archer, of
Kilkenny; and Mary, to Mr. Bathe, of Colpe, in Meath.

The elder fons and their pofterity having fallen to decay, the
family inheritance devolved on the iffue of Thomas, the third fon
of Sir Robert Dillon, of Riverftown, which Thomas appears to
be the father of Serjeant Major Arthur Dillon, who had iffue
Arthur, a Lieut. Col. in the army, and denominated of Lifmul-
len, in the county of Meath, and alfo of Dillon's-town, county
of Louth, which latter eftate of Dillon's-town, he fold to Mr.
Fortefcue, anceftor to James Fortefcue, Efq. now Knight of the
fhire for Louth. He made his will, 26 December 1684, (proved
24 April 1685) and left iffue by Mary, his wife, a daughter married to Dillon Newman, Efq. and three fons, viz Sir John, his
heir; Arthur, (of Quarter's-town, county of Cork, Efq. who
had an only fon John, and to him, by will, dated 25 February
1689, proved 17 October 1693, he bequeathed his eftates, remainder

---

[1] Rot. de A°. 2°. Jac. II. 3ª. p. f. R. 20.

(1) Maurice, to whom his father gave the castle and town of Low-Baskin, (of which he was denominated) and several other

Families of Low Baskin, Killynynen, &c.

mainder to his cousin Dillon Newman and his issue male, with divers remainders over); and George, who died 16 September 1676, in Trinity-College, Dublin, and was buried at Tarah.—Sir John, the eldest, was seated at Lady-hill, was elected to Parliament for the county of Meath, in the reign of K. William, married first in December 1684, Mary, only daughter of Morrough, Viscount Blesinton; to his second wife in February 1702, Grace, daughter of Thomas Tilson, of Dublin, Esq. and dying suddenly 21 July 1708, left issue by her, who afterwards married James Whitshed, Esq. two sons, Thomas, born in 1704, who died without issue; and Arthur, who 11 June 1730, married Elizabeth, daughter of Doctor Ralph Lambert, Lord Bishop of Meath, died in 1745, and was interred in the family burial place at Skryne, leaving issue John, his heir; Susanna, who died unmarried; and Alice, who married Rev. Nathaniel Preston, of Swainstown, county of Meath, and left issue Nathaniel, born in 1760, Arthur, Elizabeth, and Alice.—John, now Baron Dillon, the eldest son, is at present possessed of Riverstown and Odder, his paternal inheritance, also of Cardiffstown and Newtown, in county of Meath. He served in Parliament for the borough of Ratoath, and in 1782, his Imperial Majesty, JOSEPH II. was pleased to confer on him the dignity of a free Baron of the sacred Roman empire, with limitations to his issue male and female, and the Emperor's reasons for conferring this honour will appear in the following diploma, which has been duly registered, in the Supreme Chancery of the empire, at Vienna.

NOS JOSEPHUS SECUNDUS divina favente clementia electus Romanorum Imperator semper Augustus; Germaniæ, Hierosolymæ, Hungariæ, Bohemiæ, Dalmatiæ, Croatiæ, Slavoniæ, Galiciæ, et Lodomeriæ rex; Archidux Austriæ, Dux Burgundiæ, Lotharingiæ, Styriæ, Carinthiæ, et Carnioliæ; Magnus Dux Hetruriæ, Magnus Princeps Transsylvaniæ, Marchio Moraviæ, Dux Brabantiæ Limburgi, Lucemburgi, et Geldriæ, Wurtemburgæ, Superioris et Inferioris Silesiæ, Mediolani, Mantuæ, Parmæ, Placentiæ, et Quastallæ, Osveciniæ, et Zactoriæ, Calabriæ, Parri, Montisferrati, et Teschinæ; Princeps Sueviæ, et Carolopolis, Comes Habsburgi, Flandriæ, Tyrolis, Hannoniæ, Kiburgi, Goritiæ, et Gradiscæ, Marchio sacri Romani Imperii, Burgoviæ, superioris et inferioris, et inferioris Lusatiæ, Mussoponti, et Nomenei; Comes Namurci, Provinciæ Valdemontis, Albimontis, Zuthaniæ, Sarwerdæ, Salmæ, et Falkensteinii, Dominus Marchiæ, Slavonicæ, et Mechliniæ —Ea fuit multis à sæculis majorum nostrum, divorum videlicet Romanorum Imperatorum,

other town-lands; he married Mary, daughter of Sir George Fitz-Gerald, of Tecroghan, in county of Meath, Knt.

and

rum, Regum, et Archiducum Austriæ laudatissima consuetudo, ut quos vel honesta generis origine vel in patriam meritis probatos, aliisquæ virtutum ornamentis prædictos animadverterent, eosdem munificentia sua singulari præ ceteris decorandos, extollendosque susciperent, idque non tantum, ut ii virtutis suæ beneficio se condignos honores consecutos esse intelligerent, verum, ut et posteri ipsorum ampliori domesticæ laudis tuendæ, propagandæque desiderio allecti, ad paria, et majora virtutis, veræque gloriæ capessundæ conamina excitarentur, unde et Nos Dei ter optimi maximi nutu, ac providentia ad Regnorum, et ditionum nostrarum hæreditariarum gubernacula admoti nihil prius, antiquiusque duximus, quam præclara eorundem gloriosissimorum antecessorum nostrorum instituta, ac vestigia cum in aliis, tum hac ipsa in parte firmiter sequi, et bonos quoque viros, præsertim eos, singulari benevolentiæ nostræ affectu prosequi illorumque nomini, et dignitati uberius consulere, quos præter nobilium natalium decus, singularis vitæ probitas, majorum suorum merita, nec non propria, eaque assidua, in nos et Augustam domum nostram Austriacam sinceræ fidei, ac observantiæ studia commendatos, gratosque reddunt.

Perspectis igitur Joannis Dillon de civitate Lifs-Mollen in comitatu Meathensi Hyberniæ regionis sita originem suam trahentis meritis, qui Catholicam Hyberniæ nationis partem; remotis prævie cunctis, quibus impeti solita est, præjudiciis; ab omnibus hucusque formidandis persecutionibus tutam reddendo, eique plenam liberi religionis exercitii palam profitendi facultatem procurando zelosissimum intuendis humanitatis, et tolerantiæ Christianæ juribus, animum manifestavit, spectata insuper morum probitate, et summa in omni vitæ consuetudine integritate, qua apud Nos idem Joannes Dillon commendatus fuit, quarum virtutum specimina eum in posterum quoque pro indolis, officii, et datæ fidei ratione constanter editurum Nobis certo pollicemur.

Nos hisce clementiæ nostræ paginis prædictum Joannem Dillon, ejusque liberos, et descendentes utriusque sexus, legitimo thoro natos, aut nascituros, in præmium operosæ, et prospere gestorum, ac ut de benigna Nostra in eum propensione documentum nunquam deficiat, motu proprio, animo prorsus deliberato, maturo ac communicato consilio, ex certa scientia atque Cesareæ, Regiæ, et Archiducatis Nostræ potestatis plenitudine, ad statum, gradum, ordinem et dignitatem verorum, ac genuinorum liberorum Baronum evehimus, et attollimus, aliorumque sacri Romani Imperii,

nec

and had two sons and two daughters, viz. John, his heir; Gerald, Guardian of the Franciscan Friaries, in Kilkenny-

nec non regnorum, et ditionum Nostrarum hæreditariarum Baronum numero, et coetui benigne adscribimus, aggregamus, eique præterea titulum generosi, seu Magnifici, Germanice Mohlgebohnn clementer hisce largimur, ita, ut supra nominatus Johannes omnesque ejus liberi, legitime nati, utriusque sexus in infinitum ubique locorum tam in literis quam viva voce, nec non in quibuscunque actibus, rebus et negotiis spiritualibus, et temporalibus, ecclesiasticis, et profanis, ab omnibus et singulis cujuscunque status, gradus, ordinis, et dignitatis, aut conditionis existant, pro veris liberis Baronibus haberi, reputari, et existimari debeant.—Pro uti, et Nos ipsi eum talem nominamus, declaramus, et appellamus, non aliter, ac si a quatuor avis paternis; et maternis liber Baro natus et procreatus esset.

Volentes, insuper, et authoritate Nostra Cæsareo-Regia, et Archiducati expresse descernentes, præfatus Johannes Liber Baro de Dillon cum suis legitime descendentibus utriusque sexus, ubique tam in judiciis, quam extra omnibus et singulis privilegiis, indultis, immunitatibus, libertatibus, juribus, consuetudinibus, honoribus, dignitatibus, prærogativis, exemtionibus, gratiis, et favoribus, quibus alii liberi Barones in sacro Romano Imperio, regnisque, ac provinciis Nostris hereditariis utuntur, fruuntur, gaudent et potiuntur, pariter uti, frui, gaudere, et potiri valeat, quomodo libet consuetudine, vel de jure, omni contradictione, et impedimento post positis ac sublatis.—Quo vero perpetuum hujus in præfatum Joannem Dillon Baronem de Dillon et ejus legitimos descendentes collatæ dignitatis exstet documentum, eademque pleniore beneficio decorata, publico majis, magisque innotescat, præmemorata authoritate Nostra Cæsareo-Regia, et Archiducali ea, quibus hactenus usus est, armorum insignia clementer auximus, et confirmavimus, prout eadem vigore præsentium augemus, et confirmamus, ac sæpe memorato Joanni Libero Baroni de Dillon, Ejusque legitime descendentibus utriusque sexus, ea in hunc, qui sequitur, modum posthac habenda, gestanda, et deferenda benigne concedimus et elargimur. Scutum videlicet erectum, et corona Baronibus propria ornatum, in cujus area argentea tres inter angulis superioribus, nec non ad pedem scuti in medio forma nimirum triangulari sitas, leo quoque rubeus dextrorsum procedens, rictu hiante, lingua exserta, et cauda tortuose elata conspiciatur. Clypeum hunc galea chalybea aperta coronataque auro clathrata, aurea torque, et laciniis argenteis utraque extraque ex parte rubeo intertextis colore, & concinne defluentibus ornata præmiat. Ex Galea prorsus leo aureus consimilem præferens stellam dextrorsum exsurgat. Telamones sint tygrides duæ: sub
scuti

DILLON, Viscount DILLON.

Kilkenny-West and Athlone; Rose, married to ———
O'Kelly, of Aghran; and ——— a Nun. John, who
succeeded

scuti tandem pede inscriptum legatur schedulæ lemma; *Dum
spiro, spero*. Prout hæc ipsa armorum insignia in medio præsentis
Nostri diplomatis diagraphice designata videre liquet.—Statuentes, et expresse volentes ut sæpius nominatus Johannes liber Baro
de Dillon, et quilibet legitimorum suorum descendentium utriusque sexus, perpetua succestione, præscripta armorum insignia,
in omnibus, et singulis honestis, et decentibus actibus, exercitiis,
atque expeditionibus; tam serio, quam joco, in hastatorum dimicationibus, vel equestribus in bellicis, et quibuscunque certaminibus licitis, cominus et emininus, in scutis, banderiis, vexillis,
lentoriis, et cænotaphiis, sepulchris, monumentis, clenodiis, annulis, monilibus, sigillis, ædificiis, parietibus, fenestris, ostiis,
lacunaribus, tapetibus ac supellectilibus quibusvis, tam in rebus
spiritualibus, quam temporalibus, et mixtis in locis denique omnibus pro rei necessitate, et voluntatis suæ arbitrio, aliorumque
sacri Romani Imperii, regnorumque, et ditionum Nostrarum
hæreditarium liberorum Baronum more absque ullo impedimento,
vel contradictione habere, gestare et deferre, iisdemque uti quovis modo possit, et valeat; aptusque sit, et idoneus, ad recipiendum omnes gratias, libertates, exemptiones, feuda, privilegia,
vacationes a muneribus, et oneribus, quibuscunque realibus, personalibus, sive mixtis, qui sacri Romani Imperii, Nostrorumque
regnorum, et provinciarum hæreditariarum liberis Baronibus
hujus dignitatis titulo competere solent, ad utendum denique singulis juribus quibus cæteri hujusmodi ornamentis insigniti, ac feudorum capaces atque participes utuntur, fruuntur, potiuntur,
et gaudent, quomodo libet consuetudine vel de jure; Nostris tamen, sacrique Romani Imperii regnorum etiam ac ditionum Nostrarum hæreditariarum et quorumcunque aliorum juribus semper salvis.—Quapropter universos et singulos sacri Romani Imperii Electores, Principes, ecclesiasticos et sæculares, aliosque regnis, et ditionibus Nostris hæreditariis non subjectos, benigne requirimus. Nostris vero incolis, et subditis regnorum Nostrorum,
et provinciarum hæreditariarum cujuscunque status, gradus, ordinis, dignitatis, conditionis, vel præeminentiæ, sive in Regno
Bohemiæ sive in Archiducatu Austriæ iisdemque incorporatis provinciis existant, hisce serio mandamus, atque præcipimus, ut sæpius nominatum Joannem Liberum Baronem de Dillon, et omnes
ejus descendentes legitimo thoro ortos aut orituros, utriusque sexus, uti alias sacri Romani Imperii, regnorumque et ditionum
Nostrarum hæreditariarum liberos Barones habeant, reputent,
ita nominent atque honorent, ceterisque prædictis concessionibus,
immunitatibus, prærogativis, præeminentiis, honoribus, et gratiis
vigore

DILLON, Viscount DILLON.

succeeded at Low-Baſkin, married Celia, daughter of Sir John Eugan, Hugan, or Egan, of co. of Kilkenny, Knt. by whom he

vigore hujus Noſtri cæſareo regii et archiducatis diplomatis ipſis competentibus libere, quiete, et abſque ullo impedimento uti, frui, potiri, et gaudere ſinant, adeoque eos in omnibus, et ſingulis defendant confervent, et manuteneant, aliofque, ne quid in contrarium attentent, vel moliantur, pro viribus, prohibeant, et impediant, niſi indignationem Noſtram graviſſimam, et centum marcarum auri puri muletam pro dimidio fiſco, ſeu ærario Noſtro, pro reliqua vero parte injuriam paſſo, ſeu paſſis, toties quoties contra hanc Noſtræ creationis, conceſſionis, liberationis, exemptionis, et gratiæ paginam, quid factum fuerit, irremiſſibiliter ſolvendam incurrere velint.—Harum teſtimonio literarum manu Noſtra ſubſcriptarum ſigilliique Noſtri cæſareo-regii, et archiducatis appenſione munitarum, quæ dabantur in Civitate Noſtra Vienna die quarta Julii, Anno Domini milleſſimo, ſeptingenteſimo octuageſſimo tertio, Regnorum Noſtrorum, Romani vigeſimo, hæreditariiorum vero tertio.

JOSEPHUS.

But Mr. Dillon, not wiſhing to accept this mark of favour without the approbation of his ſovereign, made immediate application to the then L. L. who thereupon addreſſed the following letter To the Right Hon. Thomas Townſhend, one of his Majeſty's principal Secretaries of State :

No. 20.   *Dublin-Caſtle*, 21 December 1782.

SIR,

" John Dillon, Eſq. of Liſmullen, in the county of Meath,
" having taken an active part in the Houſe of Commons, during
" the laſt ſeſſion of Parliament, on the ſeveral meaſures adopted
" by the legiſlature for the relief of his Majeſty's Roman Catho-
" lic ſubjects of this kingdom ; his conduct engaged the grateful
" attention of the Iriſh gentlemen of that perſuaſion, reſident
" not only in Ireland, but on the Continent, who, without any
" previous communication with him, applied to his Imperial
" Majeſty, to confer upon Mr. Dillon, ſome title or dignity that
" might beſt demonſtrate the Emperor's high opinion of the li-
" beral ſentiments which have ſo much diſtinguiſhed the Parlia-
" ment of Ireland, and particularly thoſe who moved and ſup-
" ported this meaſure. And his Imperial Majeſty was therefore
" pleaſed to give directions for a diploma, conſtituting Mr. Dillon
" a Baron of the Empire. Mr. Dillon, however poſſeſſing the
" higheſt

DILLON, Viscount DILLON.

he had two daughters and nine sons, viz. Ellice or Jane, married to John Dalton, of Dalyftown, in Weftmeath, son and heir to

" higheft fentiments of loyalty and attachment to his fovereign,
" has declined to accept this mark of favor from a foreign power,
" unlefs it shall meet with the entire approbation of the King.—
" I therefore requeft you to lay this matter before his Majefty,
" and fubmit to his Majefty my humble recommendation that he
" will be gracioufly pleafed to permit Mr. Dillon, to accept the
" honor intended for him by his Imperial Majefty, and that he
" may be permitted to bear fuch enfigns of that dignity, as are
" ufually borne by perfons poffeffing the fame in Germany.—
" And if his Majefty fhall be pleafed to confent thereto, I requeft
" you will fignify to me his royal pleafure as foon as may be,
" Mr. Dillon being anxious that no time may be loft in his expref-
" fing the fenfe he entertains of his Imperial Majefty's goodnefs
" to him.

" I have the honor to be, &c.
" NUGENT TEMPLE."

" Rt. Hon. Mr. Townfhend."

To this letter his Excellency the Lord Lieutenant received the answer following:

Whitehall, 22 February, 1783.

" My Lord,
" I have had the honor of laying before the King, your Ex-
" cellency's letter, No. 20. of the 21 December.—His Majefty
" has commanded me to inform your Excellency, that the active
" part taken by Mr. Dillon, in the Houfe of Commons of Ireland,
" during the laft feffion of Parliament, on the feveral meafures
" adopted for the relief of his fubjects in Ireland, profeffing the
" Roman Catholic religion, has not paffed unnoticed by him,
" and that his Majefty has received much fatisfaction in finding
" that the liberal fentiments of that gentleman have fo defervedly
" been diftinguifhed by the Emperor.—His Majefty is well
" pleafed with the loyalty and attachment fhewn by Mr. Dillon,
" and highly approves of his accepting the honorable teftimony
" of his Imperial Majefty's moft gracious favor, and of his bearing
" the enfigns of the dignity worn by perfons poffeffing the fame
" in Germany.

" I am, &c.
" T. TOWNSHEND."

" His Excellency the Lord Lieutenant."

to Theobald, of Rowlandstown, third son of Richard of Miltown, in same county, Esq. and by him who died at Dalystown

In 1767, Mr. Dillon, married Millicent, daughter of Roger Drake, of Fernhill, in Berkshire, Esq. and by this lady who died in 1788, hath issue John, born in 1768; Charles, 1770; Arthur-Richard, 1771; William, 1774; Ralph, 1779; Robert, 1787; and three daughters, Elizabeth; Anne-Grace; and Millicent [1].

Sir Robert, of Newtown. We now proceed with the direct ancestors of the Earls of Roscomon. Sir Robert Dillon, of Newtown, near Trim, (third son of James of Riverston, and Elizabeth Bathe) in 1545, was Attorney General to K. Henry VIII. who, 20 March 1545, granted to him and his heirs for ever, the Monastery of Friars Preachers of Athnecarne in Westmeath, with the appurtenances. Q. Elizabeth also rewarded his services, 2 May 1569, with a grant to him and his heirs male, of the Monastery of Shrowell, with all its hereditaments; and by Privy Seal, dated 20 April 1570, ordered him a grant of so much land in the province of Conaught, the Annaly, or in the Dillon's and Dalton's Countries, as should amount to the extended rent of 30l. a year. 18 February 1553, Q. Mary appointed him second Justice of the Queen's Bench, and one of her Privy Council; in which post he was continued by Q. Elizabeth, 9 January 1558; and thence advanced, 3 September following, to be Chief Justice of the Common Pleas, as he was again by a new patent, 18 November 1562. He was joined in commission 28 August 1561, with Hugh, Archbishop of Dublin, and others, to preserve the peace within the English pale, during the absence of the L. L. Sussex, in his expedition to the North, against Shane O'Neile; and 13 April 1563, was, in a like commission for the counties of Meath and Drogheda, while the L. D. was engaged in a second expedition against the said O'Neile. In this reign he was Speaker of the House of Commons, one of her Majesty's Privy Council, appointed with his son Sir Lucas, and others, 21 February 1579, to make the limits of certain territories into the county of Wicklow; and was joined in several other important commissions. He married Genet, younger daughter of Edward Barnewall, of Crick's-town, Esq. by his wife Elizabeth, daughter of Sir Thomas Plunket, of Dunsoghly, Chief Justice of the Common Pleas, and had issue four sons and three daughters, viz

(1)   Sir Lucas Dillon, his heir.

Roger,

---

[1] From the original patent and attested copies of said letters, communicated by the Hon. John Baron Dillon, also the Baron's letter to Editor, Collections, &c.

Dalystown 4 January 1636, she had Richard, who married Anne, daughter of Christopher Nugent, of Dunentis in Meath,

Roger, who married Margaret, daughter of Richard Missett, (2) of Ballydromny, with whom he got the lordships of Ballydromny and Ballynecorr, in the county of Cavan, in which he was succeeded by his son James, living there in the reign of James I.

Thomas, who married first the daughter of Walter Peppard, (3) by whom he had a son Tibbot; and secondly Margaret, daughter of ——— Cushen, and by her he had a son Robert, who marrying Margaret, eldest daughter of Theobald, the first Viscount Dillon, established the families of Cannerstown, in D'llon's Country; Ballymulvey, in Roscomon; and Ballymahon, in Longford.

John, (in some pedigrees said to be a Priest) but by others (4) made founder of the families of Dremilton, in Meath, and Walterstown, in Dillon's Country.—The daughters were, Jeane, married to Sir Thomas Dillon, of Drumrany; Elizabeth, to Henry Plunket, Merchant and Alderman of Dublin; and Alison, to the Lord Slane.

Sir Lucas Dillon, of Newtown, and of Moymet, in the county Sir Lucas. of Meath (which house he built) was not only eminent in his profession of the law, but distinguished for his experience both in martial and civil affairs; insomuch as that wise Governor, Sir Henry Sidney, generally consulted him and Francis Agarde, Esq. in all matters of consequence; and found him so faithful and trusty, that he used to call him *meus fidelis Lucas*. 16 July 1568, he had a grant by Privy Seal, dated at Havering of the abbey of the Virgin Mary of Trim, with a lease of the moiety of Castlenock, and other lands, of late belonging to John Burnell, attainted; and 10 August that year, received a grant to him and his heirs male, of the towns of Ladyrath, Grange of Trim, Canonstown, Rathnally, and others in the county of Meath.

In 1567, he was his Majesty's Attorney-General, 13 October 1572, was constituted Chief Baron of the Exchequer, and one of the Privy Council; was knighted by Sir Henry Sidney, at Drogheda, in 1576; and Sir John Plunket, Chief Justice of the Queen's Bench, dying in 1583, her Majesty resolved to appoint for his successor, her trusty and well beloved servant, Sir Lucas Dillon, her Chief Baron, as a personage, whom for his very good and faithful service, and for his good deserts and sufficiency every way, she thought not only worthy of that place, but of a better; yet, upon good consideration had, and finding by himself that he was able to do her better service in the place he then had,

Meath, Esq. and other children); and Catharine, who married ——— Aylmer. The sons were MAURICE, their

had, than if he had the other, was pleafed, upon his recommendation, to appoint James Dowdall, fecond Juftice of the faid Bench, to difcharge the place of Chief Juftice; and as fome recompence to him, did, by Privy Seal[1], dated at Greenwich 5 June 1583, confer upon him the office of Senefchal (which he then held) and to his heirs male, of the Hundred or Barony of Kilkenny-Weft, over the furname of DILLON, and other the inhabitants there, with all and fingular the commodities and profits unto the fame office belonging; as alfo a leafe of fuch crown lands, fpiritual and temporal as he fhould nominate, amounting to 70l. a year, for 60 years, at the accuftomed rent; in lieu whereof, he furrendered to the Queen (30 October) all his right and title to the town and lands of Athlone, which he challenged to have belonged to the chief of the Dillons before *this* time.

In 1584 the L. D. Perrott fent him to the Queen, to give account of his proceedings in Ireland from his firft arrival, in the execution of his office; in doing which, he gave her Majefty fuch fatisfaction, that fhe made very honourable mention of him, and expreffed the high efteem fhe had for him, in the poftfcript of her letter to the deputy, dated 20 January. On 26 April 1587, he was commiffioned, with others, to diftribute the forfeited eftates in Munfter, and joined in many other commiffions of public utility during the Queen's reign. He married Jane, daughter of James Bathe, of Athcarne and Drumconragh, Efq. Chief Baron of the Exchequer, and lies buried under a monument in Newtown, with this infcription:

> Militis hic Lucæ Dillonis offa quiefcunt,
> Conciliis Regni fummus Baroque fupremus,
> Menfe Februarii decimus cum feptimus inftat,
> Tempora luftrali profufus flumine claufit,
> Terrenos linquens, cœleftes fumpfit Honores.

He had iffue by her, who died before 1581, feven fons and five daughters, viz. Sir James, created Earl of Rofcomon; Henry, of whom prefently; Chriftopher, Oliver, Alexander, and John, all died childlefs; Robert, who fettled in the King's County, and left pofterity in Munfter, and in England; Genet, married to Chriftopher, the ninth Lord Killeen, and was mother of Lucas, created Earl of Fingall; Elinor, to Robert Rochfort of Kilbride,

---

[1] Rot. A°. 26°. Eliz. D.

DILLON, Viscount DILLON. 157

heir to his father.—HUBERT, who settled at STREAMS-
TOWN and KILLINYNEN, in the territories of Dalton
and Mac-Geoghagan, assigned to him as part of
his

Kilbride, in Meath, Esq. Elizabeth; Margaret, to John Sarsfield of Shurninges, in the county of Kildare, Esq.; and Anne, to Richard Plunket, of Rathmore, Esq.

Henry Dillon, (the second son) of Kentstown, in Meath, and of Strokestown and Ardnecrane in Dillon's Country, married Elizabeth, daughter to the Lord Culpepper, and dying 18 April 1609, (or 20 April 1610) had four sons and three daughters, Henry, his heir; Theobald, (or rather Thomas Fitz-Theobald, who was seated at Waterstown, and left two daughters, one married to ——— Dillon, of Drumrany, the other to Ramsay, by whom she was mother of Colonel — Ramsay); Lucas and James, who both settled in Munster; Thomasin, married to ——— ——— Plunket, of Loghcrew in Meath, Esq.; Anne, married to George Russel, Esq. grandson of Sir William Russel, L. D. of Ireland, in the reign of Q. Elizabeth; and Margaret, married in England. Henry Dillon, Esq. the eldest son, was commonly called Harry Kittagh, or the Left-handed, and by Jane, daughter of ——— Sarsfield, of Sarsfieldstown in Meath, Esq. had Robert, of Kentstown, Henry, and two daughters. Henry, the younger son, settled in the King's County, in which and Tipperary, he was agent to Carey and Robert, Earls of Roscomon, and left James, his eldest son, now living. Robert of Kentstown, married the daughter of O'Connor Roe, and had issue Charles, knighted, and a Colonel in foreign service, who married an heiress in Flanders, and died in or about 1739, without issue; and two daughters, Magdalen, married to Edmund O'Kelly, of Lissanien; and Clare, to Michael O'Connor.

Sir James Dillon, the eldest son, who succeeded at Moymet, had a special livery of his inheritance 8 April 1595, was knighted by K. James I. from whom 15 July 1609, he received a grant of Gortmore, Cloncullen, &c. in the counties of Westmeath and Longford, to hold to him, and the heirs male of his grandfather, Sir Robert Dillon, by the 20 part of a Knight's fee, and the rent of 6l. 12s. Irish. Also 25 May 1612, a Saturday market and fair on Corpus Christi day, at the abbey of Shrowell, in Westmeath; and a grant of all the ferries and chantries in Ireland.— In consideration of the many acceptable and faithful services performed to his crown; and for his other virtues, which were eminent and worthy to be cherished; as also because his son, Sir Robert Dillon, had relinquished the errors of his ancestors, and being guided by a better judgment, conformed himself to the Protestant religion, was by Privy Seal, dated at Westminster 13

November

Family of Kentstown.

Sir James, Earl of Roscomon.

his anceftor's eftates, and to which he made confiderable additions ; he married Ellen or Ellice, daughter of Gerald Fitz-gerald,

November, and by patent at Dublin 24 January 1619, created Lord Dillon, Baron of Kilkenny-Weft, the ceremony whereof was performed by the L. D. St John in the Prefence-Chamber, on the 25 ; and the Preamble of the patent thus recites his Majefty's reafons for conferring that honour : Cum Majeftas regia Honores fons et origo exiftit, ac ut Stellarum claritas et lumen a Sole derivatur ; ita fplendidi et illuftres Tituli a fola Regis Serenitate Viris bene-merentibus communicantur : Cumque præcipua a Principe Virtus habeatur, Subditos fuos bene-merentes dignofcere, ac eorum Merita recognofcere et remunerare ; cumque etiam inter Munera et Præmia, quibus Principes Servientes fuos digniffimos onerare foleant, Honores et illuftres Tituli cætera omnia antecellant ; quia fcilicet eximiæ Virtutis perpetua exiftant Teftimonia ; et non folum ipfos, qui fic honorari meruerunt, ornatiores et ampliores, fed et alios, ipfis chariffimos, per multa fæcula feliciores reddant : Nos itaque confiderantes ac memoria repetentes Virtutes fingulares ac Merita digniffima predilecti et fidelis noftri Jacobi Dillon de Moymett in Comitatu Middiæ, Militis, Perfona idonea et optime qualificata ad recipiendum amplum Honoris Characterem, tam propter Generis claritatem, Animi fortitudinem, aliafque egregias Virtutes et quamplurima peracceptabilia Servitia nobis tam per præfatum Jacobum Dillon et Anteceffores fuos, qui Prædeceffforibus noftris in Hoc Regno noftro Hiberniæ, per multos Annos, in Locis et Gradibus Senatorum et Judicum Capitalium, bene, meritorie, integre et fideliter fervierunt ; quam etiam per Robertum Dillon, Militem, Filium præfati Jacobi, Servientum noftrum, multipliciter præftita in dicto Regno noftro Hiberniæ, quam propter amplitudinem Terrarum et Poffeffionum, quas habet in dicto Regno noftro Hiberniæ : Sciatis quod, &c. And his Majefty as a more ample teftimony of his favour, was pleafed to advance him to the dignity of Earl of Rofcomon, by Privy Seal dated Weftminfter 24 July, and by patent 5 Auguft 1622, *with this preamble* to the patent of creation Quanquam fatis amplum fibi Virtus ipfa fit Theatrum, et Summum tam Splendoris quam Voluptatis finceræ, ipfa fibi, quafi Radiis quibufdam fuis, conferat, ac placido fui et fuarum vere Opum earumque Autoris intuitu ; Evenit tamen non raro, ut etiam magna et prope perfecta Animi Indoles, novis impofitis Muniis, appofitis Præmiis, et latior excrefcat, et perfiftat lætior. Gnarum hoc Regibus, et apprime nobis, non folum quippe è Virtutibus Honores originem cepiffe, fed ex ipfis etiam Honoribus Virtutes ipfas enafci confpeximus. Nobis
autem

DILLON, Viscount DILLON.

Fitzgerald, of Pierstown in Westmeath, Esq. (by Margaret, his wife, daughter of ——— Fitzgerald, of Laragh) and

autem ipsis hoc non immerito tacita Animi Conscientia attribuere, et nobis gratulari licet, quod nos ad aliquem Dignitatis gradum evehendos susccepimus, eosdem sane aut Bonos elegimus, quod est Judicii, aut eligendo Bonis non absimiles Bonos certe fecimus, quod est Felicitatis, immo et Perspicacie, ipsam scilicet Bonitatem vel ortam persensimus sagacitate, vel orituram saltem præsensimus quodam Præsagio ; utrumque vero idque abunde præstitimus prædilecto et fideli Subdito nostro Jacobo Dillon Militi, Domino Dillon, Baroni de Kilkenny, in Comitatu nostro Westmiddiæ in Regno nostro Hiberniæ, in prædictum Baronis Dignitatem a nobis nuper evecto. Ille quidem celebri et pervetusta Familia, ac de Antecessoribus nostris et tota Hibernica Republica optime merita oriundus, in nuperrimis illis Hibernicorum Perduellium et Proditorum insultibus et populationibus, quibus universa fere vastata, est illa Regio, non tantum fidelem se, nobis et præcharissimæ Sorori nostræ Elizabethæ nuper Reginæ, exhibuit (mitantibus Anglici Cognominis et Generis non paucis, aut potius, aperte desciscentibus) sed etiam in illis Bellorum et Militiæ procellis, tam diuturnis, tam periculosis, strenuum se continuo præbuit Patriæ Adjutorem, et Rebellibus Hostem infestissimum. Marte deinde illo intestino (nostris Armis et Auspiciis) feliciter amoto, in plerisque Pacis et Togæ Artibus non pauca insignis Industriw edidit Specimina, addidit Opera. His nos et aliis compluribus illius Meritis perspectis, nec non prædilecti Subditi nostri, et in Famulitio nostro nobis Inservientis Roberti Dillon, Militis (Filii et Hæredis apparentis præfati Jacobi) in nos, Patriam et Parentes piis Affectibus pensitatis, eodemque Jacobo Præmissorum intuitu antedicti Baronis Loco et Titulo à nobis (non iniquis Hominum et Rerum Estimatoribus) insignito, eosdem iterum tanquam surculos quosdam Manibus nostris plantatos (uti non indiligentis Agricolæ) revidimus, retractavimus ; et in iisdem adeo uberes suarum Virtutum fructus, et Munificentiæ in eos nostræ, quasi autumnalem quandam Messem comperimus, ut eosdem ampliori aliquo Brabio et Honoribus (tanquam Rigatione nostra regia) fovendos certo Animi Judicio non tam moti aut ducti, quam impulsi constituerimus, ac certo constituimus. Sciatis igitur, quod nos Præmissa gratiose attendentes, dictumque Jacobum, Dominum Dillon favore prosequentes regio, ac ipsius acceptabilia in nos et Republicam Hibernicam obsequia insigniori Honoris titulo Compensare et ornare meditantes de Gratia, &c.

His lordship took his seat in Parliament 14 July 1634[1], and having the command of a troop of horse in the reigns of James and Charles

[1] Lords Jour. I. 2.

and dying at Killinynen in October 1640, was buried in Drumrany, leaving issue two sons and one daughter, viz. John,

Charles I did many singular services to his country, in that station. He married Elianor, (or Hellen) second daughter of Sir Christopher Barnewall, of Turvey, Knt. and dying in March 1641, had issue by her, who died 11 (or 12) October 1628, seven sons and six daughters, viz. Robert, Lord Dillon, his successor; Lucas, of whom presently; Thomas, Christopher, George, John, Patrick, who all died young or unmarried; Jane, married to Sir Christopher Dillon, heir apparent to Theobald, the first Viscount Dillon; Elizabeth to ——— Hussey, Baron of Galtrim; Frances, to Henry, son and heir to Christopher Burnell of Castlenock, Esq.; Margaret, to ——— Nugent, of Drumcree, Esq.; Mary, to Sir John Bellew, of Ball-Robinstown, Knt.; and Alison, to Roger O'Farrell, of Morrin, chief of his name.

The second son Lucas, was of Trinity-Island, in the county of Cavan, and of Tuaghmore, otherwise called Twomere, in Roscomon. After his father's death, being advised by letter from his brother Robert, Earl of Roscomon, so far to partake with the rebels, as to save his father's goods, he joined with those of the English pale only, the others being of different councils and affections; for which he was transplanted in 1653, from his feat and large estate in the counties of Meath and Cavan, to Tuaghmore. He married Mary, daughter of Sir John Thorp, of Rutland, by whom he had one son James, and two daughters, the elder whereof was married to John, then son and heir to Philip Reily, of Lismore, in the county of Cavan, (by his wife Mary, daughter of William O'Molloy, of Oughterheere, county of Roscomon, Esq.) by him she had two sons Philip and Luke, both officers of rank; and a daughter Mary, married to Anthony Malone, Esq.—James Dillon, of Rathwyre, Esq. the son, married Jeane, sister of Sir Anthony, and niece to Sir Patrick Mullady, of Robert's-town, in Meath, Knt. and had two sons, Lucas, who died unmarried; Patrick, who succeeded him at Tuaghmore before the year 1684; and three daughters, Mary; Jeane; and Elinor. Patrick married Dymphna, daughter of Colonel Arthur, and grand-niece to Richard Talbot, Earl of Tyrconnel, by whom he had five sons and three daughters, James; Robert; John; Arthur; Thomas, who died at Larkfield, in county of Leitrim, 16 May 1767; Frances, married to Captain Shanley; Christian, to Terence M'Dermot Roe; and the youngest to ——— Begg. —James, the eldest son, dying unmarried, Robert, the second became heir, and had he claimed the title would have succeeded the

DILLON, Viscount DILLON.

John, his heir; Edmund, (who married the daughter of Robert Dillon, Esq. and afterwards became a Canon-Regular);

the eighth Earl of Roscomon; he was Colonel of foot, and a Marshal in the armies of France, and died 24 March 1770, aged 61.

Robert, the second Earl of Roscomon, was a Nobleman of courage and bravery, and served his King and Country, with singular integrity and affection. In 1627, K Charles I. called him into his Privy Council; and 13 August 1628, appointed him a Commissioner for the granting a-new of all lands, then lately escheated to the crown in Ulster. In 1629, his Lordship, and Michael, second son of Henry Lord Folliott, had a licence, for their respective lives, to keep taverns, and sell all manner of wholsome wines, and to make and sell Aqua-vitæ, by retail or In grois, in the town of Ballyshannon. As assignee to Sir James Craige, he had two grants from the crown, the one of lands (dated 9 September 1629) in the counties of Wicklow, Tipperary, Mayo, and Roscomon; and the other (9 April 1633) of divers fairs and markets, viz. a Thursday market and fair on St. James's day, at the town of Moate in Westmeath; a Thursday market and fair on Ascension day, at Crosmullin in Mayo; a Saturday market and fair 4 August at Moylagh; a fair 4 October at Dowlary; two fairs on 8 September, and Corpus-Christi day at Killcarbarne, and a Thursday market and fair 4 August at Kingeranbane in Galway; a Thursday market and fair on the feast of St. Martin the Bishop at Synroan, and a fair on Michaelmas day, at Killean in the King's County; two fairs 15 May, and 4 October at Loughglyn in Roscomon; two fairs, 30 July and 2 October, at Ballymoate, and two fairs 31 May and 1 November, at Bricklewe in Sligo, to hold them all in fee simple, free from all rents whatever. On 8 May 1630, as an undertaker in the province of Ulster, he had a grant, with the Lord Mountnorris, of the small proportion of Latgare, containing 1000 acres, in the county of Fermanagh, with the creation thereof into the manor of Latgare; and, with James, Viscount Claneboy (as undertakers) a December 1631, of the middle proportion (1500 acres) of Derrynesogher in the same county, which was erected into the manor of Castletown, with a Monday market, and a fair there every Whitson-Monday, he took his seat in Parliament 14 July 1634 [1]. By the deed of feoffment of John Fowler, Esq dated 10 February 1634, he became seized in fee of Ballaghlerine, and other lands in the King's County; and 9 September 1639, by virtue of the commission of grace, had a confirmation of Tooregowin, Castlecorr, and many other lands in the county of Longford.—He was a member of the House of Commons;

Robert, 2 Earl.

[1] Lords Jour. I. 2.

gular); and Mary, married to Garret Dillon, of Portlick, in county of Westmeath, Esq—John, who succeeded at Streamstown

mons; and 26 May 1638, made Keeeper of the Great Seal, in the Lord Chancellor's absence: Also, 12 September 1639, one of the L. J. of Ireland, in which high post he continued until the Earl of Strafford's arrival 18 March following; after whose departure, and the death of his deputy, Wandesford, the King intended to put the government into the hands of the Duke of Ormond, but was dissuaded from his purpose by the committee of the Irish House of Commons, then in London: Whereupon, determining to appoint Lords Justices, his Majesty, at the Earl of Strafford's suit, designed Robert Lord Dillon, and Sir William Parsons for the government; but the same committee also opposed his lordship's appointment (who was a person of great parts and experience, of unquestionable loyalty, and of hearty affection to the King's service, and to the true interest of the kingdom; but who, by uniting with the Earl of Ormond in opposing their late measures in Parliament, was not agreeable to them) and represented him, in a petition to the King, as an unacceptable and unfit person, without assigning any reasons of that unfitness, or any grounds for their opinion of him.

The King, not satisfied with so general an exception against a person, who had already served him well in the same post, sent orders to his Privy Council, 15 December 1640, to cause a commission to be passed, appointing his Lordship and Sir William Parsons, L. J.; which being done, they were sworn 30 of that month; the King declaring to the committee, that he expected some particular objections before he altered his resolution. The agents set themselves to work for that purpose, and 22 December presented another petition, containing their exceptions, and desiring that some other person, against whom no objection had been offered, might be chosen. Their exceptions to his Lordship were, that when he was L. J. before, he had committed some people for selling unsealed tobacco; had been often a referree upon paper petitions; and that his son had married the Earl of Strafford's sister; which last exception Sir Richard Cox alledges, as the only cause of their discontent against him.

These matters were argued the next day before the King in Council; when he was as ill satisfied with their particular, as he was with their general exceptions; however, he told them, that he did not doubt but Lord Dillon would answer what had been objected against him; yet, to content his people, he would remove him; which was done in February following.

Being

Streamstown and Killinynen, professing the law, became an eminent Barrister; he was first made King's Council, after

Prime

Being by his enemies thus deprived of the government, the King, to balance that loss, was pleased by Privy Seal, 14 July 1641, to order a grant to be passed to him and his heirs of so many crown-lands, as should amount to 200l. English a year, according to the rents then paid into the Exchequer: But of this he was also deprived by the commencement of the rebellion soon after; which however was in some measure recovered by his son Carey, who 9 August 1661 obtained from K. Charles II. a grant of the lands of Lismortagh, &c. in the counties of Tipperary, Kildare and Louth.

In the year 1640, he was Captain of ninety-seven foot, and of sixty-three carbines; and the general rebellion breaking out 23 October 1641, he was one of the Privy Council, who that very day signed the proclamation, advertising of the discovery of the intended rebellion, and requiring his Majesty's good and loyal subjects in all parts of the kingdom to stand upon their guard, and betake themselves with all confidence and chearfulness, to their defence. In June 1642, he was made Captain of a troop of horse, to assist against the rebels, by the Earl of Ormond, against all opposition; being without exception capable of it, for his birth, religion, personal merit, and loss by the rebellion, (the family estate being in the power of the rebels, and his tenants destroying his stock of above 2500 sheep, and seven or eight score head of cattle; and when the Lord Dunsany demanded their reason for so doing, and desired them to forbear such courses, their answer was, they would not forbear; for though he was an Irishman, yet he was a Protestant, and they would take his goods again.) He served as a volunteer in all the expeditions under the Lord Ormond, from the beginning of the troubles, and expressed great forwardness to the free hazard of his life. On 1 August 1642, he was present in Parliament [1], but died at Oxmantown 27 of that month, and was buried 7 September in St. Patrick's Church.

His Lordship married three wives; to his first Margaret, daughter of David, Viscount Buttevant, by whom he had three sons, James, his successor; Lucas, who died childless; and David, who died an infant. To his second, the Lady Dorothy Hastings, younger daughter of George, the fourth Earl of Huntingdon, widow of Sir James Steuart (who was killed at Islington in a duel by Sir George Wharton) and by her he had an only son Henry, who died unmarried 21 April 1640, and was buried 23

in

[1] Lords Jour. I. 179.

Prime Serjeant, (in the reigns of James I. and Charles I.) was also a Privy Counsellor and of the Supreme Council at in Newtown, near Trim. His third wife was Anne, daughter of Sir William Stroud, of Stoake, in Somersetshire, Knt. and widow of Henry, Lord Folliott, of Ballyshannon, by whom he had one son Carey, who became the fifth Earl of Roscomon.

Sir James, 3 Earl.
Sir James Dillon, the third Earl was reclaimed, when young, (says Anthony à Wood) from the superstitions of the Romish church by Primate Usher, and sent by him into England, as a jewel of price, to be committed to the care and trust of Doctor George Hakewill; who finding him to be a young man of pregnant parts, placed him in Exeter College, under the tuition of Laurence Bodley, D. B. (nephew to the great Sir Thomas Bodley) in 1628; in which college continuing some years, he became an accomplished person. He was knighted in his father's life time; represented in 1639, the county of Westmeath in Parliament; and was as strenuous an opposer of the rebels in the county of Longford, as his father had been, on whose decease he changed his troop for that, which he had commanded, being part of the old army. On 17 November 1642[1], he took his seat in Parliament; and was a leading man in the House of Peers; was appointed 11 January 1642, one of the Commissioners to receive the propositions of the Irish confederate recusants concerning a peace; also, 26 December 1645, one of the committee of the Privy Council to take the examination of Edward Somerset, Earl of Glamorgan, about his treating of, and making a peace with the Irish; and in 1647, was one of the four hostages, sent by the Marquess of Ormond to the Parliament of England, to be surety for his performance of the articles agreed on, for the delivery to them of the city of Dublin and garrisons. For which, and his other services to K. Charles I. he was excepted (though dead) from pardon for life and estate, by Cromwell's act of parliament, 12 August 1652, for the settlement of Ireland. He married Elizabeth, third and youngest daughter of Sir William Wentworth, of Wentworth-Woodhouse, in the county of York, Bart. sister to Thomas, Earl of Strafford, L. L.; and dying at Limerick in October 1649, by a fall down a pair of stairs, left issue an only son

Wentworth, 4 Earl.
Wentworth, the fourth Earl of Roscomon, who was educated from his youth, in all kinds of polite learning; and was accounted one of the best English poets. By act of Parliament made in England, in 1660, he was restored to the estates of his ancestors, and became seized of several manors, impropriate tithes, lay-advowsons, &c. in the counties of Meath, Westmeath, King's, Mayo, Galway,

[1] Lords Jour. I. 187.

at Kilkenny. By his practice and employments, he acquired an ample estate in divers counties, which were it entire,

Galway, Sligo, Roscomon and Tipperary, of all which, in Easter term 1662, he suffered five several common recoveries to his own use for life, with power to raise 3000l. for portions of younger children, and 1000l. legacies; and after his death 1000l. a year to Francis his wife, with power of distress, remainder to the issue male of his body, and their heirs male respectively, by his said wife Frances, remainder to the heirs of his body, remainder to the use of his last will [1]. He took his seat in Parliament by proxy 10 July 1661 [2]; on 16 October following, he had a grant of the first troop of horse that should become void, pursuant to Privy Seal, 23 September preceding; was, by the interest of the Duke of York, made Captain of the Band of Gentlemen Pensioners, and afterwards Master of the Horse to the Duchess of York; both which places he quitted some time before his death. He married first, in April 1662, the Lady Frances Boyle, eldest daughter of Richard, Earl of Burlington and Cork, and widow of Colonel Francis Courtenay, by whom he had no issue; and secondly, 10 November 1674, Isabella, daughter of Matthew second son of Sir Matthew Boynton, of Barmston, in Yorkshire, Bart. but by her who remarried with Thomas Carter, of Robert's-town, in M ath, Esq [3] and died in September 1721; having also no surviving issue, and deceasing at his house near St. James's, 18 (or 20) January 1684, was buried in Westminster Abbey, having made his will 14 of that month, whereby he bequeathed all his personal estate, subject to the payment of his just debts, to his wife; and as touching the disposition of his lands, tenements, and hereditaments he devised the same to her and her heirs for ever, if he died without issue, and constituted his said wife sole executrix [4]. He was succeeded in his titles by his uncle

Carey, the fifth Earl of Roscomon, who was baptized 1 July 1627, and in the wars, unhappily begun in 1641, was a commander for K Charles I. after the restoration of whose son, and a Parliament being called in 1661, he was a Member thereof for the borough of Banagher. On 8 February 1660, he had the reversionary grant of a troop of horse, and 3 October 1691, was appointed Patent Master of the Mints [5], then to be re-established in Ireland, and worker of the same, during life, with the yearly salary of 500l. being also 13 November 1682, made Commissary General of the Horse; and 23 February 1684, sworn of the Privy-Council to K James II. from whom he had a pension, 1 January 1687, of 200l. a year; and was Colonel of a regiment of

Carey, 5 Earl.

---

[1] Lodge. [2] Lords Jour. I. 260. [3] See Leinster I. 104. n.
[4] Pre. Office and Lodge. [5] Rot. A 23°. Car. II. 3°. p. D. Memb. 27.

tire, would now yield 15,000l. a year; but in the general calamity and ufurpation of Cromwell, he loft thefe eftates, and

of foot, which he commanded 26 Auguft 1689 at the taking of Carrickfergus, and was appointed with the Earl of Drogheda, to raife men for the fervice of Ireland; for which he was attainted by K. James's Parliament, and had his eftate of 2118l. a year, and real. perfonal property fequeftered. Upon which he left the kingdom, and died in Chefter 25 November 1689.—With refpect to his eftate, he had been provided for by the acts of fettlement, and in confequence thereof, had two grants of lands; viz. 17 Auguft 1669, a grant of the fort of Bellamo in the counties of Galway and Rofcomon, which had been built by Cromwell. On 25 Auguft 1683, lands to the value of 427l. 18s. a year (part of 600l. a year in confideration of his many fervices and fufferings, were granted to him in the counties of Cork, Donegall, Mayo, Galway, Wicklow, Kildare, Meath, Weftmeath, Waterford, Tipperary, Fermanagh, Kerry, Dublin, Monaghan, Limerick, Wexford, Kilkenny, King's and Queen's Counties.—He married Catharine, daughter of John Werden, of Chefter, Efq. (by Catharine, daughter of Edward Dutton, grandfather to Sir Richard Dutton, Governor of Barbadoes) and fifter to Major-General Robert Werden, Groom of the Bedchamber to the Duke of York, and Comptroller of his Houfhold, when King, and by her (who died 24 February 1683, and was buried the 26 within the Chancel-Rails of St. Michan's Church) had two fons and two daughters, viz. a fon, who died young; Robert, his fucceffor; Lady Catharine, married in 1672 to Hugh, the fecond Earl of Mount-Alexander, and dying 26 January 1674, was buried the next day at St. Michan's; and Lady Anne, married 25 March 1675, to Sir Thomas Nugent of Taghmon, Bart. whofe widow fhe died in November 1726, and was buried the 18 at St Bride's, Dublin.

Robert, 6 Earl.
Robert, the fixth Earl of Rofcomon, was left an infant of very tender years in England, at his father's death, and coming into Ireland in the year 1700, fat firft in Parliament 21 September 1703 [1]. He married Margaret, daughter of Sir Thomas Putt, of Comb, in Devonfhire, Bart. and dying 14 May 1715, was interred the 16 at St. Bride's, having had iffue three fons and one daughter, viz. Robert and James, fucceffive Earls of Rofcomon; Thomas, born in Auguft 1706, who died young; and Lady Catharine, who died unmarried.

Robert, 7 Earl.
Robert, the feventh Earl, took his feat in the Houfe of Peers, 11 November 1717 [2]; was Cornet of a troop of horfe on this eftablifhment; married in Auguft 1719, Angel, daughter of Charles Ingoldfby,

[1] Lords Jour. II. 1.   [2] Idem. 572.

DILLON, Viscount DILLON.

and was transplanted to Stroakstown in county of Roscomon, the estate of Robert, son of Henry Dillon, then sequestered by the usurping powers; which estate, of considerable yearly value, was sold by this John's descendant to Captain Nicholas Mahon (whose family are denominated, and are now possessed of Stroakstown); Captain Patrick Plunket, and others. He married Mary or Margaret, daughter of Edmund Malone, of Ballynahown, in Westmeath, Esq. and by her had two sons and two daughters, viz. Edmund, his heir; Gerald, who succeeded his brother; Rose, (who married first to Captain Robert Dillon, then heir apparent to Sir Lucas Dillon, of Lough-Glyn, ancestor to the present Viscount, secondly to Major-General O'Farrell, and died in 1681); and Ellice, first to Captain Anthony Brabazon, of Ballynasloe, in county of Roscomon, and secondly to Theobald Dillon, of Clontowart in same county, son of the said Sir Lucas.—Edmund, the eldest son, married a daughter of Sir Richard Blake, of Ardfry, in county of Galway, Knt. Privy Counsellor to K. Charles I. and one of the Supreme Council of Kilkenny, by whom having only one daughter, who became the wife of Edmund Malone, of Ballynahown, Esq. his brother Gerald succeeded; he married first Mary, daughter of Thomas Dillon, Esq. of the family of Clonbrock, and secondly Ellice, daughter of John Aylmer, of Ballykenan, in Westmeath, Esq. by her who died 28 September 1684, he had no issue, but by his first wife had Peter, his heir; and two daughters,

Ingoldsby, of Clondiralagh in the county of Clare, Esq. (who died first September 1704) younger son to Sir Henry Ingoldsby of Beggstown in the county of Meath, Bart. and brother to Sir William, and dying without issue 9 January 1721, was buried at St. Bride's, being succeeded by his brother

James, the eighth and last Earl of Roscomon, born in 1702, who 29 August 1723, sat first in Parliament[1], and had a pension of 300l. a year, but dying unmarried 20 August 1746, at Harold's Cross, Dublin; he was interred at St. Bride's Church, Dublin. On the decease of this Nobleman, the titles continued to lie dormant, and in the year 1776, the only person who could have claimed, died in reduced circumstances at Knockrany, in county of Roscomon [2], consequently the titles being extinct, have been expunged from the list of the House of Peers.

James, 8 Earl.

[1] Lords Jour. II 737.   [2] Information of Lord Viscount Dillon.

daughters, the elder of whom married—O'Kelly, of Mullaghmore; and the younger, to Captain Patrick Mapholder.—Peter, who succeeded, married a daughter of Captain Patrick Everard, (by a daughter of — Delamere, Esq. and had issue John, his heir; Theobald, of Mount-Alba, or Mount-Dillon, Barrister at Law, who married and resided in England; and a daughter Mary, married first to George Fitz-Gerald, of Mohenny, Esq. and secondly to John Dillon, of Low-Baskin, as hereafter.—John, the eldest son of Killinynen and Randalstown, married in January 1732, Theresa, third daughter of Thomas Plunket, of Tutrath in county of Meath, Esq. and widow of Colonel Christopher Everard, of Randalstown aforesaid, in county of Meath, and by her had issue. EDWARD, (or Christopher) had settled on him the castle, town and lands of MOYVANNANE, in county of Roscomon, and marrying Mary, daughter of Christopher Jones, of Lisnegraghan, in the county of Roscomon, Esq. who died there 13 February 1639, had issue four sons, viz. John, in Holy Orders; Christopher; Gerald, also in Holy Orders; and Richard, who abandoned his country, having been concerned in the death of Pierce Dillon, Esq.—Christopher the second son succeeded, his elder brother who by becoming a Priest, became *civiliter mortuus*; he married Sabina, daughter of Redmond Bourke, of Tyaquin, in county of Galway, Esq and had issue Colonel Edward Dillon; and a daughter who married the heir apparent to John Fitz-Gerald, of Mohony, in county of Mayo, Esq. GERALD, a Priest. JAMES, who had the castle and town of Lisnegree, allotted to him, with their demesnes; he married a daughter of ——— Daly, of Lisclooney, in the King's county, by whom he was father of Gerald, who by the daughter of — O'Brennan, left James, of Lisnegree, who married a daughter of Robert Dillon, of Cannenistan (by his wife Margaret, daughter of Theobald, the first Viscount Dillon) and had issue eight sons, many of whom served in the army, with distinguished characters, whereof Robert, married Honora, daughter of Theobald Dillon, Esq (by his wife Sarah, daughter of the Viscount Mayo's family) and sister to Lucas, the sixth Viscount Dillon, and by her had issue James, his heir. THOMAS, who also had a dividend of the estate, *the custom of Gavelkind* still prevailing; he married a daughter of ——— Nangle of Kildalkin, by whom he had William, who died young; Thomas;

Thomas; and John, in Holy Orders.—The said Thomas, was father of Henry, who settled in county of Meath, and had issue Henry, who married the daughter of ——— Leonard, Esq. JOHN (or Henry) who married a daughter of O'Higgin of Gorteen, in the King's County, and his descendant, John, married Mary, daughter of Edmund Malone, of Ballynahown, Esq. and had Francis his heir, and several other sons, some of whom were religious, and other officers in the army of France, but this branch is extinct.—NICHOLAS and EDMUND were ecclesiastics.—Maurice Dillon, eldest son of John, of Low-Baskin, who succeeded to that estate, married the daughter of ——— Mac-Auley, (or Mc. Gauly) and had issue two sons, viz. Richard, his heir; Edmund, in Holy Orders; and a daughter who became a Nun.—Richard, who succeeded, married a daughter of ——— Malone, of Ballynahown, and had issue a son James; and one daughter Jane, who married first O'Ferrall Bane, of Moate, county of Longford; and secondly Maurice, fourth and youngest son of Gerald Dillon, possessor of Drumrany, until 1649, or 1652.—James, of Low-Baskin, married Rose, daughter of the said Gerald Dillon, of Drumrany, by whom he had John, his heir; and a daughter Ellice, married to ——— Browne, of Ballyrankin, Esq. whose great estate was lost during the usurpation of Cromwell, as were Dillon's Country and territories.—John, the only son of his father, was the last possessor of Low-Baskin; he married Mary, daughter of John O'Carroll, and had issue Hubert, his heir; Margaret, (who married William Davys, Esq. lineally descended from Sir John Davys, Knight-Marshal of Conaught and Munster, and Receiver-General of all the Crown Revenues in those provinces in the reign of Q. Elizabeth); and other children;—The said Hubert was father of John Dillon, living at Carramore, in county of Mayo, about the year 1768, and married to Mary, daughter of Peter Dillon, of Killinynen, as before observed.

Edmund, second son of Sir Maurice, of Drumrany, by his second marriage, had assigned to him the castle and town of Kilcornane, where he became seated, and was possessed of a considerable estate about the river Inny; he married Anne, daughter of William Pettyt, styled Baron of Mullingar, and had two daughters, one of whom became a Nun; the other married O'Ferrall, Lord of Callow, in Annaly; and three sons, viz. William, who died unmarried;

ried; Edmund, heir to his father; and James, in Holy Orders.—The said Edmund, was father of Edmund, living in 1611, who married Catharine, daughter of Thomas Dillon, of Killenfaghny, Esq. and sister to Theobald, the first Viscount Dillon, by her he had issue a son Robert and two daughters, viz. Rose, married to —— Dillon; and Mary, to —— Dalton, of Nocoval.—Robert, the heir, married Ellice, daughter of William Tuite, of Monilea, Esq. (by his second wife, a daughter of Sir Edward Tuite, of Tuitestown) and step-daughter to the said Lord Dillon, by whom he had Walter, his heir, and other children; which Walter, married Ellice, daughter of —— Hope, of Lisdistown and Hopestown, and had two sons, Richard, (married to a daughter of —— Brabazon, and had Mary, who married —— O'Reily); and Robert, who married a daughter of —— Luther, and had Walter; Theobald; and other children, of whom Theobald, was an eminent merchant in Dublin, died 18 May 1736, and having married a daughter of —— White, had issue several sons and daughters, viz. Robert, (of London, merchant, who married in November 1745, a daughter of —— Dickinson, of Woolton, in Lancashire, with a fortune of 10,000l. and died of an apoplexy, at Bourdeaux in January 1764); Thomas (Merchant and Banker of Dublin, who 23 April 1737, married a daughter of —— Hussey, Esq. and died in France in November 1764); Michael, (who married a daughter of —— Comerford, merchant of Cork, and had issue); Stephen, of London, merchant; Theobald, (who carried on an extensive trade in Rotterdam); daughter Anne (married Ambrose Ferrall, of Dublin, Esq. a very eminent brewer, who died 11 February 1741-2, leaving issue by his wife, who many years survived him, several children, of whom Richard, the eldest son, became a partner in his uncle Dillon's bank, and 19 April 1751, married a daughter of James Moore, of Ballyna, county of Kildare, Esq. and hath several children; and Catharine, the only daughter, married Patrick Latin, of Morristown-Latin, in county of Kildare, Esq. and hath several children); Mary, the second daughter of Theobald Dillon, married 2 January 1747, Captain Dennis Ferrall, alias Kelly, brother to John Kelly, of Cloonlyon, county of Galway, Esq.; and the third daughter was a Nun.

(3) Gortmore, and Highbaskin.

Richard Dillon, (third and youngest son of Sir Maurice, of Drumrany, by his second wife) had the castle, town, and lands

DILLON, Viscount DILLON.

lands of Gortmore and High-Baſkin, aſſigned to him, with divers others, in and about Ballymahon, in county of Longford, in which eſtates he was ſucceeded by his ſon Maurice, who marrying a daughter of Connell O'Farrell, of Tenelick, county of Longford, Eſq. had ſeveral children ; the eldeſt whereof Pierce, married Cicely, daughter of Garret Dillon, of Portlick, Eſq. and had Garret and Hugh, both in the army, the elder of whom married a daughter of Judge Jones, and had a ſon Pierce ; and a daughter who married Redmond Dillon, of Balleneghloghduff, ſon of Pierce, by his wife Margery, whoſe marriage articles bear date 9 and 10 May 1666.—Pierce, the ſon, was a Captain in General Dillon's regiment, and was killed in France; by his death without iſſue, this branch of the family became extinct, and the eſtates reverted to the Baron of Drumrany, to treat of whom we ſhall now proceed.

Thomas, the eldeſt ſon of Sir Maurice Dillon, of Drumrany by his firſt wife, ſucceeded to the eſtate ; he married Jane, daughter of Sir Robert Dillon, Attorney General to K. Henry VIII. and anceſtor to the Earls of Roſcomon; by this lady he had a ſon Edmund [*], Lord of Drumrany, who married

Thomas, of Drumrany.

Edmund.

---

[*] This deſcent is extracted from Mr. Lodge's Collections, (where we find that this particular branch of Drumrany, is totally extinct, or fallen to decay) appearing to be authentic, we inſert it by way of note.

Which Edmund, Lord of Drumrany, married to his firſt wife, as in text, and by her had iſſue ſix ſons and two daughters ; he married ſecondly, as in text, but the iſſue of the firſt wife were as follows : Maurice, a Capuchin Friar ; Thomas, a Franciſcan Friar ; Gerald, who ſucceeded at Drumrany ; Col. Robert, who died abroad unmarried ; John, (an eminent Lawyer, who acquired by his profeſſion, a conſiderable eſtate, and reſided at Cappagh, near Dublin, where he was ſucceeded by his ſon Sir Lucas, who was appointed a Commiſſioner 26 April 1587, by Q. Elizabeth, to ſettle the forfeitures in the province of Munſter, and to make books to the undertakers of ſaid province, which ſhould be a ſufficient warrant to the Chancellor, to paſs patents, accordingly'. He acquired ſo great an eſtate in addition to his father's, that his deſcendant's claim thereof (on the reſtoration of K. Charles II. although he was a minor during the war of 1641,) to the year 1652, when Cromwell ſettled the kingdom, was not then heard, it being adjudged too great an eſtate for a ſubject to be decreed to ; he being entitled to a great part of the city and county of Dublin, beſides Caſtle Dillon, in county of Armagh, with their appurtenances ; and divers manors and hereditaments in the North, and in the provinces of Munſter and Leinſter, as by the ſaid claims of record may be ſeen, but this branch of the family is now extinct) ; Lucas, an officer in foreign ſervice, who left no iſſue ; daughter Jane, married to ―――― Plunket, of Rathmore, in county of Meath ; and Mary, to ―――― Darcy, of Platten, in ſame county.—Gerald, the third ſon of Thomas, owing to the elder brothers taking orders, ſucceeded at Drumrany, married

' Cox, I. 395.

married first Anne, daughter of William Pettyt, Baron of Mullingar, and secondly, a daughter of Sir Christopher Plunket,

married the daughter of Bryan O'Conor Offaley, and by her had James, an Ecclesiastic; Thomas; Gerald (who settled in county of Cork, and marrying the daughter of Mac-Carthy More, was ancestor to Sir Francis Dillon, Knt.); daughter Bridget, became a Nun; and Mary, married Fitz-Gerald, of Newcastle.—THOMAS, second son and successor to his father, was knighted, and marrying Rose, eldest daughter of Thomas Dillon, Esq. and sister to Theobald, the first Viscount Dillon, had issue three sons, viz. Henry, who being sent into France, became there a Friar; Gerald; and James, who with his son Gerald, settled in Mayo, whose son Captain James Dillon, during the war in 1641, married the Lady Bingham, of Castlebar. The estate of this branch is lost, and the family in the male line, extinct.—GERALD, who succeeded at Drumrany, married Ismay, daughter of William Tuite, of Monilea (by a daughter of Sir Edward Tuite of Tuitestown) half sister to Sir Christopher and Sir Lucas, sons of Theobald, first Viscount Dillon, and by her had two daughters, Rose, a Nun, Margaret, married to ——— Reynolds, then chief of his name, in county of Leitrim; and six sons, viz. William, a Dominican Friar; James, heir to his father; Henry; and Thomas, whose lines are extinct; Gerald, an Ecclesiastic; and Maurice, who married Jane, daughter of Robert Dillon, of Low-Baskin, by her he had a numerous issue, whereof Captain Robert, and his son a Lieut. Col. died in foreign service; Richard, who left posterity, but they are extinct; and Maurice, who married the daughter of O'Kelly, and left Richard, of Curry-Drumrany, who married a daughter of Captain Molloy, and by her had Maurice; Gerald, and other children.—JAMES, of Drumrany, second son of Gerald, was bred to the study of the law, represented the county of Roscomon, in K. Charles I. Parliament, and was Captain of an independent troop, but was killed in 1649 or 1650, in his 34 year. He married Frances, youngest daughter of William Davis, Esq. son of Sr John, of county of Salop, Knight-Marshal of Conaught, Elchester and Receiver General of that province; and by her had Gerald, who died young in France, Christopher, living in the reign of K. Charles II. who became a Franciscan friar, and died in Rome; William, who lived to a great age, and died unmarried; and Richard:—Which RICHARD, succeeded, and in 1652, his mother obtained from Cromwell's commissioners (in lieu of her dower) to her, and her heirs male, 3572 acres, part of her deceased husband's estate in the county of Roscomon, as transplantation lands; but by his death, during the minority and absence of her two elder sons, and the indolence of William, her third son, no care was taken of the transplanted estate, and the whole of which (save a small pittance assigned by her to the said Richard) was lost. The said Richard married to his first wife, when under age, Rose, a daughter of ——— Dillon, of Dunimoney, and by her had William (a Dominican Friar, who after resided in London by the name of Dominick, and although civiliter mortuus, was Lord Baron of Drumrany, by the said ancient tenure Cap. per Baroniam, this branch of the family never suffering any attainder); Christopher, also an Ecclesiastic; and James Dillon, a Colonel in the army of James II. in whose service he lost his life. The said Richard, married secondly Margaret, daughter of ——— O'Molloy, of Ughterheere (by Mary his wife, daughter of Hubert Bourke) and by her had three surviving sons, viz. Gerald; Thomas, who married Mabel Dillor, widow of Alexander Robinson, Esq. but left no issue; and William, who married a daughter of said Alexander Robinson, and by her who re-married with ——— Butler, Esq. had an only son Thomas.—GERALD, Dillon, Esq. eldest son of Richard by his second wife, studied the law in the Inns of Court,

was

Plunket, Knt. by the latter of whom he had issue one son Gerald, his heir, who 12 September 1532, was made Prothonotary and Custos Brevium, of the Court of Common Pleas. On his marriage with Esina, daughter of Sir Edward Tuite, of Tuitestown, Knt. his father settled on him the lands of Dunimoney, whereof he was denominated, and had issue three sons, and two daughters, Bridget, a Nun; and Catharine, married to Sir Christopher Dalton, Knt. The sons were

Gerald, of Drumraay.

Robert, who married the daughter of O'Farrell, of Longford, by whom he had several sons, who continued to enjoy the possessions and most of the seigniory of Dunimoney, until the usurpation of Cromwell; but the bulk of the estate gavelled amongst the descendants until the reign of James II. when they followed the fortunes of that King, and attended him to France.

(1)

James, ancestor to the Viscount Dillon, and
William.

(2)
(3)

James, second son of Gerald of Dunimony, had assigned to him, as his share of the inheritance, Ballanakill, Tully, the castle and town of Lisdasiane, part of Athlone and Kilkenny-West, being then market and trading towns; and upon the dissolution of religious houses in the reign of Henry VIII he obtained a temporary lease, of divers Monasteries, Convents, and Abbies, built and endowed by his ancestors, in Athlone, Kilkenny-West, Ardnecrane, Abbey-Shruel, Holy-Island, &c. in Dillon's Country, and the respective lands thereunto belonging, whereupon, and by his protecting and continuing divers of the clergy, in the said abbies and abbey-lands, he was nicknamed *the Prior*, but Sir Lucas Dillon, Attorney-General to Q. Elizabeth, got a perpetual grant of the said abbey-lands, with all

James.

---

was seated at Dillon's Grove, in county of Roscomon, and married first Catharine, daughter of James Nugent, of Dysert, in Westmeath, Esq by whom having no surviving issue, he married secondly Honora, daughter of Pierce Aylward, of Ballynegar (a lineal descendant of Sir John and Sir Pierce of Passage and Fatlick, near Waterford, to whom K. Henry II. granted a large estate, with the duties and Royalties of Passage) by his wife Elizabeth, daughter of Christopher French, of Tyrone, Esq —He was living after 1743, and by her who died in that year, had Richard; Aylward; Mary; and Margaret.

This family bore for their coat armour pearl, a Lion rampant, ruby, holding in his dexter paw, a ducal coronet supported by a fess, saphire, all within a bordure, ermine; crest, a demi Lion rampant, ruby, issuing out of a ducal coronet, holding in his dexter paw, a like coronet.

all their appurtenances and hereditaments.—The said James married a daughter of Sir Chriftopher Dalton, Knt. of Dalton's Country, by whom he had Thomas, his heir; John and George, both Ecclefiaftics; daughter Rofe, a Nun; and Catharine, married to James Fitz-Gerald, Efq.

Thomas, Thomas, the eldeft fon, fettled in Dillon's Country, married Margery, daughter of Chriftopher Dillon, of Kilmore, by whom he had three daughters, and five fons, viz. Rofe, married to Thomas Dillon, fon and fucceffor to Gerald, of Drumrany; Catharine, to Edmund Fitz-Edmund Dillon, of Kilcornane; and Bridget, to ——— Dalton, of Moyvannane. The fons were,

(1) Gerald, who married Cicely, daughter of ——— Dillon, of High-Bafkin, and had iffue two daughters, viz. Margery, (married to a defcendant of Edward Dillon, the firft poffeffor of Balleneghloghgduff, to whom he gave the caftle and town of Lifsdaffane); and Jeane, to ——— Dillon, of Bonnoiver, whofe defcendants acquired by this marriage, part of the caftle, town, and lands of Tulla, with other poffeffions, and their pofterity exifted in 1768.

(2) Edmund, who fettled in the caftle of Ardnegragh, in county of Weftmeath, which he purchafed from Edward Dillon; he married a daughter of O'Farrell, Lord of Callow, and had iffue feveral fons, who were diftinguifhed in the army, church, and ftate. The elder branch whereof loft their eftates in the troubles of 1641, and are now extinct, but Bartholomew Dillon, a junior defcendant of the said Edmund, being a Judge itinerant of Conaught, in the reigns of K. James and K. Charles I. acquired a large eftate in the county of Mayo, and fettled in Ballacowla, in confequence however of Cromwell's fettlement, he was deprived of two-thirds of his acquired property. He married Mary, daughter of O'Kelly, and by her had Edmund, his heir; Efma, married to ——— Crofton, of Mohill, in county of Leitrim; and a younger daughter, who married Garrett Dillon, of Mayo, a defcendant of the Houfe of Drumrany.—Edmund Dillon, Efq. fettled at Lifduffe, in county of Mayo, where he was living in 1692; he married a fifter of Counfellor Richard Dillon, of the family of Clonbrock, and had two daughters, one of whom was married to Walter Jordan, of Ifland, Efq. the other to Captain Taaffe; and feveral fons, whereof only Lucas the heir, and

and Theobald, left issue. Theobald Dillon, the younger son, of Lisduffe, Gent. married 22 February, 1705, Alice, one of the daughters of Francis Slingesby, of Ballyglasse, in Galway, Esq. Lucas, the eldest son, settled at Holywell, in county of Mayo, married Juliana, daughter of Captain Josias Browne, of the *Neale* family, and had issue five daughters, and five sons, viz. Barbara, the eldest, married first to John Dillon, of Mannin, Esq. and secondly, to Christopher Bellew of Mount-Bellew, Esq.; the second, married George Hynde, of Castle-Michael, Gent.; the third and fifth, became nuns; and the fourth died unmarried: of the sons, Edmund succeeded; Josias married Mary, youngest sister, and coheir to Captain Gerald Dillon, of Mannin, and in her right inherited part of his estate; Joseph, the third, seated at Kilkelly in Mayo; the fourth became a physician; and the fifth an ecclesiastic. Edmund, the eldest son, of Holywell, married first, a daughter of Martin Blake, of Moyen, by whom having no issue, he married secondly, a daughter of John Lyster, of Corkhill in Roscomon, Esq. and had a numerous issue *.

Theobald, advanced to the Peerage. (3)

Garret, who was Captain of an independent company in (4) the reign of Q. Elizabeth, and acquired from a junior Portlick. descendant of Drumrany, the castle and town of Portlick, with sundry islands in the Shannon and Loughreagh, and a considerable estate in the county of Mayo; where he married Margaret, daughter of Mac-Costello, anciently called Nangle, Baron of Costello, so styled from the country of that name. By her he had two sons, Garret his heir, and Gerald, who settled at Ferrore, in Mayo, and married

---

* Of the other sons of Edmund Dillon of Ardnegragh, Edmund married Anne, daughter of William, the Great O'Mulloy, of Ughterheere, alias O'Mulloy's-Hall, alias Coote-Hall, Governor, and Knight of the shire for the county of Roscomon, and widow of Charles O'Conor, of Ballynegare, Esq. son to Sir Hugh O'Conor, of Ballintobber, Knt. but by her having no issue, James his brother, the younger son of Ardnegragh, became possessed of his estate, and marrying a daughter of ———— Hope, of Hopetown, had issue Dominick Dillon, who settled at Bells, part of his said uncle Edmund's estate, in county of Roscomon, he married Elma, daughter of Richard Dillon of the house of Clonbrock, and had two sons, viz. James, an eminent Lawyer, who died unmarried; Edmund also died unmarried; and three daughters, who thence became coheirs, and were Margaret, married to Colonel Thomas Daly, of Killeagh, county of Westmeath, by whom she was mother of James Daly of same place, Esq.; Clara, to John French, of the French-park family; and Alice, first to George Hynde, Gent, and secondly, to Major Edward Devenish, Governor of Courtray in Flanders. (Lodge.) •

married a daughter of George Crofton of Moate, in county of Roscomon, by whom he had three sons; Theobald (who married Marcella, daughter of George Browne of the Neale, and was father of Gerald, Recorder of Dublin, and King's Council; and 15 February 1686-7, Prime Serjeant to K. James II. whom he followed into France, and became a Colonel in that service; he married first the widow of Sir Edward Crofton of Moate, Bart. Secondly, Mary, younger daughter of George, Viscount Strabane, by the latter of whom he had a numerous issue, and Captain Theobald his eldest son, married first, Mary, daughter of Counsellor Richard Malone, by whom he had two daughters; and by his second wife, the daughter of Counsellor Read, of Dunboyne, and grand niece to Sir Richard Nugent of Dysert, Bart. he had two sons); Thomas (father of Captain Lucas Dillon, who married a daughter of ———— Kirwan, and had Theobald, whose issue male, were in remainder to Captain Theobald Dillon, as observed in another place); and Christopher, Prior of the abbey of Ballehaunes, and Provincial of the Augustins; he was interred in said abbey. Garret, eldest son of Garret, succeeded at Portlick, and marrying Mary, daughter of his cousin Hubert Dillon, of Streamstown and Killynynen, had issue Edmund his heir; Captain Gerald, who died a Dominican Friar; and several daughters. Edmund married Honora, daughter of Richard Bourke of Terlagh, Esq. and had issue Garret; John, who died unmarried; and James, who settled at Rathane, county of Mayo; married Honora, sister to Lucas the sixth Viscount Dillon, and widow of Robert Dillon of Lisnegree, Esq.; by this Lady he left male issue, who continued the eldest branch of Portlick; and his descendant, Edmond of Rathmore, married Frances, second daughter of John Dillon of Liffiane, who died in January 1692.—Garret Dillon, the eldest son, married a daughter of Sir Henry Talbot, of Mount Talbot, Knt. by whom he had Captain Gerald Dillon, of Mannin, county of Mayo; and one daughter, Margaret, married to William Kelly of Turrach, in county of Roscomon, Esq;—The said Gerald of Mannin, 17 April 1692, married Ellice, eldest daughter of John Dillon of Liffiane, in county of Mayo, Gent. and dying in 1720, had issue by her, who survived him, two sons and three daughters, viz. Edmund, born in 1696, who died unmarried; John, (who in February 1721, married Barbara, eldest daughter of

Lucas

Lucas Dillon of Holywell, in county of Mayo, Gent. and dying without issue 22 April 1731, his sisters became coheirs, and were Frances, married to James Betagh of Drimhill, in county of Galway; Margaret, to Felix Mac-Donnell of Killeigh, in county of Mayo; and Mary, to Josias Dillon, Gent as before observed.

James, fifth and youngest son of Thomas, was father of (s) James, who lived in the reign of K. Charles I. and was seated at Carrownegarry, in county of Roscomon; he engaged in the rebellion of 1641, and from this branch descended the families of Ballynakill, Tully, Portmore, Rathmoyle, Cloontowart, &c. with their cadets.

We return now to Sir Theobald Dillon of Costello-Gallen, county of Mayo, Knight, the third son of Thomas Dillon, son of James, nicknamed *the prior*, grandson of Gerald of Dunimoney, who was the son of Edmond, Lord of Drumrany by his second wife.

Sir Theobald,
1
Viscount.

Which Theobald, 25 March 1582, was appointed by patent, General Collector and Receiver of all and singular the Composition Money, within the provinces of Conaught and Thomond[1]; which employment was renewed to him by K. James, 20 August, 1 of his reign[2]. In the following year he surrendered the same, and in consideration of his assured trust and fidelity, and in regard of his divers and sundry services, the King re-granted and confirmed to him, 27 June 1604, not only the said office of Collector and Receiver General of the Composition Money, but also that of General Cessor and Collector of all and singular the several counties of Galway, Mayo, Sligo, Leitrim, Roscomon, and Clare, alias Thomond[3].—He commanded an independent troop in Q. Elizabeth's reign, and in 1559, received the honour of Knighthood in the field of battle; and his Majesty K. James I. having by the faithful service of many years, a full confession of his fidelity and merit, was pleased to advance him to the Peerage of Ireland, by creating him Viscount Dillon of Costello-Gallen in the kingdom of Ireland, by letters patent* bearing date at Westminster, 16 March 1621-2, entailing the honour on his heirs male, with

* The preamble. Sciatis quod Nos generis ac Virtutum Claritatem, ac erga Nos et Coronam nostram Constantiam et summam Fidelitatem dilecti et fidelis Nostri, Tibbotti Dillon de Costello-Gallin in Comitatu nostro Mayo in Regno Nostro Hibernia, Militis intuentes; Necnon ipsius Tibbotti in a. mis et Rebus Bellicis eximiam et spectatissimam Fortitudinem pariter et prudentiam,

[1] Rolls Off. [2] Idem. [3] Idem.

with the creation fee of 13l. 6s. 8d. out of the great and small cuftoms of the port of Dublin. He fat as a peer in Parliament, and died, as by Inquifition, 15 March 1624* at fo advanced an age, fays the pedigree, that at one time he had the fatisfaction of feeing above an hundred of his defcendants,

tiam, ac Gratiffima et ödiffema fervitia tam Nobis quam præchariffimæ nuper forori noftræ Dominæ Elizabethæ nuper Reginæ Angliæ in prædicto Regno noftro Hiberniæ, fumma cum laude preftita intime Confiderantes. Quorum omnium quamplurima non minus ardua et difficilia quam præclara in Guerris Hibernicis ad diuternam ipfius Tibbotti Gloriam extant Monumenta Volentefque proinde Ipfius Virtutes condignis Honorum Radiis compenfari, de Gratia noftra Speciali. (Rot. Pat. Canc. A°. 19°. Jac. I. 4ª. p. f. R. 14.)

* His Lordship's eftates in the counties of Mayo, Sligo, Galway, Rofcomon, and the province of Leinfter, were very confiderable. 26 June 1604, he had a grant of a weekly Monday market at Kilkenny-Weft, in Dillons Country, and county of Weftmeath, and of two annual fairs there, to be held on Whitfon Monday, and 13 Auguft, paying yearly for the fame 20 fhillings Irifh. The King alfo, in confideration of the fine of 40 marcs Irifh, did by patent, 19 July 1608, 6 of his reign, regrant, fell, and confirm to him, his heirs and affignes for ever, the entire manor, caftle, or ftone-fort and town of Killenfaghny, alias Killenfaghe, in the county of Weftmeath, with their appurtenances, and divers cartrons of land in the faid county; whereof one might defcend to him in right of inheritance, and the other might belong to him in right of his own purchafe; alfo the caftle or fort, town and lands of Ballynckilly, with their appurtenances, and divers cartrons of land, members of the faid caftle, the carrucate of Kilmacarron, containing two cartrons of Land, with many other cartrons in the faid county; the manor, caftle, town and lands of Glas-Kerne; the caftle and town of Ballyneferagh; the manor, caftle, and lands of Portlicke; the caftle, town, and lands of Ballymullon, alias Ballywolan, Roberiftown, &c. in the faid county of Weftmeath, the towns and lands of Ballymacmorchy, Clownavy, Twolaghe, Tawnaghenamrifoge, Coilloimaye, Skye, and Ballynedin; the manor, caftle, town and lands of Balbigiblane; with many other lands and hereditaments in the county of Rofcomon; the manor, caftle, and town of Caftlemore; the caftle and lands of Kilcolman; the caftles, towns, and lands of Binfadda, Ballindowe, Monyne, Illanmacgillevallye, Bealanagare, Beakan, Anagh, and Belaville; the towns of Erigg, Clonemore, and Ballyndingan; the manor, caftle, and town of Ballylahane; the caftle and town of Rathalvine, with divers other lands, rents, and hereditaments in the county of Mayo, to hold all the premiffes, by the twentieth part of a Knight's fee; (except the caftle, town, and lands of Ballymullan and Robertftown, with their appurtenances, which were to be held by Fealty, only, as of the caftle of Dublin,) with all privileges and jurifdictions, ufually granted to manors: a weekly Monday market at Kilkenny-Weft, and a yearly fair every 1 of Auguft, paying to the crown for the faid market and fair, the annual rent of 6s. 8d.

The following inquifition, taken at Charleftown in county of Rofcomon, 19 September 1623, finds that Theobald (the firft) Vifcount Dillon of Coftello-Gallen, was feized in fee of the manor, caftle, and town-land of Gally, containing three quarters, three cartrons, and half a cartron of land in faid county, viz. the quarter of Carrowancaftian; the quarter of Carrowdriftngh; the quarter of Liffechenny; the half quarter called Leggnemuky; the cartron of Cregan, and the half of a cartron; parcel of the half quarter of Cruit in Portevryn; all which premiffes were held from the King, as of the

caftle

DILLON, Viscount DILLON.

descendants, in his house of Killenfaghny. He married Eleanora, daughter of Sir Edward Tuite of Tuitestown, in Westmeath, Knight, and widow of William Tuite of Monilea,

castle of Dublin, by Knight's service.—Inquisition taken at Ballymore in county of Westmeath, 10 September 1615, finds that the said Lord Theobald was seized in fee of the following lands, &c. in the county of Westmeath, viz. the manor, castle, town and land of Killenfaghny, alias Killenfeagh, in said county, containing six cartrons of land, viz. Lackan, Clounedonnell, Annyclogla, Aghimcolle, Aghoegreny, and Agha riaghly; also the town-land of Tobberclare, containing a carucate, viz. the half cartron of Firaghmore, the cartron of Lismiskil, and Coghlea; also the castle and town-land of Ballynekilli, containing seven cartrons and an half, viz. Knockan, Clonnekahill, alias Glownekahill, Aghoe-Connorfyna, the half cartrons of Leighgneynlogh, alias Leighgnawocglagh, and of Aghreagh, alias Carraghreagh, and two cartrons in Lilduffe; also the half carucate of Kilmackcarron, viz. the cartrons of Lissintcome and of Parke; the half carucate of Tallaghan with a water-mill; half a cartron of Cartrookeyle; the island of Inshingyn in Loghree, in this county, containing one cartron; half of the island of Inshmore in said lough, containing fifteen acres, with a water-mill called Mullinglassan; also the castle and town-land of Glaiscran, containing two carucates; the castle and town-land of Ballynesscarragh and Ballybroghton, containing a cartron of land. An annual rent arising out of the lands of James Dillon Fitz-Richard, in Walterstowne. The said Lord Theobald died, seized of the premisses, 15 March 1614; and Lucas, now Lord Dillon, grandson and heir, being the son and heir of Sir Christopher Dillon, son and heir of the said Lord Theobald, was of the age of 14 years and 6 months, at the decease of his grandfather.——The said Lord was also possessed of the following lands, viz.

In Dinoragh, the quarters of Dromackoe, Clonaghmore, and Carrownecrosse; a quarter, and a third of a quarter called Treenarkilly in the townland of Kiltigeloghan; two triens, or two third parts of land, called TrienFlonghene, and Trien-Conmellente; the quarters of Calveaghe, Falleartcnon, Follen, Cloonefyn, Gawell, Carrowleggagh, the half quarter of Clooncoole; the quarter of Goorteloghan, the half quarter of Cloonemyne; the quarters of Lorge, Gortevoodegane, and Barnechange; the half quarter of Kiltycannon, the town-land of Littackry, containing four quarters, viz. Glanchaliry, Carrowbegg, Carrowhanrane, and Sonvylolan; also the quarters of Carrena, Gowlan, Carrowlinebrocke, Carrowbackcoyle, Carrnoecloghy, Carrowanmagheryarde, Carrowscolty, Carrolaggalenny, Gortleoman, Ballyan, Carrower, and Koylmore; also the town-land of Behy, containing four quarters, viz. Behed, Cloonegaronagh, Kilbragan, and Crossard; also the two quarters of Breckloone, the quarters of Gortenegaawe and Broe; also the castle and town-land of Gillenally, containing four quarters, viz. Skahum, Mirenihily, Reaskagh and Largaboy; also the quarters of Killogge, Leggan, Lisnedrougher, Cregaribracke, Koylaviony, Derrimore, Beakam, the quarter, and a third part of a quarter, called Tryea-Clooncorry; the quarter, and a third part of a quarter called Tryen-Brackloone; the quarters of Legaan, Gulshyny, Cloonebubban, Lishamske, Lissynemeatighe; the quarter, and a third part of a quarter, called Tryen-Reogh; the quarters of Pollecappull, and Grallaghnemaddy; also the town-land of Tonregie, containing four quarters, the town-land of Killougher, containing four quarters, viz. Killuugher, Coyneferns, Lorga, and Derryneeouge; also the castle of Beullanagare, with two quarters of land called Cloign-ghe, and the half quarter of Corrie; also the town-land of Ballentogher, containing four quarters, viz. Togher, Carrowreogh, Carrownkessy, and Killvaayn; also the quarters of

Adergowles,

DILLON, Viscount DILLON.

Monilea, in said county; and by her, who died at Killinure in Westmeath, 8 April 1638, and was interred in the friary of St. Francis, at Athlone; he had issue eight sons and eleven daughters, viz.

Sir

Adergowle, Carrowsemon, Carrowleisne-Rory, Donnoughmoyle, and Calldragh; the town-land of Ballidromnegarde, containing four quarters, viz. Carrowneanagh, Carroweloontorriffe, Corrownedroma, and Carrownemallaght; the town-land of Knocke, containing four quarters, viz. Carrowmere, Bruen, Cloanely and Glanfagen, and Knicon; also the precincts of the monastery of Bealahaunes, with the lands thereunto belonging; the monastery of Urlare, with the lands thereunto belonging; also the town, and six quarters of Ballendewgen, excepting eight gneves of land, parcel of the said quarter of Ballendewgen, viz. the gneves of Moyhesker, Fargarrow, Skehyneskelly, Shangarry, and Mahernyskehy, two gneves in the half town-land of Lishinbrake, and the same in the half town-land of Kilquickally, which eight are now in the tenure of Dominic French; also the rectory of Kilmurry; the advowsons of the churches of Kilcowllman, Templemore, Templemurry, Kilbeagh, Kilmory, Dinlacke, Bohola, and Killoenan; all the said premisses lye in the barony of Costello; also the manor, castle, and town-land of Ballylaghan, containing the quarters of Mullaghelare, Liffegown, the two quarters of Gortingarry, the quarters of Mullagsnrodd, and Cloonecomy; also the town-land of Knocketanbally, and Ardelowne, containing eight quarters in the barony of Gallen; a certain annual rent of five shillings English, arising out of every quarter of chargeable land in the said barony, excepting only the twelve quarters in the occupation of Gerald Dillon of Mannyn, which annual rent amounts yearly to the sum of 9l. 10s. English money; also the rectories of Gallen alias Templemore, Ballyshen alias Bohola, with all the tithes, &c.; also the castle and town-land of Rathery, containing two quarters; the town-land of Loughballyandry, containing two quarters; the town-land of Leaghballyngerran, two quarters; the town-land of Loughballyleo, two quarters; the quarter of Dromborym; the town-land of Clonbockoughter, one quarter; the quarter of Clonockaghter; the quarter of Dromderry; the quarter of Clontomcher; the castle and town-land of Bealavile, seven quarters; the quarter of Leghcarrow; the half quarters of Annaghavvaghary and Annaghkille; the small quarters, otherwise called cartrons, of Carrowocgroppan parva, Carrownskardan, Carrownacoppie, Carrowokilltowran, and Carowlsh, Duffballtraghan; two parts of the castle and town of Tullrohane; the quarters of Carrowskolty, Coshillagh, Cowllougra, Lisslelowney, Killicraghan, Brolkenny, and Eleknock; a third part of the two quarters of Montames, viz. Carrowmuck and Carrownccarnau; a third part of the quarter of Coghshelly; the quarter of Cloonmuere; the small quarters called Carrowskelly, Carrowntubber, Carrowneshancreggy, and Carrowcashell; the town-land of Tullaghanmore, containing a quarter and third part of a quarter; the town-land of Creggannefarne, containing one quarter; also seven gneves, and the third of a gneve; parcel of the quarter called Carrowcathillan-Ballyndegnen; seven gneves, a cartron, and half a cartron, in the town-land of Kiltycackally; and the land of Trientobrackan, containing one quarter and the third of a quarter; all the said lands are situate in the barony of Costello, and county of Mayo, and held from the King, as of the castle of Dublin, by the 20th part of a Knight's fee. (Rolls, and Auditor General's Office, also Liber Inquisit. post mortem penes Honoratis. W. Conyngham.)

The manor of Ballylahane, and the estate in Gallen, were sold to Messrs. Palmer in the year 1725;—but all the other lands belong to the present Lord, and contain the entire barony of Costello.

Sir Christopher, his heir apparent. (1)

Sir Lucas, from whom the present Lord Dillon descends. (2)

William Dillon of Tolchan, Esq; who had considerable (3) estates assigned to him: he married Margery, daughter of James Magawly of Ballylohloe in Westmeath, Esq. by whom he had George his heir, who died without issue; and two daughters, Margery, married to —— Walsh; and Elinor.

Thomas, on whom the estates of his nephew George devolved, he was born in the Tower of London, and styled of Brackloon. Bracklyn or Brackloon, in county of Roscomon. On the breaking out of the Rebellion in 1641, he was appointed Captain of a meeting of the Gentry of the county of Roscomon, at Ballintobber, and marrying Catharine, younger daughter of Maurice Fitzgerald of Laccagh, in county of Kildare, Esq. had issue two sons and three daughters, viz. Theobald his heir; John (sometime of Tollaghane, county of Roscomon, and after of Lissane, alias Lissyan in county of Mayo; he married Frances, daughter of Captain Anthony Brabazon, by Alice, daughter of Captain Dillon of Killyninen, and dying in January 1692, left issue by her, who re-married with Edmond Lally of Tullaghane, Esq. a daughter Ellice, married 17 April 1692, to Gerald Dillon of Mannin, Esq.; John his heir, and other children. Which John of Lissane, who was living in 1742, married in 1703, Honora, daughter of Edmund Lally, and had John who died unmarried in 1738; Patrick; Edmund; Mary, married to Gerald Dillon; Frances, to Edmund Dillon of Rathmane, in county of Mayo; and Bridget); the eldest daughter, Margery, married to Pierce Dillon of Ballyneloghdusse; the second, to —— Browne, Esq.; and the third, to Colonel Lucas Dowell of Roscomon.——Theobald, who succeeded Thomas of Bracklyn, married Sarah, daughter of Captain Anthony Brabazon aforesaid; made his will 4 September 1687, whereby he devised all his estates to Theobald Dillon then of Lough-Glyn; John Dillon of Kilmore in Roscomon; William Brabazon of Loughmask in county of Mayo, brother of his wife (and was living in 1622); and Pierce Dillon of Ballyneloghdusse, in Westmeath, Esqrs. to the uses in the said Will mentioned; bequeathed the mansion house of Brackloon to his wife, during her widowhood, or until a year after the marriage of Thomas his heir. Soon after
his

his decease, the said Sarah re-married with John Daly of
Lung, in county of Mayo, who died in April 1725, and
she died in April 1726, having had issue by the said Theobald
six sons and three daughters, viz. Thomas his heir;
Christopher (of Lungmore in county of Mayo, who pursuant
to articles dated 30 and 31 March 1696, married
Mariana, youngest daughter of Colonel John Talbot of
Belgarde, county of Dublin, by Elizabeth his wife,
daughter of Sir Henry Talbot, Knight, of Mount-Talbot
and Temple-Oge, county of Dublin; by her he had
Thomas of Lungmore, who married a daughter of Doctor
Prendergast; Anthony; Thomas; the eldest daughter married
to ———— Plunket; Sarah, the second, to ———— Dillon;
and the third became a nun); George, Gerald, James,
and William, who left no issue; daughter Ellice (married
in 1703, to Dominick O'Dowde, who left her a widow in
1737, having issue David, and other children); Elizabeth,
and Bridget, who died unmarried.——Colonel Thomas
Dillon, who succeeded at Bracklyn, married pursuant to
articles 23 March 1694, Catharine, third daughter of the
said John Talbot of Belgarde, Esq. on whom and their
issue male, the real estate of her said father was settled,
whereupon he became possessed of estates in the counties of
Roscommon and Dublin, of the yearly value of 1700l. and
dying in May 1721, had issue by her who survived him,
five sons and five daughters, viz. Henry his heir; Theobald,
Anthony, Arthur, and William died unmarried;
Ellice; Mary, who died unmarried; Sarah; Marcella; and
Bridget, who also died unmarried.——Henry Dillon of Belgarde,
Esq. married Jane, second daughter of Michael
Moore of Drogheda, Esq. and by her, who died in Capel-street,
Dublin 5 March 1762, had Thomas his heir; John;
a daughter who married ———— Trant, Esq. possessed of
considerable estates in England, she died in 1747; and several
other children.——The said Thomas married the daughter
and heir of Luke Dowell of Moyntagh, county of Roscomon,
Esq.

(5)   Edward and } Friars of the Order of St. Francis.
(6)   George,

(7)   John, who had a command in the army, and died unmarried.

(8)   Sir James Dillon, Knt. who in 1640, was Captain of a
company of 97 men, with the pay of 15 shillings a day;
and after the rebellion broke out, had a commission from
the

the State in November 1641, for the Government of the county of Longford, with another Sir James Dillon, after which he engaged in the rebellion; and we are told by the depofition of George Davis, that in his way from Dublin to the county of Rofcomon, he met at Ballymore Sir James Dillon the younger, accompanied with Henry Dillon of Ballymullen in fame county, John Edgworth, and divers others, who the next night went towards Longford, to have relieved that place, but they finding it ftrongly befieged, and all the paffages and ways blocked up, Sir James went to the caftle of Ratheline, which was alfo ready to be befieged, and having ftaid fome days there himfelf; and placed Henry Dillon there, where he continued till towards Chriftmas, and had his wife and children with him; a few days before Chriftmas, he delivered up the Caftle to Sir James Dillon the elder, one of the Governors as hath been obferved, of county of Rofcomon, and betook himfelf to his own Caftle in faid county, but before he could arrive there, Dowaltagh Mac Farry O'Hanly, Teige Mac Dermot O'Connor, and Brian Farrell, accompanied with 1000 or 1500 men, came to the faid Mr. Dillon's houfe and caftle, took away all his cattle, money, and goods, detained his caftle, and lying in wait for him, took him prifoner, and delivered him to Con O'Rourk, who came at the fame time into the county, and the faid O'Rourk kept Mr. Dillon prifoner, he going with him on foot wherever he went, until the meeting at Elphin, appointed by the faid Con and the Gentry of the county of Rofcomon, whither Mr. Dillon alfo was carried, and Con would have taken him into the county of Leitrim, but after much entreaty was prevailed on by Hugh O'Conor Dunn, to leave him in his cuftody, after which Charles O'Conor Roe, threatened to cut off, Mr. Dillon's head, if opportunity he might find; he was carried by the faid Hugh O'Conor to the meeting of Ballintobber, after which he was conveyed out of the county by the faid Hugh, and came to Dublin, his brother Garret being then engaged in the rebellion.——In April 1643, Sir James was at the fiege of Ballynakill, which furrendered 5 May, commanding at that time a regiment of foot, after which he was Lieutenant-General and Governor of Conaught and Athlone; but on the reduction of the kingdom by Cromwell, he was excepted from pardon for life and eftate by the act of parliament for the fettlement of Ireland, which paffed 12 Auguft 1652; however, after the

restoration,

restoration, he had a pension of 500l. a year, granted 25 May 1665, and became Marshal de Camp, or Major-General in the French and Spanish services. He married two wives, first Elizabeth, daughter of Thomas Plunket of Rathmore, in county of Meath, Esq. and had issue Ulick, and James, who died young; he married secondly, before 1653, Mary, daughter of Roger Jones of Sligo, Esq. and widow of Major John Ridge of Roscomon, but by her had no issue; and 24 January 1665, had his Majesty's direction to receive the profits of her jointure, she being then lately deceased.

(1) Daughter Rose, died young.

(2) Margaret, married to Robert Dillon of Cannestown, in Westmeath Esq. Justice of Peace for that county, and engaged in the rebellion of 1641; by him she was mother of James Dillon of Ballymulvey, in Roscomon, Esq. who married Jane, daughter of Robert Dillon of Clonbrock, in county of Galway Esq.

(3) Anne, to John, Viscount Taaffe of Corran, and mother of Theobald, Earl of Carlingford.

(4) Catharine, to Sir Ulick Bourke of Glinsk, in county of Roscomon, Bart.

(5) Mary, to Gerald Pettyt of Irishtown, or Molyngar, in Westmeath Esq. and dying 13 May 1634, left issue by him who died 10 March following, four sons and four daughters, viz. Thomas, who married Mary, daughter of Kedagh Mac Geoghegan; William; James; Redmond; Elinor, married to Garret Delamere; Margaret; Barbara; and Bridget.

(6) Elizabeth, to Thomas Fitzgerald of Newcastle, in county of Longford, Esq. by whom she had six daughters, viz. Margaret, married to ——— Dillon of Clonbrock, by whom she had Thomas and Elizabeth; Mary, to Conly Boy Mac Geoghegan, and had a son, Hugh; Ellin, Cicely, Anne, and Bridget, all nuns of the Order of St. Clare.

(7) Jane, to Hugh O'Conor Dunn, of Castlereagh, in Roscomon, Esq. son of Sir Hugh O'Conor, Knt.

(8) Ellen, ⎫ Nuns of the Order of St. Clare, and who
(9) Cecilia, ⎬ established the Franciscan Order of nuns in
          ⎭ Galway.

(10) Bridget, and ⎫ died unmarried.
(11) Barbara,   ⎭

Sir Christopher. Sir Christopher Dillon, heir apparent to Theobald, the first Viscount Dillon, lived at Ballylaghan, alias Eealalahin, in

DILLON, Viscount DILLON.

in county of Mayo; was President of Conaught, and of the Privy-Council, in the reigns of K. James I. and K. Charles I. but died before his father, viz. 28 February 1623-4, as by inquisition taken at Roscomon 23 August following, which found that he was seized of four quarters of the lands of Owranycluby.—He married in November 1604, Lady Jane Dillon, eldest daughter of James, the first Earl of Roscomon, and by her, who survived him, had seven sons and five daughters, viz. Lucas, who succeeded his grand-father, in the title of Viscount; Thomas, who also succeeded to the honour; Theobald, father of Lucas, the sixth Viscount; James, who died without issue; as did John, who married the widow of ——— Bingham, Esq.; Christopher, and Francis, died young; daughter Joan, married to John O'Madden, chief of his sept in the barony of Longford, in county of Galway, and at that time possessed of large estates; Elizabeth, and Mary, nuns of the order of St. Clare; Eleanora, and Mary, both died young.

Lucas, the eldest son, and second Viscount Dillon, was 14 years and 6 months old, in September 1624, when he succeeded his grandfather; and 14 December that year, his wardship and marriage were granted to Sir John King, Knt. In 1625, when 15 years of age, he married Lady Mary Mac Donnell, second daughter of Randal, the first Earl of Antrim, and dying, as by Inquisition, 13 April 1629 [1], was conveyed in a coach from Killenfaghny, and buried 14 September, in the Friary of Athlone; leaving issue by his Lady (who remarried with Oliver, the sixth Lord Louth) a son and successor,

Theobald, the third Viscount, aged 3 months, at the death of his father, and he dying in ward to the King, 13 May 1630, as by inquisition, was succeeded by his uncle,

Thomas, the fourth Viscount, who being within age, viz. 15 years old at the accession to the honour; K. Charles I. by indenture, bearing date 8 December same year, demised and to farm set, the estates then very considerable, and extending into the counties of Mayo, Roscomon, and Westmeath, to Sir Lucas Dillon of Lough-Glyn, in county of Roscomon, Knt.; and 15 March 1535-6, his Lordship having attained his full age, had livery of his lands. He was bred a Roman Catholic, but when 15 years of age, declared himself a Protestant, and was present in the Parliament held at Dublin, 16 March 1639-40 [2], and 23 October

Lucas, 2 Viscount.

Theobald, 3 Viscount.

Thomas, 4 Viscount.

[1] Rolls. [2] Lords Jour. 1. 99.

ber 1640, we find him a Lord of the Privy-Council[1]: 16 February that year, he was of the Committee of Grievances, and in November 1641, he, and the Lord Viscount Mayo, were appointed Governors of the county of Mayo, which for some months they kept free from all disturbances, without any assistance from the state. Soon after which, the two Houses of Parliament, considering of more effectual methods to quell the rebellion than had been hitherto taken, to prevent its growth, to remove the discontents of the nation, and restore the peace of the kingdom; did thereupon assent to a representation to the King, and in certain instructions given by the Lords (13 February 1641-2) then in town, after the prorogation of the former Parliament, the Lord Dillon was charged with presenting them to the King, and to press for speedy and effectual orders therein. His Lordship was well qualified for this important trust and commission, being a member of the Privy Council of Ireland, a Protestant, a man of extraordinary parts and demeanour, generally beloved and esteemed, well affected to the Crown, and very acceptable to his Majesty, who had lately received and treated him with singular marks of esteem and kindness; and at this time the House of Lords recommended it to the King, that he might have some command in Conaught, where his power and interest were considerable. He embarked a few days after the prorogation, in order to go to England, and execute this employment; but being driven by a storm as far as Scotland, landed there, and making all possible expedition to London, with Lord Taaffe, who accompanied him, was seized on the road at Ware in Hertfordshire, by an order of the House of Commons, dated 3 November, all his papers taken away, and himself secured with the Lord Taaffe, remained in custody several months, till it was of no consequence to keep them longer in restraint; and then being negligently guarded, they made their escape and went to the King at York, too late to offer a remedy, when the rebels were strengthened with foreign supplies, and the rebellion was become almost universal. We are told by Doctor Borlace, in his history of that time, that his Lordship in his private instructions, had orders to move, that no forces might be sent over out of England, but that the whole work might be left to the remonstrants,

[1] Lords Jour. I, 134.

remonstrants, and that they would then undertake to suppress the rebels themselves.

After his return home, he was made a Lieutenant-General, and the King reposing especial trust and confidence in the great industry, judgment, abilities, and good affection of his Lordship, and Henry, Viscount Wilmot, did 27 April 1645, appoint them joint Presidents of Conaught[1], and Governors of the Fort of Athlone, but that Fort being suppressed by Father George Dillon, in favour of the Nuncio's party, and his Lordship being very uneasy at the loss of his Government, and hoping to recover it, went to Kilkenny for that purpose, where 6 December 1646, he was reconciled by the Nuncio, to the Church of Rome, according to the Roman Pontifical in St. Mary's Church before a vast concourse of people; upon which, the Supreme Council resolved to deliver back to him Athlone, whither he went in the middle of December; but O'Neill's forces refusing to obey the order for giving him possession, he was then disappointed. He afterwards joined the Marquess of Ormond, who then commanded the army of the confederates, and 25 July 1649, was left by him with 2000 foot, and 500 horse, to block up the city of Dublin on the North; but the attack on the army by Michael Jones, being made on the East, prevented them from action. Although he had been disappointed of the Government of Athlone, yet he afterwards was Governor of that Castle, which he held and maintained till 18 June 1651, when articles were agreed on between Sir Charles Coote, Lord President of Conaught, and Sir James Dillon, on his Lordship's behalf, concerning the surrender thereof, for the use of the Parliament of the Commonwealth of England [*].—His Lordship's estates, consisting of several manors, lands, and heredi-

---

[*] The articles were, 1. That Sir James did covenant and agree, that the said castle should be surrendered, with all arms, ammunition, artillery, and stores therein contained, unto such persons as the Lord President should appoint to receive the same.—2. That the officers and soldiers then in garrison, should have liberty to march away with their arms, colours flying, drums beating, bandaliers full of powder, with matches lit at both ends, bag and baggage, and with a safe convoy to any such garrison within the province of Conaught, as the Governor should direct, or elsewhere.—3. That whereas the Lord Viscount Dillon of Costello, has desired to submit to the Government of England, as being of an English descent and extraction; the said Sir Charles Coote,

[1] Rolls Off.

hereditaments, in the counties of Westmeath, Roscomon and Mayo, being seized and sequestered by the usurped powers of the Commonwealth of England, on account of the rebellion, he was expelled by the said powers, out of his said estate, for his adherence to K. Charles I after which he went abroad, and with four of his sons lived in exile in France, Spain, &c. On the restoration he returned home, and by a provision in the acts of settlement, was restored unto and vested in all the estates whatsoever, whereof he, or any to his use were seized and possessed, on 22 October 1641, or after, in pursuance whereof he exhibited his claim, 5 November 1662, before the Commissioners appointed to execute the said act, who, by their decree bearing date 19 August 1663, did restore him to the several manors and other hereditaments he laid claim to, viz. Bracklyn, Ballintogher, and many others in the counties of Mayo, Roscomon, and Westmeath [1]. The number of acres in the county of Mayo, amounting to 53,301, of profitable land, plantation measure; 5864 of the same land and measure in Roscomon; and 5030 in Westmeath [2]; and new quit rents being imposed upon the same by the acts of settlement and expla-

Coote, Lord President of Conaught, by authority of Parliament, with advice of the Council of War, did engage and undertake to Sir James Dillon, that he will answer and accordingly settle with the Parliament, that the Lord Dillon, his wife, children, and servants, be *indempnified* for all things done by him during the war of Ireland, provided he act nothing henceforth to the prejudice of the Parliament of England, their Army, or Garrisons.—4. That the said Lord Dillon shall have liberty to reside at Portumna, or Loughreagh, with such a competency of land allowed unto him, as shou'd be convenient to maintain a stock, for the maintenance and support of his family.—5. That in regard, the said Lord Dillon is *disshenbabled* suddenly to pay his debts, he shall be protected from arrests and suits, for any debts formerly contracted by the space of 3 years.—6. That he shall have a pass to go into England, or into a foreign country, when he shall desire the same.—7. That he shall have liberty to transport 1000 or 2000 of the Irish, if he can make condition with any Foreigner, in Amity with the Parliament of England.—8. That this condition be continued to his Lady and family in his absence.—9. That the inhabitants of the town of Athlone, shall have quarter for their lives, with assurance to enjoy their estates and goods, and remain in the said town, paying such contribution as others do, whilst they remain within the English quarters.—10. That such of his friends or kindred as shall make their particular obligation, shall be received upon reasonable conditions.—11. That the Castle of Athlone, shall be delivered according to the before mentioned articles, by Sir Robert Talbot, Governor thereof, at or before Sunday next, at 10 of the clock aforenoon, and that Captain Bellew, and Captain Fitzgerald, be sent forth *this morning*, as hostages for them. (Rot. O. Cromwell. 9. p. f.)

[1] Rolls, Aud. Gen. Chief Rememb. and Forfeiture Off. 20 Car. II. 10. p. f. [2] Enrolled 19,

explanation; he had a releafe of part thereof 11 November 1663, and by his Majefty's directions of 17 November 1669, and 3 May 1670 had a further abatement of the faid quit rents; the Government of Conaught having been conferred upon his Lordfhip, and the Lord Wilmot for life, and to the furvivors of them; and his Lordfhip authorifing the Lord Wilmot, did, 9 March 1660-1, in confideration of a competent fum of money, and for divers other good caufes, and valuable confiderations, furrender the faid poft of Prefident of that Province, to K. Charles II. by whom, in 1662, he was made Cuftos Rot. of the county of Weftmeath.

Before 1636, he married Frances, daughter of Nicholas White of Leixlip, Efq. with whom he had a fortune of 3000l. and dying in 1672, or the year after, had iffue by her (who died in Winetavern-ftreet, and was buried in St. James's, 9 January 1664) fix fons, viz.

Charles, his heir apparent, born in or before 1636, he (1) ferved as a General in the armies of France, Spain, and Flanders; alfo in England and Ireland, during the exile of K. Charles II.; whilft abroad he was appointed Governor of Tournay, and in obedience to an Englifh Act of Parliament he returned home, and retired to his eftate, where he died before his father, unmarried, and was interred in Hare, or Holy Ifland, in Loughrea.

Chriftopher, who died in Winetavern-ftreet, unmarried, (2) and was buried by his mother 20 June 1663.

Rupert, who, whilft Page of Honour to K. Charles II. (3) being from his addrefs and figure confidered an object of envy, was fet upon, fays the pedigree, by the other pages, and flain in the Palace yard.

Thomas, who fucceeded to the honour, and became the (4) fifth Vifcount.

Ormond, and } died young. (5)
Nicholas, } (6)

Thomas, the fifth Vifcount Dillon married Elizabeth, *Thomas* eldeft daughter of Sir John Bourke of Derymaclagtny, in *5* county of Galway, Knt. (by his wife Lady Mary, fecond *Vifcount.* daughter of William the feventh Earl of Clanricarde) and by her, who after married Sheffield Grace of Courtftown, in county of Kilkenny, Efq. he had one fon, Thomas, and one daughter, Elizabeth, who both died young, and his Lordfhip deceafing in 1674, the honour devolved on Lucas Dillon, eldeft fon of Theobald, third fon of Sir Chriftopher Dillon, eldeft fon of Theobald, the firft Vifcount.

Which

Which Theobald, married Sarah Bourke of the Viscount Mayo's family, and had issue the said Lucas; Captain James Dillon, who died without issue; daughter Honora, married first to Robert Dillon of Lissnagragh, or Lissnagree, secondly, to James Dillon of Rathmane, Gent.; and Bridget, the younger daughter, married ―――― Dillon of Mayo.

Lucas, 6 Viscount.

Lucas, who succeeded, and was the sixth Viscount, settled, on the last day of February 1674-5, a rent charge of 600l. a year, on the widow of Thomas the fifth Lord, during her life, to be issuing out of his estates in the counties of Mayo and Roscomon; and being high in the favour of K. Charles II. his Majesty in consideration of the many services and sufferings of his family, did by his letter, dated 22 September 1675, direct a grant to be made under the Great Seal (which was accordingly done 10 January following[1]) whereby he remitted, released, and for ever quit claim, to the yearly sum of 455l. 13s. 10h. of the new quit rents, amounting together to the yearly sum of 700l. 18s. 10. passed by the acts of settlement, on the estates decreed to Thomas the fourth Lord; of which estates he levied fines, and suffered recoveries to the use of himself, his heirs and assignes[*].—He married to his first wife, Ursula, daughter of

---

[*] 2 September 1682, his Lordship made his last Will, and thereby bequeathed his Soul to his Saviour and Redeemer Jesus Christ, through whose merits and sufferings he hoped for a free remission of all his sins, and to become partaker of everlasting glory; and his body to be buried where, and after such decent and becoming manner, as his Executors and Trustees should think fit and appoint. He gave and bequeathed all his estates whatsoever in the several counties of Westmeath, Roscomon, and Mayo, to Garret Moore of Muraine, in said county of Mayo, Esq. and Denis Daly of Aghriane, in county of Galway, Esq. Counsellor at Law, and their heirs, to such uses, and subject to, and chargeable with all such rents, rent-charges, debts, dues, legacies, and estates really due and payable, that are not by him particularly mentioned and expressed, for them to have and to hold, all the aforesaid premisses, with their appurtenances, to the sole use, benefit and behoof of his dearly beloved wife, Anne, Lady Viscountess Dillon for her life, and also to be paid the yearly rent of 400l. during her life: he bequeathed likewise to the said Garret Moore, and Denis Daly, all the number of acres, lands, tenements, and hereditaments in the county of Mayo; passed in certificate and letters to his beloved kinsman, Theobald Dillon of Loughglin, in the county of Roscomon, Esq. in trust for, and to his own use, together with the town and lands of Monymore in the said county of Mayo, to hold the last mentioned premisses, to the use of Theobald Dillon for life, and after to the heirs male of his body to be begotten; remainder to John Dillon of Ballyglost, in county of Roscomon, Gent. and his heirs male, lawfully to be begotten; remainder to Theobald Dillon of Killmore, in said county of Roscomon, and to his heirs. He gave and bequeathed in like manner to the said Garret Moore, and Denis Daly;

[1] Rolls and Aud. Gen. Off.

of William, Viscount Dongan, and Earl of Limerick; and to his second wife, about the latter end of the year 1681, the Lady Anne Nugent, eldest daughter of Richard, Earl of Westmeath, with whom he had 1500l. fortune, and settled a jointure on her of 400l. a year, but in a few months after his marriage, being seized with a dropsy, or some such lingering distemper, he died in September or October 1682, at Killenfaghny in Westmeath, the usual mansion-house of the family, and having had no issue by either of his Ladies, the title and estates descended to Theobald Dillon of Kilmore, Esq. the next heir male of the body of Theobald, the first Viscount, viz. the eldest son of Robert Dillon, Esq. eldest son of Sir Lucas Dillon, Knt. who was the second son of Theobald, the first Viscount Dillon.

Which Sir Lucas, was settled at Lough-Glyn, in county of Roscomon, where he had a considerable estate settled on him by his father, and where he lived (says the Pedigree) in

Lough-Glyn.

Daly; the town and lands of Rathbelvine, and Graslaghbegg, in county of Mayo, to the use of Onor Fitz-Morori, alias Dillon, her heirs and assignes, until she be paid the sum of 400l. together, with the lawful interest thereof, according to 10 per cent. He wills further, that 400l. be paid and raised out of his said estates in Mayo, to be paid over to his wife for the following uses, that is to say, 100l. to be applied to such uses as his wife, and one Doctor William Bourke should think fit; 300l. to be distributed to such friends as his wife, and Edmund Nugent of Carlanstown in Westmeath, Esq. should think fit; and 300l. to be applied towards his burial and funeral charges. He wills, that his beloved kinsman Henry Dillon, son and heir to Theobald of Kilmore, shall during his father's life, hold and enjoy all his ecclesiastical livings, or impropriate tithes in the county of Mayo, and as for his personal estate, having before by other writings, given and assigned over the same to Thomas Nugent, Esq. his loving brother in law, for the use of his said wife, by deed bearing date 17 April last past, he ratified and confirmed the same by his will, and further bequeathed unto her, her heir and assignes, the town and lands of Drumrany, in county of Westmeath, containing 300 acres or thereabouts, for ever, subject nevertheless to the payment of 250l. to one Fletcher, to whom the premisses were mortgaged for the said sum; and after the determination of the aforesaid uses and limitations, he wills the said estates to descend to Theobald Dillon of Kilmore for life, and after his decease, to Henry his eldest son for life, and after, to the heirs male of his body lawfully to be begotten; remainder to Christopher, another son of the said Theobald, and his heirs male; remainder to the other sons which the said Theobald might have, and their heirs respectively; remainder to Theobald Dillon of Lough-Glyn; remainder to John Dillon before named, brother of the said Theobald; remainder to Theobald Dillon of Brackloone for life; remainder to his eldest son Thomas, and his heirs male; remainder to the other sons which the said Theobald Dillon might have; remainder to John Dillon of Tulkhan, brother to the said Theobald of Brackloone, and their respective issue male; remainder to the right heirs male of Sir Theobald Dillon, the first Lord Viscount Dillon. He appointed his wife sole executrix, and the said Thomas Nugent, Edmund Nugent, Thebald Dillon of Lough-Glyn, and Denis Daly, trustees. (Prerog. Office, and Lodge.)

in splendour, and in universal esteem. He was of the Privy-Council to K. James I. and Charles I. until the rebellion of 1641 (in which it appears by the deposition of Hugh O'Conor, taken 11 February 1642-3) that in or about Christmas 1641, he, with others of the county of Roscomon, were persuaded and prevailed with, to join, by Hugh Oge O'Conor, and certain others employed (as they said) by Sir Lucas Dillon for that purpose, affirming to them, that Sir Lucas well knew it was the King's pleasure, that the said Gentry should take up arms; for, that the pretended Parliament of England, would otherwise destroy them; and further alledged, that they should within one quarter of a year, see his Majesty himself, and the said Parliament in arms, one against the other. Yet afterwards, the said Sir Lucas repaired unto the President of Conaught, and professing his fidelity, obtained his Lordship's protection, under colour whereof he played into both hands, and at the meeting of all the Gentry of the county of Roscomon, at Ballintubber, there were present Sir Lucas Dillon, Sir Ulick Bourke, William O'Molloy, Alexander Nugent, Thomas Dillon, Hugh Oge O'Conor, Charles O'Conor Roe, Teige O'Conor, &c. who all of them took an oath (which was first taken by Sir Lucas) and the substance of it was, for the maintainance of the King's prerogative, and for the establishing of the Romish religion, in and throughout the kingdom of Ireland; at which meeting it was also agreed and concluded on, that the said Sir Lucas, and Hugh Oge O'Conor, should repair unto the Earl of Clanricarde, with an offer from the county to make his Lordship their General, which was accordingly done by them, who returned his Lordship's answer to this effect, "That he "could not accept of any such charge, until he had un- "derstood his Majesty's pleasure," and the said deponent understood also from sundry persons, that the purpose and meaning of the principal Actors in the Rebellion was, to have the kingdom of Ireland freed from all persons besides the Irish, and that the plot thereof was contrived, and set on foot, at the late meeting of Parliament at Dublin, and at the aforesaid meeting at Ballintubber, there were appointed Colonels and Captains, amongst whom Thomas Dillon, brother to Sir Lucas, was appointed a Captain.— Sir Lucas was afterwards a member of the Supreme Council of Kilkenny; and 4 January 1647-8, was with the Lord Athenry, and Sir Roebuck Lynch, appointed a Resident

Council

DILLON, VISCOUNT DILLON.

Council in the interval of the General Assembly for Conaught; for all which he had his estates seized and sequestered by Cromwell, and in 1653, was imprisoned in the city Marshalsea of Dublin; but surviving these distracted times, was in 1662, high Sheriff of the county of Mayo. He married Jane, daughter of John Moor of Brees, or Bryess, also of Cloghan and Ball in county of Mayo, Esq. and had issue eight sons and three daughters, viz. Robert his heir; Theobald Dillon of Lough-Glyn, Esq. (to whom and his heirs, the four quarters of Lough-Glyn, and the four quarters of Ballymacmorough, in county of Roscomon, being the sequestered estate of his father were set out, he was Colonel of a regiment of foot, and married Alice, daughter of John Dillon, Esq. Counsellor at Law, but died without issue); John, of Kilmore (who, with all his younger brothers, were Captains of Independent troops of horse, or companies of foot, in the service of K. Charles I. and II. he married Bridget, daughter of ―――― Bourke of Ballyglass, in county of Roscomon); Christopher, Gerald, Edward, Arthur, Lodowick, all died unmarried; Bridget, married to Francis, Lord Athenry; Barbara, a Nun of St. Clare; and Mary, married to John O'Carrol, of Elye O'Carrol, Esq.

Captain Robert Dillon, the eldest son of Sir Lucas, married Rose, eldest daughter of John Dillon of Streamstown, or Killynynen, Esq. Serjeant, and Privy-Counsellor to K. James I. and K. Charles I. as before mentioned, and deceasing at an early period of life, left issue by his Lady (who remarried with General John O'Farrell of Tyrlekin, and died in 1681) two sons and three daughters, viz. Theobald his heir, and the seventh Viscount Dillon; Lucas, who died unmarried; Alice, or Elizabeth (married to James Ferrall of Callows, in county of Longford, Esq.); Jane (first to ―――― Lally of Tullynedaly, Esq. by whom she was mother of Brigadier General Lally, Colonel of an Irish regiment in the French service, and was wounded at the battle of Fontenoy; the said Jane married secondly, John Mac-Hubert Bourke); and Mary, to ―――― Dillon of Sinoghweny, in county of Mayo, Gent.

Theobald, the eldest son, succeeding to the title, was the seventh Viscount Dillon. He resided chiefly at Kilmore, and was Lieutenant-Colonel to the Earl of Clanricarde's regiment of Guards, in the army of K. James II. and for his services to that King, was outlawed, in or about the

Robert.

Theobald, 7 Viscount.

the year 1690¹, which outlawry was reversed by his son, as will appear. He married Mary, daughter of Sir Henry Talbot of Temple-Oge, in county of Dublin, and of Mount-Talbot, in county of Roscomon, Knt.; and his Lordship deceasing in 1691, left issue by his said Lady (who was killed by the second bomb thrown into Limerick by K. William's army) six sons and two daughters, viz. Robert, who died before him, unmarried; Henry, his successor in the honour; Arthur, father to Charles the ninth Viscount; Captain Christopher, James, and Lucas, who were all in foreign service, and died unmarried; daughter Jane, married to Sir John Bourke of Mitford, Bart.; and Bridget.

Henry 8 Viscount. Henry, the eighth Viscount Dillon, represented the county of Westmeath in K. James's Parliament, held at Dublin 7 May 1689, in which year he was Lord Lieutenant of the county of Roscomon; he was soon after appointed Governor of the town of Galway, and was Colonel of a regiment of foot in that King's army.—4 July 1687, articles of marriage were concluded on, between his Lordship and Frances, second daughter of George, Count Hamilton (by his wife Frances, eldest daughter and coheir to Richard Jennings of Sandridge, in county of Hertford, Esq. who after became the wife of Richard Talbot, Duke of Tyrconnel) with his said wife, having 3000l. fortune, he settled on her 400l. a year, at the same time making a settlement of the estate, whereby it was entailed on their issue male; remainder to his Lordship's brothers, Arthur, James, and Lucas, and their respective issue male; remainder to Theobald Dillon of Lough-Glyn; remainder to John Dillon of Kilmore; remainder to Theobald Dillon of Bracklyn, then lately deceased; remainder to John Dillon of Bracklyn, brother to the said Theobald; remainder to Edmund Dillon, some time of Ardnegragh, brother to Sir Theobald the first Viscount; remainder to Garret Dillon, some time of Portlick*, another brother of the said first Viscount,

---

* From Garret here mentioned, descended James of Portlick, whose nephew Gerald, 17 April 1692, married Elice, daughter of John Dillon of Lifsane, county of Mayo, Gent. who died soon after his daughter's marriage; the said Gerald lived at Mornin in said county, and had two sons, Edmund his heir,

¹ Case, presented to the House of Lords, on the claim of Lord Dillon.

DILLON Viscount DILLON.

Viscount, and their issue male respectively. After this period it appears by a rule book of the Court of King's Bench, in Trinity Term (6 Will. and Mary) that the outlawry against his father was reversed by the judgment of said Court, and which judgment was duly entered up and enrolled, and also examined by the House of Lords, 2 December 1697, when the Lord Viscount Massareene reported, that the said outlawry was reversed[1]. He is said to have had summons to Parliament as a peer[2]; made his will 12 January 1713-14*, and departed this life on the following day, viz. 13 January; he was buried on 23 at Ballyhaunis, in county of Roscomon, in the tomb of Christopher Dillon, prior of that friary, leaving issue by his said lady (who after married Patrick Bellew, then son and heir apparent to Sir John Bellew, Bart.) an only son

Richard the ninth Viscount Dillon, who was born in 1688; 16 January 1715, in obedience to an order of the House of Lords, 12 December preceding, he appeared in that House, delivered his writ of summons in the usual manner, and took the oath of allegiance, but being asked whether he would

Richard, 9 Viscount.

---

heir, born in 1696; John; and several daughters; also a sister Margaret, married to William Kelly of Turnach, county of Roscomon, Gent.—The said John of Lisliane, lived some time before at Tullaghane, county of Roscomon, and died in January 1692, leaving by Frances his wife, whose sister married Edmund Laily of Tollaghane, Esq. the aforesaid Ellice, and John of Lisliane, Gent. living in 1719, (Lodge.)

* Whereby he devised all his lands, tenements and hereditaments in the respective counties of Westmeath, Roscomon, and Mayo, wherein, or whereof he was seized of any estate of inheritance, of fee simple, absolute or conditional; or of any estate in equity, or wherein he had any equitable, conditional, or other just right, to Denis Daly of Aghrane, in Galway, Esq. his heirs and assignes, to be forthwith sold, to the intent and purpose, and upon trust and confidence that he the said Denis should and would, out of the first money that should come, or arise by sale of the said lands, pay, satisfy and discharge, debts due by judgment, bond, or other contracts, and for which there was then no real security, by mortgage from him, or any of his ancestors, lineal or collateral, standing out, or of force; and after the payment of such debts, that the surplus money arising by the said sale, should be applied towards the discharging of the mortgages, or other real securities, either in law or equity, affecting, charging, or encumbering all or any part of the jointure, by him or his deceased father, or either of them, settled on his Lady Frances, or any of the lands, tenements, and hereditaments, settled upon or secured to her by a late act made in England, in lieu and satisfaction of, or as an equivalent for her jointure, or any part thereof, and appointed his Lady sole executrix. (Prerog. Office.)

[1] Claim ut antea and Lords Jour. I. 675. [2] Case ut antea, and Lords Jour. I. 693.

DILLON, Viscount DILLON.

would take the other oaths, and make and subscribe the declaration pursuant to the statute, his Lordship was pleased to say he would consider of it, and withdrew¹. His Lordship died in the year 1737², and having married in 1720, the Lady Bridget Bourke, second daughter of John ninth Earl of Clanricarde, left an only daughter Frances, married to Charles Dillon her own cousin-germain, and her father's successor in the title, which Charles, was eldest son of Arthur, third son of Theobald the seventh Viscount³.

Which Arthur went into France, where before he was 20 years of age, he commanded an Irish regiment. In 1705, he was made a Marshal de Camp, was Governor of Toulon, and distinguishing himself in the field, was advanced to the rank of Lieutenant-General, in which station he acquired still higher reputation, being esteemed by all the great Generals of his time, and universally beloved by the soldiery. —He married Christiana, daughter of Ralph Sheldon, Esq. and niece to General Sheldon: and deceasing, 5 February 1732-3, N. S. left issue by his Lady who died, 5 August 1757, aged 73, five sons and three daughters, viz.

(1)(2) Charles and Henry, } successive Viscounts.

(3) James, who about the year 1740, was made a Knight of Malta, and Colonel of Dillons Regiment, at the head of which he lost his life, at the battle of Fontenoy, in 1745, when his regiment was given to his brother

(4) Edward, then 25 years old, who was wounded in the battle of Laufelt, and soon after died at Maestricht; and the King of France, considering the services rendered to him by this family, was induced to declare, that he would not give the command of that regiment (which he put on English pay) to any person save of the name of DILLON, and agreeable to the recommendation of the family.

(5) Arthur, the youngest son, was first made Bishop of Evreux, in Normandy, thence promoted to the Archiepiscopal See of Toulouse, and lastly, to that of Narbonne. He is a Commander of the Order of the Holy Ghost, Primate of The Gauls, and President of the States of Languedoc*.

Daughter

---

* To this Prelate, the Literati of *this* country confess much obligation, he has manifested a liberality of principle almost hitherto unknown, and through his enquiries and exertions, the antiquities of Ireland have been lately much elucidated.

¹ Lords Jour. II. 491. ² Cafo. ³ Idem.

DILLON, Viscount DILLON.

Daughter Frances, a Carmelite Nun, died at Pontoife. (1)
Catharine, alfo a Carmelite Nun, died at St. Denis in
1754, and (2)
Bridget, married to the Baron Blaifel, a Lieut. General
in the fervice of France. (3)

Charles, the eldeft fon, fucceeded his coufin germain, *Charles,*
and became the tenth Vifcount; he was Colonel of a regi- *10*
ment in France, which regiment he commanded upon the *Vifcount.*
Rhine, againft the Germans in 1734. 16 January 1734-5,
he married Frances, only daughter of Richard the ninth
Vifcount Dillon, and in September 1736, came into Ireland
and took poffeffion of his inheritance, which he enjoyed till
his deceafe. By his faid Lady, who died in London 18
January 1738-9, he had an only fon Charles, born 9 or 10
November 1738, who died in May 1739; and his Lordfhip
deceafing in London 24 October 1741, was fucceeded in
title and eftates by his brother.

Henry, the eleventh Vifcount, who ferved as Major of
Dillon's regiment whilft under the command of his brother, *Henry,*
and afterwards as Colonel, which command he refigned be- *11*
fore the act for preventing Britifh fubjects from entering into *Vifcount.*
foreign fervice, arrived in London 13 May 1744, and 26
October 1744-5 married Lady Charlotte Lee, eldeft daughter of George-Henry, the second Earl of Litchfield*, and
deceafing in 1787, left iffue by her Ladyfhip, four daughters,

---

* The family of LEE took its furname from the Lordfhip of *Lee* in the Parifh of Wibenbury, and county of Chefter, whereof Sir Walter at Lee, Knt. (who lived towards the clofe of K. Edward III. reign) left iffue Sir John, of Lee-Hall, whofe fon and heir John, was father of Thomas, and to him fucceeded John of Lee-Hall, who married Margery, daughter of Sir Ralph Hocknell of Hocknel-Hall, in Chefter, Knt. and had two fons, Thomas, who fucceeded at Lee-Hall; and Benedict, who, in the reign of K. Edward IV. removed from Chefhire, to Quarendon in county of Bucks, and by Elizabeth, daughter and heir to John Wood of county of Warwick, Efq. had Richard his heir, who bore for his coat armour, *Argent, a Fefs be-tween three Crefcents, Sable* ; and had iffue by Elizabeth his wife, daughter and coheir to William Sanders, of the county of Oxford, Efq. three fons, viz. Sir Robert of Burton, Knt. (father of Sir Anthony, who married Mar-garet, daughter of Sir Henry Wyat, Knt. and had Sir Henry, made a Knight of the Garter by Q. Elizabeth, and he lies interred in Quarendon Church, where at the upper end of the chancel, is a black marble fixed againft the wall, with an infcription); Benett anceftor to the Earl of Litch-field ; and Roger, of Pightefton in Bucks, anceftor to the family of Bin-field.—Benett the fecond fon, married to his laft wife, Elizabeth, daughter of Robert Cheyne of Chefham-Boyes, in Bucks, Efq. made his will 21 Febru-ary 1545, wherein he bequeathed divers charitable legacies; to his wife Elizabeth;

ters, and three sons, viz. Frances, born 6 October 1747, married in June 1767, to Sir William Jerningham, of Norfolk,

zabeth, the profits of all his lands in county of Northampton, and at Stony-Stratford, Huncote, Beerston, Brownton, and Oving in county of Bucks, for term of her life, and after to his executors, towards finding his children till they came of age; to his godson, Benett Lee, his damask gown, and all his best apparel; to Margaret, daughter of his brother Roger, 20 marcs; and constituted Paul Dayrell, Christopher Wescott, and Ralph Harri, executors; Sir Anthony Lee, Knt. and Henry Bradshaw overseers, to each of whom he bequeathed 10l. The probate of his will, bears date 1 July 1547. His issue were, Robert his heir; Mary, first wife of Sir George Tyrrel of Thornton, in Bucks, Knt.; and Jane.—Robert the son was knighted, and his son, Henry of Quarendon, became heir to his cousin Sir Henry, Knight of the Garter; which Henry, was first knighted, and 29 June 1611, was created a Baronet. He married Eleanor, daughter of Sir Richard Wortley, of Wortley in Yorkshire, Knt. and died in 1631, leaving Sir Francis his heir; Eleanor, married to Maurice Berkley, Viscount Fitz-Harding; and Elizabeth, to Sir Samuel Tryon, of Boys-Hall in county of Essex, Bart.—Sir Francis, second Baronet, of Ditchley in Oxfordshire, and Quarendon aforesaid, married Anne, eldest daughter of Sir John St. John, of Lydiard-Tregoze, in county of Wilts, Bart. and died about 1641, leaving by the said Anne (who remarried with Henry Earl of Rochester) two sons, Henry, and Francis-Henry, successive Baronets.—Sir Henry, third Baronet, married Anne, eldest daughter of Sir John Danvers of Cornbury in Oxfordshire, Knt. and sister and coheir to John Danvers, Esq. had two daughters his coheirs, viz. Eleanor, married to James Bertie, Earl of Abingdon; and Anne, to Thomas Lord Wharton; and dying without male issue, was succeeded by his brother Sir Francis-Henry, the fourth Baronet, who married Elisabeth, daughter and heir to Thomas Pope, Earl of Downe, and by her (who remarried with Robert, Earl of Lindsay in Scotland) he had Sir Edward-Henry his heir; and Francis-Henry Lee of the Temple, Esq.—Sir Edward-Henry, fifth Baronet, 5 June 1674, was created Baron of Spelsbury in Bucks, and Earl of the city of Litchfield. He was L. L. and Custos Rot. of county of Oxford, L. L. of Woodstock-park, High-Steward of the borough of Woodstock, a Lord of the Bedchamber; Colonel of a regiment of foot; after Colonel of the first regiment of Foot-Guards; and died 14 July 1716. He married Lady Charlotte Fitz-Roy, natural daughter of K. Charles II. by Barbara, Duchess of Cleveland, and by her (who died 17 February 1717-18) had twelve sons, and five daughters, viz. Charles, who died young; Edward-Henry, born in 1681, who died 21 October 1713, being then a Colonel in the Royal regiment of Foot-Guards; James (born 13 November 1682, Captain of the Litchfield man of war, and having married Sarah, daughter of John Bagshaw of London, died at Brasil in 1711 without issue); Francis, died young; Charles-Henry, born 5 June 1688, died at the Temple 3 January 1708; George-Henry, who succeeded to the honours; Francis-Henry-Fitz-Roy, died young; Fitz-Roy-Henry (born 2 January 1699, made a Lieutenant in his Majesty's fleet in 1721; 25 October 1728, sworn Captain of the Loo man of war; 4 February 1730-31, appointed to the Pearl man of war; 25 February 1733, to the Falkland; and 28 July 1738, to the Pembroke of 60 guns. In May 1735, he was constituted Governor of the Island of Newfoundland, which he resigned 3 June 1738, and died 15 April 1750, being then Vice-Admiral of the Red); William was made Governor of Cape Coast Castle, 12 May 1738, and he died without male issue; Thomas, and John died unmarried; Robert (married 21 January 1717-8, to Catharine, sister of Sir John Stonehouse,

DILLON, Viscount DILLON.

folk, Bart.; Catharine, born 4 June 1752; Laura, born 21 April 1754; and Charlotte, born 11 September 1755, who became the first wife of Hon. Valentine Browne, only son of Thomas, Lord Kenmare, and she died in 1782[1]. The sons were,

Charles, who succeeded to the honour. (1)

Arthur, born at Braywick in Berkshire, 3 September (2) 1750; a Major-General in the French service, Governor of Tobago, and Colonel proprietor of Dillon's regiment. In the late war, he distinguished himself at the taking of Grenada, St. Eustatia, Tobago, and St. Christopher's, which latter island he held, till it was restored to the English at the peace; he was likewise at Savannah, and second in command under Count d'Estaing.—He married first, Lucy, daughter of Count de Rothe, Lieutenant-General in the French

house, of Radly in Berkshire, Bart.); Lady Charlotte (married 2 January 1698-9 to Benedict-Leonard Calvert, Lord Baltimore); Lady Anne; Lady Elizabeth (married first to Colonel Lee, by whom she had one son, and a daughter married to Henry, eldest son of Henry V. Palmerston, and secondly, 27 May 1731, to Rev. Edward Young, Rector of Welwyn in Hertfordshire, Chaplain in Ordinary to his Majesty, and a celebrated poet; she died 29 January 1739, leaving Arthur Young, Esq. F. R. S. who has acquired much fame in the literary world); Lady Barbara, married in May 1715, to George, only son of Sir Charles Brown, of Riddington in Oxfordshire, Bart.; and Lady Isabella, who died young.——George-Henry, L. L. D. the second Earl, was born 12 March 1689, he sat as a peer 18 September 1716, and was made Custos Brevium of the Court of Common Pleas. He married Frances, daughter of Sir John Hale, of Woodchurch, in county of Kent, Bart. and deceased in February 1742-3, leaving issue by his Lady who died in London, 25 February 1769, three sons, and four daughters, viz. George-Henry, Viscount Qarendon; Edward-Henry, who married a daughter of —— Derander, and died without issue; Charles-Henry, who died 7 July 1740, at St. Mary le Bon; Lady Charlotte, married to Henry Viscount Dillon, as in text; Lady Harriet, (in 1749 to John, Lord Bellew, and dying in April 1750 without issue, was interred in South-Audley Chapel, Westminster); Lady Anne, born in February 1730, and married 17 December 1749, to Hugh Lord Clifford; and Lady Mary married in August 1742, to Cosmus Nevile, of Holt in county of Leicester, Esq. by whom she had issue.—George-Henry, third Earl, received his education at St. John's College Oxford, and 27 February 1739, was chosen to Parliament for that county, was elected Chancellor of that University, and complimented with the degree of L. C. D. He was sworn of the Privy Council 14 July 1762; married Diana, daughter of Sir Thomas Frankland, Knt. one of the Lords of the Admiralty, and dying in September 1772, without issue, bequeathed all his estates to his uncle Robert, the fourth Earl of Litchfield, for life, remainder to his nephew Charles, he to assume the surname, and quarter the arms of Lee. The said Earl Robert, died in November 1776, when the title of Litchfield ceased, and the estates vested in the Rt. Hon. Charles Dillon-Lee, now Lord Viscount Dillon. (Collins edit 1756, II. 473, 475, 476, 477, and 478, collections, and information of Lord Dillon.)

[1] See Title Aylmer. n.

French service, and Colonel Proprieter of Rothe's regiment; by this lady who died in September 1782, he had one son who died young; and a daughter married in 1786, to Count de la Tour du Piu Gouvernet, a French Nobleman of very high rank.—He married secondly in 1784, the relict of Count de le Touche, and daughter of ——— Girardiue; by this lady who was born at Martinico, and is possessed of considerable estates in that island, he hath issue two daughters.

(3) Charles, 12 Viscount.

Henry, born 28 June 1759.

Charles, Dillon-Lee, the twelfth and present Viscount Dillon, was born in London, 6 November 1745, and conformed to the established church 4 December 1767; was appointed a Lord of the Privy Council in Ireland, during the administration of Simon, Earl Harcourt, who commenced L. L 30 November 1772; but was not sworn till the administration of the Duke of Rutland. In 1776, on the decease of Robert, Earl of Litchfield, he succeeded to the estates of his maternal ancestors, and was appointed High Sheriff of Mayo, in 1787: In which year on the decease of his father, he succeeded to the estates and honour of his ancestors, and 22 January 1788, presented a memorial to his Excellency, George Grenville-Nugent-Temple, Marquefs of Buckingham, and L. L. praying that a writ of summons should be issued for calling him to take his seat as a Peer of the realm in the Parliament then assembled, which memorial was referred by order, dated same day, to his Majesty's Prime Serjeant, Attorney General, and Solicitor General, who examined said memorial, and made their report 26 February 1788, which report (briefly stating the pedigree) being transmitted by the said Marquefs of Buckingham, L. L. to the King, his Majesty was pleased to refer the same to the House of Peers of Ireland [1], and 18 March following, pursuant to an order of reference from the L. L. 11 of same month, Lord Ranelagh reported from the Lords committees, for privileges to whom the memorial was referred, that, "it is the opinion of the committee, that the Rt. Hon. "Charles Dillon-Lee, hath fully proved his claim to the "title and honor of Lord Viscount Dillon, of Costello- "Gallen, in Ireland, and that he hath a right thereto." Upon which report and resolution the question being put that this House do agree therewith, it was resolved that the Lords

---

[1] Collections and Case.

DILLON, Viscount DILLON.

Lords Spiritual and Temporal in Parliament assembled, *nemine dissentiente*, that this House doth agree with the com-
" mittee of privileges, in their report upon the memorial
" of the Right Hon. Charles Dillon-Lee, to his Excellen-
" cy the Lord Lieutenant, and by his Excellency referred
" to this House, by his Majesty's order, claiming the
" title and honor of Lord Viscount Dillon, of Costello-
" Gallen, in the county of Mayo, in this kingdom.

" Ordered, that the Lord Chancellor do attend his Ex-
" cellency with the said report and resolution of the said
" committee, and the resolution of the House thereon, and
" their desire that the same be transmitted to, and laid be-
" fore his Majesty, as the opinion of this House, on the
" said memorial and reference[1]."

The said resolutions were accordingly transmitted to the King, who established the claim of his Lordship, and directed a writ of summons to be forthwith issued, which bears date 2 May 1788, calling him to take his seat in Parliament as a Peer of the realm[2]. His Lordship has been enrolled amongst the Fellows of the Royal Society, and is also a Member of the Royal Irish Academy. In 1787, he was High Sheriff of the county of Mayo, and 21 June 1788, was appointed a Governor of that county. 19 August 1776, he married at Brussels, in the Dutchy of Brabant, the Hon. Henrietta-Maria Phipps, daughter of Constantine-John, late Lord Mulgrave, and by this lady, who deceased 1 September 1782, he has Henry-Augustus, born at Brussels 28 October 1777; and Charlotte-Frances, also born at Brussels, 17 February 1780[3].

TITLES.] Charles Dillon-Lee, Lord Viscount Dillon, of Costello-Gallen, in the county of Mayo.

CREATIONS.] So created 16 March 1621-2, 19 Jac. I.

ARMS.] Quarterly, 1st and 4th pearl, a Lion passant between three crescents ruby, for Dillon. 2d and 3d, pearl, fess between three crescents, diamond, for Lee.

CREST.] A demi-lion, ruby, holding between his paws an etoile pearl.

SUPPORTERS.] Two angels proper, vested pearl, with wings elevated, the dexter having a sash over her shoulder, saphire, each holding in her dexter hand a palm branch, proper.

MOTTO.] DUM SPIRO SPERO.

SEATS.]

---

[1] Extracted from the MS. Journals of the House of Lords. [2] Hamper Office. [3] Pedigree from his Lordship.

NETTERVILLE, Viscount NETTERVILLE.

SEATS.] Lough-Glyn, in county of Roscomon, 89 miles from Dublin; Ditchley, in county of Oxford, 79 miles from London; and Lillies, in county of Buckingham, 44 miles from London.

NETTERVILLE Viscount NETTERVILLE.

5.   **T**HIS noble family is said to derive its pedigree from Charles, Duke of Normandy, and to have come into Ireland, on the first reduction of the kingdom, in the reign of
Sir Formal.   Henry II. in the person of Sir Formal Netterville, who marrying Philadelphia, daughter of the Lord William de Vesey, (by his wife Isabel, daughter of William, Earl of Salisbury, natural son of K. Henry II. by Rosamond, daughter of
Richard.   Walter, Lord Clifford) was father of Richard Netterville, who married Catharine, daughter of Hugh de Lacie, L. J.
Henry.   of Ireland, and had issue Henry, who by Agnes, daughter of Richard de Burgo, ancestor to the Earl of Clanricarde,
Nicholas.   was father of Nicholas, the father by Catharine, daughter
John.   of Sir Luke Fitzgerald, Knt. of John, who married Susanna, daughter of Sir Christopher Darcy, of Platten, in
Sir Luke.   the county of Meath, Knt. and had issue Sir Luke Netterville, who married Anne, daughter of Sir Oliver Plunket,
John.   of Killeen, and had John, his heir, whose wife was Anne,
John.   daughter of Sir Richard Nugent, by whom he had John Netterville, which John was seated at Kirkstown, married Anne, daughter of Sir John Barnewall, and was father by
Luke.   her, of Luke Netterville, Esq. who by Catharine, daugh-
Nicholas.   ter of John Fleming, Baron of Slane, had Nicholas, his heir, who marrying Elizabeth, daughter of John, Earl of Kil-
Sir Luke.   dare, had issue Sir Luke Netterville, which Luke married Anne,

NETTERVILLE, Viscount NETTERVILLE.

Anne, daughter of Sir John Bellew, by whom he had two sons, John, his heir; and Luke, Archdeacon of Armagh, and in 1217*, chosen by the chapter Archbishop of that see, whereupon he repaired to England, for the King's consent, who refusing to confirm the election, because made without his approbation or licenfe, the Monks compounded for 300 mares of silver and 3 of gold, for liberty of election; and repeating their choice, he was invested with the pall, and consecrated by Stephen Langton, Archbishop of Canterbury. In 1224, he founded a Dominican friary at Drogheda, and dying 17 April 1227, was buried in the Abbey of Mellefont.

Sir John Netterville, of Douth, the elder son, married Mary, daughter of Sir Patrick Bellew, of Castletown, and left Luke, his heir, who married Anne, daughter of Sir John Cruife, of the Naul, in the county of Meath, by whom he was father of Sir Patrick Netterville, who marrying Jane, daughter of Sir John Barnewall, of Trimleftown, left Sir Richard Netterville, of Douth, who took to wife Jane, daughter as we presume of Richard Plunket, Lord of Rathregan, ancestor to Patrick, Lord Dunfany, and had issue Sir Nicholas Netterville, who in 1309, sued Waryn Mulys, to give his account, whilst he was his Bailiff at Drynan. He married Elizabeth, daughter of Sir Christopher Darcy, of Platten, and had Luke, his heir, who by Marian, daughter of the Lord of Howth, had Sir Nicholas, his successor, who married Mary, daughter of Patrick Plunket, the first Baron of Louth, and had John Netterville, of Douth, who was Justice of the Court of Common-Pleas, and married the daughter of Christopher Barnewall, the second Lord Trimleston, by whom he had three sons, Patrick, of Douth; George; and Thomas, who was also a Judge of the Common-Pleas.

George, the second son, married Margaret, daughter of Henry Dowdall, of Terfeighan, in the county of Louth, Esq. and had George, his heir; Patrick and Laurence, who both died childlefs; and Alifon, second wife to Thomas Cufack, of Gerardftown, Esq. by whom she had Patrick

Sir John.
Luke.
Sir Patrick.
Sir Richard.
Sir Nicholas.
Luke.
Sir Nicholas.
John.
Family of Caftleton-Kilpatrick.

---

* In this deduction, we have followed the pedigree of the family, but there seems to be too many descents (viz. 12 in number) for so short a period, as from the arrival of Sir Formal, at sooneft in 1169, to the year 1117, which being only 48 years, they muft have succeeded each other every fourth year, a circumftance by no means probable. (Lodge.)

trick Cusack, Esq. who married Frances, daughter of Bartholomew Dillon, Esq.[1] —— George, the eldest son, was of Castleton-Kilpatrick; married Anne, daughter of Thomas Fitz-John, of Byanston, and left John Netterville, of the same place, Esq. who married Margaret, daughter of Luke Netterville, as will follow, and had issue two sons, James and Richard, and six daughters, viz. Alison (married to Sir William Talbot, of Cartown, Bart. and by him, who died 16 March 1633, was mother of Sir Robert Talbot, Bart. of Richard, Duke of Tyrconnel, and other children); Jane, the second daughter, (to Christopher White, of Clongill, county of Meath); the third, (to —— Balfe, of Galmerston); the fourth, (to —— Everard, of Randalston); the fifth, (to —— Drake, of Drakeston); and the sixth, (to —— Weldon, of Raffin, Esq.)—James, the elder son, married, and had issue three daughters, viz. Anne, married to William, brother to Maurice Eustace, Lord Chancellor; Elinor, to Walter Barnewall, of Stackallan, Esq.; and Margaret, first to —— Plunket, of Morestown, and secondly, to Captain James Wyers, High Sheriff of the county of Meath.—Richard Netterville, the younger son, died without issue, and bequeathed his estates to Lord Netterville's family, saving only a rent-charge of 400l. on the lands of Ballymore, as a legacy to his nephew, Henry White, of Ballymore, Esq.[2].

Patrick.   Patrick Netterville, Esq. who succeeded his father at Douth, married Anne, daughter of Peter Travers, of Cortilagh and Ballykey, Esq. by his wife Elizabeth, daughter and coheir to Sir Robert Hollywood, of Tartaine, and had John, his successor, who 26 April 1499, was constituted one of the commissioners of the peace for the barony of Slane; married Alice, eldest daughter of Nicholas, Lord of Howth, and by her, who after married Patrick Whyte, of Malaffen, second Baron of the Exchequer, in 1532, had issue Lucas, of Douth, who 19 October 1559, was made second Justice of the King's-Bench, and marrying Margaret, daughter of Sir Thomas Luttrell, of Luttrellstown, Knt. had four sons, and two daughters, viz.

John.

Lucas.

(1)   John, his heir.
(2)   Richard, of Corballies, who in 1576, was sent, with Barnaby Scurlock, and Henry Burnell, by the Lords of the

---

[1] Lodge Collect.   [2] Idem.

the Pale, to Q. Elizabeth, to seek redress from the burthen
of the Cesse, imposed by the L. D. Sidney, who in his letter on that occasion to the Queen, dated at Kilmainham
20 May 1577, thus describes them : " They are not able,
" they say, to geve to youer Majestie ether Stuffe or Money
" for synding your soldiours. But to furnishe that Trium-
" virat, now sent to suppresse your Majestyes Prerogatyve,
" they can make above 1000l. if they have gather'd so
" muche as they made their Reckninge for, whereof I wishe
" it would please your Majestye to give Order, that they
" may be examined. And of their own estates, in respect
" of their Parentage; first for Scurlocke, I am sure he hath
" purchased more, and buylded more, than ever his Fa-
" ther, Graundfather, or all his surname ever did ; and
" his cheife Creditt and Meane to gett this, was by being
" Attorney to your Sister and yourself, from which Office,
" for his Negligence and Wilfulnes, in the time of my
" Lord of Sussex Governement, he was displaced : Since
" which Time (as he might) he never ceased to impugne
" Inglishe Governement, and in espetiall your Majestyes
" Prerogative. Nettervill is the younger sonne of a meane
" Family and second Justice of one of the Benches, borne to
" nothinge and yet onelye by your Majestyes Bountye lyveth
" in better Countenaunce, than ever his Father did, or his
" elder Brother dothe ; and notwithstandinge that all he hath,
" he holdeth of your Highnes in Effecte, yet is he (your sa-
" cred Majestye not offended with so bad a Terme as his
" *Lewdness* deserveth) as sedicious a Varlett, and as great
" an Impugner of English Governement, as any this Land
" bearethe. Burnell's Father is alyve, and an old Man ;
" but neither in Youth nor Age lyved, or was able to lyve,
" in halfe that appearaunce that this Man dothe. He
" thirsteth earnestlye to see the Englishe Governement with-
" drawen from hence : But, for aught I knowe, he is the
" least unhonest of the three. By theise, it may please
" your Majestye to judge of the rest : I do not meane for
" Malice, but for Wealthe and happie Estate ; which,
" indede is universall, as farre as your Authoritie is ex-
" tended, savinge the verie base Tenaunt who lyveth mise-
" rablye, and not so moche for any Burden of the Sol-
" diour as thorough the Gredines of his covetous Landlord,
" for no where lyve they more wretchedlye, than where the
" Land is freed from the Soldiours."

He then proceeds to shew the effect of this universal conspiracy (as he terms it) to deny any support for the army; and says, "As confidentlye as I can conceive of any thinge, which sensiblye by sight or feeling I have not, so probablye am I persuaded, that if Nettervill had not bene, I had before this tyme assured your Majestye of above 10,000 Marcs of increase of Revenue yearelye more than I found you possess'd of; for I held a streighter Hand in the Matter of *Cesse*, the rather to bringe theim to a certeine Rent for the Release of the same." And therefore, in his instructions and memorial sent to the Queen the same day, desires, "that he may, for this respecte, and his other lewd, presumptuous, arrogant, and undutiful Dealings to me, the State, and Governement, be more severelye dealt withal, above the rest, for example's sake; and his Companions to fynd as little Favour for their Presumption, and bold Attempt against me and the Governement, as in Reason, Equitie and Honnor, may any Ways be shewed theim [1]."—Hereupon they were committed to close confinement, for impugning the Queen's Royal Prerogative to take *Cesse*, and affirming that none could be imposed but by Parliament, or Grand Council, and that whatever was otherwise set down, was against law, and the ancient customs and statutes of the realm: But they were released in August 1577, by reason of the plague then in the Fleet-Prison, upon entering into good bonds to remain either in the city, or within ten miles thereof; and before the end of the year were pardoned, and the *Cesse* reduced to five marcs the plowland, upon their offering, with all humility, to do unto the Queen and her realm, true and faithful service.—In 1585, he and the said Henry Burnell were Knights in Parliament for the county of Dublin; and having married Alison, daughter of Sir John Plunket, of Dunsoghly, made 12 October 1559, Chief Justice of the Queen's Bench, died 5 September 1607, and was buried at Donabate, in county of Dublin [2], and leaving no issue by her, who deceased 1 of that month, he bequeathed his estates to Nicholas [3], son of his elder brother John.

(3) George, who succeeded his brother at Corballies, left also no issue.

(4) Thomas.

Daughter

[1] Sidney's Letters, I. 181, 183. 186. [2] Lodge Collect. [3] Ulster's Office.

Daughter Margaret, married to John Netterville of Castleton-Kilpatrick, before mentioned. (1)

Alison, to Alexander Barnewall of Robertstown in Meath, Esq., and had Thomas Barnewall of the same place, Esq. who died 25 December 1633, having married first Margaret, daughter of James Plunket, of Dunsoghly, Esq. by whom no issue; and secondly Margaret, eldest daughter of Sir Walter Dongan, of Castletown, in the county of Kildare, Bart. by whom he had Gerald, Walter, Alison, Elinor, and Anne, with others who died young. (2)

John, who succeeded at Douth, was representative, with Richard Barnewall, of the county of Meath, in the Parliament of 1585; and 31 May 1601, making a settlement of his estate, died at Douth 20 September following; and having married Eleanor, second daughter of Sir James Gernon (frequently called Garland) of Kilmacoole in the county of Louth, Knt., by his wife Anne, younger daughter and coheir to Thomas Plunket, of Kilsaran, Esq. left issue by her, who died 29 January 1620, an only son

Nicholas, then 20 years old *, a person of many good qualities, and on that account considered by K. James I. as one, worthy to be advanced to the Peerage of Ireland, who accordingly by patent †, dated at Westminster 3 April 1622,

---

* For the fine of 50l. he had a confirmation 16 December 1611, of the messuage and land of Corbally; the castle and lands of Jordanstown, with divers others in the counties of Dublin, Meath, Carlow, Wicklow, Wexford, Roscomon and Westmeath; Also, 1 March following had a special livery, as heir to his father and uncle Richard, of Corballie, for the fine of 37l. 6s. Inquisition 20 August 1621, find that he was seised in fee of the town-land of Cloan Mc. Gillevante, in county of Westmeath, containing 80 acres of land. And by virtue of the commission for remedy of defective titles, dated 11 October 1634, he had a grant 11 May 1636 of the castle, manor, lake, fishing, mill, &c. of Ballymore-Loughtewdy, with a Wednesday market, and fair there on 4 October, and many other lands in Westmeath, to hold by the service of a Knight's-fee and the rent of 17l. 5s. English, no rent being reserved to the crown before. And also 20 May 1639, he had another grant, in virtue of the same commission, of the lands of Burnestown and others in the county of Meath, and elsewhere. (Lodge.)

† The Preamble. Ad Regni decus et Ornamentum conducere nihil mag's arbitramur, quam Viros, insignes Virtutibus pariter et Majoribus claros, qui de Rege & de Republica bene meriti sunt, et laudabilia præstiterunt Obsequia, condignis Honoribus augere. Hinc enim Videmus indies Virtutem al., atque et in Animis generosis ac illustribus Industriam et Alacri atem ad Res præclaras peragendas foveri. Perpendentes igitur quod dilectus nos Nicholaus Netterville

‡ Inq. post mortem patris and Lodge Colect.

1622, created him Viscount Netterville of Douth, with the fee of 13l. 6s. 8d. payable out of the customs of the port of Dublin. He took his seat in the Parliament, which met 14 July 1634 [1], but gave his attendance only a few days, having leave, the 26, to retire into the country for that session, in regard of his lady's sickness.—He was again present the first day of the second session (4 November) as he was in the Parliament, opened 16 March 1639, when four subsidies being granted to the King by the Commons, who intended to publish a declaration to serve his Majesty with their bodies and estates, he was appointed by the Peers, 24 of same month, one of the managers, to agree and join in the form of that declaration.—Being in the country at the breaking out of the rebellion 23 October 1641, he repaired to Dublin the day after, and waited on the L. J. with great professions of his loyalty, and readiness to assist in suppressing it [2]; but his offer of service not being accepted, he retired into the country, and joined with the Lords of *the Pale*; for which he forfeited his estate; was outlawed 17 November 1642, and by the Commissioners for executing the act of settlement was adjudged *Nocent*.

He married first Elenor, daughter of Sir John Bathe of Drumconragh, county of Dublin, and Athcarne, in the county of Meath, and she dying 27 October 1634, was buried 9 November, in the church of Douth; his second wife

---

Netterville de Douth in Comitatu Meath in Regno nostro Hiberniæ Armiger, ex illustri et antiqua Prosapia et Genere ortus et prognatus sit; quodque primus istius Familiæ in dicto Regno nostro Hiberniæ Antecessor, existens Nepos Hugonis de Lacy quondam Comitis Ultoniæ et Domini de Conaught et Meath in dicto Regno Hiberniæ, extra hoc Regnum Angliæ in dictum Regnum Hiberniæ, sub auspiciis clarissimorum Progenitorum nostrorum, ad Gentem Hibernicam in Coronæ regiæ dicti Regni nostri Angliæ Jugum et Obedientiam subigendam transfretavit, et ibidem cum præfato Hugone Clarissimi Servitia perpetravit; a tempore cujus Subactionis et Conquestus Antecessores præfati Nicholai Netterville antiquam hæreditatem eis et Meritorum suorum præmium adtunc impensam, hucusque tenuerunt, et eandem hæreditatem idem Nicholaus jam possidet. Considerantes insuper singularem ipsius Familiæ erga Coronam nostram Angliæ Fidem, utpote, in tot sæculis, et tantis Regni istius turbis, nullam Sanguinis attincturam aut Corruptionem unquam passa est. Observantes etiam summam Fortitudinem, Prudentiam, Dexteritatem, Industriam, Constantiam et Fidelitatem ipsius Nicholai Netterville erga nos et Coronam nostram, volentesque proinde eundem Nicholaum Netterville condignis Honoribus et regalibus Præmiis ornare, et ampliare, Sciatis quòd, &c.

[1] Lords Jour. I. 2. [2] Temple p. 31.

wife was Mary, *, daughter of Alderman Brice of Drogheda, widow of John Hoey, Esq. Serjeant at Arms, and also the relict of Sir Thomas Hibbots, Chancellor of the Exchequer, by whom he had no children; and deceasing in 1654, was buried at Mountown in the county of Dublin, having issue eight sons and five daughters, viz.

Sir John Netterville, his successor. (1)

Lucas, of Corballies, in the county of Dublin †, who being engaged with the Irish in their first insurrection, was at the head of those, who sent an answer to the state 10 December 1641, when the L. J. inquired into the reason of their assembling and taking arms. He died in the rebellion; and for that reason the Parliament of England[1] 3 August 1648, granted the capital messuage, town and lands of Corballies, with so much of his estate adjoining, as should amount to 400l. a year, English, to Anne, Lady Harcourt, widow of Sir Simon Harcourt, who lost his life in that war.—He married Mabel, daughter of Sir Patrick Barnewall of Turvey, and had issue Richard, who died young; and Francis, a Colonel in the Irish army, who after the reduction of the kingdom by Cromwell, was employed 1651, by Don Francisco Friscott, who was licensed by the L. D. General to raise and transport 2000 Irish soldiers for the King of Spain's service. He married Mary, daughter of General Thomas Preston, and had one son and one daughter, Thomas and Mary, who both died young.

(2) Family of Corballies.

Patrick

---

* She lived at Cotlandstown in the county of Kildare, and, as appears from her deposition, suffered much by the rebellion; being between 1 November 1641 and 31 January, robbed and deprived by the rebel, there and elsewhere, of 2000 sheep, which she accounted to be worth 600l. 70 milch cows, worth 210l. 42 oxen and 3 bulls, 135l. 40 horses, 120l. corn in haggard, 360l. corn in ground 300l. 1200 stone of sheep's wool, 100 stone of lamb's wool, and 40 stone of lockes, 7 ol. houshold goods, 200l. yearly rents, 700l. debts, 5000l. so that she had then lost 8951l.

† Which estate he possessed, pursuant to the will of his uncle Richard Netterville, of same place, Esq. dated 11 April 1607, (soon after which he died) whereby his trustees by his settlement of 16 June 1606, were to stand seized of his lands of inheritance in the county and city of Dublin, to the use of his wife Alison for life; remainder to Luke, second son of Nicholas, Viscount Netterville in tail male; and of his leases and farms in the counties of Kilkenny and Tipperary, for the payment of his debts, and afterwards to Patrick and Robert, third and fourth sons of the said Viscount in tail male. (List of Claims 1662.)

[1] Lodge Collect.

(3) Family of Longford.
Patrick Netterville, of Miltown, in Tipperary, Efq. who was alfo engaged in the rebellion; and by Mary, fifter of Sir Thadeus Duffe, Knt. had a daughter married to Mr. Keravan; and four fons, Nicholas; Lucas; Richard, who married Honeftas, daughter of Chriftopher Netterville, of Fethard, and left no iffue; and John, a Prieft. —Nicholas, the eldeft fon, together with his mother, had a grant of lands in the county of Galway, 24 March 1676, and became feated at Leighcarrow, in that county; and marrying Mary, daughter of Sir Redmund Burke, had three fons, Luke, who left no iffue; Patrick; James (who by Mary, his wife, left Chriftopher Netterville, a lunatick, in 1731[1]); and feveral daughters, the fecond of whom, Mary, was firft married in April 1674, to Sir Edmund Burke, of Glinfk, Bart. to whom fhe was third wife, and after to Roger O'Shaghnaffey, of Caftlegarre, county of Galway, Efq.—Patrick, who fucceeded, was feated at Lecarrow, and Longford, in the county of Galway; married Margaret, fifter to James Ferrall, of Killmore, in the county of Rofcomon, Efq. and dying in 1735, had three fons and four daughters, viz. Edmund, of Longford, and of Glafnevin, near Dublin, fheriff of the county of Galway, for the year 1745; (who married Margery, eldeft daughter of Frederick Trench, Efq. Member of Parliament for the faid county, and died in June 1777, leaving two children, Frederick; and Margery, who married in Auguft 1760, Walter Lawrence, of Woodfield, county of Galway, Efq.[1]); James and Patrick, who both died unmarried; Cicely, married to Sir Henry Burke, of Glinfk, Bart.; Margaret, to John Fallon, of Ballyglafs, in Rofcomon, Gent.; Catharine, deceafed; and Bridget, married in 1744, to James Tully, of Dunmore, M. D. and died in 1748.

(4) Family of Crucerath.
Robert, of Crucerath, and of Knockcumber, in Meath, who married Jane, daughter of Sir William Rigdon, of Rigdon-Hall, in Lincolnfhire, Knt. and had fix fons and four daughters, viz. Nicholas, his heir; John, who married Sarah, daughter of Sir Thomas Offeley, Groom-Porter, and died after 1722, childlefs; William, a Lieutenant in the army, who married the Lady Frances Ridgeway, elder daughter of Wefton Pitt, third Earl of Londonderry, which title is extinct, and died 20 February 1709; Robert,

[1] Lodge Collect.

Robert, James, Patrick, Mary, Alice, Jane, and Elizabeth, who all died young.—Nicholas, of Crucerath [1], in February 1676, married Catharine, daughter of William, Viscount Fitz-William, and by her, who died in 1741 [2], had three sons and three daughters; William; Nicholas; John, of London; Alice; Dorothy, who died unmarried; and Mary, married to James Barnewall, Esq. and died in 1728.—William, the eldest son, married Mary, daughter and heir to Robert Preston, of Charestown, in the county of Dublin, Gent. (who died 22 June 1716, by his wife Alice, niece to Thomas Hussey, of Cullmullen, in Meath, Esq.) and had issue Robert, to (whom his grand-mother Alice, who died in 1733, left the benefit of her farm of Charestown, and who 20 October 1755, married Margaret, daughter and coheir to Sir Andrew Aylmer, Bart. and relict of —— Luttrell [3]); Catharine; and Mary.—Nicholas Netterville, of Hollymount, alias Rathallin, in Meath, Esq. (the second son of Nicholas) 7 June 1719 conformed to the established church, and 31 January, 1727, had his Majesty's warrant for an annuity of 80l. a year, and the sum of 324l. He married first Elizabeth Jones, widow of Henry Luttrell, of Luttrellstown, Esq. father of Simon, late Earl Carhampton [4], and she dying in 1723, he married 20 August 1724, Joyce [5], widow of Sir Ignatius Nugent, Knt. and had one son Nicholas, made an ensign of foot in 1747, and one daughter Catharine [6].

Richard, who in 1640, commanded a company of 97 foot, at 15s. a day [7].

Christopher, a Jesuit.

Captain Thomas Netterville, of Black-Castle [8], who being in England, when the troubles began in Ireland, had a pass from the King in November 1641, to return to his native country; but was stopped in his journey by the Mayor of Chester, and by an order of the House of Lords, (17 January) taken prisoner to London; but some time after being released, he came into Ireland, and was engaged in the rebellion; after which he resided at Black-Castle, married Catharine, daughter of Thomas Betagh, of Moinalty, in Meath, Esq. and had Matilda or Maud, who married Richard Everard, of Randalstown, in Meath, Esq. and had several children, of whom the eldest son Thomas, by his wife Anne, daughter of Thomas Barnewall, of Rowston, in Meath, Esq. had issue two sons Matthias and Christopher.

Nicholas,

---

[1] Articles dated 22. Court of Prerogative. [2] Her will was proved 15 Feb. that year in the Court of Prerog. Office. [3] Lodge Collect. [4] See that title. [5] Prerog. Office. [6] Lodge. [7] Id. [8] Id.

(8) Nicholas, a Jesuit, and Chaplain to L. D. Tyrconnel, in 1688.

(1) Daughter Mary was married to Sir Luke Fitz-Gerald, of Tecroghan, Knt. and was mother of George, who married, Jane daughter of Sir Thomas Carey, of Portlester, and had an only child Mary.

(2) Margaret, in 1626, to Pierce Butler, son and heir to Edward, of Grange, the first Viscount Galmoy, and by him, who died in 1650, had Edward, successor to his grandfather in that title.

(3) Alison, to Walter Chevers, of Mountown, in the county of Dublin, Esq.

(4) Ellen, or Eleanor, to Thomas Fleming, of Cabragh, in the county of Cavan, Esq.

(5) Jane, to Matthias, Lord Trimleston [1].

Sir John, 2 Viscount. Sir John Netterville, the second Viscount, was knighted in his father's life-time, and in 1540 commanded a half standing company of 97 men at 15s. a day; with whom, on the breaking out of the rebellion the year after, he accompanied the Lord Moore, into Drogheda, 26 October, for the defence thereof against the Northern rebels: But his religion inclining him to favour their insurrection, he declared much virulency in his affections, by giving groundless alarms, raising false rumours, and infusing evil dispositions into the minds of the townsmen; who, as it afterwards appeared, were but too forward to take part with the rebels. It was believed, they had in the very beginning concerted to cut off the Lord Moore, and seize upon his troop, and that Sir John Netterville's part was to begin a mutiny; which he attempted the night he was to be upon the watch, by giving ill language and endeavouring to make a quarrel with his Lordship; which that Lord very discreetly passed over, and so carefully looked to the guards, that they could take no advantage to execute their design. —After this, he retired to his own house, till he was forced by the rebels to quit it, and throw himself into the King's protection, by repairing to the Earl of Ormond, at Garretstown; but upon his arrival in Dublin, he was committed prisoner to the castle, and there continued, until, upon his petition to the King, giving an account of his conduct, (the substance whereof is inserted below)

[1] See V. Kingsland a.

NETTERVILLE, Viscount NETTERVILLE.

low *,) he was enlarged in April 1643; in which very month, he accompanied the Irish army to the sieges of Ballynekill and Borrass in the Queen's County; and, after the reduction of the kingdom by the Parliament, was, with his

---

* In his petition he sets forth, that in the beginning of these troubles he was at his dwelling-house, distant some few miles from Drogheda, to the siege whereof the rebels came upon a sudden in such numbers, that he could make no way into the town, and so was forced to maintain his House within a mile of the enemy: But their multitudes so increased, that he was no way able to resist them, and they broke and forced into his house in great parties once or twice, and resided there against his will: But abhorring their ways, he determined to leave his house, and come to his Majesty's forces with the first opportunity, which was when the Earl of Ormond came to Garretstown, within ten miles of his dwelling; to whom, of his own free desire and accord he immediately repaired (though with much hazard of his life) and humbly submitted and presented himself to his Majesty's obedience and service, and so came to Dublin to his service and protection; where, on his coming, the Lords of the Council, 12 March 1641, committed him prisoner to the castle, and soon after he was indicted of treason in the King's Bench, chiefly for receiving the rebels into his House, whereas he was not able to resist them: And being the fourth or fifth that presented themselves, after his Majesty's proclamation from Westminster 1 January, and the number of them that so came exceeded not 14 or 15 persons in the whole kingdom; yet all were committed and indicted; some put to the rack and otherwise afflicted, so as many were deterred from submission (as it may be conceived) by the severity extended to those few, that of their own accord came to his protection and service. Having in great distress remained in prison, above 12 months, bail being refused, his request was, that the King would consider the inevitable necessity of his receiving the rebels into his House, for which cause chiefly he was indicted of high treason, and the indictments found by such men, against whom he had legal exceptions, and some of the examinations taken against him were extorted by menaces with the rack and such like punishments, and that himself, in examination, was much enforced, by leaving out all that might lawfully mitigate or excuse his offence; and that it was conceived, his Majesty's proclamation, and the order of Parliament, with his humble submission and coming to Dublin, as soon as possibly he could, would in honour and justice give pardon to greater transgressions. The benefit of all which he implored, and to be released upon bail, that so he might preserve that little fortune, which was not as yet possessed by the rebels, whereby to keep his wife and children from starving.—This was confirmed by the following certificate;

"We, whose names are underwritten, are ready to depose upon oath, whensoever we shall be thereunto required, that Sir John Netterville did voluntarily come in, and submit himself in such manner and form, as in his petition is set forth. Witness our hands this 5th day of April 1643.

JOHN DONGAN.
EDMUND BUTLER.
HENRY TALBOT."

And all the articles of his petition he defended by the attestations of credible witnesses.

his father, 12 August 1652, excepted from pardon for life and estate.—However, his lady 20 April 1653, obtained an order of government to enjoy a fifth part of the profits of the estate, over and above contribution, towards the better subsistence of herself and children ; and five days after, in regard she was an English-woman, and a stranger in the country, that fifth part was discharged from contributing to the reparation of losses and robberies, committed by the Irish in rebellion, and from debts contracted by her husband during the time of the rebellion : Also, 12 May, upon her petition, desiring to be continued in the possession of *Douth* and *Proudfootstown*, as part of her fifths, the same was allowed her, in regard she had no other place to resort unto, for the accommodation of herself and family.

She was the Lady Elizabeth Weston, elder daughter of Richard, Earl of Portland, Lord High-Treasurer of England, and Knight of the Garter, by his first wife Elizabeth, daughter of William Pincheon, of Writtle, in Essex, Esq. They were married in 1623[1], and his Lordship dying in September 1659,[*] was buried in the church of St. Giles in the Fields, London, having issue by her, who died in 1656, and was buried in the same church, seven sons and four daughters ; Nicholas, his successor ; Richard, who died in Italy ; Hierome, a Priest ; James, a Lieutenant in the army, who married Eleanor, daughter of Sir William Talbot, of Cartown, Bart. and widow of Sir Henry O'Neile ; Lucas, Patrick, and Robert, died infants ; Mary, married in 1661, to Henry, the second Viscount Kingsland ; Frances ; Margaret, to William Archbold, of Timolin, in the county of Kildare, Esq. and Eleanor, who died young [†].

Nicholas, 3 Viscount.

Nicholas, the third Viscount Netterville, being entitled to the estate of the family in tail, which had been seized and sequestered by reason of his father's and grandfather's engagements

---

[*] By his will, dated 2 September 1659, (prov:d 27 July 1663) he commends his body to be buried as near to the body of his deceased lady, as conveniently might be. (Prerog. Office.)

[†] After the reduction of the kingdom by Cromwell, a pension of 50 shillings a week was granted to Hierome and seven more of his Lordship's children, for their support.

[1] Pursuant to deed dated 17 February 1623.

engagements in the rebellion, was particularly mentioned and taken care of, as one of the 36 *nominees*, by the King's declaration for the fettlement of Ireland, 30 November 1660, and in confequence thereof, in 1662, put in his claim before the commiffioners for executing the act of fettlement, but had the misfortune to be judged *Nocent* by them 23 March, upon the evidence of perfons, who were all, or moft of them, after detected of, and punifhed for perjury, contrary to univerfal expectation, and to the opinion of feveral that were thought to be convinced of his innocence ¹; whereupon his brothers and fifters claimed their refpective portions, appointed by their father's marriage-fettlement, dated 27 February 1623, and his brothers their refpective remainders after his death without iffue male, they were accordingly decreed thereto in 1663, and had a grant thereof by patent in 1666; and when the faid portions fhould be fatisfied, Edward Smith, Sir Courtenay Pole and others, entitled to the eftate, fo long as his Lordfhip fhould have iffue male, were to continue their poffeffion.— Being thus ftripped of his eftate, he repaired to England, and applied to the King, who was fo well fatisfied of the hardfhips caft upon him; fo well affured of the loyalty of him and his anceftors to the Royal Family; fo defirous that all juft interefts fhould be provided for; and fo willing to extend his mercy to his Lordfhip, as far as might ftand with his juftice, that he was pleafed to have it enacted by the act of explanation, that the commiffioners for execution thereof, fhould fet out to the faid Edward Smith, Sir Courtenay Pole, and others, their refpective two-third parts, and then reftore his Lordfhip to all the eftate his father, or grandfather had enjoyed on 22 October 1641 (fpiritual livings and tithes, rectories and parfonages, impropriate and appropriate tithes excepted) to hold the fame as if he had been adjudged *innocent*, and that he fhould be thereby reftored in blood to all intents and purpofes.—But notwithftanding this, he could never get into poffeffion of more, than about a fifth part of the eftate, for which he paffed patent 18 June 1666, after vaft trouble and expence.

He was of the Privy-Council to James II. in whofe reign and *that* of his brother he had a penfion; and being in that King's army before the city of Derry, was taken prifoner 6 May 1689, and outlawed; he made his will 3 April fame

---

¹ Lodge.

same year, and dying soon after ¹, his children preferred a petition to K. William and Q. Mary, setting forth, that he was erroneously indicted of high treason before the grand jury in the county of Westmeath, some months after his decease, and judgment of outlawry given against him: Upon consideration whereof, the Queen sent her letters from Whitehall 31 March 1692, ordering the reversal of his outlawry, which was reversed accordingly; and in the act of Parliament, passed 9 K. William, to hinder the reversal of several outlawries and attainders, it was provided, that nothing therein contained should extend to attaint Richard, late Earl of Tyrone, Theobald, late Viscount Dillon, and Nicholas, late Viscount Netterville, who died during the late rebellion, before the third day of October 1691.

² In April 1661, he married Margaret, daughter of Thady O'Hara, of Crebilly, in the county of Antrim, Esq. (by his wife Catharine, sister to Daniel O'Neile, Page of Honour to K. Charles II. Captain of the first Troop of Guards, Privy-Counsellor and Post-Master-General) and had issue four sons and four daughters; John, his heir; Nicholas, who died when about 16 years of age; Luke, born in 1679, (who 12 ³ June 1707, conformed to the established church, and by the intercession of the house of Peers ⁴, obtained a pension of 200l. a year on the Civil List. He married Anne, daughter of Mr. Stanley, of Drogheda; died in 1742, and was buried with his ancestors in the church of Douth, leaving issue Nicholas, Hierome, and Margaret); James, died in his infancy; Mary, Elizabeth; Catharine, (married to Major John Bird, of Drogheda); and Honora; one of which daughters was first wife to Nicholas Plunket, of Dunsoghly, Esq.

John, Viscount. John, the fourth Viscount Netterville, at his father's death, was in foreign parts for his education, and after the reduction of Ireland in 1692, returned home, being then under age. 19 January 1715, he took the oath of allegiance ⁵. On 30 May 1704, he married Frances, eldest daughter of Richard, Viscount Rosse, and died of a fever at Liege in Flanders, 12 December 1727, in the 54 year of his age, leaving an only son

Nicholas,

¹ Lodge. III. 818.   ² Articles dated 1 April, 2500l. fortune.   ³ Lords Jour.
⁴ Lords Jour. II. 758. 762. 818.   ⁵ Idem. 494.

NETTERVILLE, Viscount NETTERVILLE. 217

Nicholas, the fifth Viscount,* born in 1708, who, after two years stay in the University of Utrecht, returned to Ireland in August 1728; took his seat in the House of Peers, 25 February 1729¹, and 28 of that month 1731, married Catharine, born 25 May 1712, only daughter of Samuel Burton, of Burton-Hall in the county of Carlow, Esq.² and his Lordship departing this life 19 March 1750, was buried at Douth, leaving by his lady, who died 24 May 1784, an only son John, and two daughters, viz. Frances, born 5 September 1733, married to —— Blake, Esq. and died at Marseilles in May 1764³; and Anne, born in 1738, who died in December 1756.

John³, the sixth and present Viscount, born in 1744.

TITLE.] John Netterville, Lord Viscount Netterville, of Douth, in the county of Meath.

CREATION.] So created 3 April 1622, 20 Jac. I.

ARMS.] Pearl, a Cross, Ruby, Frettee, Topaz.

CREST.] On a Wreath, a Demi-Lion Rampant, Ruby, Bezantee.

SUPPORTERS.] The Dexter, a Sea-Horse, parti per fess, Ruby and Proper, the Mane, Legs, Fins and Tip of the Tail, Gold. The Sinister, a Lion Guardant, Ruby, Bezantee.

MOTTO.] CRUCI DUM SPIRO FIDO.

SEAT.] Douth, in the county of Meath, 25 miles from Dublin.

Nicholas, 5 Viscount.

John, 6 Viscount.

---

* His Lordship was indicted 1 August 1743, for the murder of Michael Walsh, in county of Meath, and 3 February following was tried for the same, by the House of Peers, and honourably acquitted. (Lords Journals, IV. 579.)

¹ Lords Jour. III. 119. ² See Title Conyngham. ³ Ulster's Office.

NEEDHAM.

NEEDHAM, Viscount KILMOREY.

6. THIS family of NEEDHAM, NEDEHAM, NEDHAM,
hath been of great note in the counties of Salop and Chef-
William. ter, and is defcended from William de Nedham, Lord of
Staunton in the laft mentioned county 1102 (3 Hen. I.) whofe
William. fon William, living 1154 (1 Hen. II.) had Roger his heir,
Roger. living in the year 1200, the father of William, the father of
William. John, the father of John de Nedeham, living 1330 (4 Edw.
John.
Thomas. III.) whofe fon Thomas Nedeham, of Nedeham in the coun-
ty of Derby, living 1337, (11 Edw. III.) had iffue two
fons, Thomas his heir, and William, anceftor to Vifcount
Kilmorey, and of whom hereafter; Thomas, the elder fon
was living in 1353, he married Maud, daughter of Roger
Melure, of Thornfet in county of Derby, and had iffue,
Robert Needham, living in 1381 (5 Ric. II.) whofe fon
Needham, of Needham (4 Hen. V.) had John Needham of
Thornfet (2 Hen. VI.) the father of Otwell, of Thornfet,
who had Chriftopher his heir, and Margery, married to
Thomas Whittington of Pantley, Efq.—Chriftopher fuc-
ceeded at Thornfet, and married Elizabeth, daughter of
John (alias Thomas) Shalcrofs, of Shalcrofs, and had iffue
Otwell his heir; Edward, Arthur, Humphry,- Chriftian,
which four died unmarried; Agnes married to John Gref-
well of Chefter; and Ifabel to John Radifh.—Otwell was
feated at Thornfet, Needham, and Chowley, and marrying
Elizabeth, daughter of Nicholas Cadman, of Colly, had
iffue eleven fons, and five daughters, viz. William his heir;
Richard of Senetorton (who married firft Elizabeth, daughter of Henry Sacheveral, by whom he had no iffue; and fecondly, Dorothy, daughter of Henry Eyre, of Highlow,
and by her had three fons, Humphry, John, and William);
Humphry (who married Grace, daughter of William Ellis,
and had a fon Richard) ; Henry (who by Anne, daughter of
—— Hazlewood, had an only daughter, Anne, married
to Laurence Blandefton of Southampton); Edward, who
died

died young; George (who by Ciare, daughter of —— Jafper of Antwerp, had a fon Francis); Otwell (who by Elizabeth, daughter of —— Weftby, had William his heir); Arthur, Triftram, Anthony, and John, all died unmarried: daughter Elizabeth, married to Robert Radcliffe of Mellor; Letitia, to Richard Windefley, of Windefley; Dorothy, to John Dakin; Grace, to William Bullock of Ounfton; and Eleanor.——William Needham of Thornfet, the eldeft fon, married Margaret, daughter and heir to Nicholas Garlick of Whitfield, Efq. and had Otwell; and George (who married Catharine, daughter of Stephen Eyre).—Otwell left iffue Henry of Benhes, who married firft, Mary, daughter of Owen Williams, of the county of Caernarvon, and by her had William, and Dorothy; and he married fecondly, Hefter, daughter of John Tedcaftle of London, and had iffue, Henry (who continued the line in county of Derby); and two daughters, Elizabeth and Sarah [1].

William, the younger fon of Thomas of Needham, living in 1375 [2], was Juftice of Chefter, and married Alice, daughter and heir to William (or Henry) Cravach, of Cravach, living there 3 Ric. II. 1379, and had Robert his heir, living 1417, who had two fons, Robert; and Thomas, father (by Catharine, daughter of Humphry Hill) of Humphry Nedeham, who left a fon Robert.

William.

Robert.

Robert Nedeham of Cravach, Efq. the elder fon, living 18 Rich. II. married Dorothy, daughter of Sir John Savage of Clifton in Chefhire, Knight of the Garter, by his wife Catharine, daughter of Thomas Stanley, and dying in 1448 (26 Hen. VI.) was buried in Holme-Chapel, leaving by her, who deceafed in 1430, four fons and one daughter, Anne (or Agnes) married to John Starkey of Oulton, in the county of Chefter, Efq. whofe fon and heir Hugh, died in 1526, and by Margaret, daughter of Philip Egerton, of Egerton, was father of Hugh Starkey, Efq. who built the church of *Over*, in 1543, and died in 1555, without iffue. The fons were,

Robert.

Thomas, his fucceffor. (1)

Sir John Nedeham, who in 1449 was chofen Serjeant of London, for which city, the next year, he was Member of Parliament, and in 1452, was Lieutenant-Juftice of Chefter, of which, in 1461 he was made Juftice, and afterwards confti- (2)

---

[1] Pedigree Penes J. L.   [2] Idem.

constituted a Judge of the Court of King's Bench. He married Margaret, youngest daughter of Randal Manwaring, of Over-Pever in Cheshire, Esq. widow of William, the son of Sir John Bromley, of Badington, and dying without issue, in 1480, was buried in Holme-Chapel; having settled the lands, called Hallum-Lands in the county of Chester (which he had purchased in 1471, from Thomas Chickford, who had married Elizabeth, daughter and heir to Robert de Hallum) and the rest of his estate on his next brother

(3) Robert of Atherley, whose descendants lived at Shavrington (or Shavington) in Salop, and failed of issue male, in 1578 (21 Eliz.) whereby the estate devolved on Robert Needham, of Shenton, Esq. and is now enjoyed by the Lord Kilmorey.

(4) Hugh, of whom we find no farther mention.

Thomas. Thomas Needham, of Crevach, Esq. the eldest son, married Maud, daughter of Sir William Brereton, of Brereton (by his wife Maud, daughter of John Dutton, of Dutton, Esq. and widow of Sir William Booth, of Dunham) and deceasing in 1463, was buried in Holme-Chapel, having issue Sir William his heir, and a daughter Anne, married to Robert Greene, of Congleton in Cheshire, Esq.

Sr William. Sir William Needham, of Crevach and Shavington, Knt. married Isabel, one of the three daughters, and coheirs to Sir John Bromley, who died in 1487, by Joan his wife, daughter and heir to William Hexstall, descended from Sir Walter Bromley, living in the reign of Henry III. and by

Sr Robert. her left Sir Robert Needham, Knt. who in 1506 (22 Hen VII.) purchased the estate of Shenton, and in the 20. 27. and 32 years of Henry VIII. was sheriff of the county of Salop.——He married Agnes, daughter of John Manwaring of Baddeley, Esq. and died in 1556 (the probate of his will bears date, 30 July 1557) having issue Thomas his heir, and four daughters, ———, married to Robert Cholmondeley, of Chorley, Esq.; Jane, to Sir Andrew Corbet of Morton, and was mother of Sir Vincent Corbet; Mary, to John Winnington of Pantley; and Maud, to Sir Thomas Venables of Kinderton, Knt.

Thomas. Thomas Needham of Shenton, Esq. married Anne, daughter of Sir John Talbot, of Grafton in the county of Worcester, and had issue three sons, and three daughters; Robert, Thomas, John; Anne, married to Sir Richard Bulkeley of Beaumaris; Margaret, to Richard Stevenson
of

NEEDHAM, Viscount KILMOREY.

of Dothell; and Margery, to George Coney, of Coney, Esqrs.———Robert, the eldest son, in the 6. 28 and 37 years of Q. Elizabeth, was Sheriff of the county of Salop, and in her reign, had considerable commands during the war in Ireland; after which he was made Vice-President of the Council, in the marches of Wales; and by Frances, youngest daughter of Sir Edward Aston of Tixhall, in the county of Stafford (by Joan, daughter of Sir Thomas Bowlefs, Baron of the Exchequer) had two sons and six daughters, viz. *Robert.*

Robert, created Viscount Kilmorey. (1)

Thomas of Poolpark, in county of Derby, who married Ellen, daughter of Sir Henry Bagenal, Knight-Mareschal of Ireland, and widow of Sir Robert Salisbury, by whom he had issue, Sir Robert Needham of Poolpark (who married Mary, daughter and heir to ——— Hartop of Surry, and left posterity) Richard, also of Poolpark; Arthur of Cambridge; Thomas; and Francis, both of London, and a daughter Elizabeth, living in 1633[1]. (2)

Daughter Maud, married to John Aston, of Aston in Cheshire, Esq Sewer, or Steward to Q. Anne, wife of K. James I. and by him, who died 13 May 1615, had three sons and three daughters, whereof the eldest son, Sir Thomas Aston, was created a Baronet 25 July 1628, and was ancestor to the present Sir Willoughby Aston. (1)

Jane, to James Collier of Darleston, in Staffordshire, Esq. who sold *Stone* and *Darleston* to his father-in-law. (2)

Anne, to Robert Powell of Park, Esq. (3)

Dorothy, second wife to Richard Chetwode, Lord of Chetwode Wood-hall, and Warkworth, in the county of Bucks, and had five sons and six daughters, viz. Robert; Thomas; John; Tobias; Francis: Grace; Mary; Dorothy; Jane; Beatrix; and Abigail[2]. (4)

Mary, first to Thomas Onslow of Beraton; and secondly, to Sir Robert Vernon of Hodnet, both in Shropshire, and was mother of Sir Henry Vernon, created a Baronet 25 July 1660. (5)

Elizabeth, died unmarried.

Sir Robert Needham, who succeeded at Shenton, was knighted by K. James I.; served the office of Sheriff for the county of Salop in 1606; was appointed 12 November 1617, of Council to William, Lord Compton, President of (6) *Sir Robert,* 1 *Viscount.*

---

[1] Lodge'. Collect. [2] Idem.

NEEDHAM, Viscount KILMOREY.

of Wales; and by K. Charles I. created a Peer of Ireland, by letters patent, dated 18 April 1625. He married to his first wife, Jane, daughter of John Lacy, Esq. Alderman of London, she dying 16 July 1591, was buried at Atherley in Shropshire, without issue; he married secondly, Catharine, daughter of John Robinson of London, Esq. relict of George Huxley, of Wyrehall in Middlesex, Esq. who left her a widow 30 April 1627; and by her he had two sons and four daughters; Robert his successor; Alexander of Newstead; Anne, Elizabeth, both died unmarried; Elenor, wife to William Owen of Shrewsbury, Esq.; and Frances, to Sir Rowland Cotton.

Robert, 2 Viscount.

Robert, the second Viscount, married first Frances, third daughter of Sir Henry Anderson, Sheriff and Alderman of London in the reign of Q. Elizabeth, by whom he had Robert his heir; Ellen; and Frances, the first wife of Thomas, son of George Cotton of Cumbermere, Esq. and had one son, George, who by Mary, daughter of Sir Thomas Smyth, of Haugh in Cheshire, Knt. had an only daughter, who died young before him.——His Lordship's second wife was Eleanor, daughter and heir to Thomas Dutton of Dutton, Esq. Widow of Gilbert, Lord Gerard of Gerard's Bromley, and dying at Dutton, 12 September 1653, had issue by her, who died there 12 March 1665, æt. 69, and was interred the 16 at Great-Budworth, four sons and eight daughters, viz.

(1) Charles, successor to his half-brother Robert in the honour.
(2) George, who died at Chester without issue, in 1544.
(3) Thomas.
(4) Arthur, overlaid by his nurse.
(1) Daughter Anne, died in her infancy.
(2) Eleanor, first married in 1638, to Peter Warburton of *the Lodge* in Cheshire, Esq. she being then but 11 years old, but he dying without issue, and under age, of the small-pox at Oxford, 1 August 1641, she became the second wife in 1544, of John, the first Lord Byron, then Governor of Chester, who died in France without any issue by her, in 1652; and she, who is described to have been a Lady of such beauty, sweet disposition, and general repute, that she scarce left her equal, died at Chester, 26 January 1663, about the age of 36 years, and was buried in Trinity Church.

Susan,

Sufan, married in 1652, to Richard Scriven, of Fordfley (3)
in Shropfhire, Efq. where fhe died 'n Auguft 1667.
Catharine, died unmarried at Dutton, 11 March 1665, (4)
the day before her mother, and was buried in the fame
grave.
Mary, died after the year 1669, unmarried[1]. (5)
Penelope, in 1653, became the firft wife of Randal Eger- (6)
ton, of Betley in Staffordfhire, Efq. and dying in 1670, lies
buried in the North-Aile of K. Henry VII. Chapel, Weftminfter Abbey, under a monument with this infcription;

PENELOPE,
Filia é pluribus lectiffima
ROBERTI Dom. NEDHAM Viceco. de KILMURRAY
et
HELENÆ antiquifs. DUTTON de DUTTON
In Comit. Palat. Ceftr. Hæredis unicæ,
Conjux mœftiffimi
RANDOLPHI EGERTON de Betley Ceftr. Confinio,
Carolino nuper in Exercitu Majoris (ut vocant) Generalis,
Supremoque nunc Regni Confilio (Parliamento regio)
Staffordienfium Delegati. (fidem
Cujus in utrumque Carolum Britanniar. Monarchas immobile
Refque præclare geftas, Pofteri non tacebunt.
(Cui nunquam nifi moriendo gravis)
Heic juxta EGERTONORUM Infignia
(Illuftrifs. Baronum de MALPAS)
Una cum RANDOLPHO Filiolo
Pofita eft ex voto.
(Quin ab illâ magis (credite) fe pofitum voluit Maritus,
Neque vita functum alibi ponendum optat)
Filiolæ dans vitam perdidit,
XIII. Kalend. April. Anno } Humanæ M. D. CLXX°.
Reftitut.   } Britannicæ X°.
Stat fine pede Virtus.

Her hufband died 20 October 1681, and was buried with
her.
Dorothy, died unmarried at London, in June 1669. (7)
Elizabeth. (8)
Robert, the third Vifcount Kilmorey, married Frances, Robert,
fecond daughter of the aforefaid Gilbert, Lord Gerard, by 3
the Vifcount.

[1] Lodge's Collect.

the said Eleanor Dutton, and had an only child, Eleanor, which died an infant in 1643; and his Lordship deceasing in January 1657, was buried at Atherley, when the honour descended to

Charles, 4 Viscount.
Charles, his half-brother, and the fourth Viscount, who in 1659, met at Warrington in Lancashire with the Earl of Derby, and Sir George Booth, in a small party, to prepare for the restoration of K. Charles; having a speedy accession of great numbers of the Gentry, which encreased to 500 men, they marched to Chester, and by the interest of Colonel Werden, had the gates opened; but (5 August) General Lambart being dispatched against them with a good body of men, took them prisoners to London, where his Lordship died in 1660; and having married Bridget, daughter and coheir to Sir William Drury, of Besthorp in Norfolk, Knt. had issue by her, who became the second wife of Sir John Shaw of London, Bart. three sons, viz. Robert, and Thomas, who succeeded to the honour, and Byron, who was educated at Cambridge, and in 1681, incorporated A. M. in the University of Oxford.

Robert, 5 Viscount.
Robert, the fifth Viscount, born in 1655, succeeded his father, and dying 29 May 1668, a minor, was interred in the chancel of the church of Besthorp, in Norfolk, with the following inscription over the vault;

Memoriæ
Prænobilis Domini
Roberti Nedham
Vicecomitis de Kilmorrai,
Carolo vicecomite (in utrumque Carolum Britanniarum Monarchas temporibus Monarchomachis, fidelissimo)
Ac Brigetta vicecomitissa superstite,
Gulielmi Drury equitis Aurati et dominæ Mariæ filia
Prognati:
Eximia tam virtute, quam eruditione, nobilitatem
Geminantis:
Proceritate, venustate, pulchritudine,
Ostenti:
Amoris publice ferreo sæculo,
Magnetis
Ingenio præcoci maturæ vitæ spem
Frustrantis:
Anno Dom. 1668°, ætatis 13° maii 29.
Sole, comite et exemplo, ut alibi luceret,
Occidentis:

Anastasia

NEEDHAM, Viscount KILMOREY.

Anaſtaſin Paſchatis diem, qui anno hujus
Obitus conſcio defuit, æternitate penſaturam
    Præſtolantis:
  Hoc monumentum dicavit avia
    Quotidie viſitatura.
Dum jacet hic tumulo, manet hæc tumulata dolore [1].

Thomas, the ſixth Viſcount, who ſucceeded his brother, had his education in Chriſt-Church, Oxford, and 4 Auguſt 1677, welcomed the Duke of Ormond, Chancellor of that Univerſity, with a ſpeech, to his lodgings in the ſaid College.——He married Frances, daughter and heir to Francis-Leviſon Fowler of Harnage-Grange, in Shropſhire, Eſq. (by his wife Anne, ſecond daughter of Peter Venables, Eſq. Baron of Kinderton) and by her, (who remarried firſt, 2 May 1690, with Theophilus, Earl of Huntingdon, and ſecondly, with the Chevalier de Ligondes, Colonel of horſe, one of the French priſoners taken with Mareſchal Tallard at the battle of Hochſtet; by the latter of whom ſhe had one ſon the father of Anne-Conſtantia Ligondes, who became the firſt wife of the Right Hon. John Beresford, ſecond ſon of Marcus, Earl of Tyrone [2]; and her Ladyſhip deceaſed 27 December 1723) had iſſue

Robert, the ſeventh Viſcount, who was under age at the death of his father, and lies buried in the church of Atherley in Shropſhire, under a monument thus inſcribed;

> Near this place is interred the Right Honourable Robert, Lord Viſcount Killmorey;
> He left four ſons, Robert, Thomas, Francis, And John; and four daughters, Anne, Mary, Elizabeth and Henrietta, by the Right Honourable Mary his wife, daughter of John Offley of Crew, in the county of Cheſter, Eſq.
>   Deceaſed October 2 1710,
>   Then aged 28 years.

Robert, the eldeſt ſon, and eighth Viſcount, dying unmarried, 19 February 1716, his next brother Thomas,

---

[1] Blomfield's Hiſt. Norfolk, I. 335.   [2] See that title.

NEEDHAM, Viscount KILMOREY.

Thomas, 9 Viscount. Thomas, became the ninth Viscount, and 29 June 1730, married the Lady Mary Shirley[1], born 25 September 1712 in Dublin, she was third daughter, and coheir to Washington, Earl Ferrers, (by his wife Mary, daughter of Sir Richard Levinge, Bart. Justice of the King's Bench in Ireland) and his Lordship dying 3 February 1768, without issue, by his Lady who deceased 12 August 1784[2], was succeeded by his next surviving brother,

John, 10 Viscount. John, the tenth and present Viscount Kilmorey; in July 1737, he was made Colonel and Captain of a company of grenadiers, in the second regiment of foot guards, which he resigned in November 1748.—11 January 1758, his Lordship married Anne, relict of Peter Shakerley, in county of Chester, Esq. and had issue, Thomas, who died 19 April 1773, unmarried; Robert; Francis, married to the daughter of ——— Fisher, Esq.; and a daughter Mary.

TITLE.] John Needham, Lord Viscount of Kilmorey, in the county of Clare.

CREATION.] So created, 18 April 1625, 1 Car. I.

ARMS.] Pearl, a bend, saphire between two bucks heads caboffed and attired, diamond.

CREST.] On a wreath, a phœnix in flames, proper.

SUPPORTERS.] The dexter, a horse bay coloured mane and tail, diamond; the sinister, a buck, proper.

MOTTO.] NUNC AUT NUNQUAM.

SEAT.] Shenton-Hall, in County of Salop, 130 miles from London.

---

[1] Ulster's Office.   [2] Lodge's Collect.

BOURKE,

BOURKE, Viscount MAYO.

IN our account of the Earl of Clanricarde, the antiquity of this family is evidenced[1]; and in *that* of the Earl of Mayo[2] we have shewn, that Edmund Bourke, second son of Sir Thomas *Mac-William-Oughter*, is direct ancestor to the Viscounts Mayo, which Edmund (*Barbatus*, called by the Edmund. Irish nv scsoig, i. e. bearded) succeeded his brother in the title of Mac-William, and enjoyed the same to his death in 1458, being succeeded therein by his next brother Thomas.——In 1443, the said Edmund, and his confederates, both English and Irish, raised a powerful army, to fight Ulick (Oge) Fitz-Ulick-Rickard-Mac-William of Clanrickard; but the battle was prevented, by the latter going to the former's house, and making a submission, because he had not at that time a sufficient force to defend his country, and a peace was concluded, on condition of Clanrickard's delivering to him 400 cows, a horse and a mare.——He died in the latter end of the year 1458, with this character, " That he was Lord of the English, and many Irish in " Conaught, and the only Englishman in Ireland, worthy " to be chosen Chief, for his resolution, proportion of per- " son, generosity, hospitality, constancy, truth, gentility " of blood, martial feats, and all qualities, by which a " man might merit praise."——He married first Honora, daughter of Ulick (Roe) Mac-William of Clanrickard; secondly, the daughter of O'Flaherty, by whom he had three sons, viz David (Duffe) of Gosydin; John; and William of Ilean-an-Caca, or *the dirty Island*: having also three sons by his first wife, Sir Rickard his heir; Ulick, from whom the Lord Mayo derives; and Thomas (Roe) ancestor to the Bourkes of Ballinghana in Tyrawly.

[1] I. 127.   [2] See that title in III.

BOURKE, Viscount MAYO.

Familes of Caſtlebar, Tyrawly, Newtown, Ballintobber, &c.

Sir Rickard Bourke, the eldeſt ſon, (ſtyled O'Courſkey from his being a great warrior, and uneaſy to his neighbours in this and other kingdoms) was elected Lord Mac-William Oughter in 1469, on the reſignation of Rickard Bourke of Turlogh; and by Celia, daughter of Mac-Jordan, had certainly ſix ſons, Edmond, Walter, Thomas, John, Rickard-Oge, and William, who died without iſſue; ſome alledging he had four other ſons, Ulick, David, Theobald, and Meyler. His five ſons who left poſterity were,

(1) Edmond of Caſtlebar, who was murdered 2 February 1513, in the monaſtery of Rathbran, by the ſons of his brother Walter, leaving three ſons, Ulick, David (Bane) who both left poſterity; and William, who had no iſſue.

(2) Walter, who had five ſons, of whom Theobald (Reagh) by a daughter of Theobald Fitz-Ulick Fitz-Edmond Barbatus, had Ulick, who left iſſue.

(3) Thomas Baccagh (Lame) whoſe three ſons Edmond (Buy), John, and William left poſterity.

(4) *Family of Tyrawly.* John of Tyrawley, who in 1506, was ſlain in the monaſtery of Ballintobber, by his nephew David Fitz-Edmond, and had iſſue a daughter, married to David Fitz-Edmond Bourke, anceſtor by her to the family of Partry; and many ſons, whoſe poſterity are all extinct, except *that* of Oliver, who by the daughter of O Donnell, had eight ſons, Sir John, his heir; Sir Richard of Newtown, of whom preſently; Thomas, of Caſtle-Cloghans, in Tyrawly (who had five ſons, Edmond (Buy) Walter, Theobald, John, a Friar, and Richard); Edmond, anceſtor to the family ſometime ſeated at Roppagh; David of Rathroe, progenitor to the Bourkes of Rathroe, Iniſcoe, Carrukill, and others; Ulick, Anthony, and Walter (the Giber) who all left iſſue.

Sir John Bourke of Tyrawly, Ardnaree, &c. Lord MacWilliam, was commonly called *Joannes Magnus*; and 14 June 1570 fought Sir Edward Fitton, Preſident of Conaught, and Rickard, Earl of Clanrickard, at Shruel, who (he thought) were encroaching too far upon the county of Mayo, on that ſide. In 1577 he was Sheriff of that county; and 24 June 1580, had a ſingular grant from Meiler Barret (or Bareith) to him, his ſons, grandſons, and all his poſterity, of the caſtle of Croſincorlina, for certain conſiderations, eſpecially for the publick good, and that the country might be reduced to civility. He died that year, leaving eight ſons, viz. Walter (Kittagh) left-handed, of Bellecky, in Tyrawly, of whom preſently; Oliver, of Iniſcoe (who firſt married Una, daughter of Cathald O'Conor

O'Conor Sligo, and had two sons and one daughter; Thomas (Roe) who in 1638, made over his estate to Miles, Viscount Mayo; and Walter, who both died childless; and Una, married to Sir George Boyle, brother to Richard, Archbishop of Tuam. By his second wife he had John, ancestor to the Bourkes of Iniscoe); Ulick (Roe) of Crossmelina; John-an-Thleive, i. e. of the mountain; William (Fadha) the Long, of Castlelacken; David; Rickard; and Thomas (Ciach) the Blinker.

William, the fifth son, was accidentally killed in 1591, by one Alexander Mac-Donnell, leaving two sons, John, and Richard of Ainhagh. John married a daughter of Sir Hubert Burke of Glinsk, and was slain in 1642, leaving William his heir; and Edmond, who died in Spain.—— William, married first the daughter of Rickard Bourke of Newtown, by whom he had an only son, Thomas, who also died in Spain; and secondly, Mary, daughter of —— Sweeny, and by her had five sons, Edmond, Rickard, William (whose eldest son Edmond, left three sons, William Thomas, and Walter, living in 1750); John, and Walter, who died unmarried in Spain.——Edmond, the eldest son, by Catharine, daughter of Edmond Bourke of Ballintobber, Esq. had two sons and two daughters; of whom Thomas, the elder was seated at Moyne, near Killala in Tyrawly; and married Bridget, daughter of Michael Cormick, of Mullinmore, Esq. but had no issue in 1754.

Family of Castlelacken.

Walter (Kittagh) Bourke of Bellecky, Esq. the eldest son of *Joannes Magnus*, married the daughter of —— O'Donnell, Lord of Tyrconnel, and had three sons and four daughters; of whom Theobald, the eldest son, by the assistance of O'Donnel, was made Mac-William in 1595; but that title, and the succession by tanistry having been discountenanced by the Government some years before, during the rule of Rickard Mac-William, Bourke of Newtown, (after the death of Rickard Mac-William, father of the first Viscount Mayo, and the surrender of Mac-William Eighter, by Ulick of Clanrickard) Sir John Norris, assisted by the Earls of Clanrickard and Thomond, marched against him with a considerable army, and encamped at Ballinrobe in 1596; whom, by the aid of his cousin Theobald-ny-Lung, O'Flaherty, O'Maly, and O'Donnel, he obliged to decamp and quit the country, after leaving garrisons at Conge and Galway: but soon after, the said Theobald-ny-Lung (upon a disgust, chiefly taken at his entertaining many of O'Donnell's men in his service, whereby the country

try was harrassed, and burthened with free quarter) deserted him, and drawing after him O'Flaherty, his half-brother, O'Conor Sligo his brother-in-law, and O'Maly his near relation, joined the forces of Sir Coniers Clifford, Governor of Conaught, and expelled him the province; whereupon he and his adherents were attainted, and seeking a sanctuary in Spain, were kindly received by Philip II. who created Theobald, Marquefs of Mayo, and settled a pension upon him and his posterity, suitable to that dignity, which he and his son Walter (Kittagh) enjoyed, who dying without issue, left it in the custody of his half-brother, Colonel Plunket, until it should be claimed by some of his heirs general.

Family of Newtown.

We now return to Sir Richard Bourke of Newtown in Tyrawly, second son of Oliver Fitz-John of Tyrawly. He was Lord Mac-William, after his cousin Rickard (Iron), and by the daughter of O'Dowde had three sons, William his heir; Moyler, who married Johanna, daughter of Mac-Dermot of Carrick; and Ulick, who by Honora, another daughter of Mac-Dermot, had two sons and two daughters, Walter; Edmond; Honora, married to Edmond Bourke of Rathroe; and Sarah, to ———— Bourke of the family of Turlogh.————Walter, the elder son, married Celia, daughter of William Bourke, younger son of Oliver, of Roppagh, and had William, who by Margaret, daughter of Theobald Fitz-Moyler Bourke, had four sons and four daughters, Walter, Thomas, David, Michael, Celia, Mary, Cicely and Winifred.————Walter, the eldest son, married Anne, sister to Roger Palmer, of Palmerstown, Esq. and had two daughters, Mary, and Frances, and three sons, William, who married Anne, daughter of Edmond Palmer of Moylagh, in Tyrawly; Oliver, unmarried; and Walter, whose wife was the daughter of John O'Donnel, of Irrus.

William Bourke of Newtown, Loughmeasg, and Ardnaree, the eldest son of Sir Richard, married Catharine, daughter of Rickard (Iron) Mac-William Oughter, and had five sons, Sir Thomas, who died childless; Oliver (Kittagh); John; Ulick; and David. Oliver, by his wife Catharine Browne, had two sons, John (who married Agnes, daughter of Gregory Nolan, of Ballinrobe, Esq. and had five sons and two daughters, viz. Colonel Thomas Bourke, who by Joanna, daughter of ———— O'Shaghnasy, had one son, who died a Captain in Spain; and four daughters, Marian,

Marian, Lady Archdeckne in France; Agnes; Clare; and Margaret, a Nun; Richard, and Captain John, both died childlefs; Counfellor Oliver Bourke, who married Julian, daughter of John Bodkin of Carrowbegg, in Galway, Efq. William, a Captain in France, died in Italy; Alice, married to Colonel David Bourke, as hereafter; and Clare, to Edmond O'Flaherty, of Ballynahenfy); Rickard, who married Catharine, one of the feven daughters of Major John Browne, of the Neale, and had two fons and two daughters, Oliver (who married Agnes, daughter of William Skerret, Efq. and ha*. iffue William, Francis, Patrick, Catharine, Joanna, and Celia); John; Celia; and Joanna; who married Edmond Bourke, of Urey.

Rickard (Oge) youngeft fon of Sir Rickard O'Courfkey, had iffue fix fons, whereof Rickard (Oge) the fifth was of Ballintobber, and had Edmond (Buy) the father of Rickard, who had two fons, viz. Edmond, Buy (of Ballintobber, who by Mary, daughter of William Bourke of Roppagh, had Thomas, a Captain in Flanders, in Q. Anne's wars; Oliver, David; Catharine, married to Edmond Bourke, of Caftlehacket; and Bridget, to David, younger fon of Ulick Bourke, of Inifcoe); Thomas, who married Mary, daughter of Mac-Donnell, and had two fons, Rickard, a Captain in Flanders in Q. Anne's reign; and William, a Captain in the Duke of Lorain's fervice. *(5) Family of Ballintober.*

We now proceed with Ulick Bourke, fecond fon of Edmond (Barbatus) anceftor to the Lord Mayo. He married a daughter of Saba O'Kelly, of Callow, and had three fons, Edmond; Walter Fitz-Ulick, anceftor to the Bourkes, called Sloght-Illiac, or the offspring of Ulick; and William, an Abbot.—Edmond, who fucceeded, had alfo three fons, David; William of Corran; and Rickard, who died in Spain, leaving a fon of his own name, called Captain Tringus.——David, the eldeft fon, married firft, the daughter of John Fitz-Oliver Bourke of Tyrawly, by whom he had Walter (Fadda, the Long) of Partry, of whom prefently; fecondly, Finola O'Flaherty, and by her he had two fons, Rifdaird an Iarain (Iron Dick) anceftor to the Lord Mayo; and William, called by the Irifh Theabb-Kiagh, or the blind Abbot, who in 1584, with the fufpected Bifhop Malachias Annalone, renounced the Pope before the L. D. Perrott, fwore to the King's Supremacy, and the Friar quitting his habit, they both publifhed their recantation, and a profeffion of their faith. His third wife was the *Ulick. Edmond. David.*

daughter

daughter of David Fitz-Edmond Bourke of Turlogh, by whom he had one son Ulick ny-Timchil, or the Visiter, whose son Thomas, by warrant, dated at Greenwich, 5 July 1602, had a new grant of his estate, but his issue is now extinct.

Family of Partry.
Walter (Fadda) the son by the first wife, married a daughter of Mac-Philbin, originally a Bourke, and had issue Miles; and Theobald, whose posterity hath ceased. Miles married Margaret, daughter of Murrough O'Flaherty, and had David, who by Honora, daughter of Macnamara of Cratilagh, had a daughter Mary, married to Thady O'Conor Sligo; and Colonel Rickard Bourke of Partry, who married Mary, daughter of Bryan O'Flaherty, of Aghnamar in the county of Galway, Esq. and dying in 1687, left three sons and two daughters, David his heir; Miles (who by Bridget O'Maly had three daughters; and three sons, Bartholomew, Patrick, and Richard); Captain Thomas, (who first married Bridget, elder daughter of Francis, Lord Athenry, widow of Colonel James Talbot, of Mount-Talbot; and secondly, Mary Lynch, and had no issue by either); Celia, married to Captain William Bourke of Rathroe; and Bridget, to Colonel Miles Bourke, great grandson of Theobald, the first Viscount Mayo.——David Bourke of Partry, Esq. by Sarah, daughter of ——— Crofton, had four sons and five daughters, viz. Richard, a Captain in the King of Spain's army, and killed in the battle of Almanza, 1707; John, died a Captain in Spain; Walter became heir; Thomas, a Captain in the Spanish service, and slain in the battle of Campo-Santo in Italy, 8 February 1742; Mary and Elizabeth, both unmarried in 1754; Honora, married to Rowland Bourke of Iniscoe, Esq.; Elinor, to William Mac-Andrew of *the Back* in Tyrawly, by whom she had three sons; and Clotilda, to John Fitz-Edmond Costello, and had two sons, Edmond and Jordan. ——Walter, the third and only son, who married, was also a captain in the Spanish army, and lost his life in the same battle with his brother Thomas, leaving by his wife, the daughter of ——— Sweeny, one son David, and two daughters, Sarah and Mary.

Sir Rickard.
We return here to Sir Rickard (an Iarain) Fitz-David Bourke, ancestor to the Lord Mayo. In the reigns of Edward VI. and Elizabeth, he performed considerable services to the state, and became a singular ornament to his family, in that early time of reforming the natives to civility and order, as appears by the testimonies of two *Great Men,*
the

the Lord Chancellor Cufack, and L. D. Sidney.——In 1552, he was called the fecond Captain of moft power in Conaught, and (fays Sir Thomas Cufack, in his letter to the Duke of Northumberland, concerning the ftate of the kingdom) " is a perfon of honeft conformity, and doth
" hinder none of the King's Majefty's fubjects, and is
" ready to join with the Earl of Clanrickard, and every
" other Captain, to ferve the King's Majefty, in any place
" in Conaught; fo as a Prefident, or yet a Captain, with
" a competent number of men, continuing at Galway, will
" caufe all the country to be good fubjects; and he, with
" the Earl of Clanrickard, and a Captain, will be able to
" rule all Conaught, which is the fifth part of Ireland."

And the L. D. Sidney, in his account to the Lords of the Council, of the ftate of affairs in the province of Conaught, dated 28 April 1576, informs them, that Mac-William Ewghter very willingly came in to him, " and I
" found him (fays he) verie fencible, though wantinge the
" *Englifhe* tongue, yet underftandinge the *Lattin*; a lover
" of quiet and civylitie, defierous to holde his landes of
" the Queene, and fuppreffe Irifh extorcion, and to ex-
" pulfe the Scotts, who fwarme in thofe quarters; and in-
" deede have almoft fuppreffed theim; in fome prooffe
" whereof, he taried with me moft of the time I remayned
" at Galway, and thence went with me to Athlone, and de-
" parted not till I went from thence, where, verie reve-
" rentlye, by othe, he fhewed his feaultye, and did his ho-
" mage, as humblye bynding hymfelfe, as well by othe as
" indenture, ever hereafter to hold his lands of her Ma-
" jeftie, and her crowne, and to pay yerelye 250 mares,
" fterlinge, and to fynde 200 foldiors, horffemen and foote-
" men, for two monethes by the yere, and to geve them
" foode in that proporcion, as, I truft, in tyme fhall fuf-
" fice both for their meate and wagies. In one of his pe-
" ticions exhibited unto me, he humblye befought (doubt-
" inge that I would have taken away the Bonnaught from
" the Clandonells, which they have of him and his coun-
" try) that they might (with-drawinge it from him) holde it
" of the Queene. This devife was underhand practized
" by me, and they, verie glade of this overture made by
" hym, humblye defiered to holde it of her Majeftye, and
" fo, by indenture paffed betwixt the *Galloglas* and the
" Queene, they prefentlye doe. This, my Lords, is an
" entraunce of no fmall confequence, bothe for the reduc-
" inge

"inge of the countrie to her Majesties obedience, and no
"small increase may be made besides to her commo-
"ditie, and the augmentacion of her revenue. He
"received his countrie at my hands, by way of Se-
"neshallshipp, which he thankefullye accepted. The
"order of knighthoode I bestowed upon hym, where-
"of he semed verie joyous; and some other little niffles
"I gave him, as tokens betwene hym and me, where-
"with verie well satisfied he departed. This is all
"I thought necessary to write of Mac-William, savinge
"that he was desierous I should sende thither an Englishe
"Sheriffe, as I have likewise donne in all the other coun-
"ties within that province, which, of late, hath bene
"omitted: Mac-William protested he would obey him I
"sent, and geve hym findinge for a sufficient strength of
"men on horseback and foote, which I accomplished ac-
"cordinge to his desier, and sent one with hym. Surelye,
"my Lords, he is well wonne, for he is a great man; his
"land lyeth a longe the West-North-West coast of this
"realme, wherein he hathe maney goodly havens, and is
"a Lorde in territorie, of three tymes so much land as the
"Earle of Clanrickarde is. He brought with him all his
"bretheren, Mac-Phillipin, who in surname is a Bourke;
"as he is; and, besides theim, a great nomber of owners
"of landes and castlles, lienge in the same countrey;
"O'Maylle came lykewise with hym, who is an originale
"Irisheman, strong in galleys and seamen; he earnestly
"sued to hold of the Queen, and to pay her rent and ser-
"vice [1]."

That year (1576) he joined the Deputy in his march, to suppress the insurrection of the Earl of Clanrickard's sons, who had wasted his country; and by his assistance and advice, the deputy dividing his army, routed several parties of the rebels, executed some, killed many more, dispersed the Scots who had joined them, and returned to Dublin, after he had strengthened and restored Mac-William to many of his castles, and left Sir Nicholas Malby, Governor of Conaught, possessed of the houses of Roscomon and Athlone, and all the Lord Clanrickard's houses in Clanrickard. In his relation of these transactions to the Lords of the Council, from Galway 20 September, the L. D. writes, that Mac-

---

[1] Sidney's Letters, I. 104.

Mac-William in that rebellion was the only man of power in Conaught, that shewed himself loyal, and had done best service upon the rebels; and in his Lordship's dispatches from Dublin, 27 January following, he relates "that after "he understoode that his Lordship's force was entred into "his countrie, whereof the Scotts stoode moche in doubt, "he gathered his strength and people together, and foorth- "with gave a charge upon the Scotts, and cried *Bowes*, "*Bowes*, which voice so soddeinely geven, and they think- "inge it indede to be true) it stricke soche a terror into the "amased mynds of the beggarly Scotts, as they leaft all "the pray behynde them, and saved theimselves by flyeng "and ronninge away. I delyvered to hym the castle of "Ibarrye, I had taken from the two sons of one Edward "Bourck (who were sent from the Earl of Clanrickarde's sons to entertain the Scots, to come into Conaught, to the aid of those rebels) to kepe it to her Majesties use, "and all the castlles and piles besides he was dispossessed "of; settled him quietlye in his owne, with such creditt "and countenaunce, as I hope he shall be hable to main- "teine hymself, in despite of all his enemies, that shall "hereafter attempt any thinge against him [1]."

In 1585 he surrendered his estate in the county of Mayo, upon the composition then established in Conaught, died in that year (though some say, in 1583) and having married Grany-na-Male, (that is, Grace O'Maly) daughter of Owen O'Maly of *the Owles*, an ancient *Irish Chief*, and widow of O'Flaherty (a lady much renowned by the natives of Co- naught, who relate many adventures and remarkable actions of her courage and undaunted spirit, which she frequently performed on the sea) he had three sons and one daughter, viz. Sir Theobald his heir; Walter and Edmond, neither of whom left issue; and Catharine, married to William Bourke of Newtown.

Sir Theobald Bourke (called Tibbot-ny-Lung, or of the ships, because he was born at sea) in the reign of Q. Eli- zabeth commanded a company in her Majesties pay, from which he was cashier'd, for defeating and hanging Dermoid O'Conor, in his way from Conaught to Munster, as he was marching with the President's protection, in order to perform singular service in that province, on the arrival of the young Earl of Desmond. In 1597, he was sent into England by Sir

Sir Theo-
bald,
Viscount.

[1] Sidney's Letters, I. 149. 150.

BOURKE, Viscount MAYO.

Sir Coniers Clifford, Governor of Conaught; and after his return, did, with his followers, maintain, in 1599, 600 foot, and 60 horse, against the crown in the county of Mayo; but, upon the King of Spain's landing some considerable forces, in conjunction with the Pope's Nuncio, at Kingsale, to support the rebel-party against the Queen, he levied at his own expence 160 men, and fought there in the head of them, under the Lord Mountjoy, when a glorious victory being gained, he was knighted for his gallant and loyal behaviour: and on the accession of K. James I. he exhibited a petition in behalf of himself, and his two brothers by the half-blood, Murrogh and Donnell Ikeggie O'Flaherty of Ieherconaght, praying his Majesty to accept of their respective surrenders of their estates, and to regrant the same by letters patent; to which the King (desiring his subjects should hold their own according to English tenure, and that their possessions should be settled in a certain and perpetual course of descent, for their encouragement to live in a civil way, to the benefit of their lawful progeny) condescended, and by Privy Seal from Winchester, 25 September 1603, ordered a commission to issue, to inquire what lands they held by descent, or other lawful means; then to accept of their surrenders, and confirm the same to them by patent, to hold by knight's service.

In 1613, he represented the county of Mayo in Parliament; and being possessed of a large estate, and distinguished for his eminent affection to the crown, K. Charles I. esteemed him worthy of a place among his Peers of Ireland [*], and accordingly advanced him to the title of Viscount Burke of Mayo, by Privy Seal dated at Westminster, 8 February 1626, and by patent 21 June 1627 [†].—— He married Maud, daughter of Charles O'Conor Sligo, Esq.

---

[*] Either he, or his son, was created a Baronet of Nova Scotia, in the reign of K. Charles I. "but it must have been (says Mr. Lodge) after he "was created a Viscount, yet certain it is, that the eldest son of the Vis-"count Mayo, enjoys the title of Baronet, and is styled, Sir during his fa-"ther's life.

[†] The preamble. Cum dilectum nobis Hiberniæ Regnum tum patris nostri felicissimæ Memoriæ, tum nostris temporibus quamplurimum effloruisse; et magis quam anteactis sæculis, tam Civilitate quam Opulentia auctum novimus, ut singulare Dei Beneficium agnoscimus; its multum gratulamur esse illam nobis oblatam Occasionem, quâ Magnifici Principis erga suos subditos extet Testimonium, præsertim cum inter cætera, quæ multum intersunt Reipublicæ ad nostrum et subditorum Emolumentum, ex illa emicuerunt haud pauci Viri, qui pro Possessionum amplitudine sustinere, et pro Generis splendore,

BOURKE, Viscount MAYO.

Esq. and sister to the aforesaid Dermoid (who in the year 1500, killed Richard and Thomas Bourke, the third and fourth Lords Castleconnell, but was soon after killed by his brother-in-law) and dying 18 June 1629, was buried with his ancestors at Ballintober, having issue four sons and three daughters, viz.

Miles, his successor. (1)

David, who died without issue. (2)

Theobald (Riabbach, the Strong) of Cloghans in Tyrawly, married the daughter of Walter Bourke of Turlogh, Esq. and died in Spain in 1654, leaving three sons and three daughters, viz. Colonel David Bourke, who married Alice, daughter of John Bourke of Loughmeasg, Esq. and died in France in 1694, whose posterity is extinct; Theobald-oge, who by Catharine, daughter of Edward Fitz-Dominick Browne, had five daughters; Walter died childless in Flanders; and of the daughters, one was married to ——— Mac-Jordan, and the other two died unmarried. (3) Family of Cloghans.

Rickard (commonly called *Iron Dick*) had issue Theobald Bourke, Esq. who married first Grany, daughter of ——— O'Maly, and by her had one son Colonel Miles Bourke, who died in 1715, and was buried at Ballintober, leaving no issue by his wife Bridget, daughter of Richard Bourke of Partry, Esq. Theobald married secondly, Celia, daughter of John Birmingham of Turlovaughan, Esq. by whom he had three sons, Rickard Iron (who married Mary, daughter of ——— Lynch, of Barna in the county of Galway, Esq. and had Theobald, who died unmarried; Miles, who went into the French service; Patrick; Thomas; Luke; (4)

---

dore, et heroicæ virtutis claritate altioris Honoris Titulos demereri possint. Quocirca cum Theobaldus Burke Eques Auratus, ex illustrissima olim in Anglia Prosapia oriundus, non solum Latefundiis et Generis sui Nobilitate, sed præcipue sinceræ erga nos et Antecessores nostros Fidelitate et Bellicosâ virtute inclaruit, quorum alterum in immota Animi Constantia etiam cum Regnum intestinis incendiis deflagraverit, alterum Rebus in Hispanos non ita pridem appellentes fortiter gestis emicuerit; æquum censemus et utriusq; nomine reportet subditi digni ac de suo principe optime merentis Præmium. Cumque autem nihil repertum fuerit Honorum Titulis clarius aut eminentius quo principes subditos suos bene-meritos et pro Rebus ante gestis, remunerare, et ad altiora stimulari possint, et soleant, quia et Caracter indolibile favoris regii et virtutis subditi futuris sæculis permaneant. Nos ex regia nostra favore et munificentia statuimus dictum Theobaldum in numerum Parium Regni nostri Hiberniæ adscribere, et ad Vicecomitis hæreditarii gradum promovere. Scitis igitur quod nos, intuitu Præmissorum, dictum Theobaldum continuo favore nostro prosequentes gratioso, ac ipsius benemerita Honoris Titulo compensare et nobilitare volentes in hoc dicto Regno nostro Hiberniæ, de Gratia nostra speciali, &c. (Rot. A°. 9 Car. I. 2. p. f. R. 8.)

Luke; and Apollonia); Theobald Reagh (married firſt the daughter of O'Dowde, by whom he had no iſſue; and ſecondly, the daughter of Ulick Bourke of Caſtlehacket, and by her had four daughters, living in 1754); David, who married Mary, daughter of Richard Fitz-Maurice, near Balſ in Mayo, Eſq. and dying in 1741, was buried at Aghagowr, near Weſtport, leaving Theobald (who left one ſon and one daughter, living in 1754); Patrick; Richard; John; Stephen; and Miles.

(1) Daughter Mary, married to O'Conor (Dun) of the county of Roſcomon, deſcended from Roderick O'Conor, the laſt Iriſh monarch of that family.

(2) Honora, firſt to Murrogh O'Flaherty of Aghnamurra in the county of Galway, Eſq. (whoſe grandſon and ſucceſſor married Bridget, daughter of Theobald, Lord Mayo, as hereafter) and ſecondly, Ulick Bourke of Caſtlehacket, Eſq. whoſe deſcendants are now denominated of Ower in the county of Galway

(3) Margaret, to Theobald, eldeſt ſon of Walter Bourke of Turlogh.

Sir Miles, 2 Viſcount. Sir Miles Bourke, the ſecond Viſcount, took his ſeat in Parliament, 4 November 1634 [1]*; and being a Proteſtant, was, on the breaking out of the rebellion, appointed by the ſtate, with Thomas, Viſcount Dillon, joint Governor of the county of Mayo, and had a commiſſion for the ſuppreſſing thereof, and the preſervation of all his Majeſty's loyal ſubjects in thoſe parts: by virtue of which, he raiſed in that

* His Lordſhip preferred a petition to K. Charles I. ſetting forth, that by reaſon there was no certain place appointed within the county of Mayo, for the holding of the aſſizes, goal-delivery, ſeſſions, and other publick meetings of the Miniſters of Juſtice about the affairs of that county, and that the goal being kept in Conge, in the moſt remote part of the county, the inhabitants did not only ſuffer in their eſtates, by the journeying of the diſorderly priſoners with their guard through the country, to the place where the judges met; but juſtice alſo many times was prevented by the ordinary eſcape of notorious malefactors; and whereas the town of Ballincarra, otherwiſe Bellcarra, was a fit place in all reſpects for the ſaid publick meetings: His Majeſty being graciouſly pleaſed to embrace all fit occaſions to expreſs his royal care of the good and caſe of his well affected ſubjects, ſent his directions from G. eenwich, 10 July 1632, to the L. D. Wentworth, requiring him to conſult the Judges concerning his Lordſhip's petition; and finding the convenience as ſet forth, to grant the ſame by patent for 31 years, unleſs in time of general contagion and ſickneſs [1].——And, 21 December 1637, he had the grant of a weekly Thurſday and Saturday market, and a fair at that place on the feaſt of St. Matthew.

[1] Lords Jour. I. 25. [2] Rot. A°. 10 Car. I. 2. p. ſ.

that county six companies of foot, consisting of 300 men, besides officers, and for some months kept it free from all disturbances, without any assistance from the Government. But (as Sir Richard Cox observes in the preface to his history) there being, during those distractions, no less than five different armies in Ireland, each pursuing different interests, *that*, in which his Lordship served, among other exploits, laid siege to Castlebar; which he took, and upon the surrender, agreed by articles, that the English should march away with their arms, and be safely convoyed to Galway.——But many of them being murdered by the way, 13 February 1641, at the Bridge of Shrule, which divides the counties of Mayo and Galway, whither his Lordship had safely conducted them; his son Sir Theobald was brought to his trial for that massacre, after the kingdom was reduced by the Parliament; and they were both excepted from pardon (though he was dead, having departed this life in 1649) by Cromwell's act of Parliament, passed 12 August 1652, for the settlement of Ireland.——His Lordship's conduct, during this rebellion, having never been set in a clear light, we shall shew in the notes, by what steps he forsook his religion, and how far he was instrumental in the said massacre *.

He

* Mr. John Gouldsmith, incumbent of Breshowle in the county of Mayo, in his deposition before the Privy Council and Commissioners authorized for that purpose, informs us, that between 3 and 4 years before the rebellion began, Francis Gouldsmith his brother (who was a Romish Priest of good account, being Capitian Majore of the Castle of Antwerp in Brabant) sent him a letter by one father Riccard Barret, a Jesuit and Spanish Preacher, and (as he had heard) an agent for the Irish in those parts; by which his brother required him, by many earnest and attractive arguments, to leave Ireland; and, removing all impediments, delay, and excuses, thus concludes, " I " wonder, brother, you will live in so base a kingdom; you'll say, you have " wife and children, and cannot come; sell the little goods you have, and " come away with your wife and children." And about the latter end of July, before the rebellion began, he observed that certain *Irish Smiths* had in a short space made a multitude of *Skeins*, whereby he conceived that some sudden mischief and insurrection would ere long ensue, and which would amount to no less than such a rebellion, which, as he suspected, had been discovered to his brother.

The first man robb'd in the county of Mayo, was one Mr. Perceval, whereupon the Lord Mayo, with a certain number of men, pursued those rebels, that had taken his cattle; and coming to a pass through a ford at Ballyhowner, the rebels had there fortified a mill against them with musqueteers, their army being not far off prepared for battle: but after some intercourse between his Lordship and them by messengers, he gave them a protection; and then, after much shouting and joy on both sides (both parties being intermingled) they lodged that night at the abbey of Ballyhowner, among a company of friars,

BOURKE, VISCOUNT MAYO.

He married first, Honora, daughter of Sir John Burke of Derrymaclaghtny, in the county of Galway, Knt. by the Lady

friars, by whose instructions they then broke forth into all inhuman practices, barbarous cruelties, and open rebellion. Upon which, the deponent in his distress, came with his wife and family to the Lord Mayo, who then had in his house of Bellcarrow, Mr. Gilbert, a distressed Minister, with his wife and family, and three other gentlemen, all which he entertained at his table, and then made his complaint in what a despicable case the state had left him, without help or succour, he having sent to them for relief.

About that time, news came from the rebels, that they would have the Lord Mayo go with them into open action and hostility against the Protestants; and quickly after, there came a report, that upon a certain night his castle should be beleaguer'd; wherefore about midnight his Lordship went forth with his men for the encounter, but the rebels came not. His Lordship was miserably perplexed in the nights with anxious thoughts; but not long after he propounded a question to Mr. Gouldsmith and Mr. Bringhurst, whether he, in this great extremity, having no relief from the State, might not take these men in rebellion into protection, and make use of them as he thought fit for his Majesty's service? The former opposed this step; but his Lordship's intentions being to subdue those of Costiloe by the men of Gallen, and those of Gallen by the rebels that lived in the Carragh, sent to Sir Henry Bingham, and desired a consultation with him and his council in Castlebar about this matter; but Sir Henry (fearing some interruption in the way) dared not to give him a meeting; upon which, my Lord propounded the matter in writing; desiring, that if he and his council should approve it, they would put their hands unto it. Sir Henry approved and signed it, with Mr. Barnard, Mr. Buchanan, and Dean Varges; and his Lordship having received this, it was also signed by Archdeacon Gilbert, Mr. Bringhurst, and Mr. Gouldsmith.

Immediately upon this, Mr. Gouldsmith perceived motions towards popery in his Lordship's house; Popish books of controversy were sent to him; and Laughlin Kelly, the titular Archbishop of Tuam, came and reconciled his Lordship to the Romish Church: about which time, Sir Henry Bingham sent him a letter to this effect. *I understand your Lordship is gone to Mass; I ask your Lordship's servant in what way soever your Lordship shall walk.* And all the English in the country following their example, there remained not in the whole county of Mayo one clergyman or layman, to preserve the memory of the Protestant religion, ten persons only excepted, viz. the Viscountess Mayo, the Lady Bourke, Mrs. Burley, Mr. Tarbock, Mrs. Hammer, Owen the butler, Alice the cook-maid, Mr. and Mrs. Gouldsmith, and Grete, their child's nurse; so that those of the laity, who turned to mass, did amount to 1000 in number in that county; (the clergy, some being fled, some murder'd, and the rest turned to mass) but Mr. Gouldsmith, by his Lordship's permission, continued his ministry in the house, disputed with priests that came to seduce the ladies, and publickly answered such Popish books of controversy, as they put in their hands, insomuch that his Lordship was greatly maligned and persecuted about him; and the said titular Archbishop reproved his Lordship for keeping him to exercise his ministry, and maintain his religion, saying, *be must deliver him up to them.* What will you do with him? (says my Lord) We will, said the bishop, send him to his friends; you will, said my Lord, send him to Shrule to be slain, as you did others; but if you will give me six of your priests, to be bound body for body, for his safe conveying to his friend, I will deliver him to you. The Bishop refused that motion; yet so far prevailed, that he was confined to a private part of the house, and of a long time dared not publickly to exercise his ministry, or shew himself in the house, for fear of being murdered. Nevertheless, on sabbath-days he exercised

BOURKE, Viscount MAYO.

Lady Margaret Burke, daughter of Ulick, the third Earl of Clanrickard; and secondly, Isabella, daughter of —— Freake,

eised the same privately, sometimes in the presence of but one, and seldom to more than two; till at length the Lady Mayo perceiving that her servants heard divine service privately, grew to such earnest impatience and boldness, that she plainly told her Lord, she would not be an atheist, but would again enjoy the ministry; wherein she prevailed so far, that from thenceforth he more publickly performed his function to those few remaining Protestants, until he came from thence.

But whilst he stay'd there, Sir Henry Bingham's castle of Castlebar being beleaguer'd by the rebel Edmond Bourke, Sir Henry desired the Lord Mayo to take that castle from him, and to keep it for his use, for that he himself could hold it no longer; whereupon he went thither with his forces, but the rest of the castle not assenting to part with it, he returned home. About which time, the Bishop of Killala [Dr. John Maxwell] having formerly lost his castle and good, contracted with Bourke of Castleleaken to give him a safe convoy; but he must perfidiously brought him into the hands of the said Edmond Bourke (as he was besieging Castlebar) who proposed to have put him upon the engine or Sew, which he had prepared for undermining and breaking down the castle, purposely that if the besieged should shoot against the Sow, they might hit the Bishop their friend: whereof the Lord Mayo having notice, wrote a letter to Bourke the convoy, blaming his perfidiousness, and signifying plainly unto him, that if he did not deal with the Bishop according to his promise, he would deal with him as an enemy, wheresoever he met him; whereupon, Bourke brought the Bishop within sight of his Lordship's house, and there left him. His Lordship then went to meet the Bishop, and took him and his family home, where he kindly entertained them, and gave him a band to put about his neck, and a shirt which he wanted, and kept him, with his wife, three children, servant, and five or six of his ministers, for 8 or 10 days. At that time Sir Henry Bingham again desired his Lordship to come and take his castle, which he could no longer keep; whereupon, he marched thither with an army, drove away Edmond Bourke, and entered and possessed the castle, upon quarter, and his promise to convoy the garrison safe to Galway. Whereupon, Sir Henry, with his company, the Bishop of Killala, and many of the neighbouring English, above 60 in number (whereof some fifteen were Ministers) were taken to be convoyed to Galway, his Lordship covenanting with one Edmond Bourke for their safe convoy up in a certain day, in whose custody he left them at Shrule; but was not gone far, when Bourke drew out his sword, directing the rest what they should do, and began to massacre these Protestants; some whereof were shot; some stabb'd with skeins; some run through with pikes; some cast into the water and drowned; and the women, that were stripped naked, lying upon their husbands to save them, were run through with pikes; so that very few escaped; among whom was the Bishop of Killalla, but was wounded in the head; and Mr. Crowd, a clergyman, was so beaten with cudgels on his feet, that he died thereof shortly after, the other Ministers being slain.

This bloody affair is more distinctly specified in the deposition of Henry Bringhurst, of Kilkeran in the county of Mayo, Esq. who deposeth, that his Lordship, with his son Sir Tibbot Bourke, did personally accompany the said unhappy people from Castlebar, Kinturk, and Bellcarrow, with five companies of soldiers, for their better security, to the town of Shrule, where two companies were to receive them over the bridge, being in the county of Galway; and for their more safe convoy, the titular Archbishop of Tuam faithfully promised his Lordship to accompany them with his letter, and several

Freake, and widow of Sir ―― Benboe, Knt. and by her, (who is called Ellis, in an order of government 29 March

ral Priests and Friars, to see them safely delivered at the fort of Galway: And being all come to Shrule on Saturday night, 12 February 1641, the Lord Mayo provided for them at the House of Serjeant Robert Lambert and others, and the next day for their dinner, lying that night in one bed with the Bishop of Killala, whose wife and children, according to his desire, lay in the next chamber. The next day being Sunday, (that bloody day) the gentlemen of the barony of Kilmaine, finding themselves much burthened by the soldiers (having lain upon them four nights) entreated to be eased of them, by sending them to their homes, for that they had brought them to the end of the county of Mayo, where they were to be received by the companies of Murrough-na-Doe O'Flaherty, and Ulick Bourke of Castlehacket, who lay that night within two miles of Shrule, and appointed to meet the company at Kilnemanagh, about a mile from Shrule, on Sunday morning. Upon which earnest request of the gentry, the Lord Mayo dismissed his companies (except one under the command of Captain Walter Bourke, who lived within a mile of Shrule, or little more) which company being then commanded by his brother Edmond, was appointed to convoy the company to Killnemanagh, to the two companies there ready to receive them; and it being almost twelve o'clock, and the march long (14 miles) and having no place nearer for the poor travellers to lodge at that night than Clare, which was ten miles, the said Edmond Bourke having, with his wicked company, been at Mass, and the titular Bishop having failed to send either Priests, Friars, or letter, and the town not able to provide for the company another night, the said Bourke desired to be going, undertook for their safe delivery at Killnemanagh, and the company being desirous to get to Galway, the Lord Mayo furnished them with his own and his son's horses, so that his son had not a horse left to go with him; and having seen the Bishop, with his wife and children, and the rest that had horses, mounted, he took leave with them; and accompanied only by two or three horsemen, rode away towards Conge, Sir Tibbot Bourke's house, 6 miles from Shrule; who (notwithstanding that he rode a good round pace, for the weather was very cold) intending to stay for his son at the house of one Andrew Lynch, 2 miles short of Conge, a messenger, as he was ready to dismount, came and told him, that presently after he was out of sight, the said Edmund Bourke and his men fell upon the Bishop and his company, had wounded and stripped him, with his wife and children and all the rest, had murdered some, and were about to murder the remainder. Whereupon, his Lordship went instantly into a chamber, and there wept bitterly; pulling off his hair, and refusing to hear any manner of persuasion or comfort, or to be patient, having no means at that time left him to be revenged of that inhuman bloody massacre; fearing besides the loss of his son, and that now they were entered into blood, they would fall upon himself, being then a Protestant, with the few English he had under his protection. And within half an hour after came Sir Tibbot, his son, who with tears related the tragedy, but could not certainly tell who was killed, or who escaped: But being demanded by his father, why he would ever come away, but either have preserved their lives, or have died with them? Answered, that when they began the slaughter, they charged him, (having his sword drawn against them) both with their pikes and musquets, and would have killed him, but that John Garvy, the Sheriff of the county of Mayo, (who was brother-in-law to Edmond Bourke, the principal murderer) came in betwixt him and them, took

him

March 1654, allowing her, an English gentlewoman, the sum of 25l. on account of her old and decrepid age, and her low and necessitous condition, to bear the charges of her voyage to England, and 12 May following she had another order for 10l. on the same account [1]; she died in 1663.) he had no issue, but by the first had three sons, Sir Theobald his successor; John, Edmond, engaged in the rebellion, both died childless; and a daughter Margaret, married to John Moore, of Bries, in the county of Mayo, Esq. by whom she had no issue.

Sir him in his arms, and by the assistance of others, forcibly carried him over the bridge, brought him a horse, and caused him to be gone after his father, for that he could there do no good, but would be killed or endangered, if he opposed them, whereupon he came away. The next day his Lordship going to Conge, lay in bed two or three days, without taking any sustenance; but the third day went to the house of the titular Archbishop (being within a quarter of a mile) where he was that day received to Mass, and with a two days after took his way to a great meeting of the county at the town of Mayo; from which time he was ever (or for the most part) under the command of the Romish clergy; and 1 August 1642 was chosen, with the Lord Clanmorice, to represent the county of Galway in the provincial council for Connaught; by which, held at Ballinrobe that month, he was elected Governor of the county of Mayo, having for his guard and attendants 100 foot and 50 horse allowed him in pay; and that year, was appointed one of the Supreme Council at Kilkenny. About which time, the Clan-Jordan, Clan-Steevens, and Clan-Donells came to Strade and Ballylaban, and gathering together all the British they found there, closed them up in a house (in the same manner as had been done at Sligo, where a butcher, with his axe, flew to in one night) with an intent that night to murder them; but notice thereof being given to the Lord Mayo, he prevented their wickedness, and preserved the poor innocent people from slaughter. And being quite weary of his engagement with the Irish, he made his escape in January 1644, from the Supreme Council at Kilkenny, vowing he would never be under their obedience.—Sixty-five persons were killed at Shrule, among whom were two women great with child, and were all tumbled into two pits, close by the high-way, without any ceremony or order.

This narrative is confirmed by the depositions of Sir Theobald Bourke (then Lord Mayo) taken at Galway 15 November 1652; of William Baker, taken there 10 January following; and of Edmond Dooney, otherwise Bourke, servant to Miles, Lord Mayo; who saith, that his Lordship gave him 5l. and bade him deliver it to the Bishop of Kilala, when he should part with him at Galway-Fort; and with Miles Rochford, another servant, was ordered to carry with them the Bishop's two daughters: But after they came over the bridge, a shot was made from between the bushes, whereupon Edmond Bourke drew his sword; and the examinant spurring his horse, rode back to the bridge with the Bishop's child behind him, where he was charged with pikemen, but was rescued by Walter Bourke Mac Rickard Mac-Thomas Roe, who drew his sword and made way for him, and so he got clear, with the child safe, as Miles Rochfort did with the other. (Lodge)

[1] Council Office, Lib. A. I. 140. 190.

BOURKE, Viscount MAYO.

Sir Theobald, 3 Viscount.

Sir Theobald Bourke, the third Viscount Mayo, was educated in the University of Oxford, under the great Archbishop Laud, who, at his trial, boasted of having brought up that young Nobleman in the Protestant religion. In 1639, he was Knight in Parliament for the county of Mayo; and during the course of the rebellion, performed many good services to the King by his courage and prudence; and, among the rest, persuaded his Kinsman, Rickard Burke in 1649, to quit the Nuncio's faction, and return to the King's obedience; who no sooner did so, than as a testimony of his sincerity, he discovered to Sir Theobald a combination between Prince Rupert, then Admiral of the fleet in the Irish seas, and some officers in Ireland, of forming a scheme to serve their country, religion, and King in an opposite way to the L. L. which Sir Theobald immediately communicated to the Marquess of Clanrickard, who made it known to the L. L. whereby it was prevented.—But in 1652, after the kingdom was reduced by Cromwell, and the military service in a manner finished, the Commissioners of Parliament began their civil administration, by erecting a High Court of Justice (as they called it) to try those, who were accused of the barbarous murders committed in the rebellion. The commission for holding *that* in Conaught bore date 17 December 1652; was signed by Fleetwood, Ludlow, and Jones; and directed to Sir Charles Coote, Peter Stubbers, Humphry Hurd, Francis Gore, John Desborough, Thomas Davis, Robert Ormsby, Robert Clerk, Charles Holcroft, John Eyre, Alexander Staples, and others, who sat upon the trial of his Lordship, for the aforesaid massacre at Shrule, which they began 30 December, and ended 12 January, when he was condemned by the vote of seven of the Commissioners, (Gore, Davis, Clerk, and Holcroft dissenting) to be shot to death, which was executed upon him the 15 in Galway, where he was buried. The soldiers, appointed to shoot him, missed fire three times, but at last, a Corporal, blind of an eye, hit him.

His Lordship's first wife was the daughter of ———— Talbot, of the county of York, Esq. descended from the Earl of Shrewsbury and Waterford's family, by whom he had two sons and two daughters; Theobald and Miles, who both enjoyed the honour; Margaret, married to Sir Henry Lynch, of Galway, Bart. but died without issue;

and Maud, to John Brown, of Westport, in the county of Mayo, Esq. ancestor to the Earl of Altamont. His second wife was Eleanor, daughter of Sir Luke Fitz-Gerald, of Tecroghan, in the county of Meath, Knt. and by her, (who 15 April 1653, was permitted to enjoy so much of her jointure, as was then waste and undisposed of, and to receive the rent reserved upon so much thereof, as was then set, until further order, paying contributions; to enjoy also the personal estate, whereof her husband died possessed; was allowed a pension, in 1656, of 40 shillings a week, and died in 1693) he had a son Luke, who died young.

Sir Theobald, the fourth Viscount, being left a minor, preferred a petition, upon his father's death, to the commissioners of Government for a maintenance; who declared, 15 April 1653, that if he would repair to Dublin, and make application to them, they would take care that he should be decently educated, and maintained. He came to Dublin accordingly, and 1 July, Mr. Samuel Winter and Alderman Thomas Hooke, were ordered to consider of some godly and religious family, where he might be provided with diet and other necessary accommodations, and to agree for his diet and schooling at the Free-School; which they did, and he was placed under the tuition of Mr. John Stephens, Master of the Free-School in Dublin [1], with an allowance of 20l. a year, for his education and diet; and 20 August 1656, in consideration of a letter from the L. D. in his behalf, 30l. a year was allowed for his maintenance, to commence from 25 March preceding; some time after which, he was sent for to England by his mother's relations, with whom he lived till the restoration of the King.

On 14 May 1661 he took his seat in the House of Peers [2], and 18 July, delivering a petition to be restored to his estate, it was ordered by the House, that he should be recommended to the agents in England, particularly to supplicate his Majesty on his behalf, being comprised in his declaration; and 30 June 1662, the Lords addressed the L. J. that they would cause to be inserted in the act of explanation a clause, for the better securing such as had been innocent of the rebellion, and yet lost their estates; in compliance

Sir Theobald, 4 Viscount.

[1] Council Office. Book of Orders, A. I. 216.   [2] Lords Jour. I. 134.

compliance wherewith a proviso was inserted, and he was decreed to his estate, by the Commissioners for putting that act in execution, 11 April 1666, and 30 August following, had a grant of the benefit of that decree, consisting of 50,000 acres of land, and 5 manors in the county of Mayo. —He married first Ellen, daughter of Sir Arthur Loftus, of Rathfarnham; and secondly, the Lady Owens, some short time before his death, which was occasioned by too large a quantity of laudanum, to compose him to rest, after taking physick in a fit of sickness: He died 5 June 1676, was buried 8 of that month, in St. Patrick's, Dublin, and leaving no issue, was succeeded by his brother

Sir Miles, 5 Viscount.

Miles, the fifth Viscount, who married Jane, youngest daughter of Francis, Lord Athenry, and for some time after his marriage, having no prospect of issue, was prevailed on to sell his estate, for the discharge of some debts he had contracted; dying at Castle-Bourke in March 1681, he was buried at Ballintober, having issue by her, who died at Turlovaughan, her father's seat, 6 June 1687, an only child

Sir Theobald, 6 Viscount.

Theobald, the sixth Viscount of Mayo, born 6 January 1681, who conformed to the established church 19 June 1709, being Trinity Sunday, and two days after took his seat in the House of Peers [1]— He married to his first wife, 8 July 1702, his first cousin Mary, youngest daughter of the aforesaid John Browne, of Westport, Esq. by whom he had three sons and five daughters, viz. Theobald, his successor; Miles, who died young; John, after Lord Mayo; Jane (married to Murrogh-Morgan O'Flaherty, of Lemonfield, in the county of Galway, Esq. and had five sons and one daughter, viz. Brian, who died in 1750; Sir John, who married Miss Royse, of the county of Limerick, and had Thomas, and Anabella; Thomas, who married Susanna Bourke, of same county, and had a son John-Bourke O'Flaherty, L. L. D and Member of Parliament for the borough of Callan); Patrick; Michael; and Mabel, married to Captain William Patterson [2]); Maud, died young; Elizabeth, married William Mitchel, of Carshalstown, in county of Surrey, Esq. she was upper housekeeper of Somerset House, and died 9 June 1770; Mary,

[1] Lords Jour. II. 276.   [2] Information of J. B. O'Flaherty, Esq.

Mary, died young; and Bridget, married 11 October 1731, to John Gunning, Esq. then of the Middle-Temple, eldest surviving son and heir to Bryan Gunning, of Castle-Coote, in the county of Roscomon, Esq. and had one son Sir John, and four daughters, Mary, married 5 March 1752 to George-William, Earl of Coventry; Elizabeth 14 February 1752, first to James, Duke of Hamilton and Brandon, and secondly, 3 March 1759, to Colonel John Campbell, who after became Duke of Argyle; Catharine; and Liffy, who died 1 January 1753, in the ninth year of her age.

In June 1731, his Lordship married secondly Margaret*, eldest daughter of the said Bryan Gunning, Esq. and deceasing in Dublin 25 June 1741, without issue by her who died in 1771, was buried at Ballintob er, being succeeded by his eldest son

Sir Theobald Burke, the seventh Viscount, who took his seat in Parliament 6 October 1741 [1], and in March 1726, married Ellis, elder daughter of James Agar, of Gowran, in the county of Kilkenny, Esq. whose grandson James, hath been advanced to the Peerage, and by her, who re-married with Francis, Lord Athenry, had two sons Theobald and Agar, who died in their infancy; and his Lordship departing this life in London, was interred at Ballintober,

Sir Theobald, 7 Viscount.

---

* She had been thrice married, namely, first to John Edwards, of Dublin, Esq. Attorney at Law, who was killed by endeavouring to get out of the Four Courts, 16 June 1721, upon a false report of their being on fire. By him she had a daughter Catharine, married 8 November 1726, to Robert Gunning, of Cloondera, county of Longford, Esq. and had issue Robert, of Cloondera, who died 30 June 1750; and William. She married secondly, William Lyster, of Athleague, in county of Roscomon, Esq. by whom she had Margaret; Jane; and Elisabeth, married 17 February 1753, to William Dwyer, Esq. Barrister at Law, and was left enciente of a son John, born in November 1722, who dying unmarried 28 November 1753, his estates devolved on his two married sisters, their husbands using the name of Lyster, viz. on the said Margaret, married to William Dwyer, Esq. and Jane, who married Christopher Kirwan, now Kirwan-Lyster, Esq. She married to her third husband in 1727, Captain Francis Houston, of Ashgrove, in Roscomon, Esq. who dying in 1731, she became the wife of Lord Mayo, and died 9 June 1771. (Lodge.)

[1] Lords Jour. III. 479.

Ballintober, where his Lady erected a monument to perpetuate his memory, with this inscription:

> A faithful Friend, a dutiful Son,
> An affectionate Brother,
> And a tender Husband;
> He passed through Life
> With unblemished Honour, beloved and esteemed
> By all that knew him
> His manners were easy;
> His Temper gentle and humane;
> The knowledge of his high Birth
> Had no other Effect upon him,
> Than to make it his Study, in all the Offices of Life,
> To live up to the Character, to which he was born;
> Being sensible that the truest Nobility
> Is that of the mind;
> And to possess it in the highest degree,
> Is to walk steady in the paths of Virtue;
> Which he did to the day of his Death.
> He died at London the 7th day of January 1741,
> In the 36th year of his Age,
> Much lamented; but by none more sincerely
> Than by his much beloved and afflicted Consort,
> Ellis, Lady Viscountess Mayo,
> The eldest Daughter of James Agar
> Of Gowran in the county of Kilkenny, Esq;
> And of Mary his wife, daughter of Sir Henry Wemys,
> By whom he had two sons, Theobald and Agar,
> Who both died young.
> In Testimony of the affectionate Respect,
> Which his Lady
> Most deservedly retains for his Memory,
> This Monument was by her erected.

His Dowager was in 1758, created Countess of Brandon.

Sir John, 8 Viscount. His only brother John succeeding to the honour, was the eighth Viscount of Mayo, and took his seat in the House of Peers 10 November 1743[1]. He married Catharine, daughter and heir to Major Whitgift Aylmer, of the West-Indies (descended from Dr. John Aylmer, Bishop of London, and from Dr. John Whitgift, Archbishop of Canterbury, both in

---

[1] Lords Jour. III. 542.

BOURKE, Viscount MAYO.

in the reign of Queen Elizabeth) widow of Mr. Hamilton, of the county of Galway, and had issue one son Sir Aylmer Bourke, born 17 November 1743, who died 21 July 1748, and was buried in the church of Irishtown, near Dublin; and one daughter Bridget, married 11 May 1758, to Edmund Lambert, of Boyton, county of Wilts, Esq. pursuant to articles dated 28 April 1758, and died in May 1773, leaving by him a son Aylmer-Bourke Lambert. His Lordship died in Pall-Mall, London, 12 January 1767, (since when the title has lain dormant) and Catharine, his lady, re-married in July 1770, with Edmond Jordan, of Legan, county of Mayo, Esq. and died in January 1776[1].

TITLES.] Sir —— Bourke, Lord Viscount of Mayo, and Baronet.

CREATIONS.] Baronet of Nova-Scotia, by K. Charles I. and V of the county of Mayo, 21 June 1627, 3 Car. I.

ARMS.] Parti per Fess Topaz and Ermine, a Cross, Ruby, the first Quarter charged with a Lion Rampant, Diamond, and the second with a dexter Hand couped at the Wrist and erect, Ruby.

CREST.] On a Cap of Maintenance, a Lion sejant, Pearl, gorged with a golden ducal Collar.

SUPPORTERS.] The Dexter, an Harpie guardant, with wings and a Lion's body, Topaz; a human face, neck and breast, proper, and armed, Ruby. The Sinister, a Man in Armour to the middle of his thighs, having a sword, proper, in a belt, Ruby, and about his neck a square white band, his hands naked, sandals, diamond, and in his exterior hand a battle-axe, proper.

MOTTO.] A CRUCE SALUS.

[1] Collections.

LUMLEY, Viscount LUMLEY.

<small>Osbert.
Liulph.</small>

THIS noble family takes its name from Lumley-Castle, situate on the banks of the river Weare, in the bishoprick of Durham; and is descended from Osbert de Lumley, of Lumley-Castle, whose son Liulph, a considerable nobleman in the time of K. Edward the Confessor, married Algitha, younger daughter of Aldred, Earl of Northumberland, son of Earl Uchtred, by his wife Edgina, youngest daughter of K. Ethelred II. —— Liulph, in respect of his parentage, possessions and good qualities, became the favourite of the inhabitants of the bishoprick of Durham, and grew into such esteem with Walcher, Bishop of Durham, and Earl[1] of Northumberland, that he consulted him in the management of all his temporal affairs; whereat Leofwyn, his Chaplain (finding himself less frequently called to Council) conceived such envy, that he procured one Gilbert (to whom the Bishop had committed the care and oversight of the Earldom) to murder Liulph by night, in his manor-place not far from Durham, in the year 1080; but his death was soon revenged by the people, who put the murderers and the Bishop himself to a tragical end.

He had issue four sons, Uchtred; Osbert, whose only child Ormonda, was married to Robert de Peshale; Adam, to whom the Conqueror gave the lands of Uldell and Gilcruce; and Odo, to whom he gave Talentire and Castle-

<small>Uchtred.</small>

rigge, with the forest between Galtire and Græca,—Uchtred, the eldest son, had issue Sir William; and Matthew, of Lumley-Magna, the father of Martin, whose wife was

<small>Sir William.</small>

named Christiana.—Sir William de Lumley, had a grant from Hugh, Bishop of Durham, of the same immunities and privileges, his other palatine Barons enjoyed, which K. Henry by charter confirmed; and in gratitude for so

great

[1] Collins, IV. 115.

great a favour, he gave to that See his village of Dicton, in Alverton. He married Judith, daughter of —— Hefilden, of Heyfilden and was father of Sir Will. de Lumley, who had two fons, William his heir; and Marmaduke, the father of John Fitz-Marmaduke, Lord of Horden, in the bifhoprick of Durham, who 12 February 1301 [1], 29 Edward I. was one of thofe Barons, that withftood the papal ufurpation, and fubfcribed a memorable letter * to the Pope (in anfwer to a haughty bull he had fent the King, wherein he fet himfelf up for judge of the controverfy betwixt him and the Scots, and commanded him to forbear further proceedings againft them, claiming foverеign authority over them, in right of the church) wherein they owned and claimed the dominion of Scotland, and peremptorily concluded, *that the King fhould in no wife undergo his Holinefs's judgment therein*; which was accompanied by a very fmart reply from the King himfelf, afferting his fovereignty over that kingdom. *Sir William.*

William, the elder fon of Sir William and Judith de Lumley, married the daughter and coheir of Sir Walter D'Andre, of Morton-D'Andre, in the bifhoprick of Durham, and left iffue Sir Roger de Lumley, who by Sybil, eldeft daughter and coheir of Sir Hugh de Morewyc, an eminent Baron in Northumberland, who died 45 Henry II. left two fons, Sir Robert; and Sir Roger (anceftor to the families of Harlefton and Clipfton in the county of Northampton); and a daughter Margaret. *William. Sir Roger.*

Sir Robert de Lumley in 1298, on the death of his mother (then the widow of Laurence de St. Maur) fucceeded to her eftate, viz. the manors of Weft-Chivington, Morewyc, and Bamburgh-Caftle, with divers other lands in Northumberland, being then 26 years of age, of which the next year he had a fpecial livery, for the fine of 5 marcs, fterling; and married Lucia (rather Ifabel) eldeft daughter of Marmaduke de Thweng, a great Baron, Lord of Thweng and Kilton Caftle, with feveral other manors in the *Sir Robert.*

---

* An exemplar of this inftrument, with their feveral feals affixed, is preferved in Corpus-Chrifti College Library in Oxford, and the feal of this John Fitz-Marmaduke, is a fefs, between three parrots, circumfcribed *Johannes Filius Marmaduci*; which arms the family ftill retain. (Collins IV. 117.)

[1] Collins IV. 116. and Lodge Collect.   [2] Lodge Collect.

252   LUMLEY, Viscount LUMLEY.

the counties of York, Lancaster and Westmoreland *, and coheir to her brothers Thomas, William, and Robert, by whom he had three sons, Sir Marmaduke, Thomas, and William.

Sir Marmaduke.   Sir Marmaduke married Margaret (or Mary) daughter and heir of ——— Holland, and assuming the coat-armour of his mother, his posterity has used the same to this day. He died in 1370, (44 Edward III.) having four sons, Robert, Ralph, Thomas, William, and a daughter Isabel, *Robert.* married to Sir William Fulthorp.—Robert de Lumley, the eldest son, being under age at his father's death, was in ward to William, Lord Latimer, 48 Edward III. when a partition was made of the lands of Thomas de Thweng, Baron of Kilton-Castle, whereof he had the manors of Moressome-Magna and Parva, with divers others in the county of York, and Roveley, in Northumberland; of which he died seized 12 December 1374, (48 Edward III.) leaving *Sir Ralph.* Ralph, his brother and heir, then 13 years old, who in 1385 (9 Richard II.) was a Knight, and in the retinue of Henry de Percy, Earl of Northumberland, in the expedition to Scotland, when he behaved so well, that he was made Governor of Berwick upon Tweed the ensuing year, and so continued until he was taken prisoner by the Scots, two years after; being in 1391, Deputy-Governor of the same place, under the last Earl.—In 1392, he obtained licence to make a castle of his manor-house at Lumley; and was summoned to Parliament among the Barons, from 8 Richard II. to 1 Henry IV. inclusive; being attainted next year of treason by Parliament, and had his lands seized, for being concerned with Thomas de Holland, Earl of Kent, and other Lords his confederates, who not assenting to the deposal of Richard II. joined in a confederacy against Henry IV.

---

* Marmaduke Thweng, of Kilton, married Lucia, daughter of Peter de Bruce, of Skelton, a great Baron in the reign of K. Henry III. and coheir to her brother Peter, by whom she had Sir Robert de Thweng, living in that reign, who by Maud, daughter of Gilbert Hansard, had Sir Marmaduke, who married Isabel or Dorothy, daughter of William Ros, and had Robert, whose wife was Margaret, daughter of Sir Bryan Say, (by Maud, daughter and heir to John Monceux) and sister to Patrick Say, Governor of the Marches of Wales in 1258, and had issue the said Marmaduke de Thweng, who had three sons, Thomas, a Priest; Sir William, and Robert, who died without issue; and three daughters, who became coheirs and were the said Lucia, or Isabel; Margaret, married to Robert Hilton, of Sweyne, in Westmoreland; and Catharine, to Ralph Daubigny, ancestor to the Lord Daubigny. (Lodge Collect.)

IV binding themselves by indenture, to be diligent and faithful to each other in their undertaking, and to attend carefully upon the execution of it. But their design having miscarried by an unforeseen accident, and being afterwards discovered to the King by Edward, Duke of Albemarle and Earl of Rutland, they resolved to pull off the mask; and as they knew how the people stood affected, dressed up Magdalen, one of K. Richard's Chaplains, who very much resembled his master, in royal robes, and gave it out that the King had made his escape from prison: Whereupon the people flocked so hastily to *their* colours, that in a few days they amounted to 40,000 men, and narrowly missed surprising K. Henry at Windsor: After which miscarriage being afraid to attack him, who waited for them upon Hounslow-Heath with 20,000 men, they resolved to retire towards Wales, which was well disposed in Richard's favour, and encamped without the gates of Cirencester; but some of the principal commanders having the imprudence to lodge within the town, they were surprised in the night by the Mayor, who cut off two of their heads; and the army without being terrified by the noise of that transaction, and dispersed, thirty-one Lords, Knights, and Gentlemen, the chief leaders of the rebellion, were taken to the King at Oxford, who immediately caused them to be executed: But the Lord Lumley died in the field of battle, which is evident from the record, whereby his estate, real and personal, was adjudged in Parliament to be forfeited.

His wife was Eleanor, daughter of John Lord Nevil, of Raby, and sister to Ralph Nevil[1], the first Earl of Westmoreland, by his wife Jane, daughter of John of Gaunt, grandson of K. Edward III. and their surviving issue were four sons and three daughters, viz.

Thomas, who was attainted with his father, and died a minor, 31 May 1404, seized of many manors in the bishoprick of Durham, and in the counties of York and Northumberland, notwithstanding that John, Earl of Somerset, had a grant of so much of the estate, as amounted then to 360l. a year. (1)

Sir John, heir to his brother, being then 20 years old. (2)
William, or George. (3)
Marmaduke, rector of Stepney in Middlesex, elected in 1429, Master of Trinity-Hall, and Chancellor of the University (4)

---

[1] Collins IV. 119.

verfity of Cambridge; 16 April 1430, he was confecrated Bifhop of Carlifle, being alfo conftituted 18 December 1446, Treafurer of England, and after he had fat 20 years in that fee, was tranflated to Lincoln, which he enjoyed fcarce a year, deceafing in his attendance on the King at London. He contributed largely towards the building of Queen's-College, Cambridge, and beftowed 200 marcs [1] a confiderable fum at that time, upon its library, with many valuable books.

(1) Daughter Margaret, was married to Sir John Clervaux, of Croft, in county of York, and was mother of Richard Clervaux, Efq. who by Elizabeth, daughter of Henry Vavafor, Efq. had two fons, Marmaduke, who married Elizabeth, daughter of Sir John Stranguifh, (and had a fon John, whofe daughter Elizabeth, was married to Thomas, Lord Hilton); and John, who by Jane, daughter of John Huffey, of Sleaford, in county of Lincoln, Efq. had a daughter Margaret, married to John Fitz-William, of Sprotborough, Efq.

(2) Catharine, to Sir John Chideok, of Chideok, in county of Dorfet, Bart. [2] and had two daughters, coheirs, Catharine, married to Sir John Arundel, of Langherne, in Cornwall; and Margaret, to William, Lord Stourton.

(3) Elizabeth, to Adam Tyrwhit, of Kettleby, in Lincolnfhire, whofe fon Sir Robert, by Elizabeth, daughter of Sir Richard Warburton, was father of Sir William Tyrwhit, who married Anne, daughter of Sir Robert Conftable, and had Sir Robert, who married the daughter of Sir Gilbert Talboys, and was father of Sir Robert Tyrwhit, who by Elizabeth, daughter of Sir Edward Oxenbridge had an only child Catharine, the wife of Sir Henry D'Arcie, Knt.

Sir John. Sir John Lumley, heir to his brother Thomas, doing his homage in 1405, 6 Henry IV. had livery of all the eftate, whereof his father was feized at the time of his attainder, and being reftored in blood by act of Parliament, 13 Henry IV. was knighted that year for his fervices in the wars of Scotland and France. He alfo fignalized himfelf with K. Henry V. in his wars, but in the laft year of his reign, loft his life in the field of battle with Thomas, Duke of Clarence, the King's brother, Governor of France, who,

[1] Collins, IV. 120. [2] Idem. 119.

who, being betrayed by his Scout-Master Andrew Forgufa, a Lombard, who misrepresented the enemy's numbers, precipitated himself into a battle at Baugie in Anjou, on Easter-Eve 1421, and was slain by the Earl of Buchan, (who had brought 7000 Scots to assist the Dauphin) with the Lords Lumley, Tankerville, Angus, and Ross, who disapproved of this rash design, yet testified their duty, by obeying their General, while living, and their valour, by accompanying him in his death.—He married Felicia, daughter of Sir Matthew Redman, Governor of Berwick, and had issue Thomas, his heir; Edmond; and Maud, married to Sir Henry Thirkeld, of Cumberland, Knt. [r]

Thomas, Lord Lumley, in 1432 (10 Henry VI.) had a special livery of his estate; was knighted for his services in the wars, and concerned in divers negociations.—In 28, 29, and 31 years of Henry VI. he was one of the King's guarantees in three several treaties with the King of Scots; and his Majesty, having experienced his fidelity, prudence and conduct, constituted him in 1453, Governor of Scarborough-Castle for life. In 35 Henry VI. he was again employed to treat with the Scots; and two years after was also a guarantee in another treaty.—On the accession of K. Edward IV. to the crown, he petitioned the Parliament for the reversal of his grandfather's attainder; which was accordingly reversed in the first year of that King's reign, and he had summons to Parliament among the Barons in the 3. 7. 12. and 22 years of that King.—In 1465, he was appointed a Commissioner to treat of a marriage betwixt some person of the King's allegiance, and James, King of Scotland; and concerning certain mutual breaches of the truce: About which time he was at the siege of Bamburgh-Castle, in Northumberland, held out, with some other Northern garrisons, by the Lancastrians; and 10 October 1466, in regard of his fidelity, circumspection, and industry, was chosen a Commissioner, to treat at Newcastle upon Tyne, with the deputies of the King of Scots, concerning certain grievances between the two nations.—He married Margaret, daughter of Sir James Harrington, brother of Sir William Lord Harrington, Knight of the Garter, and dying in 1484, had issue George, his successor, and three daughters; Joan, married to Bertram Harbottle, of Northumberland; Margaret,

[r] Collins, IV. 111.

three sons, Thomas; Roger (who married the daughter of Sir Richard Ratcliffe, and had a son of his own name); and Ralph (or John) Lumley.

Thomas, the eldest son, when the three estates of the kingdom were summoned to meet at Westminster 27 October 1495 (11 Henry VII.) appeared on behalf of the clergy and commonalty of the diocess of Durham; and 14 Henry VII. the King having called a like assembly for their assent to the peace, made with France 3 November, he and Sir George Manners were the two specially deputed by the Lords and Commons of the said diocess, to meet the King and give their assent thereto.—He died before his father, and having married Elizabeth Plantagenet, natural daughter of K. Edward IV. by the lady Elizabeth Lucy[1], had issue four sons and three daughters, viz. Richard; John; George; Roger, (who had three daughters, his coheirs, Agnes, married to John Lambton, of Lambton, in county of Durham; Isabella, to Richard Conyers, of Horden, in same county; and Margaret to Thomas Trollop, of Thornleys, Esqrs.); Anne, married to Ralph, Lord Ogle, of Bothal, and was mother of Robert, Lord Ogle; Sybil, to Sir William Hilton, Baron Hilton, of Hilton, in the bishoprick of Durham, whose son Thomas, Lord Hilton, married Elizabeth, daughter and heir to John Clervaux, of Croft, Esq.; and Elizabeth to ——— Creswall, of Northumberland, Esq.

Richard. Richard, the eldest son, succeeding his grandfather, had summons to Parliament 1 Henry VIII. and died on Trinity Sunday 26 May 1510, (2 Henry VIII.) seized of the manor and castle of Kilton, in the county of York, and of the manors of Kirkby, Kendale, Hessington, &c. He married Anne[*], daughter of Sir John Conyers, of Hornby-Castle, Knight of the Garter, by his wife Alice, daughter of William Nevil, Lord Falconbridge, and Earl of Kent, and had two sons and two daughters; John, his heir, then 18 years of age; Anthony, ancestor to the Viscount Lumley; the eldest daughter, married to Richard Grey; and the youngest to ——— Conyers, of Scarborough.

John,

[*] On the monument at Cheam, in Surry, for John Lord Lumley, she is called Ann, daughter of William Lord Coigniers. (Collins IV. 124. a.)

[1] Collins IV. 123.

John, Lord Lumley, in 1513, (when James IV. of Scotland, invaded the kingdom of his brother-in-law, Henry VIII. whilst he was at the siege of Therouenne, in France, and made himself master of Norham-Castle) brought a considerable strength to the Earl of Surry, Lieutenant of the North, who had marched to York with 500 men only, and was a principal commander of the van-guard in the battle of Flodden-Field (fought 9 September) where the King of Scotland fell, and his army was defeated.—In 6 Henry VIII. he was summoned to Parliament, as Lord Lumley, and the ensuing year had livery of his inheritance. In 1520 he was present at the meeting between his Sovereign and the Emperor Charles V. at Canterbury; and crossing the seas the same year, attended the King to his interview with Francis King of France, between Ardres and Guisnes.—In 1523, he was in the army under the Earl of Shrewsbury, to invade Scotland, had not a peace ensued; and the next year, in the expedition under the Earl of Surry against the Scots, who, with a supply of 3000 foot and 1200 men at arms from France, having entered England were put to flight, with the loss of Jedburgh and other places.—In 1530, he had summons to that Parliament, which gave the first stroke to the dissolution of the monasteries in England; and the next year signed that memorable letter to Pope Clement VII. intimating, that unless he complied with the King in his divorce from Q. Catharine, his elder brother's widow, the acknowledgment of his supremacy in England would be much endangered: But notwithstanding this, in 1537, he was among the chief of those Northern Lords, who appeared in the insurrection, called *The Pilgrimage of Grace*; and a pardon being offered by the Duke of Norfolk, General of the army sent to suppress them, he was delegated to treat with the Duke at Doncaster, and so well accommodated matters, that all concerned in the tumult were permitted to repair to their respective habitations, without being questioned for their offence, which was confirmed by the King.

He married Joan, daughter of Henry, Lord Scrope of Bolton, by Elizabeth, daughter of Henry Percy, Earl of Northumberland, by whom he had an only son George, who being engaged in an insurrection with the Lord Darcy, Sir Thomas Percy brother to the Earl of Northumberland, and others, was apprehended with them, committed to the Tower,

Tower, arraigned at Westminster in June 1537, before the Marquess of Exeter, High Steward of England, and being found guilty of high treason, suffered death.—Having married Jane, second daughter and coheir to Sir Richard Knightley, of Upton, in county of Northampton, Knt. by Jane, daughter of Sir John Spencer, Knt. he left issue by her, who remarried with John Knottesford, of Malvern Priory in county of Worcester[1], John, successor to his grandfather; Jane, married to Geffrey Markham, Esq. who died childless; and Barbara, first to Humphrey Lloyd, of Denbigh, Esq. the Antiquary of Wales*; and secondly to William Williams, of Cloghwillane, in Wales, Esq.

John.

John, Lord Lumley, the only son, was an infant at his grandfather's death; but, upon his petition 1 Edward VI. setting forth, " that he was a person in lineage and blood " corrupted, and deprived of all degree, estate, name, " fame, &c. by reason of his father's attainder;" it was enacted, " That he and the heirs male of his body should " have, hold, enjoy and bear the name, dignity, state and " preheminence of a Baron of England."—On 29 September 1553, two days before the coronation of Q. Mary, he was made a Knight of the Bath, being first knighted by the Earl of Arundel, his father-in-law, Lord Steward of the Houshold, commissioned by the Queen to confer that honour. He and his lady attended the coronation; he amongst the Barons, and she, one of the six principal ladies dressed in crimson velvet, that sat in the third chariot of state; next to whom rode ten ladies in the like dress, their horses trapped with the same; coaches in that age not being used by any of the nobility, and, as Stowe relates, were not brought

into

---

* He was the only son of Robert Lloyd, otherwise Rossindalle, of Denbigh, Esq. and had issue Henry Lloyd, of Cheam, in Surry, Esq. who by Mary, daughter of Robert Prowe, of Bromfield, in Essex, had Henry, his heir, who married Isabella, daughter of Sir Isham Parkyns, of Bunney, in Nottinghamshire, and had Henry Lloyd, of Cheam, Esq. who died 3 December 1704, æt. 66, leaving by Elizabeth, daughter of Benjamin Goodwin, of Stretham, Esq. (who died in November 1705, and was buried with him in the church of Cheam) three daughters, Elizabeth, Susan, and Catharine, and one son Dr. Robert Lumley Lloyd, Rector of Covent-Garden, who in 1723, laid claim to the ancient Barony of Lumley, but which claim was not allowed by the House of Lords, and he died in November 1730.

[1] Collins. IV. 125.

into England till the year 1564. She alfo rode in the proceffion at the funeral of that Queen; and his Lordfhip 24 April 1556, with the Lord Talbot, introduced Ofep Napea, Ambaffador from the Emperor of Ruffia, to his audience of leave, who brought rich prefents from his mafter, and concluded a treaty of amity and commerce, being the firft Ambaffador to England, from that Court.

In 1559 (1 Elizabeth) he was appointed a Commiffioner to receive the claims of fuch, as held of the Queen by the tenure of *Grand Serjeanty*, and were required to perform their refpective fervices at her coronation. In 1566 he was employed to treat with *Cofmo Medicis*, Duke of Florence, about the fum of 11250l. due to K. Henry VIII. which the Queen received with intereft.—In 1570, he was taken into cuftody, with his father-in-law, for being privy to divers tranfactions relating to the Queen of Scots, and to her defigned marriage with the Duke of Norfolk; but in 1587, he was commiffioned with other Lords, for the trial of that Queen, and fat in judgment on her in Fotheringay-Caftle; being alfo the following year in the commiffion for the trial of Secretary Davifon, for contempt towards the Queen, breach of his allegiance, and neglect of his duty, in fending the warrant for putting the Queen of Scots to death, without her Majefty's knowledge; and the commiffioners differing in their fentiments about him and his punifhment, his Lordfhip declared, that the fentence was juftly pronounced againft that Queen; but that never in any age was there fuch a contempt againft a Prince heard or read of, that the Queen's Council, in the Queen's palace, in the Council-Chamber, near the Queen, who was, as it were, Prefident of the Council, fhould refolve upon a matter of fuch confequence, without her advice or knowledge, when both they and Davifon might have had fo eafy accefs to her: Protefting, that if he had but one only fon, and he were in the fame fault, he would cenfure him to be feverely punifhed. But being perfuaded of the man's ingenuous and honeft intention, he would inflict no heavier punifhment upon him, than the reft had done before; which was, that he fhould be fined 10,000l. and imprifoned during the Queen's pleafure; to which the majority of the commiffioners affented.

In 1582, his Lordship and the learned Richard Caldwell, M. D. founded a publick lecture in chirurgery, to be read in the college of physicians, to begin 6 May 1584, and to continue for ever, twice a week, viz. on Wednesday and Friday.—In 44 Eliza. he was one of the Peers for the trial of Robert Devereux, Earl of Essex; and on the accession of K. James I. appointed one of the Commissioners for settling the claims at his coronation, and making Knights of the Bath.—He was, as Camden writes, " a person of " entire virtue, integrity, and innocence, and in his old " age a complete pattern of true nobility; had so great a " veneration for the memory of his ancestors, that he caused " monuments to be erected for them in the collegiate " church of Chester, on the street (opposite to Lumley-" Castle) in order, as they succeeded one another, from " Liulphus, down to his own time; which he had either " picked out of the demolished monasteries, or made new." —Having no issue, he took care that his estate should descend to one of his own name and blood, by his last will, which he made 28 January 1605, and by deeds of settlement. By his will, he ordered his body to be buried in the church of Cheam in Surry, whereof he was patron, with as little extraordinary charge, as conveniently might be; and bequeaths to his kinsman and heir male Richard, son and heir apparent to Roger Lumley, Esq. son of Anthony, brother to John, Lord Lumley, his grandfather, his castle of Lumley, and all such manors, &c. as he had made a lease of in trust, 20 February 1594; and ordered 200l. to be distributed amongst the poor.

He married first Jane, elder daughter and coheir to Henry Fitz-Alan, the last Earl of Arundel, of that surname, who died 25 February 1579, æt. 68. (the other daughter Mary being married to Thomas Howard, Duke of Norfolk, the Earldom of Arundel still subsists in that illustrious family) and had issue Charles, Thomas, and Mary, who died infants, and lie buried with their mother in the chancel at Cheam. His second wife was Elizabeth, only daughter of John, Lord D'Arcie, of Chich, in Essex, and sister to Thomas, created Earl Rivers, who survived him without issue, and lies buried at Cheam, under an arch of white marble, supported with white fluted pilasters, with her effi-

gies

gies lying at full length, and over her, in capitals this inscription:

> Elizabethae nobili Darceorum Familia
> Oriunda, Johanni Baroni de Chiche unica
> Filia, Johanni Baroni de Lumley secunda
> Conjux, omni Virtutum et Honoris splendore
> Cumulata, Corporis reliquias huic Monu:
> :mento, Animam multo pretiosissimam bea:
> :torum Sedibus Paradisi Gaudiis commendavit.

His Lordship deceased 10 April 1609, æt 76, and was buried in the vault with his first lady, having a noble monument of white marble erected to his memory, against the north-east side of the chancel, adorned with the arms of the several families his ancestors had married into, with a long inscription*, expressing his virtuous qualities and high descent, concluding with these lines;

> Conscia Mens Recti, Mentis spes, Anchora Sanctæ
> Spei chara Mater, vel Soror alma Fides,
> Præsentis Vitæ Comitesque Ducesque fuere,
> Æternæ Vitæ pignora certa manent.

The ancient Barony of Lumley being thus extinguished, **Anthony.** we must return to Anthony Lumley, Esq. younger son of Richard, Lord Lumley, by Anne, sister to William, Lord Conyers, ancestor to the Viscount Lumley, as before observed.—He married the daughter of Richard Gray, of Northumberland, Esq. and was father of Roger Lumley, **Roger.** who by Anne, daughter of ———— Kurtwyche, Esq. left Richard, his heir; George; and John †; and several daughters, one of whom was married to Sir John Conyers of Horden, in the bishoprick of Durham; and Elizabeth, to Sir William Langley, of Higham-Gobions, in Bedfordshire,

---

* Against the East wall of the chancel is very curiously painted on a wooden tablet, his Lordship's Bust; which, with a figure of the monument and the inscription at large, may be seen in Sandford's Genealogical history of the Kings and Queens of England, folio, p. 422, 423. Edit. 1707.

† Collins. IV. 131.

shire, and of Stainton, in Yorkshire, created a Baronet 29 May 1641, and was mother of Sir Roger Langley, who succeeded to the title in 1651, and resided at Sheriff-Hutton-Park, in the county of York.

Sir Richard, Viscount.

Sir Richard, who succeeded his father, was the chief heir male of the family, after the decease of John, Lord Lumley, in 1609, and inherited the greatest part of the estate, by his Lordship's deed of settlement and last will.—On 19 July 1616, he was knighted at Theobalds, by K. James I. created Lord Viscount Lumley, of Waterford, by patent, bearing date 12 July 1628; and 4 November 1634, took his seat in the House of Peers[1].—In the time of the civil war he adhered to the King, and made his house of Lumley-Castle, a garrison; was a principal commander under Prince Rupert, with whom he marched into the West of England; was at the siege of Bristol, and remained there when it was surrendered to the Parliament forces 10 September 1645, he afterwards compounded for his estate at the sum of 1955l. 10s.[2]. He was also among those loyal Peers, who subscribed a memorable declaration just before the meeting of that Parliament, which restored K. Charles II. and which very much contributed to it, by appeasing the minds of many, who had incurred guilt.

He married Frances, daughter of Henry Shelley, of Warminghurst-Park, in Sussex, Esq. and by her who died in February 1657, and was buried in Westminster-Abbey, had one son John, and a daughter Julia, married first to Alexander Jermyn, of Lordington, in Sussex, Esq. (by whom she had Frances, first married to Francis, son and heir to Sir Henry More; and secondly to John Shuckburgh, of Barton, in Warwickshire, Esq.) and by her second husband, Sir Christopher Conyers, of Horden, in the palatinate of Durham[3], Bart. had also an only daughter Julia, first married to Sir William Blacket, of Newcastle, and of Wallington, in Northumberland, Bart. and secondly, to Sir William Thompson, Recorder of London, and Baron of the court of Exchequer.

John Lumley, Esq. the only son, married Mary, second of the three daughters and coheirs to Sir Henry Compton, of Bramble-Teigh, in Sussex, Knight of the Bath (youngest son of Henry, the first Lord Compton, ancestor to the Earl

of

[1] Lords Jour. L. 26.   [2] Collins, IV. 131.   [3] Id. 132.

of Northampton) by Cicely, daughter of Robert Sackville, Earl of Dorset, and dying in 1658 (before his father, who lies buried with his kinsman John, Lord Lumley, at Cheam) was interred 9 October, in the church of St. Martin's, London, having issue two sons and three daughters, Richard; Henry; Elizabeth, married to Richard Cotton, of Watergate, in Sussex Esq.; Frances; and Anne, who died unmarried.

Henry Lumley, Esq. the younger son, embraced a military life; was a very brave and good officer; served in the wars of Ireland, at the revolution; and 10 August 1692, was made Colonel of the King's regiment of horse, on the death of Sir John Lanier, at Steenkirk, in which station he distinguished himself in several campaigns, particularly at the battle of Landen, where his regiment, by the noble *stand* they made, saved the King from being taken prisoner. On 7 May 1694, he was made a Major-General, and served under the Duke of Marlborough, during the course of Q. Anne's wars; by whom 24 February 1702-3 [1], he was constituted a Lieutenant-General, and in April 1703, Governor of Jersey, being also in January 1710, made a Lieutenant-General of the horse in Flanders, as he was again 5 April 1712; and appointed 12 December 1714, of the board of general officers for the regulation of the army.—He married first Elizabeth, daughter of ———— Thimbleby, of the county of Lincoln, Esq. and secondly, in July 1713, Anne, daughter of Sir William Wiseman, of Great Canfield-Hall, in Essex, Bart. by his second wife Arabella, daughter of Sir Thomas Hewet, of Pishiobury, in Hertfordshire, Bart. sister and heir to George, Lord Viscount Hewet, of Gowran, in whose family-vault at Sabridgeworth, they lie buried under a neat marble monument, thus inscribed:

Here lieth
The Honourable Henry Lumley, Esq.
Only brother to Richard, Earl of Scarborough,
Who was in every battle, and at every siege,
As Colonel, Lieutenant-Colonel, or General of the Horse
With King William, or the Duke of Marlborough,
In twenty campaigns in Ireland, Flanders and
Germany, where he was honoured, esteemed and
Beloved by our own armies, by our allies, and even

By

[1] Collins, IV. 132.

By the enemies, for his singular politeness and
Humanity, as well as for all his military virtues
And Capacity.

He sat long in Parliament [for Arundel]
Always zealous for the honour of the crown, and
For the good of his country, and knew no party, but
That of truth, justice and honour.

He died Governor of the Isle of Jersey the
18th of October 1722, in the 63d year of his age.

Here lieth also
Mrs. Frances Lumley, his only dear and beloved
Child, of great beauty and greater hopes, who
Died the 13th of October 1719, in the 6th year of
Her age; sometime the joy, then the anguish of
Her fond parents.

Here lieth also
Dame Anne Lumley, daughter of Sir William
Wiseman, Bart. of Canfield, in Essex, who set
Up this monument in 1723, in memory of the
Best of husbands, and her dear child, near whom
She was deposited, An°. 1736-7.
She died on the 4th of March 1736-7 in an
Advanced age. She was a lady possessed of all
Those amiable qualifications, which adorn her
Sex, and rendered her, whilst living, the delight
Of all those, who had the happiness of her
Acquaintance, by whom her death was greatly
Lamented, as well as by the poor, to whom she
Was, living and dying, a most bountiful
Benefactress.

Richard, a Viscount. Richard, the second Viscount Lumley, who succeeded his grandfather, having all the advantages of education, at home and abroad, rendered himself so acceptable from his first setting out in the world, that he was particularly taken notice of by K. Charles II. and distinguished amongst the most polite men of that polite age.—On 11 September 1680, he was appointed Master of the Horse to Q. Catharine, and in that station so far recommended himself, that the King, in consideration of his great merit, approved

fidelity

fidelity and high defcent, advanced him to the Peerage of England, by the title of Baron of Lumley-Caftle, in the county of Durham, 31 May 1681, with limitation of the honour to the heirs-male of his brother, but was not introduced in the Englifh Parliament, until 19 May 1685 [1].

On the Duke of Monmouth's infurrection in the Weft, he was appointed (31 July 1685) to the command of the King's regiment of carbiniers, and had a principal fhare in the victory of Sedgemore; the Duke, with his companions the German Count, and the Lord Grey, being by his vigilance difcovered, furrendered prifoners to his Lordfhip. Neverthelefs, when he obferved that K. James's defign was to introduce Popery, and to fubvert the eftablifhed laws of the country, he forfook the Court; appeared on the behalf of the feven Bifhops at their trial; and was among the chief of the nobility, who had the courage to confult with Mr. Dykvelt (whom the Prince of Orange entrufted to manage his affairs in England) and to conceit fuch meafures, as might be fit for the Prince to govern himfelf by; and often met at the Earl of Shrewfbury's to confult how to proceed; and drew the declaration, on which they advifed his Highnefs to engage; being alfo chiefly entrufted by the Earl of Orford, who went to Holland, and had the Prince's direction for the management of the revolution.

When matters were concluded, the Lords of Devonfhire, Danby, and Lumley undertook for the North; and retiring into their refpective counties, his Lordfhip, by his intereft and friends, fecured the important town of Newcaftle, which declared for the Prince foon after his landing. He was no lefs inftrumental, by his arguments in Parliament, in gaining the vote, *that the Throne was vacant*, and that the Prince and Princefs of Orange fhould be declared King and Queen of England. For which fervices, the day after their proclamation (14 February 1688) he was fworn of the Privy Council, declared a Gentleman of the King's Bedchamber, and 2 April 1689, made Colonel o. the firft Troop of Horfe-Guards; being alfo, before their coronation, created Vifcount Lumley, of Lumley-Caftle, by patent, dated 10 April 1689; and further advanced 15 April 1690, to the title of Earl of Scarborough.

On 16 January 1689, he attended K. William into Ireland; was at the battle of the Boyne; waited on his Majefty

[1] Collins, IV. 133.

jesty to the great Congress of Princes at the Hague, and returned with him to England. In 1691, he went again to Holland, and attended the King in his campaigns in Flanders until the peace of Ryswick; was made a Major-General 1 April 1692; Lieutenant-General, 24 October 1694; and in that reign was L. L. and *C. Rot.* of the county Palatine of Durham, county of Northumberland, the town and county of Newcastle upon Tyne, and Vice-Admiral of those sea-coasts; in which posts he was continued by Q. Anne, until he resigned them on 20 April 1712; of whose Privy Council he was sworn 10 May 1708; was one of the Commissioners to treat of a union between England and Scotland; 2nd Surveyor of the customs and subsidies, inwards and outwards, in the port of London.—On the accession of K. George I. his Lordship was one of the Peers, entrusted by his Majesty with the Government, until his arrival, his name being written with the King's own hand; and 1 October 1714, he was sworn of the Privy Council; appointed (the 9) L. L. of the counties of Durham and Northumberland; constituted, 21 November, one of the Court-Martial, to examine into the state of the army, to settle the seniority of the several regiments, and the ranks and claims of the officers; and 9 March 1715-16, made Chancellor of the dutchy of Lancaster, which he resigned in May 1717, and thereupon had a grant (the 31) of the office of Vice-Treasurer, Receiver and Paymaster-General, and Treasurer at War in Ireland, jointly with Matthew Ducie Morton, Esq.—He departed this life by an apoplexy 17 December 1721, and was buried, with his ancestors, in the church of Chester in the Street; and having married Frances, daughter and heir to Sir Henry Jones, of Aston, in the county of Oxford, who distinguished himself and was slain in the wars of Flanders (whose wife was Frances, sister to Thomas, Earl of Falconberg) inherited in her right, among other lands, the manor of Farmington, in Gloucestershire; and by her, who was a Lady of the Bedchamber to their Majesties, Mary and Anne, and died 26 November 1737, had issue seven sons and four daughters, viz.

(1)   Henry, Lord Lumley, elected to Parliament in 1702 for the county of Sussex, and in 1709, for the borough of Arundel, who died of the small-pox 24 July 1710[1], and was

---

[1] Collins, IV. 135.

was buried with his grandfather at St. Martin's in the Fields.

Richard, who succeeded to the honours. (2)

William, killed at sea, in the *Mediterranean*, 9 April (3) 1709, having both his legs shot off, on board the Mary-Galley.

Thomas, who also succeeded to the honours. (4)

Charles, who in May 1724, was made Groom of the (5) Bed-Chamber to K. George II. when Prince of Wales; served in Parliament for Chichester, and died 11 August 1728.

John, appointed 5 December 1728, Groom of the Bed- (6) Chamber to his Royal Highness Frederick, Prince of Wales; chosen 23 February 1727, Member of Parliament for Arundel, in Sussex; was a Captain in General Honeywood's dragoons, whence in November 1731, he was promoted to a company in the Coldstream Regiment of Foot-Guards; was made 23 April 1734, Avenar and Clerk-Martial of the King's Stables, and in 1736, Gentleman of the Horse to his Majesty; but died in London 16 October 1739, and was buried near his brother Henry.

James, chosen in February 1728, Member of Parliament (7) for Chichester, and in May 1741, for Arundel; appointed in May 1727, Equerry to the King, and in 1736, succeeded his brother John, as Avenar and Clerk-Martial, being also Groom of the Bed-Chamber to Frederick, Prince of Wales; and died 14 March 1766, unmarried.

Daughter, Lady Mary was married to George, Earl of (1) Hallifax, and died 10 September 1726, in the 35 year of her age.

Lady Barbara, in August 1716, to the Hon. Charles (2) Leigh, of Leighton-Beaudesert, in the county of Bedford, brother of Thomas, Lord Leigh, which county he represented in two Parliaments, and died 28 July 1749, and she died 4 January 1755, without issue.

Lady Anne, in October 1727, was made a Lady of the (3) Bed-Chamber to the Princess Anne, and in 1735, to the Princesses Amelia and Caroline; 19 February 1738, she became second wife to Frederick Frankland, Esq. late Member of Parliament for Thirsk, in the county of York, a Commissioner of the Revenue in Ireland, and a Commissioner

sioner of Excise in England, brother to Sir Thomas Frankland, Bart.; and deceasing 29 February 1739-40, was buried 4 March, with her brother the Earl of Scarborough, in St. George's Chapel, Audley-Street.

(4) Lady Henrietta, died unmarried in 1757[1].

Richard, 3 Viscount. Richard, the third Viscount Lumley, from the seventh year of Q. Anne's reign, served in Parliament for the boroughs of East-Grinsted and Arundel; and 10 February 1710, received from her Majesty a Captain's commission in the army.—On 21 September 1714, he was appointed a Gentleman of the Bed-Chamber to George, Prince of Wales, and in November, Master of the Horse, being 8 February following, made Colonel of the first Troop of Grenadier Guards, which he resigned in December 1717. On 10 March 1714, he was summoned by writ to the English House of Peers; was nominated 20 June 1715, one of the Commissioners for establishing the houshold of the Prince and Princess of Wales; and 2 May 1721, had the honour to represent his Royal Highness Ernest-Augustus, Duke of York, at the baptism of William, Duke of Cumberland.—On 26 December that year he succeeded his father, as L. L. and *C. Rot.* of Northumberland and Newcastle; and 22 June 1722, was constituted Colonel of the second regiment of foot-guards; was elected 4 July 1724, a Knight of the Garter, and installed 28 at Windsor; appointed 14 June 1727, Master of the Horse to his Majesty, which he resigned 22 February 1733; was sworn of his Privy Council; and in September 1727, made L. L. and *C. Rot.* of Northumberland, and Vice-Admiral of the county of Durham.—On 18 December 1735, he was made a Major-General; and 2 July 1739, a Lieutenant-General; but died *

unmarried

* His Lordship's character is thus drawn by a masterly pen, in a pamphlet, written on the occasion of his death, intituled, *The Court Secret, a Melancholy Truth.* "There was yet about the Sultan, one man of the race of Ali Etc. " Asra, who scorned the Vizier as much as he loved his Sovereign; who " seemed to be left as an example to *the Great*, of all the virtues they ought " to imitate; fond of fame, but more of virtue; loyal, but not for reward; " free in the delivery of truth, but gentle in the manner; modest in defend- " ing himself, resolute in the defence of others; not void of human frailties, " but not too proud to acknowledge them; incapable of flattery, though to " oblige the woman he loved, or temporize with the Prince he revered; of " such exemplary honour, that no consideration, though of life itself, was of
" any

[1] Collins, IV. 136.

unmarried 29 January following, and was succeeded by his brother.

Sir Thomas Lumley-Saunderson, the fourth Viscount Lumley, who in several Parliaments represented the county of Lincoln; was elected 25 May 1725, a Knight-Companion of the Order of the Bath; appointed in 1721, Envoy-Extraordinary to the King of Portugal; and 28 November that year, Clerk of the dutchy Court of Lancaster; 28 November 1728, was chosen Knight of the shire for Lincoln; also in May 1738, was made Treasurer of the Household to the Prince of Wales, and Steward of the Lordship of Kirton, in Lindsey, Lincolnshire; was one of the principal Surveyors of the port of London; was a Commissioner of the navy; and Lieutenant-Colonel to a regiment of foot, raised to suppress the late rebellion.—On 22 May 1723 James Saunderson, Earl of Castleton, dying at Richmond without issue, æt. 56. bequeathed his estate to him, on condition that he took and used the name of Saunderson, which he did by act of Parliament.—He married the Lady Frances Hamilton[1], second daughter of George, last Earl of Orkney, and by her, who was a Lady of the Bed-Chamber to the Princess of Wales, had issue Richard, Lord Lumley; George, who died 11 December 1739; and three daughters, Lady Anne; Lady Frances, married in June 1753, to Peter Ludlow, of Ardsallagh, county of Meath, Esq. who was created Earl Ludlow; and Lady Henrietta, who died 6 November 1747, aged 16.

His Lordship departed this life 15 March 1752, and was succeeded by his only son,

Richard,

" any weight in the scale against it: In a word, he was in all things the re-
" verse of the *Vizier*; and therefore, until he was undone, the *Vizier* never
" thought himself safe."

His Epitaph.

" With the best Virtues of a private State;
With the best Talents of the truly Great;
In Courts he liv'd without one slavish Fear,
Nor lost the *Briton* in the *British* Peer;
Honour'd and lov'd by all the World beside,
One Man accus'd him, and the base one lied."

[1] Ulster's Office.

Richard, 5 Viscount.

Richard, the fifth Viscount, who in July 1765, was appointed Cofferer of his Majesty's Houshold, and on the 12 of same month, sworn of his Majesty's Most Honourable Privy Council, in Great Britain, his Lordship was also Deputy Earl-Marshal of England, to Edward, ninth Duke of Norfolk, Colonel of a battalion of the Lincolnshire Militia, at the General Election in 1774, he was chosen to represent the city of Lincoln, and 10 April 1782, was appointed one of the joint Vice Treasurers of Ireland ; 12 December 1752, he married Barbara, sister to Sir George Savile, of Thornhill and Rufford, in county of York, Bart. and deceased 12 May 1782, having had by her who died at Bath in January 1773, six sons and two daughters, viz.

(1) George-Augustus, who succeeded to the honours.
(2) Richard, born 3 April 1757, to whom his uncle Sir George Savile bequeathed his estates, on condition of his taking the sirname of Savile.
(3) Thomas-Charles, born 22 June 1760, now in Holy-Orders.
(4) John.
(5) Frederick.
(6) William, born 28 August 1769.
(1) Lady Frances-Barbara-Ludlow, born 25 February 1756, died young.
(2) Lady Mary-Arabella, born 1 June 1758[1].

George-Augustus, 6 Viscount.

George-Augustus, the sixth and present Viscount, who was born 22 September 1753, and was baptized 24 October following, his present Majesty (then Prince of Wales) the Princess Augusta, and the Marquess of Hartington, after Duke of Devonshire, being sponsors.

TITLES.] George-Augustus Lumley-Saunderson, Earl of Scarborough, Viscount Lumley, of Waterford, and Viscount and Baron Lumley, of Lumley-Castle.

CREATION.] V. Lumley, of Waterford, 12 July 1628, 4 Car. I. B. Lumley, of Lumley-Castle, in the Bishoprick of Durham, 31 May 1681, 33 Car. II. V. of the same

Collins IV. 138. and Supplement.

LUMLEY, Viscount LUMLEY.

same place, 10 April 1689, 1 Will. and Mary; and E. of Scarborough, in the county of York, 15 April 1690, 3 Will. and Mary.

ARMS.] Pearl, a Fess, Ruby, between three Parrots, Emerald, collared, as the second, being the bearing of the ancient Barons, *Thweng*, and were assumed by Sir Marmaduke Lumley, son of Sir Robert Lumley and Isabel Thweng; the ancient arms of Lumley, being Ruby, 6 Martlets, Pearl.

CREST.] On a Wreath, in her nest, proper, a Pelican feeding her young, Pearl, vulned, proper, as the first.

SUPPORTERS.] Two Parrots with wings expanded, Emerald, Beaks and Members, Ruby.

MOTTO.] MURUS ÆNEUS CONSCIENTIA SANA.

SEATS.] Lumley-Castle, in county of Durham, 196 miles from London. Stansted, in Sussex, 56 miles from London; and Sandbeck, near Tickhill, in the West Riding, of Yorkshire.

SMYTHE,

SMYTHE, Viscount STRANGFORD.

9
John.

Thomas.

HIS Lordship derives his descent from John Smythe, of Corsham, in Wiltshire, Esq. (whose ancestors were of good antiquity in that county) living there in the reign of Henry VIII. who left issue Thomas, his heir, and a daughter Elizabeth.—Thomas Smythe, Esq. removed from Corsham, into the county of Kent, and seated himself at Ostenhanger, now generally called Westenbanger, which he purchased in Q. Elizabeth's reign, from Sir Thomas Sackville, and very much improved, by augmenting the buildings of the house, &c. which had been damaged by fire. He also purchased the manor of Postling, from Sir Anthony Aucher; Halden from Robert, Earl of Leicester; and the manor of North-Ash, which last he settled on his second son: and being customer, or farmer of the customs in that reign, acquired a very considerable estate, which he further increased by his marriage with Alice, daughter and heir to Sir Andrew Judd, of Ashford, in the same county, thereby obtaining the manors of Ashford, and Westure; and deceasing 7 June 1591, was buried in the church of Ashford, leaving three sons and three daughters.

(1) Sir John, ancestor to the Lord Strangford.

(2)
Family
of
Bidborough

Sir Thomas Smythe, of North-Ashe, (by his father's settlement) who purchasing from the Lord Berkeley, in the reign of James I. the manor of Bidborough, in Kent, made it the place of his residence.—He was also customer to Q. Elizabeth after his father's death, and had such a share in the favour of her successor K. James, that 19 March 1604, he sent him Ambassador to the Empress of Russia; after his return from which honourable employ, he was made Governor of the society of Merchants, trading to the East-Indies, Muscovy, the French and Summer Islands, and Treasurer for the colonies and companies of Virginia. During this appointment, he resided at Deptford, where his magnificent house was burned 30 January 1618; so that in April following,

following, he resigned those employments.—He married Sarah, daughter and heir to William Blount, Esq. and by her who became the second wife of Sir Robert Sidney, the first Earl of Leicester, had issue two sons; the elder of whom, Sir John Smythe succeeded him at Bidborough; was also farmer of the customs ; and married the Lady Isabella Rich, youngest daughter of Robert, the first Earl of Warwick, by his first wife the Lady Penelope Devereux, daughter of Walter, Earl of Essex, and left Robert Smythe, Esq. his successor at Bidborough, who was also seated at *Sutton-at-Hone*, and at *Bounds* in Kent, and 8 July 1652, married the Lady Dorothy Sidney, eldest daughter of Robert, the second Earl of Leicester, (by the Lady Dorothy Percy, eldest daughter of Henry, the ninth Earl of Northumberland, by the Lady Dorothy Devereux, his wife, daughter of Walter, Earl of Essex) and widow of Henry, Earl of Sunderland, and had Robert Smythe, Esq. Governor of Dover-Castle, who married Catharine, daughter of William Stafford, of Blatherwick, in the county of Northampton, Esq. and had Henry his heir, father of Sir Sidney-Stafford Smythe, of Bounds, Knt. appointed in 1750, one of the Barons of the Exchequer in England, whose wife was Sarah, eldest daughter of Sir Charles Farnaby, of Kippington, in Kent, Bart.—The younger son of Sir Thomas Smythe, of Bidborough, and Sarah Blount, in November 1618, marrying the daughter of Charles Blount, Lord Mountjoy and Earl of Devonshire, by the aforesaid Lady Penelope, Countess of Warwick, without the consent of his father, left England about the middle of July following, upon some discontent, without taking leave either of father or wife.

Sir Richard Smythe, who married Jane, daughter and heir to John White, of London, Esq. who dying in 1607, lies buried in the parish church of St. Stephen, Coleman-street, (to the poor whereof he gave 100l. a year, for provision of sea-coal) where, on a pillar in the choir, is erected a handsome monument, with this inscription : (3)

> Here lieth Dame Jane, Daughter and sole Heir of
> John White of this Parish, Esq. first married
> To Samuel Thornhill of Bromley in the county
> of Kent, Esq. by whom she had issue two sons,
>   Timothy

SMYTHE Viscount STRANGFORD.

Timothy and John, and one daughter named Elizabeth. She secondly married Sir Richard Smythe, Knt. son of Thomas Smythe of Oftenhanger In the county of Kent, Esq. and had issue by Him one but daughter named Mary. The said Dame Jane died the 13th of October 1607, being About the age of 33 years.

In whose remembrance her said husband Caused this monument to be made, 1608.

(1) Daughter Catharine, was the second wife of Sir Rowland Hayward, Lord Mayor of London, who died 5 December 1593, having issue five sons and five daughters, of whom the survivors of their infancy were, George, John, Alice, Catharine, Mary, and Anne.

(2) Elizabeth, first married to Simon Horsepoole, of London, Esq. free of the Drapiers company, and of the ancient Wool-Staple; Merchant-Adventurer of the Old-Hanse and Muscovy Companies; Sheriff of that city in 1591; and by him, who died 14 January 1601, æt. 75, she had three sons and three daughters, William, Simon, Thomas; Elizabeth, married to Alexander King, Esq. one of the Auditors to Q. Elizabeth; Hawys, to Francis Donington, Merchant of Tripoli; and Joan, to John Whitebrooke, Gent.—Her second husband was Sir Henry Fanshaw, as in the note.

(3) Jane, second wife to Thomas Fanshaw, of Ware-Park, in Hertfordshire, Esq.* Remembrancer of the Exchequer, and

---

* This branch of the family descended from the Fanshaws, of Fanshaw-Park, in Derbyshire, John Fanshaw of that place having two sons, Henry and Thomas, successive Remembrancers of the Court of Exchequer; the latter of whom purchasing Ware-Park from Catharine, Countess of Huntingdon, about the year 1570, resided there; and by his first wife Mary Bourchier, had an only son Henry, who in 1600, succeeded him in the office of King's Remembrancer of the Exchequer; was knighted; died 10 March 1615, and married as in the text, by whom he had ten children, but only left Sir Thomas; and Sir Simon, who married Catharine, daughter to Sir William Walter, of Wimbledon, and widow of Knighton Ferrers, son to Sir John Ferrers, of Beyford, in Hertfordshire, Knt. and Sir Richard, an eminent Poet, and an accomplished Gentleman, who in 1635, was appointed Resident to the Court of Spain, whence being recalled in 1641, he adhered to the royal cause; was created in 1644, Doctor of the Civil Law ot Oxford; made Secretary to the Prince of Wales, whom he attended in his flight to Jersey; was in 1648, made Treasurer of the Navy, under Prince Rupert; was created a Baronet

and by him, who died in February 1600, had issue Thomas; William; and Alice, married to Sir Christopher Hatton, Knight of the Bath, by whom she was mother of Christopher, created Baron Hatton, of Kerby, and grandmother of Christopher, created Viscount Hatton.

Sir John Smythe, the eldest son, of Oestenhanger and of Ashford, Knt. received his education in the University of Oxford, and 42 Elizabeth, was High Sheriff of the county of Kent. He married Elizabeth, daughter and heir to John Phineux, of Hawhouse, in Kent, Esq. (Sheriff of that county 29 Elizabeth, and son to Sir John Phineux, by Elizabeth, daughter and heir to the family of Apuldorfield, of Hawhouse) and thereby considerably augmented his estate, obtaining the manors of Whitstaple, Bonnington and Northcourt, with a descent in blood, from

Sir John.

a Baronet in 1650, and sent Envoy to Spain; whence being recalled into Scotland, he served there in quality of Secretary of State; was made prisoner in 1651, at the battle of Worcester, but being released on account of his health, he repaired to the King at Breda, in February 1659, who knighted him in April following, and after the restoration made him Master of the Requests, and Secretary of the Latin Tongue. In 1661, he was chosen to Parliament for the University of Cambridge (where he received his education) was sworn a Privy Counsellor of Ireland; sent Envoy to Portugal, and shortly after Ambassador to that Court, where he negotiated the marriage of K. Charles II. and the Infanta Catharina, daughter of K. John IV. to which Court he returned Ambassador in 1662, and the next year was sworn of the Privy Council in England; being also in February 1664, sent Ambassador to Philip IV. of Spain, died at Madrid 16 June 1666, æt. 69, and was buried in a vault, made for himself and family in the church of Ware, near which a handsome monument is erected to his memory, setting forth that he married Anne, eldest daughter of Sir John Harrison, of Balls, in Hertfordshire, Knt. by whom he had six sons and eight daughters, of whom only one son and four daughters survived him.—Sir Thomas Fanshaw, the eldest son of Henry, succeeded him in estate and office; was invested Knight of the Bath at the coronation of Charles I. served in Parliament for the borough of Hertford, under James and Charles I. and continuing firm in his loyalty to that unhappy King, supplied him with great sums of money, and quantities of arms, for which he was imprisoned, with his son, and his estate sequestered; but on the restoration, he was chosen to Parliament for the county of Hertford, and for his eminent services, created 5 September 1661, Baron Fanshaw, and Viscount Fanshaw, of Dromore; in which he was succeeded by his eldest son Sir Thomas, who represented the borough of Hertford, in the aforesaid Parliament, and sold Ware-Park to Sir Thomas Byde. He married first the only daughter and heir of Knighton Ferrers; secondly Sarah, daughter and heir to Sir John Evelyn, of Wiltshire, and was succeeded by Charles, Viscount Fanshaw, who in October 1680, was sent Envoy Extraordinary to the Prince Regent, of Portugal, and was Chief Remembrancer of the Exchequer; in which and his honours he was succeeded 28 March 1710, by his brother Simon, who died 23 October 1716, and the titles are now extinct, by the death of his successor Evelyn, Viscount Fanshaw.

from the famous family of Apuldorfield, and a right of quartering their arms, with those of Phineux.—He departed this life in the beginning of the year 1609, and was buried with his father in Ashford church, leaving issue.

Sir Thomas, 1 Viscount.
Sir Thomas Smythe, of Oestenhanger, who purchased the manor of Otterpool, from Sir Edward Hales, and also the manor of Peckmanston; and being a person of distinguished merit and opulent fortune, was made a Knight of the Bath in 1616, at the creation of Charles, Prince of Wales; and was further advanced by that Prince, when King, to the dignity of a Peer of Ireland, by the title of Viscount Strangford, by letters patent, bearing date 17 July 1628.—He married the Lady Barbara Sidney, seventh daughter of Robert, the first Earl of Leicester (by his first wife Barbara, daughter and heir to John Gammage, Esq. of Coyttie, in the county of Glamorgan) and niece to the learned and memorable Sir Philip Sydney; and his Lordship deceasing 30 June 1635, was buried in his chapel, adjoining to the church of Ashford, leaving issue by her, who was born in 1559, and re-married with Sir Thomas Culpeper, of St. Stephens, near Canterbury, one son Philip, and a daughter married to ——— Burrows, of the county of Suffolk, Esq.

Philip, 2 Viscount.
Philip, the second Viscount Strangford, resided at Oestenhanger, until he disposed of it, with other lands, to the family of Finch; and 22 August 1630, marrying his first cousin the Lady Isabella Sidney, seventh daughter of Robert, the second Earl of Leicester, was father of

Thomas, 3 Viscount.
Thomas, the third Viscount, who died in August 1708, at his seat near Canterbury, and was buried at Ashford; leaving

Philip, 4 Viscount.
Philip, the fourth Viscount, who married Mary, daughter of George Porter, of the county of Middlesex, Esq. eldest son to Endymion Porter, Groom of the Bed-Chamber to K. Charles I. by his wife Olivia, fourth daughter of John, Lord Butler, of Brantfield; and dying in September 1715, left issue Endymion, his heir; and several daughters, of whom Catharine, was the first wife of Henry Roper, Lord Teynham, had two sons Philip and Henry, who both succeeded to that title, and died at Kensington 16 April 1711; Elizabeth, was married to Henry Audley, of Bear-Church, in Essex, Esq. whose widow she died 25 January 1732, and

and was buried 4 February at Charf, in Kent; and Olivia, married to John Darell, of Calehill, in Kent, Esq. died his widow 15 January 1753, in the 82 year of her age.

Endymion, the fifth Viscount, took his seat in Parliament, 12 November 1715[1], married Elizabeth, daughter of Mr. Le Larget, of St. Martin's, London; died 8 September 1724, and was buried the 10 in St. Peter's Church, Dublin, leaving by his said Lady, who died in Holland, 28 June 1764, one daughter and one son

Endymion, 5 Viscount.

Philip, the sixth Viscount Strangford, born in 1715, who took his seat in Parliament 9 October 1739[2]; and 11 April 1742, entering into Holy Orders, was presented that day in 1743, to the prebend of Killafpugmullan, and the rectories of Templeufque, Kilkoan and Kilroan, otherwise Ballydelogher, in the county of Cork; being also 26 May 1746, collated to the Precentorship of the Cathedral Church of Elphin; created 22 October 1751, Doctor of Laws, by the University of Dublin; and 7 April 1752, presented to the Deanery of Derry, which he afterwards resigned.—In 1741, his Lordship married Mary, daughter of Anthony Jephson, of Moyallow, in the county of Cork, Esq. and had one son Lionel, his heir; and two daughters, Mary and Anne. His Lordship died 29 April 1787, and was succeeded by his only son

Philip, 6 Viscount;

Lionel, the seventh and present Viscount, who was born at Londonderry, 19 May 1753, entered into the army at an early period of life, and served many campaigns in North-America, but retired from the military profession; in 1785, he entered into Holy Orders, and was presented in 1788, by George, Marquess of Buckingham, L. L. to the living of Kilbrew, in the diocess of Meath. 5 September 1779, his Lordship married at New-York, in North-America, Maria-Eliza, eldest daughter of Frederick Philips, of that province, Esq. and hath issue two sons and two daughters, viz. Percy, born in London, 31 August 1780; Lionel, 28 March 1783; Eliza, 5 September 1781; and Louisa, 2 March 1785[3].

Lionel, 7 Viscount.

TITLE.]

---

[1] Lords Jour. II. 451. [2] Idem III. 440. [3] Information of Lionel, Lord Strangford.

WENMAN, Viscount WENMAN.

TITLE.] Lionel Smythe, Viscount of Strangford, in the county of Downe.

CREATION.] So created 17 July 1628, Car. I.

ARMS.] Pearl, a Cheveron ingrailed between three Lions passant, Diamond.

CREST.] On a Wreath, a Leopard's Head erased, Pearl, gorged with a plain Collar and Chain, affixed, Diamond.

SUPPORTERS.] The Dexter, a Lion, Topaz, Guttee de Larmes. The Sinister, a Leopard, Pearl, gorged and chained, as the Crest.

MOTTO.] VIRTUS INCENDIT VIRES.

WENMAN, Viscount WENMAN.

10. Henry.

THIS family of Wenman hath been long seated in the counties of Oxford and Berks; of which was Henry Wainman, or Wenman, Esq. (for the name was diversly written) of Blueberry, county of Berks, who in 1482, married Emmotte, daughter and heir to Sympkin Hervey, of the county of Hereford, Esq. and died in the reign of Edward IV. leaving issue by her, (who after married Thomas Fermor, of Witney in Oxfordshire, whom she also survived) two sons and two daughters, viz. Richard, his heir; John (who by Alice his wife left a son Thomas, and a daughter Alice); Alice; and Elizabeth, married to Lawrence Fermor of the same county, by whom she had William, Joan, and Mary.

Richard.

Richard Wenman, Esq. the elder son, married Anne, daughter of John Bush of the county of Gloucester, by

whom

whom he had two sons and three daughters, Thomas, William, Alice, Joan and Mary.——Thomas was knighted by Thomas. Q. Elizabeth, and married Ursula, daughter and heir to Thomas Gifford, of Twyford in the county of Bucks, Esq. by which marriage he became possessed of the manors of Twyford, Pounden, and Chamton, in that county; and his issue were, Sir Richard, Henry, William, Anne, and Elizabeth

Sir Richard, who succeeded, was Sheriff[1] of the county Sir Richard. of Oxford, in 1562, (5 Eliz.) and marrying Isabel, elder daughter and coheir to John, Lord Williams of Thame*, left issue Sir Richard his heir; Sir Thomas; and a daughter married to ——— Tasburg.

Sir Thomas Wenman of Dublin, Knt. the younger son, 18 February 1627, obtained the directions of K. Charles I. to have the first vacant company in his army, after former warrants were supplied; was made 18 November 1628, Governor of the fort, then lately erected at Cork; and 7 July 1629 Provost-Mareschal of the province of Munster, with the pay of 5s. 7h. a day for himself, and 16d. a-piece for 12 horsemen, during life.——He died in 1637, having made his will 3 September 1636, wherein he leaves his wife Margaret, relict of Sir Francis Aungier, Master of the Rolls[2], executrix, and residuary legatee; devises to his nephew Philip,

---

* John, Lord Williams of Thame, was the second son of Sir John Williams, of Burfield in Berkshire, by his wife Elizabeth, daughter and coheir to Richard Moore of that place, Esq. and by his several preferments in the reigns of Henry VIII. Mary, and Elizabeth; of Treasurer of the Jewel House, and Court of Augmentation, Lord Chamberlain, of the houshold to K. Philip, and President of the Council in the Principality of Wales, acquired a very considerable estate, and 5 April 1554, was created Lord Williams of Thame. —He married Elizabeth, daughter and coheir to Thomas Bedlow, Esq. widow of Andrew Edmonds, of Cressing-Temple in Essex, and dying 14 October 1559, was buried at Thame under a white marble tomb, where he had founded and endowed a beautiful school and alm-house.——His issue were two daughters, Isabel, Lady Wenman; and Margaret, wife to Henry Norris, created Lord Norris in 1572, whose grandson by her was created Viscount Thame, and Earl of Berkshire; but he leaving only a daughter Elizabeth, she became the wife of Edward Wray, Esq. Groom of the Bedchamber to K. James I. (third son to Sir William Wray, of Glentworth in Lincolnshire, Bart.) by whom having an only child Bridget, second wife to Montague Bertie, the second Earl of Lindsey, she was mother of James, Lord Norris of Rycote in her Right, created Earl of Abingdon.——And, in the division of the estate, Thame-park, &c. falling to Lady Wenman, hath continued the chief seat of this noble family.

---

[1] Fuller's Worthies. [2] See Countess of Longford, n.

Philip, and the heirs male of his body (after his Lady's deceafe) the manor of Ballintogher, and all his eftates in the counties of Sligo and Leitrim; remainder to his nephew Sir Thomas, and his heirs for ever; bequeathing legacies to his nieces Penelope, Jane, Elizabeth, and Agnes.

Sir Richard. Sir Richard Wenman, who fucceeded at Thame-Park, ferved the office of Sheriff for Oxfordfhire, 13 Eliz.[1] and married Jane, daughter of William, Lord Delawar; by whom he had Richard, created Vifcount Wenman, and the faid children mentioned in their uncle's will, viz. Philip, who fucceeded his nephew in the title; Thomas, whofe only daughter Mary, was married to Francis Wenman, as hereafter; and of the daughters, Agnes, the youngeft, was married to ———— Clarke; Elizabeth, to ———— Floyde; Jane, to ———— Goodwin; and Penelope, a lady of great fidelity and courage, was the fecond wife of Sir John Dynham (grandfon of Thomas Dynham, Gent. by Catharine, fole daughter and heir to Leonard Rede, Efq. grandfon and heir to Edmund Rede of Borftal, living in 1487) and by him, who died 16 February 1634, had three daughters his coheirs, Mary, Alice, and Margaret, the eldeft of whom was then the wife of Lawrence, fon and heir to Sir Robert Banaftre, whofe only daughter and heir Margaret, was married to William Lewis of *the Van*, in the county of Glamorgan, Efq. in 1648, and had iffue Edward, who died unmarried, in 1672; and two daughters, of whom the eldeft, Mary, married firft William Jephfon, Efq. who dying on Trinity Sunday 1691, fhe remarried with Sir John Aubrey of Leantrithed, in county of Glamorgan, Bart. fon of Sir John, grandfon of Sir Thomas, and great grandfon of William Aubrey, L. L. D. a perfon higly efteemed in the reign of Q. Elizabeth.

Sir Richard.
1 Vifcount. Sir Richard Wenman, the eldeft fon, who fucceeded at Thame-Park, for his gallant behaviour at the taking of Cadiz, in 1596, where he ferved as a Volunteer, and Sheriff of the county of Oxford for the year 1627[2]; was honoured with knighthood; and by letters patent *, dated at

---

* The Preamble. Et Solii regii fulgor, et Regni uniufcujufque Gloria fingularem adipifci folent acceffionem, cum Viri infignioribus eminentiorum Virtutum, clarorum Natalium, amplique, et quod fuftinendis Dignitatibus par fit, Patrimonii, Meritis confpiciendi, ad altiores Honorum Gradus evocantur,

[1] Fuller's Worthies. [2] Idem.

WENMAN, Viscount WENMAN,

at Canbury, 30 July 1628, created Baron Wenman of Kilmaynham, and Viscount Wenman of Tuam, with the annual creation fee of 13l. 6s. 8d. Irish, payable out of the customs of the Port of Dublin.

His loyalty and duty inclined him to the interests of K. Charles I. during the Civil war, whose service he promoted to the utmost of his power; and in his Lordship's family it was, that Doctor Seth Ward, the great ornament of England, (Bishop of Exeter, and of Salisbury after the Restoration) when he had been expelled Sidney-College in Cambridge, and long harassed for his allegiance, found an asylum, his incomparable learning and obliging temper, making way for a kind and generous reception from the Lord Wenman.——His Lordship married Agnes, eldest surviving daughter of Sir George Fermor, of Eston-Neston in the county of Northampton, ancestor to the Earl of Pontefract, and

centur, atque ejusmodi illustrantur Titulis, qui velut perpetui veræ Dignitatis Testes et præsenti Ævo sint, et ad Posteros transmittantur. Nam ut ingens Reipublicæ felicitas ex id genus Virorum copia nascitur, ita è publica atqt principali eorum Agnitione, quæ Honoribus sit rite dispensandis, augetur ille fulgor Solium circumstipans, cujus diffusiori Luce non solum alacriores fiunt eorum Animi, et excitatiores qui in Actu et administratione positi Rem optime gerunt ; sed etiam alii, qui nondum Virtutis Specimina edidere, ad Res præclara capessendas, ut ejusmodi etiam Præmia sortiantur, non mediocriter incenduntur. Hæc serio nos recolentes egregia Merita Viri clarissimi Richardi Wenman de *Thame-Park* in Comitatu nostro *Oxoniæ* Militis intuemur, cujus sive Natalium splendorem, sive Patrimonii amplitudinem, sive Animi fortitudinem, prudentiam, Morumque præstantiam consideremus, eum talem agnoscimus esse Virum, qualem ad altiores Honorum Gradus cum Primis evehendum esse censemus. Natalium ejus splendorem (præter eum, qui Equestri vetustæ sibique ipsi Cognomini Familiæ debetur) variatim auxerunt Matrimonia à Decessoribus ejus serie continua cum Familiis aliquot Illustribus, unde ipse lineatim extrahitur, contracta; Ursula scilicet ejus Proavia, Uxor nempe Thomæ Wenman ejus Proavia filia erat unica et hæres Thomæ Gifford de Twiford in Comitatu nostro Buckinghamiæ, cujus Majores, unde ipse originem traxit, et Baronum Parliamenti Regni nostri Angliæ, et Comitum de Longa-Vill in Normania, atque Comitum dicti Comitatus nostri de Buckinghamia titulis quondam floruerunt Isabella Avia ejus filia erat primogenita atque Cohæredum altera Johannis Williams Militis, Baronis olim de Tame ; et demum Jana, Mater ejus, filia erat Willielmi nuper Baronis Delaware ; nec vero tantæ Natalium Claritati eximia Animi fortitudo defuit, quam largiter exhibuit ipse in celeberrima illa *Gadium* sub Regina Elizabetha direptione, in quâ, ut famâ audivimus, se Virum bellicosum et Honoris adjectione plene dignum præbuit. Hisce, velut Corona accedit inviolata fides, quam erga Patrem nostrum gloriolæ Memoriæ, atque erga nos-ipsos et Negotia nostra nunquam non servavit, et permanenter et summo cum Judicio præstitit ; adeoqne, ut nec quidquam Ei decesse, necessarium est ut agnoscamus quo minus amplioribus Honoribus jure optimo sit donandus : Quocirca eum in Statu, Gradu, Honores, et Titulos et Baronis et Vicecomitis in Regno nostro Hiberniæ creandum et evehendum meritissimum duximus. Sciatis igitur, &c. (Rot. A°. 4 Car. I. 5. p. f. R. 54.)

and had issue Thomas his heir; and Elizabeth, married to Grevile Verney, Esq. who died 9 December 1648, leaving her with child of a son, born 26 January following, and named Grevile.

Thomas,
2 Viscount.

Thomas, the second Viscount Wenman, was one of the adventurers in Ireland, when the kingdom was reduced by the English Parliament, and subscribing the sum of 600l. had an allotment of 617 acres, 1 rood, 15 perches of land plantation measure, amounting to 1000 acres, statute measure, in the barony of Garrycastle, and King's County: he was appointed by Parliament one of the Commissioners to carry the Propositions for peace to the King at Oxford, in 1644, and was again appointed Commissioner for the treaty at Uxbridge that year; as he was for the treaty at Newport in 1648; and was one of the 41 members, who, for giving their vote, " That the concessions of his Majesty to the pro- " positions upon the treaty at Newport, were sufficient " grounds for the house to proceed upon, for the settlement " of the peace of kingdom," were seized by the army, and. committed to close imprisonment. In the year 1645, he was considered as one of the sufferers, and received 4l. a week, by order of the Parliament, for the damages he suffered on his estates in the county of Oxford, by the King's forces [1]. This Nobleman had his introduction to the House of Peers of Ireland by Lord Aungier, his proxy, 13 July 1661 [2]: but leaving only daughters, Frances the eldest was married to Richard Samwell, of Upton in Northamptonshire, Esq.. (by whom she had Sir Thomas Samwell created a Baronet, 22 December 1675, and several daughters, of whom Mary was married to Adolphus Oughton, Esq. and was mother of Sir Adolphus Oughton, of Tetchbrooke in Warwickshire, Bart. and Frances was wife to Sir Thomas Wagstaffe, Knt. whose only daughter and heir Frances, was first married to Sir Edward Baggot, of Blithfield in Staffordshire, Bart.; whose son and heir Sir Walter Wagstaffe Baggot, represented that county in the British Parliament, and was succeeded by Sir William, created Lord Bagot; and secondly, to the said Sir Adolphus Oughton, Bart.) and Penelope was married to Sir Thomas Cave of Stamford, created a Baronet 30 June 1641, by whom she had Sir Roger, and other children.

Philip,
3 Viscount.

To Thomas, Lord Wenman, succeeded Philip his uncle, the third Viscount, who, after the death of his only son, without

---

[1] Salmon's Peerage.   [2] Lords Jour. 1. 301.

out issue, by Barbara his wife, eldest daughter of Sir Edward Villiers, and sister to William, the first Viscount Grandison, procured from K. Charles II. 30 January 1683, a new entail of the honours on his next heir male, Sir Richard Wenman, Bart. in reversion after his own death, with the same precedency that he enjoyed; who accordingly succeeded to the title.——He derived from the family, seated at Caswell, in the county of Oxford; whereof Francis Wenman, in the reign of Q. Elizabeth came into Ireland, where he died, and left issue Sir Francis Wenman, Knt. then of very tender years, whose wardship was granted, 6 August 1603 to Allen Apsley, Esq. but after he attained his full age, he had a special livery of his estate, 17 February 1623, and 13 April 1640, represented the county of Oxford in Parliament.—He married Anne, third daughter of Sir Samuel Sandys, of Omberslade in Worcestershire, Knt. and had Francis his heir; and a daughter Anne, the first wife of Sir John Fettiplace, of Childry in Berkshire, created a Baronet, 30 March 1661, by whom she had five sons and five daughters.

Francis Wenman, Esq. 29 November 1662, was created a Baronet, and married Mary, daughter of Thomas Wenman, Esq. before-mentioned; which Lady lies buried in the church of Witney, in Oxfordshire, under a marble monument, with this memorial;

To the memory of
Mary, late wife to Francis Wenman of Caswell, Esq. daughter to Thomas Wenman of Thame:
:Parke, who departed this life the 13th of November Anno Dn"i 1657, being the twenty-fourth year of her Age. She had issue Thomas, Francis, Ferdinando, Elizabeth and Richard.

Sir Richard, the youngest son, by the decease of his brothers, succeeded to the title of Baronet, as he did to those of Baron and Viscount Wenman: and in the Parliament, which met at Oxford 21 March 1680, represented the town of Brackley, in the county of Northampton, for which place he had served before, as he did in the reign of K. William, being on that account excused his attendance (20 October 1692) in the Parliament of Ireland.

He married Catharine, elder daughter and coheir to Sir Thomas Chamberlayne of Wickham, and Northbrooke, in
the

Sir Richard, 4 Viscount.

the county of Oxford, Bart. (son and successor of Sir Thomas Chamberlayne, created to that dignity 4 February 1642) by his wife Margaret, daughter of Edmond Prideaux of the Inner-Temple, Esq. and by her (who in 1698 re-married with James, the first Earl of Abingdon, and after his decease, on 22 May 1699, with Francis Wroughton of Heskett in Wiltshire, Esq.) had issue Sir Richard his heir, and two daughters; Catharine, first married to Robert Bertie of Benham in Berkshire, Esq. fourth son of the aforesaid Earl of Abingdon, who leaving her a widow without issue, 16 August 1710, she became the wife of Sir William Osbaldeston, of Chudlington and Nethercote, in Oxfordshire, Bart., and by him, who died 17 September 1736, had Sir Charles his successor.—The younger daughter was married to John Wicksted, Esq.

Sir Richard, 5 Viscount. Sir Richard Wenman, the fifth Viscount, married Susana, daughter of Seymour Wroughton, of Heskett, Esq. sister to his mother's third husband, and departing this life at his seat of Thame, 28 November 1729, was there buried with his ancestors, leaving issue two sons, Sir Philip his successor; and Richard, who in 1773, married Jemima, relict of Colonel Caulfield.

Sir Philip, 6 Viscount. Sir Philip, the sixth Viscount, was born 23 November 1719, served in the British Parliament for the city of Oxford, married 13 July 1741, Sophia, eldest daughter and coheir to James Herbert, of Tythorpe, in county of Oxford, Esq. and deceased 16 August 1760, having had by his said lady, who died 20 June 1787, four sons and three daughters, viz. Sir Philip, who succeeded to the honours; Thomas-Francis, born 18 November 1745; Richard, born 13 November 1746; and Henry-Herbert, born 18 July 1749, died young; daughter Sophia, (born 7 August 1743, married in 1768, William-Humphry Wykham, of Swalcliffe in county of Oxford, Esq. and by him who is deceased had William; Philip; Sophia; and Harriot); Susanna, born 10 November 1744, died young; and Mary, born 27 March 1748, died in 1757 [1].

Sir Philip, 7 Viscount. Sir Philip, the seventh and present Viscount, was born 18 April 1742, and married 7 July 1766, to Eleanor, fifth daughter of Willoughby, Earl of Abingdon [2].

TITLES.] Sir Philip Wenman, Lord Viscount Wenman of Tuam, Baron Wenman of Kilmaynham, and Baronet.

CREATIONS.]

[1] Ulster's Off.   [2] Idem.

TAAFFE, Viscount TAAFFE.

CREATIONS] B. Wenman of Kilmaynham in the county of Dublin, and V. Wenman of Tuam in the county of Galway, 30 July 1628, 4 Car. I.; Baronet, 26 November 1662, 14 Car. II.

ARMS.] Parti per Pale, ruby and faphire, a crofs patonce, topaz.

SUPPORTERS.] Two greyhounds, ruby, gorged with plain collars, gold.

CREST.] On a wreath, a cock's head erazed, faphire, crefted and jelloped, topaz.

MOTTO.] OMNIA BONA BONIS.

SEATS.] Thame-Park 37 miles from London: Cafwell, near Witney in the county of Oxford; and Twyford in the county of Buckingham, 52 miles from London.

TAAFFE, Viscount TAAFFE.

THE family of Taaffe hath been of great antiquity and considerable repute in the counties of Louth and Sligo, and hath produced many eminent perfons, among whom was Sir Richard Taaffe, who flourifhed in the time of K. Edward I. and died in 1287; contemporary with whom was the Lord Nicholas Taaffe, who by deed, dated at Clantarffe, Craft' Animarum 1284, gave in pure alms to God, the Blefled Mary, and the Knights Templars in Ireland, his lands of Killergy; and died 30 October 1288, (16 Edw. I.) leaving iffue John Taaffe, Archbifhop of Armagh, who died in 1306, and Richard Fitz-Nicholas Taaffe, againft whom, by virtue of his father's said charter, Adam, Prior of the Holy Trinity, in Dublin, recovered 400 acres of land in Killergy, with 20 mares coft, in Hillary term 1291,—He left iffue (probably) two fons, Richard; and Nicholas, who about 1310, gave and confirmed the manor of Donacumper, in the county of Kildare, to

the

the priory of St. Wolftan; and in 1334 (8 Edw. III.) had a grant from the crown of lands in Kenlys, &c. to the value of 10l. a year, during pleafure, for his profecution of Sir Richard de Mandeville, John Cogan, and others, the murderers of William de Burgo, Earl of Ulfter.

Richard.   Richard Taaffe, Efq. was feated at Ballybraggan, and Caftlelumpnagh, and in 1315 (9 Rich. II.) was Sheriff of the county of Louth, when Hugh de Lacie, the younger, Earl of Ulfter, for inciting Edward Bruce to invade Ireland, for joining him with all his force, caufing him to be proclaimed King, and committing divers murders and outrages, was condemned to be drawn with horfes, afterwards to be hanged and quartered, one quarter, with his head, to be fet up in Dublin, and the others in Drogheda, Dundalk, and Trim, and his bowels to be burned: But the Archbifhop of Armagh and others interceding with the L. J. to refpite his execution, until the King's pleafure might be known, his body was delivered for fafe cuftody to this Richard Taaffe, who kept him, until he was ordered to be hanged at Drogheda.—On 19 March 1336, by the name of Richard Taaffe, of Caftlelumpnagh, he obtained the King's Writ of Eafe; being excufed by patent, during life, from attending, or being put on affizes, Juries, &c.

He was founder of the families of Ballybraggan, Athclare, Bolies, Stormanftown, Cookftown, Stephenftown, Ranitty, Dromin, and Harleftown, from the laft of which the Lord Vifcount Taaffe derives.—By his wife Joan (who after married John Rochford, and pleaded her dower in 1384, againft her fon of 40 meffuages, two mills, 8 carucates of land, 80 acres of meadow, 200 of pafture, 200 of wood, 500 of moore and bogg, and 12 pence rent in Ballybraghan, Duncafhell, Athclare, Mandevilftown, Dromyng, Rathefkyr, Wodeton, Drakefton, &c. in county

John.   of Louth) the faid Richard, left John Fitz-Richard Taaffe, who in 1349, was the King's coroner, being then ftyled John Taaffe, *fenior*, of Ballybraghan, Lifcartan, and Rath,

John.   near Platen; and by Rofe his wife, was father of John Fitz-John Taaffe, who in 1342, purchafed half a carucate of land, in Kiltaltyn, from Michael Bath, and Mariot

Thomas.   his wife, and his iffue were Thomas Fitz-John; Nicholas
Nicholas.   Fitz-John Taaffe, of Rathmolyn (who by Joan his wife had Adam Fitz-Nicholas of the fame place, his fecond fon, his eldeft being probably Simon, who was living in 1363, which Adam, in 1368, pleaded 300l. againft Walter Cufack);

fack); and Richard Fitz-John of Gibfton, who had iffue Nicholas Fitz-Richard his heir; and John Fitz-Richard, of Ballybraggan, and of Lifcahan, who in 1411, fued William More of Bermeath, coufin and heir to John Taaffe, of Caftlelumpnagh for 1000l. which John was living in 1382, and probably is the fame perfon who was Sheriff of Louth in 1377, and maried Alicia, who on his deceafe, remarried with John Talbot. Nicholas Fitz-Richard, the eldeft fon, fucceeded at Ballybraggan, and was father of Richard Fitz-Nicholas, his fucceffor there, living in 1355, the father of Walter Fitz-Richard, living in 1365, whofe fon Nicholas, in 1414, 2 Hen. V. was appointed one of the Keepers of the Peace in the county of Louth, with power to affefs men, horfes and arms: and to him fucceeded Sir Nicholas Taaffe, who in 1441, was fheriff of Sir the county of Louth, when he did great fervice to the Eng- Nicholas lifh Government in Ireland; and his fon Sir Robert, 13 Sir Robert, April 1468, with 70 horfe, joined the Mayor of Drogheda at Ardee, who, with 500 archers, and 200 pole-axes, marched againft O'Reily and his fon, Mac-Cabe and Mac-Brady, who had entered and wafted Louth with 2400 men: At Malpas-bridge they came to an engagement, where O'Reily, his fon and 400 men were flain; for which fignal fervice, K. Edward IV. the next year gave the town of Drogheda a fword, to be carried before the Mayor, and the annual fum of 20l. for the maintainance thereof.

To him fucceeded Sir Lawrence Taaffe, Knt. who in Sir 14-2 was one of the 13 honourable and moft faithfully dif- Lawrence. pofed perfons in the counties of Kildare, Dublin, Meath, and Louth, eftablifhed by act of Parliament a fociety, by the name of *the Captain and Brethren at Arms, or the Brotherhood of* St. George, for the prefervation of the *Englifh Pale.*—From him defcended Peter Taaffe of Ballybraggan, Peter. Efq. whofe fon and heir Nicholas, in 1552 (6 Edw. VI.) Nicholas. had a fpecial livery of his inheritance, and reprefented the county of Louth in the Parliament, which met 2 January 1559.—He left iffue John Taaffe, of Ballybraggan and of John. Harlefton, Efq. who had three fons, viz.

Chriftopher, to whom a fpecial livery of the eftate was (1) granted, 4 March 1606. He married Sufanna, third daughter of Luke, the firft Earl of Fingall, and was fucceeded in his eftates by his fon, John of Braganftown, who had a like livery by patent, 5 Auguft 1633; but he, with his fon Chriftopher, being engaged in the rebellion of 1641, the fame was forfeited.

(1) Sir William, anceftor to the Lord Taaffe.
(3) Peter, of Dromin in Louth, who, during the rebellion in Q. Elizabeth's reign, was murdered in his own houfe, and left iffue, Jenico, the father of John; and Lawrence, who in 1583, lived at Moymet, and 31 March that year, received a warrant from the Queen, to have the firft penfioner's place that fhould fall void, (after the preferring of Richard Wood and Roger Lucas) and that in the mean time he fhould be otherwife relieved, the manner of which relief fhe referred to the Deputy's difcretion, who could beft judge what was meet to be done, for the prefent neceffity of the poor Gentleman, whom fhe was induced to relieve for his good fervices, fundry times done, both before and in the time of the rebellion, following therein his father's fteps, who was murdered in his own houfe, and had his goods carried away, and his houfe burned and fpoiled, in revenge of a fpecial good piece of fervice performed to her by his faid fon; And K. James I. for the fame reafon, by patent, dated 16 October 1624, purfuant to Privy Seal at Weftminfter, 17 July, gave and confirmed to him and his heirs, the caftle, town, and lands of Peppardftown in the county of Louth, which were then, and had been for many years in the occupation of him and his anceftors.

Sir William. Sir William Taaffe of Harlefton, of Ballymote, and of Smarmore, the second fon of John Taaffe of Harlefton and Ballybraggan, diftinguifhed himfelf by his fervices to the crown, during the courfe of Tyrone's rebellion.—On 1 November, 1597, he was made Conftable of St. Leger's caftle; and after the Spaniards in 1601 had landed at Kingfale, and, in order to fubfift, had taken a large prey of cattle and fheep, which were in a feeming ifland, on the South fide of the town beyond the water, not to be entered, but by a march to a neck of land, of 8 or 9 miles about, Captain Taaffe ufed fuch expedition, that he attained the place before night, and by a hot fkirmifh recovered the prey, although under the cover of Caftlenyparke, mann'd purpofely to fecure them.—On 10 February 1601, the Lord Barry and he routed Donogh Moyle Mac-Carthy's men; and at the fiege of Kingfale he behaved with fuch fingular courage and conduct, that he was knighted; and in December 1602 commanding the Irifh in the Queen's pay in Carbery, he engaged a band of rebels under the Apoftolick Vicar Owen Mac-Egan (whofe barbarity was fuch, as to caufe every Irifhman,

Irishman, that served the Queen and fell into his hands, to be confessed and absolved, and then instantly executed) whom he killed, 5 January with 140 of his men, near the river Bandon, took all their cattle, and (upon O'Suillevan's flight) wasted his country and reduced his castles; whereby and the Nuncio's death, the Mac-Carthies of Carbery submitted to mercy.—By this success over the Irish, the kingdom was settled in a state of peace; and when K. James ascended the throne, he put such methods in execution, as he judged most conducive to the establishment thereof; the principal of which was the plantation of the forfeited lands, and the disposition of them to such persons, as he was assured not only deserved a reward for their past services, but would continue to promote the tranquility of the kingdom, and secure it from future commotions: Among whom, Sir William Taaffe had not the least share of his Majesty's Bounty, as well as *That* of Q. Elizabeth, having served them both with great fidelity *.

On 21 April 1630, he makes his will, and thereby bequeaths his body to be buried in the chancel of the church

---

* The Queen, in reward of his service, by her letter from Greenwich 6 July 1592, ordered him a lease, or leases in possession or reversion, of so many crown lands in Conaught, as should amount to 30l. a year, for 30 years, without fine; and K. James by patent, 9 January 1603, granted to him in fee-farm the Rectory of Ballykilly, parcel of the Priory of Inistiock, lately demised to Sir Lucas Dillon, the Precinct of St. Mary *de Insula vitæ* in O'Carrol's country, with other religious possessions in the counties of Waterford and Cavan; and 20 of that month, the manor of Smarmore in the county of Louth; the town and lough of Ballinlowre, in the county of Dublin; the Abbey of Odorney in Kerry; the Rectories of Odorney, Mollahiffe and Rathreogh, with other hereditaments in those counties, and in Cork, Waterford, Sligo, Longford, Meath, Westmeath, Kildare, Mayo, Tipperary, and Queen's county, to hold by the 20 part of a Knight's fee, and 37l. 8s. 6d. rent.——Also, 16 July 1604, he had a grant of the entire territory or country of Ichouloe in the county of Cork, containing 28 small carucates of land, each consisting of 120 acres, lying in Muskery, to hold by the like tenure, and the rent of 5l. 1s. Irish.—Farther, he passed patent 20 January 1610 for 1000 acres of escheated lands in Cavan; and 2 July 1617 the King gave him the town and land of Ballintogher, Drumcongragh, and many others in the baronies of Corren and Tirrerill in the county of Sligo, to hold as of the castle of Athlone by Knight's service; in which patent is contained a grant to his son and heir John, (then of Cotletstown) his heirs and assignes, of the castle, town and lands of Cotletstown and divers others in the said last county; some parts of which having been by former grants given to Francis Edgeworthe of Dublin, Esq. from whom Sir William Taaffe at a great expence, for the better security of his estate, had acquired them, and some of them being pretended to lie in the county of Leitrim, he passed a new patent (to avoid all doubts and questions) 17 April 1620, of the lands of Ballintogher, &c. to hold in capite, which were erected into the manor of Ballintogher.

of Athirdee, where his ancestors lay, and directs his well-beloved son Sir John Taaffe, immediately after his death, to cause to be erected a monument over his burying-place, for effecting whereof he left 50l. if in his life-time the same was not finished; and that his son, the second year after his decease, should pay the sum of 170l. to such persons and pious uses, as his trusty and well-beloved cousin and friend, Walter Evers of Bingerston, in Meath, Esq. should distribute and appoint, &c.—He married to his first wife Elizabeth, daughter of Sir William Brett, of Tulloch in Fingall; secondly, Ismay, daughter of Sir Christopher, and sister to Sir John Bellew, Knts; and dying 9 February 1630, was buried in Ardee, leaving issue by his second wife [1], Sir John his heir; Mary, married to John Taaffe of Arthurston; and Eleanor, to Richard Taaffe of Cookstown, both in the county of Louth.

Sir John, Viscount.

Sir John Taaffe was knighted in his father's life-time, and the King (as he expresseth himself in his Privy Seal, dated [2] at Westminster 27 June 1628) having received special commendation of his virtues and abilities; of his father's long services, in the wars of Ireland with much valour and reputation; and that he was a principal gentleman of an ancient English family, and well affected to his Majesty's interests; was pleased to advance him to the dignities of Baron of Ballymote, and Viscount Taaffe of Corren, by patent *, bearing date at Dublin, 1 August 1628; and 14 July

---

* The preamble. Cum ad Coronæ regiæ honorem et claritatem nihil magis conducere videatur, quam ut Heroum et clariorum Virorum copia in omnibus Regni partibus stabiliatur, utpote eorum Consiliis, Prudentia, Virtutibus et Fidelitate, solium Regis non solum firmatur, et quasi tot Columnis aureis undique suffulcitur, verum etiam eorum nitore et splendore, tanquam Radiis à Majestate regia derivatis, estimatio Principis apud rudes et agrestiores Subditos magis veneranda efficitur, et in remotioribus Regni Partibus sacra redditur. Notque dilectum et fidelem nostrum Johannem Taaffe de Ballymote in Comitatu Sligo Militem, gratiose intuentes, in ipsoque non solum Familiæ suæ Antiquitatem, ex illustrissima olim in Anglia Prosapia oriundam, verumetiam Possessionum amplitudinem et latifundum, necnon heroicæ Virtutis tum ipsius, tum Patris sui Willielmi Taaffe Militis, qui sinceram et immotam Animi Constantiam erga Coronam nostram, tam in nuperrimis intestinis hujus Regni Seditionibus, quam in Acie Knsalien̄si contra Hispanos præstitit, ubi prædictus Willielmus Taaffe non solum strenui Militis, verum etiam sagacissimi Ducis Gloriam reportavit; de quibus omnibus per amplam Testimonium recepimus: Nos prædictum Johannem Taaffe Militem, non

---

[1] Pedigree communicated to J. L. by Nicholas Lord Taaffe in 1761.
[2] Rot. A°. 4. Car. II. 1. p. D. R. 26.

July 1634, he took his seat in the House of Peers[1]. After the commencement of the rebellion, he received a letter at his seat of Ballymote, written by friar Peter Taaffe, and signed by Sir Phelim O'Neile at Braganstown, in February 1641, to this purpose: "That his Lordship, with the rest of the Roman Catholick confederates in the province of Conaught, should vigorously prosecute the war, according to their first undertaking, until all the Hereticks were routed out; and that if they did not unanimously proceed in that business, he would, as soon as he had reduced Drogheda, march thither with his army, to spoil and destroy all those that were refractory, for that they were all as deeply engaged in the business as he was, and should not withdraw when they pleased." If the contents of this letter were true, his Lordship was soon freed by death from his engagements, for he departed this life before 9 January 1642[2], and was interred at Ballymote, the burial-place of the family.—By Anne, daughter of Theobald, the first Viscount Dillon, he had fourteen sons, and three daughters, viz.

Theobald, created Earl of Carlingford. (1)

Christopher, who died unmarried after the year 1625, in the 21 year of his Age. (2)

Lucas, who during the rebellion was a Major-General in Conaught, and in October 1649, made Governor of Ross, with 1500 foot, to defend the place against Cromwell; after whose reduction of the kingdom he submitted, with his brother Francis, and the forces under their command, upon the articles concluded at Downemore; yet was excepted from pardon for life and estate, and being forced to retire, served for some time as a Colonel in Italy and Spain; but deceased in Ireland, and was buried at Ballymote.—He married first Elizabeth, daughter of Richard Stephenson of Dunmoylin, in the county of Limerick, Esq. and left an only child Mary, married to Rickard Burke of Derrymaclaghtny, in the county of Galway, Esq. and secondly, Annabella, fifth, and youngest daughter of Thomas Springe, Esq. (3)

---

non modo prædicti Willielmi filium natu maximum, sed etiam paternarum Virtutum Hæredem, a'tioribus Honorum titulis infigniendum, et in Classem Nobilitatis collocandum, ipsumque et hæredes masculos de Corpore suo procreatos et procreandos, in numerum Heroum et Parium hujus Regni Hiberniæ adscribendum statuimus. Sciatis igitur, &c.

[1] Lords Jour. I. 2. [2] Depositions of the Protestants.

Esq. (the first of that name in Kerry, by his wife Annabella, eldest daughter of John Browne of Awny, Esq.) by whom he had one son Christopher, a Captain in the regiment, whereof Dominick Ferreter was Major, in the time of K. Charles's exile in Flanders, with whom having some angry words, the Major commanded two of Doctor Field's sons his kinsmen, then in their company, to shoot Captain Taaffe, if he did not quit the place, which one of them accordingly did.——By the daughter of ——— Fitz-Gerald of Ballynasquiddane he left one son Lucas, a Captain in the Irish army, who retired into France upon the revolution, and by Elizabeth Gunter his wife, left one son Abel Taaffe, of Tipperary.

(4) Francis, a Colonel in the rebellion of 1641, died at Naples, and having married an Italian Lady, left a son Charles.

(5) Edward, died unmarried.

(6) Peter, a Canon of the Order of St. Augustine, and was killed at Drogheda, 10 September 1649.

(7) Jasper, married the daughter of Sir William Hill, Knt. and was killed in battle, without issue.

(8) Captain William, ancestor to the present Viscount Taaffe.

(9) Thomas, married in Flanders, and had three sons and one daughter; Lucas; Theobald, who died unmarried; Charles; and Anne.

(10) Charles, was Abbot of the Cistercian Abbey of Boyle, in the county of Roscomon,

(11) Patrick, died in the 14 year of his age.

(12) John, a Capuchin Friar, died in Italy.

(13) George died in the 16 year of his age.

(14) James, was a Franciscan Friar.

(1) Daughter Ismay, was married to Bryan Mac-Donogh of the county of Sligo, Esq.

(2) Eleanor, a Nun of the Order of St. Clare.

(3) Anne, a Nun of the Order of St. Dominick.

Sir Theobald, Viscount, and Earl of Carlingford

Sir Theobald Taaffe, the second Viscount, in 1639 represented the county of Sligo in Parliament, and during the course of the rebellion, was constituted General of the province of Munster; of which post being deprived by the peace, concluded by the Marquess of Ormond with the Irish in 1646, and the Earl of Carlingford, he remained without employment until April 1649; when, upon the death of Sir Thomas Lucas, he was made Master of the Ordnance; a charge, for which he was well qualified

by

by his capacity and experience, and which he well deserved by his extraordinary affection and services to the crown. ——In 1651 he was sent, with Sir Nicholas Plunket, and Geffrey Browne, by the Marquess of Clanrickard, the King's Deputy, to the Duke of Lorain, to solicit his aid in favour of the (then) unhappy kingdom of Ireland; and was excepted from pardon for life and estate, by Cromwell's Act of Parliament for the settlement of Ireland: But, after the Restoration, until the King's Order for restoring him to his estate could be executed, he had his Majesty's Letters of direction, dated 17 August 1661, to the L. J. to grant him 800l. a year towards his immediate support, to be paid monthly out of the treasury.—But notwithstanding, his Lordship being detained from the possession of his estate, and the said annuity being stopped, he addressed the King for relief, who 30 November that year, required his Chief Governors, to use all diligence for the restoring him to his estate; and in the mean time, from the date of his said former order, to allow him the said annuity, or otherwise the immediate possession of his estate, with the rents due, according to former orders.—Accordingly, by the Acts of Settlement he was restored to his estate, together with those of Christopher Taaffe of Braganstown, and Theophilus Taaffe of Cookstown, which they had respectively forfeited; and had the benefit of his provisoe confirmed by patent 16 April 1667, and by several future patents a discharge of the new quit-rents, imposed by those acts.

"His Majesty having a particular esteem for his Lordship,
" was pleased, as an especial mark of the gracious sense he
" had of his eminent services for him and his interests, to
" honour him with the dignity of Earl of Carlingford
" in the county of Louth, entailing that honour on
" the heirs male of his body," by Privy Seal, dated at Whitehall 17 June 1661 [1], and by Patent [*] 26 June 1662, he was accordingly advanced to that title with the creation

---

[*] The Preamble. Cum regiam nostram Majestatem optime decet, ut qui Obsequio & Fidelitate nobis se libere obtulerunt, præcipuis Honoribus Imperii nostri regalis primò dignarentur; nos regia mente commemorantes eximia Merita et Servitia prædilecti et perquam fidelis Consanguinei nostri Theobald,

[1] Rot. A°. 13 Car. II. 1. p. D.

creation fee of 20l.; and for the better support of the honour, his Majesty, by patent, dated at Tedington, 25 August 1670, gave him 4000l. of the rents, payable to the crown out of the retrenched lands of adventurers and soldiers, during such time as the same remained in the common stock of Reprisals, and out of forfeited jointures, mortgages, &c.; and also 4 August 1676 settled on him a pension of 500l. a year.

His Lordship married first Mary, daughter of Sir Nicholas White of Leixlip, with whom he had a large fortune, and by her had six sons and one daughter; and his second wife was Anne, daughter of Sir William Pershall, Knt. but by her, who in 1693, re-married with Randal, Lord Dunsany, he had no issue; and dying 31 December 1677, was buried at Ballymote.—His children were, William and Robert, who both died unmarried; Nicholas and Francis, successive Earls of Carlingford; Dillon, who died without issue; John, father of Theobald, late Earl of Carlingford; and Lady Anne, first married to Sir Joseph Throckmorton, secondly, to Nicholas Plunket, Esq. second son of Christopher, Earl of Fingall, and died in July 1742, in the county of Monaghan.

Nicholas, 3 Viscount, and 2 Earl

Nicholas, the third Viscount Taaffe, and second Earl of Carlingford, was of the Privy Council to K. James II. and sent in 1689, his Envoy or Ambassador to the Emperor Leopold; but the next year commanding a regiment of foot in his army, lost his life (1 July) at the battle of the Boyne; and leaving no issue by his wife Mary, daughter of ——— Wild of Wildhouse, Esq. was succeeded by his brother

Francis, 4 Viscount and 3 Earl.

Francis, the third Earl, the famous Count Taaffe of the Empire, who was above 30 years in the Imperial service, being Colonel of the Royal Cuirassiers, and Lieutenant-General of the horse.—He was placed by his father to prosecute his studies, in the city of Olmutz in Germany, where his talents

---

Theobaldi, Domini Vicecomitis Taaffe de Corren, Baronis de Ballymote in Provincia nostra Conaciæ in dicto regno nostro, Hiberniæ, nobis et Antecessoribus nostris præstita et impensa, tam in remotis Partibus et transmarinis, quam in Dominiis nostris et sub regali nostra Potestate, ipsum Theobaldum in eminentiorem Dignitatis titulum promovere decrevimus; non solum ut insigni regio magis publice decoretur, sed ut quibus Gratia et Affectu propter indefatigata Fidelitati suæ Servitia nobis et Domi et apud Exteros præstita indulgamus, universi cognoscitur; manum enim esse censemus, ut qui nobiscum in a tve fis publice comprefsus sit, in Secundis etiam nobiscum publice su citetur. Sciatis igitur, &c.

lents were so great, that to this day his portrait is preserved
there. The Emperor Ferdinand made him one of his Pages
of honour; and Charles the fifth Duke of Lorain, gave
him a Captain's commission in his own regiment of cuirassiers, which regiment he afterwards bestowed upon him, and
committed to his care the education of all his children, particularly of his eldest son, Leopold: His conduct being
equally conspicuous in the cabinet and the field; he in
his younger days, obtained the golden key, as Chamberlain to the Emperor, was advanced to be a Marshal, Counsellor of the State and Cabinet, and obtained from the King
of Spain, the Order of the Golden Fleece. He was so
highly esteemed by most of the crowned heads in Europe,
that when the hereditary honours devolved to him on his brother's death, he was exempted from forfeiture, by a special
clause in the English Act of Parliament, 1 Will. and Mary;
and in the Act, passed in Ireland, 9 of that reign, to hinder
the reversal of divers outlawries and attainders, it was provided, that nothing therein contained should extend to attaint or convict of High Treason, Nicholas, late Earl of
Carlingford, or his brother John Taaffe, Esq. or to vest in,
or forfeit to the crown their estates.—But his Lordship dying * without issue, in August 1704, the honours descended
to his nephew Theobald, son of his brother John. Which
John, in December 1671, married Lady Rose Lambart,
third daughter of Charles, the first Earl of Cavan, and being a Major in K. James's army, was killed before Derry
in April 1689, leaving issue the said Theobald; Lambart,
killed at the siege of Cremona in Italy, in 1701; and a
daughter Mary.

Theobald, the fifth Viscount, and fourth Earl, married
Lady Amelia Plunket, youngest daughter of Luke, third
Earl of Fingall, and 25 April 1737, receiving a pass from
the Government to go into Germany, died at Lisle in Flanders, 24 November 1738, O. S. without issue (by her who
died 4 October 1757, at Brussels) and was buried the 26
in the chapel of the college of Lisle, whereby the Earldom
of

Theobald,
5
Viscount.
and
4
Earl.

---

* His death was very much lamented at the Imperial Court, and especially by Charles the fifth Duke of Lorain; who, to express his concern for the
loss of so great a man, and one that had been so faithful and serviceable to
his Highness's family, and to the Emperor and Empire in general, ordered the
Cathedral church of Nancy to be hung with black, and his corpse to lie in
state the space of a month, attended by his guards.

of Carlingford became extinct; but the titles of Baron and Viscount devolved on his next heir-male, Nicholas Taaffe (descended from William, eighth son of John, the first Viscount) whom, by his will, dated 7 May 1737, he constituted his heir, residuary legatee, and joint executor.

Which William Taaffe, Esq. married Margaret, daughter of Conor O'Kennedy Roe (Dynast of Ballyartil in Ormond, by his wife Eleanora, daughter of ———— Purcell, titular Baron of Loughmoe, in county of Tipperary) by whom he had one son Francis, and three daughters; Elizabeth, married to Hiberus O'Hara of Ballyhara, in the county of Sligo, Esq.; Elinor, to John, son of Major Walter Philips of Ballinduth, in the county of Mayo; and Mary, who died young.—Francis Taaffe, Esq. married Anne, daughter of John Crean, of O'Crean's-Castle in Sligo (by his wife Sarah, daughter of William Ormsby, Esq. by his wife Mary, of the family of Mapolder[1]) and by her, who after married Mr. Philips of Ballinduth, in the county of Mayo, and died in 1736, had Nicholas, Viscount Taaffe, and two daughters; Anne (married to John Brett, of Rathdoony in the county of Sligo, Esq. by whom she had several sons, all deceased, and four daughters, Anne, married to Roger Irwin, of Lisballin in the said county, Esq.; Sarah; Mary; and Elizabeth); and Mary, to Theodore, son of Major Christopher Verdon, of Clunigashell, and died childless.

Nicholas, 6 Viscount.

Nicholas, the sixth Viscount Taaffe, Count of the Holy Empire, was educated in Lorain, appointed Chancellor to Leopold, father to the Emperor Francis I. from thence he entered into the Austrian service, where he was raised to the rank of L. General. He obtained the Golden Key from the Emperor Charles VI. as he did from his successor, which mark of distinction both his sons enjoyed[2]; his Lordship was Colonel of a regiment of fusiliers; and possessed a considerable estate in Silesia.—He distinguished himself, by the name of Count Taaffe, during the war in 1738 with the Turks, and behaved at Belgrade with such remarkable bravery, that he gained the victory with great honour.—He married Mary-Anne, de Spendler, or Spendley, Countess of the Empire, daughter and heir to Count Spendler of. Lintz in Upper-Austria, of an ancient and illustrious family of the Empire, a Lady of the bed-chamber

[1] Pedigree. [2] Idem.

chamber to her Imperial and Hungarian Majesty, and by her, who died 21 November 1769, æt. 69, at the castle of Elischan in Bohemia, had issue two sons, viz.

(1) John, who was born 1 Jan. 1740-1, in Soho-square, London, appointed in 1761 a Counsellor Imperial Aulick of the Empire. He had the honour to attend the Emperor and Empress from Vienna to Inspruck, in August 1765, and was present at the celebration of the marriage of the Infanta of Spain, with the Archduke Leopold, which marriage he was appointed by their Imperial Majesties to notify to the Court of Naples; and died, before his father, upon his return, at Gortz, 10 December 1765, of a fever. He married Maria Choteck, Countess of the Empire, and left issue Rodolphus, successor to his grandfather, another son, and a daughter.

(2) Francis, younger son of Nicholas, is Colonel Commandant of the regiment of Deux-Ponts, a Lord of the bedchamber, or Chamberlain to their Imperial Majesties, a General in the Austrian service, and a Count of the Sacred Roman Empire. In January 1772, he married at Brussels, the eldest daughter of John, late Lord Bellew, but hath no issue.

His Lordship deceased 30 December 1769, at the castle of Elischan, being succeeded by his grandson,

Rodolphus, the seventh and present Viscount Taaffe, in the Imperial service, and now in Hungary. His Lordship is married, and has issue two sons.

Rodolphus, 7 Viscount.

TITLES.] Rodolphus, Taaffe, Lord Viscount Taaffe of Corren, and Baron of Ballymote, both in the county of Sligo.

CREATION.] So created 1 August 1628, 4 Car. I.

ARMS.] Ruby, a cross, Pearl, Frettee, Saphire.

CREST.] On a wreath, a dexter arm in armour embowed, brandishing a sword, all proper.

SUPPORTERS.] The dexter, a horse, pearl, semée of estoils, diamond. The sinister a Wyvern, or sea-dragon, with wings expanded, proper.

MOTTO.] IN HOC SIGNO SPES MEA.

JONES,

JONES, Viscount RANELAGH.

12. THE family of Johns or Jones, anceſtors of this noble Lord, had their reſidence in the county of Lancaſter, from whence deſcended Sir Roger Jones, Knt. Alderman of London, father of Thomas Jones, who received his education in Chriſt Church College Cambridge, where he took the degree of M. A. but that of D. D. was conferred upon him at Dublin, in 1614; was ſucceſſively Chancellor and Dean of St. Patrick's Cathedral, in Dublin, from whence he was promoted by letters patent 10 May 1584, to the epiſcopal ſee of Meath, was conſecrated two days after, and 8 November 1605[1], he was tranſlated to the archiepiſcopal ſee of Dublin, purſuant to Privy Seal, 8 October preceding, in which the King thus writes, " Whereas ſince the death " of the late Archbiſhop of Dublin, we have given no " order for ſupply of that ſee, becauſe the ſame being a " place ſo eminent within the kingdom, we took time to " adviſe of a meet perſon for it, we have ſince, upon con- " ference with divers of our Council, found no one more " fit for the preſent time, than the Buſhope of Meath, in " regard of his long experience in the kingdom, both in " the eccleſiaſtical ſtate as a Buſhope, and in civil affairs as " Counſellor, (having been ſworn a Member thereof in " June 1584) wherefore we have made choice of him, and " we are further pleaſed that he ſhall hold in commendam, " a prebend which now he hath in poſſeſſion, which he will " nominate unto you[2]." He held the ſaid prebend, viz. that of Caſtlenock, and the rectory of Trim, in commendam, with this ſee, and for the reaſons contained in the ſaid Privy Seal, was made Lord Chancellor of Ireland in October 1605[3], which high office he filled until his deceaſe.

18 May

---

[1] War. Bp. 156. and Lodge. Bp. 354. 355.   [2] Rolls Offi. and Editor's copy of War.
[3] Id.

18 May 1608, he obtained a licence to hold a yearly fair at Ballymore, in Weftmeath, on the feaft of the affumption of the bleffed Virgin, at the rent of 6s. 8d. Irifh, and in 1612, a cuftodiam was granted to him of the bifhopricks of Kilmore and Ardagh [1].

He married Margaret, daughter of Adam Purdon, of Lurgan-Race, in county of Louth, Efq. relict of John Douglas, Gent. (by whom fhe had a numerous iffue) and deceafing 10 April 1619, was buried in St. Patrick's Cathedral, under a monument of black and white marble, compofed of feveral columns, pillars and pyramids, and two infcriptional plates of white marble, with his ftatue on its knees reprefented under an arch above the tomb, and on the monument this infcription:

> THOMAS JONES, Archiepifcopus Dublin,
> Primas et Metropolitianus Hiberniæ,
> Ejufdem cancellarius, nec non bis é Juftitiariis unus,
> Obiit decimo Aprilis, anno reperatæ falutis humanæ
> 1619.
> Margareta, ejufdem Thomæ Uxor Chariffima,
> Obiit decimo quinto Decembris,
> Anno a partu Virginis, 1618 *.

The iffue of the Archbifhop were fix children, three of whom died young, and thofe who furvived, were Sir Roger, his heir; Margaret, married to Gilbert Domvile, Efq. Clerk of the Hanaper, and died 5 July 1615; and Jane, married to Henry Piers, of Triflernagh, in county of Weftmeath, Efq.[2].

Sir Roger Jones, of Durhamfton, in county of Weftmeath, Knt. fucceeded to the eftates which his father had formed, and purfuant to Privy Seal at Weftminfter, 21 July, and patent † at Dublin, 25 Auguft 1628, was created a Peer

Sir Roger, 1 Vifcount:

---

* This monument was repaired by the family in 1731, through the folicitation of Jonathan Swift, Dean of St. Patrick's. (War. Bps. 355.)

† The Preamble. Cum in dilecto neftro Rogero Jone, equite aurato, eximiam quandam propenfitatem et alacritatem ad res noftras promovendas jamdiu animadvertimus et ex antiquorum parentum meritis, et virtut.but fuis in fequile

[1] Rolls Off. and Editor's Copy of War. Bps. 354. 355. [2] See Fitz-Maurice, Earl of Kerry, a.

a Peer of Ireland, by the titles of Baron Jones, of Navan, and Viscount of Ranelagh, and his Lordship sat first in Parliament, 14 July 1634[1].

He married first Frances, second daughter of Gerald Moore, the first Viscount of Drogheda, she dying 23 November 1620, was interred in the family vault, at St. Patrick's, and he married secondly Catharine, daughter of Sir Edward Longueville, of Wolverhampton, in county of Bucks, Knt. and dying in 1628, had issue by her a daughter Elizabeth, married to Colonel Robert Sandys, son of Sir Edwyn Sandys, of Narbonne, county of Kent, Knt.

The issue by his first wife, were two sons and two daughters, viz.

(1) Arthur, who succeeded to the honours.
(2) Thomas, from whom the present Viscount descends.
(1) Daughter Margaret, married to Sir John Clotworthy, Viscount Massareene.

Mary,

negotiis nostris assidue prestitis abunde exploratum habemus prædictum Rogerum ad altiora et magis et ardua Regni negotia suscipienda et peragenda, per habilem fore utpote qui per multos exinde annos retroacta secretioribus consiliis nobis, et pro charissimo Patri nostro beatæ memoriæ extiterit, ac in iisdem prudentia, Integritate, et fidelitate apprime pollentem se semper prestiterit; reperientes etiam in dicto Rogero per eximia merita et virtutes propriis sibi militaribus memoriæ defuncti, coronæ nostræ multipliciter prestitis et impensis qui per multos annos curriculos non solum Cancellarius dicti regni nostri Hiberniæ, magna cum integritate et equali justitiæ distributione inter subditos hujus Regni feliciter gessit, verum ut etiam primitus consiliarius et dicto Patri nostro ac nuper Reginæ Elizabethæ in dubiis et vacillantibus intestini belli temporibus rebus publicis hujus Regni faustissime presidebat ac locum tenentis officio vacante supremi magistratus sive unius supremorum justiciarum munere semel atque iterum perfunctus est, ac in iisdem omnibus exequendis prudentia, gravitate et provida circumspectione celebri inclaruit, ac senatorum prestantissimi, necnon omnibus, numeris absolutis (in perennium nominis sui elogium) gloriam ut portavit horum intuitu, ac ut tempore omnibus quem futuris seculis innotescat, qualis erga dictum Rogerum propter merita prædicti nostri fuerit affectus, qualis apud nos meritorum ipsius Rogeri existimatione eaque intentione ut caudere et munificentia nostra prædictum Rogerum de nobis et patria bene meritum ad altiora excitent dictusque Rogerus quodcunque munus sibi a nobis imposteris concreditum fuerit honorificentius geratum et alacrius exequatum dictum Rogerum in numero Parium et heroum hujus Regni nostri Hiberniæ adscribendum et in gradum Baronis et Vicecomitis hereditarium hujus regni promovendum censuimus. Sciatis igitur quod nos de gratia nostra speciali, &c. Jour. I. 81.

[1] Lords Jour. L 2.

Mary, married first to John Chichester, Esq. of the family of Donegal; and secondly, to Colonel Christopher Copley.

Arthur, the second Viscount, took his seat in the House of Peers, 5 February 1644[1]. He married Catharine, daughter of Richard, first Earl of Cork, died 17 January 1669 *, and was buried the 14 at St Patrick's, having issue Richard, his heir, and three daughters, viz. Catharine, (married first to Sir William Parsons, of Bellamont, county of Dublin, Bart. and secondly to Hugh, Earl of Mount-Alexander, which title is extinct); Elizabeth, to —— Maultster, Valet de Pe, and had issue; and Frances, died unmarried, or without issue.

Richard, the third Viscount Ranelagh, was chosen to the English Parliament for the borough of Castlerising, in Norfolk, also for Westlowe, in county of Cornwall, was appointed Vice-Treasurer of Ireland 4 June 1674, 17 of that month, Constable of the Castle of Athlone, and was created Earl of Ranelagh.—He was several years Pay-Master to the army; was sworn of the Privy Council to K. William, 1 March 1691; 3 November 1704, appointed one of the Governors of Q. Anne's bounty for the augmentation of the maintenance of the poor clergy, and departed this life 5 January 1711 †. He married first Elizabeth, daughter of Francis,

(a)

Arthur, 2 Viscount.

Richard, 3 Viscount, and 1 Earl.

---

* About the last day of December 1669, he declared his last will, nuncupative, and appointed Sir John Cole, executor, in trust for his three daughters, to each of whom he bequeathed 2000l. for their portion; that his daughter Mount-Alexander be first paid; and that Elizabeth and Frances, should have their portions, on condition they married with the consent of his daughter Mount-Alexander, his son and Sir John Cole, or any two of them; and in case either of them died unpreferred, her portion to accrue to his son, he paying 500l. to his surviving sister. (Prerog. Off. and Lodge.)

† By his will, made 10 February 1710, he ordered that whatsoever remained of the effects assigned for the payment of his debts should be divided (his said debts, funeral charges, and legacies, being first paid thereout) into four equal shares or parts; one of which he devised to his eldest daughter Kildare, by his first wife; and by a codicil of the same date, left her two of his silver salvers, gilt and godroned about the brims, marked No. 1. and No. 2; and four of his 12 silver gilt plates, godroned about the brims; and his dear mother's picture hanging up in his closet at Chelsea. To his cousin the Lady Catharine Fitzgerald, of whose hearty friendship to him and his, he was always sensible, he bequeathed his chagreen case, with a gilt spoon, knife, fork and a spoon for eggs and marrow, in it. (Prerog. Off. and Lodge.)

---

[1] Lords Jour. 1. 217.

Francis, Lord Willoughby, of Parham; and secondly, Margaret, daughter of James Cecil, third Earl of Salisbury, relict of John Lord Stawell; by the last lady he had no issue, but by his first, had two sons, viz. Arthur and Edward, who died young; and four daughters, viz. Elizabeth, who died young; Elizabeth, married to John, eighteenth Earl of Kildare; Frances, to Thomas, Earl Coningsby, being his second wife; and Catharine, who died unmarried 12 or 14 April 17—, at Chelsea, in an advanced age; the title of Earl thus became extinct; but those of Viscount Ranelagh, and Baron of Navan, having lain many years dormant, were revived in the persons of

Charles Jones, the lineal heir and fourth in descent from Thomas Jones, second son of Sir Roger, the first Viscount, which Thomas Jones took to wife, Elizabeth, daughter of John Harris, of Winchester, Esq. and had issue two sons, Roger; and Thomas, who died without issue. Roger, the eldest son, served in the English Parliament for the city of Winchester; married Martha, daughter of the Rev. Mr. Gulston, Rector of Waltham, and Prebendary of Winchester, and by her had issue a son Charles, and three daughters, viz. Elizabeth, married to William Whitacre, Esq.; Martha, to Joseph Etherfea, Esq.; and Anne, to John Devile, Esq. Charles, the only son, was several years a Cornet in the regiment of Dragoons, commanded by George, Lord Carpenter: He married Elizabeth, daughter of James Douglas, of Haddington, in Scotland, Esq. and died in Ireland, leaving issue a son Charles, and three daughters, viz. Martha; Margaret, married to Thomas Garden, Esq.; and Wilhelmina, to Doctor John Hill, of London.

Charles, 4 Viscount.
Charles Jones, the present Viscount Ranelagh, sat first in the House of Peers, on the death of his cousin Richard, late Earl and Viscount Ranelagh, 16 October 1759 [1]. On 22 July 1760, he obtained an annual pension of 300l. and 10 October 1764, his Majesty was pleased to augment the same to 400l. per annum [2]. 16 May 176—, It was "re-
"solved by the Lords Spiritual and Temporal in Parlia-
"ment assembled, *nemine contradicente*, that an humble ad-
"dress be presented to his Excellency, the L. L. that his
"Excellency will lay before his Majesty the request of this
"House,

[1] Lords Jour. IV. 149. [2] Pension List.

"House, that his Majesty will be graciously pleased to grant to the Right Hon. Lord Viscount RANELAGH, the sum of 1000l. in testimony of their approbation of his Lordship's particular merit and faithful service in these four last sessions of Parliament, as Chairman to the several committees appointed to consider the bills that have passed this House [1]." 21 December 1771, and 28 February, 1774 we meet similar resolution [2]; 18 December 1775, a like resolution passed in his Lordship's favour, augmenting the sum to 1600 [3], which was repeated 22 December 1777, and 21 December 1779 [4]. 15 December 1781, and 15 December 1783, resolutions passed in his Lordship's favour, augmenting the sum to 2000l. [5], and 4 April 1785, 13 March 1786 [6], and in 1787, like resolutions passed in his Lordship's favour for the sum of 1400l. sterling. He married Sarah, daughter of Thomas Montgomery, Esq. Member of Parliament for Lifford, in county of Donegall, and had issue ten sons and three daughters, viz. Charles, born 29 October 1761; Thomas, born 2 February 1763; Richard, (born 23 March 1764, married 13 September 1785, Sophia, only daughter and heir to the late John Giddart, of Blakeley-hunt, in county of Lancaster, Esq.); John, born 15 January 1768, died young; Benjamin, born 8 September 1770; John, born 1 June 1772; Roger, died young; William; Richard-Montgomery, born 13 September 1776; Alexander, born 9 March 1778; Robert, born 30 March 1780, died young; daughter Mary, born 15 June 1766; Sarah, born 7 September 1767; and Margaret, born 9 May 1769, who died young [7].

TITLES.] Charles Jones, Baron Jones, of Navan, in county of Meath, and Viscount Ranelagh, in county of Dublin.

CREATION.] So created 25 August 1628. 4 Car. I.

ARMS.] Saphire, a cross, topaz, charged with 5 mullets, ruby, between 4 pheons, of the second.

CREST.] A dexter arm couped and armed, holding a dart, proper.

SUPPORTERS.] Two Griffins party per fess, emerald and pearl.

MOTTO]

---

[1] Lords Jour. IV. 487.   [2] Idem. 608. 725.   [3] Idem 813.
[4] Idem. V. 26. 148.   [5] Idem. 255. 417.   [6] Idem 585. 704.
[7] Ulster's Off.

FITZ-WILLIAM, Viscount FITZ-WILLIAM.

Motto.] CŒLITUS MIHI VIRES.
Seat.] Monkstown, county Dublin, 5 miles from Dublin.

FITZ-WILLIAM, Viscount FITZ-WILLIAM.

23. THE prime descent of this family may be seen under the title of Earl Fitz-William; one whereof (whose christian name is now lost) attending K. John into Ireland, when Chief Governor of the kingdom, founded this branch, which hath flourished from that time to the present, as the following records, made in their favour, fully demonstrate.

John. In the year 1282, John Fitz-William, the elder, son of Richard and Margery, recovered six messuages in Swerdes, from William Wycombe; and 29 August 18 Edward III. Philip Fitz-William, and William Fitz-Bernard, entered into a recognizance before the Chancellor at Cork, to pay to the Prior of St. John, of Jerusalem, and his successors, 40s. in fifteen days after St. Martin, the Michaelmas Term next ensuing, with power of distress, and the forfeiture of roos. in case of non-payment.

Richard. Richard (or Robert) Fitz-William, of Ballymon, living in the reign of Edward II. left issue by Ellena, his wife,
William. two sons, William; and Robert, living in 1342.—William, the elder, in 1348, (22 Edward III.) was pardoned by the King, all transgressions and murders, he had, or might have committed in the exercise of martial law upon the Irish, who bordered on the *English Pale*; to restrain whose incursions,

fions, he built the castle of Wicklow, of which he was made Constable; and in 13-5, 49 Edward III. appointed Chief Commander and Governor of all that part of the country. He was also in 1367, Lord of Kilkenran, and left issue a daughter Elizabeth, married to Sir Thomas de Musgrave; and a son

William, who in 1381, and 1382, was Sheriff of the county of Meath, which office he served by commission, dated at Cork, 13 January 1381, for the county of Dublin; and two days after was commissioned to arrest, and in safe custody to keep the persons of Richard White and Reginald Talbot, late Sheriffs, and Robert Lichteburgh, late Escheater of Ireland, who were endeavouring to go beyond sea, without rendering an account to the King, into the Exchequer, for the several debts due to him in respect of their offices.—On 8 March following, he and Sir Richard Talbot, Nicholas Houthe, Richard Netterville, and others, were appointed, jointly and severally, Keepers of the Peace in the county of Dublin; and he was made Seneschal of all the Temporalities in that county, with power to appoint his Deputy.—On 16 June 1382, he was constituted Constable of the Castle of Wykynglow (Wicklow), with the annual fee of 20l.; which patent being renewed to him 15 August 1385, a *mandamus* issued to Anastacia, late wife of Richard Netterville, Thomas Netterville, and John Humfray, Chaplain, Keepers of the said castle, to deliver it up to him, with the arms, armour, and all other things thereto belonging.—By patent, dated at Trim 20 September 1385, he was made Keeper of the Great Seal of the Exchequer, with liberty to name a Deputy; and by commission, dated at Tristledermot, 8 May 1389, he and Sir Richard Talbot, John Cruys and Thomas Marward were appointed, jointly and severally, Keepers of the Peace in the county of Dublin, and to render an accompt before the Prior of the Holy Trinity, and the Mayor of Dublin, and not into the Exchequer: with which authority he was solely invested in 1391; to arm the inhabitants at pleasure for its defence; to punish offenders, and to do all such things as he should think fit, and conducive to that end: Being also again made Sheriff of the county for the years 1394 and 1397; had the custody of the *Staines*, near Dublin, in order to preserve the water-course free and clean, for the benefit of the city; and was made Keeper of all the Lands and Tenements in the marches of Leinster, which James, Earl of Ormond had held for life.

FITZ-WILLIAM, Viscount FITZ-WILLIAM.

John. In this last mentioned year of 1397, he died, and the King granted a pardon to his son John, for all transgressions; who being slain the next year, left issue by Christiana, his wife, Henry Fitz-William, Esq. who by his petition to K Henry IV set forth, That he had undergone divers great expences and labours in the King's service, and the wars in Leinster, in which he was wounded, without any consideration or regard from the King, to the manifest detriment of his fortune; and that he had a lease of certain lands and tenements in the Nardenesse, Berragh and Fingowere, in the marches of the county of Dublin, which were the King's demesnes, and which he preserved at very great expence and care, and were not worth maintaining against the Irish, without the assistance of the state; in respect whereof, and of his said services, the King committed unto him the custody of those lands for 20 years, with the fee of ten marcs a year thereout, by patent, dated at Dunboyne, 14 June 1403.

Henry.

Thomas. To him succeeded Thomas Fitz-William, who in the said King's reign, was Constable of the town of Swordes; and had issue a daughter Felicia, married to Walter, third son of Sir Robert Cruise, of Grallagh and Tirrelston, (by his wife Elinor, daughter of Simon Geneville) whose eldest son was Simon Cruise, Esq.*; and a son Richard Fitz-William, who was living at Donnybrook, near Dublin, in 1432; and (we presume) was father of Philip Fitz-William, Esq. to whom K. Henry VI. granted a certain sum of money out of the crown rents, which he was to pay for his manor of Thorn-Castle, in order to enable him to build a fort there, which in 143?, had been destroyed by the King's Irish enemies.—In 1442, he was living at Merryong; and in 1440, being one of the Counsellors and Servants to Richard, Duke of York, had a remittal of all the chief rent he was to pay the King, during life.

Richard,

Philip.

Stephen. To this Philip succeeded Stephen Fitz-William, who in 1463, held the manor of Thorn-Castle; and to him William Fitz-William, who married Anne, only daughter of Thomas Cruise, of the Naull, in the county of Dublin, Esq. by

William.

---

* By him the said Thomas Cruise, Esq. who by Joan, daughter of Richard Dardits, had a daughter Lysine, married to John Roche, of Noby; and a son John Cruise, Esq. who married Joan, daughter of Peter Bellew, of Platten, and had William, who left no issue, and a daughter Elizabeth. (Lodge.)

FITZ-WILLIAM, Viscount FITZ-WILLIAM.

by his wife Elizabeth, daughter of Robert Hollywood, of Tartaine, Esq.* and left Richard, his heir, who married **Richard.** Genet (or Margaret) Hollywood, of the same family, and had Thomas Fitz-William, Esq. of Meryon, Brey, and **Thomas.** Baggotrath in the county of Dublin, of which county he was Sheriff in 1511 (3 Henry VIII.) and is proved by inquisition to have died in 20 of that reign, 1529.—He married Eleanor†, daughter of John Dowdall, Esq. third son of

---

* Which Thomas, was son and heir to said Simon Cruise, of Grallagh, Esq. (eldest son o Sir Robert) by his wife Margaret, daughter and heir to John Cruise, of the Naull, Esq.—The said Thomas, father of Anne Fitz-William, had two sons William, (who married Margaret, daughter of Henry Betagh, of Moynalty, Esq. died 1 November 1438, and left three daughters Maud, Joan, and Anne, his coheirs); and Christopher, who died in France, in the time of Henry V. without issue. (Lodge.)

† The Bill in Chancery, filed by T. Fitz-William, of Baggotrath, his grandson, in Michaelmas Term 35 Henry VIII. proved this his marriage, that his son and heir was Richard, and his grandson named Thomas, who was found rightful heir of the bodies of John Dowdall, Gent. and Dame Margaret Jenico, his wife, by the answer upon oath of Sir Walter Delahide, of Moyclare, Knt. of the age of 40 years, who deposed, that a certain time Sir Maurythe Eustace, of Ballycotlande, Knt. and Dame Johan Eustace, his wife; Sir John Plunket, of Bewlye, Knt. and Dame Maud Eustace, his wife, the said Sir Walter Delahyde, and Dame Jenet Eustace, his wife, daughter of the said Dame Margaret Jenico, and the said T. Fitz-William, of Baggotstrath, Gent. grandfather to the first above-named T. Fitz-William, being then married to the aforesaid Elianore Dowdall, daughter and heir to the said John Dowdall, and Dame Margaret Jenico, their bodies lawfully begotten, as aforesaid, repaired and went together to one William Godynge's house in Dublin, to search upe certain evidences concerning the said Dame M. Jenico's lands and tenements; and after that they had searched awhile, the said Sir Maurice Eustace, being somewhat practised and learned in the laws, perceiving a certain suit of deedes, whereby the said Dame M. Jenico made a suretie of all her said lands and tenements to herself and the said John Dowdall, and the heirs of their two bodies together, he secretly conveyed the said fute of deeds with him, and so immediately they all departed from thence. And forthwith the said Sir Maurice and Johan his wife, Sir J. Plunket and Dame Maud his wife, Sir Walter Delahyde and Jenet his wife, went together to the said Sir Walter's chamber, then being in the late Gray Freres, besides the said city of Dublin, and as soon as they came to the said chamber, Sir Maurice said, that he had found a thing in the said chest, that did make very much for all their purpose; and they asked him what it was? He answering, said that it was a suit of deeds whereby Dame Margaret Jenico made a surety of all her whole lands to herself and the said J. Dowdall, and the heirs of their two bodies together; which suit of deeds if the said T. Fitz-William had, he would, in the right of the said Elyanore Dowdall, his wife, take all the said lands from them, whereunto the said Dame Johan his wife answering said, it were better that all they together, being sisters, should inherit and have the said lands as heirs to the said Dame, M. Jenico their mother, than that the said E. Dowdall should have all the said whole lands. Thereupon they concluded forthwith to burn the said suit of deeds; but Sir William Delahyde

of Sir John Dowdall, of Newtown, and coheir to her mother Margaret, daughter and heir to Sir Jenico D'Artois, a Gascoign, by his wife Maud, daughter of Christopher, Lord Killeen, and widow of Richard Talbot, of Malahyde, Esq.[1] and had issue three sons and two daughters, viz.

Richard,

---

lahyde would not in any ways consent or agree thereunto, but desired them to keep the same secret and sure, and not to burn them. And so upon this communication betwixt them, the bell in the said Freres church began to knolle to the sacrynge of mass, and Sir Walter departed, and went then to the church to the sacring and to hear mass. And so he being then absent, Sir Maurice and the rest immediately called for a faggot to the chimney, which being put a fyre, they forthwith, according to their conclusion burned all the said suit of deeds, left the same at any time ever might be had, or come to light; which thing the said Dame Jenet his wife shewed him immediately after he heard the said sacring and mass, and came to his said chamber, wherewith he was very sorry and discontented. And the next Lent after, he and his wife being sore moved in their conscience to keep the burning and imbesselynge of the said deeds secret, went to a Frere of the said house of Gray Freres to shryfte, and so declared entirely the same matter unto him, who required and counselled them, in discharge of their conscience afore God, to manifest and declare the same unto them that rightfully was entitled and ought to have the said evidences of lands.—Whereupon Sir Walter, being in estimation and favour with the late Earl of Kildare, and knowing that the said Richard Fitz-William late of Baggoterath, Gent. kinsman and servant unto the said Earl, was rightful inheritor to the said lands, moved the Earl of the circumstances and effect of all the said matter, and desired him to speak to the said Richard, and to further and bring the matter to pass after such sort, that said Richard should make Sir Walter and his wife and their heirs sure of the portion of the said lands, which was at that time in their possession, in consideration that by the manifesting and declaring of the truth, as is aforesaid, unto the said Richard, he might the sooner attain the right and possession of all the residue of the said Dame Margaret's lands, which then was out of his possession, whereupon the said Earl, Sir Walter and wife handled the matter after such sort and fashion in the true declaration of the whole circumstance of the enbeselinge and burning of the said deeds, so that the said Richard by means thereof, and by the advice of other his trusty kinsmen and friends, made a surety to Sir Walter and wife and their heirs of the portion then in their possession.—And Sir Walter, further deposed, that his wife, long afore this time, in the life of the said Richard Fitz-William, in presence of the said Earl and many others, examined upon the Holy Evangelists, testified the full effect and force of the whole contents of this testimonial to be true; whereupon there was then an instrument made thereof subscribed with the said Earl's hand, and others there being present. All which matters aforesaid the said Sir Walter, without mede, reward, or any other manner of occasion or means, saving only to discharge his conscience afore God in declaring of the truth in that behalf, hath deposed and testified to be true, by the Holy contents of his oath aforesaid. (Rot. 34 Hen. VIII. D. R. 6.)

[1] Lodge.

Richard, of Baggotrath, his succeffor. (1)

Sir William, of the Great-Park at Windfor [1], appointed 26 Auguft 1532, Clerk of the Hanaper, and reprefented the county of Carlow, in the Parliament held 12 January 1559, (2 Elizabeth) having iffue by Jane, his wife, four daughters, Mabel, Elizabeth, Catharine, and Elizabeth, whereof Catharine, was the firft wife of Chriftopher, Vifcount Gormanfton, and died in 1595. (2)

Sir Nicholas, a Prieft, Prebendary of Ballymore, and Treafurer of the Cathedral of St. Patrick, Dublin, to whom after the diffolution of that church, viz. 26 June, firft of his reign, K. Edward VI. granted a penfion of 66l. 13s. 4d. Irifh for life. (3)

Daughter, Margaret, was married to William (Mac-Theobald) Walfh, of Carrigmaine, in the county of Dublin, Efq. and had a daughter Joan [2], and a fon Richard, who by Eleanor, daughter of William Euftace, of Clongoofewood, Efq. by his wife Margaret, daughter of Maurice Fitz-Gerald, of Alnoon, county of Kildare, Efq. [3] was father of Howell Walfh, whofe wife was Elinor, daughter of Michael Fitz-William, of Dunore, hereafter mentioned. (1)

Alifon, firft married to Chriftopher Ufsher, Bailiff of Dublin, in the year 1500, twice Mayor thereof in 1518 and 1524, and by K. Henry VIII. in 1525, made Cuftomer and Collector of that port. * Her fecond hufband was Sir James Fitz-Symons, of Dublin, by whom fhe had a fon Nicholas; and her third was Alderman James Sedgrave, but by him fhe had no iffue [4]. (2)

Richard Fitz-William, of Baggotrath, Efq. in 1527, (19 Henry VIII.) was one of the Gentlemen of the King's Bedchamber, and that year made Senefchal for life of his Majefty's four manors of Newcaftle near Lyons, Efker, Taffagard, and Cromlin, with power to fubftitute a deputy, and to yield no accompt.—He married Catharine, daughter Richard.

---

* She was his fecond wife, and mother of John Ufher, Mayor of Dublin in 1561, who by Alifon, daughter of William Newman, was father of Sir William Ufher, Clerk of the Council, knighted by the L. D. Carew, 23 April 1603, who married Ifabel, daughter of Dr. Adam Loftus, Archbifhop of Dublin, and Lord Chancellor, and had Arthur, his heir, drowned at Dunfybrook.

[1] Ulfter. [2] Idem. [3] Lodge. [4] Ulfter.

ter of Robert Bathe, of Kepoke, in the county of Dublin, Esq. by his first wife Rose Woodlocke, and had three sons, Sir Thomas, Michael, and John; the second of whom Michael was seated at Donamore (or Dunore) in the county of Meath, and in the reigns of K. Edward, Q. Mary, and Q. Elizabeth, was Surveyor-General of the Crown-Lands; for his services in which station, and in respect of the singular favour, which the Queen bore to his uncle Sir William Fitz-William, deceased, her Majesty by Privy-Seal, dated at Greenwich, 25 May 1560, granted him a lease in reversion, of the manor and rectory of Donamore, for 21 years, after the end of his former interest of two years to come. He married Mary, daughter of Jenico, the third Viscount Gormanston, and had issue William who, as by inquisition, succeeded at Donamore, married, and had issue Elizabeth, who married first Edward Plunket, of Loghgor; and secondly, Peter Taaffe, Esq.[1]; Patrick; Eleanor, married to Howell Walsh, Esq. above-mentioned; Catharine, the second wife of George King, of Clontarfe, Esq. who died without issue by her, 13 July 1631; Jane; and Elizabeth, married to Gerald Fitz-Gerald, executed for murder in the time of the rebellion.

Sir Thomas. Sir Thomas Fitz-William, of Meryon, and of Baggotrath, the eldest son, had a grant of a special livery, a pardon of licence of alienation, and a pardon of intrusion, as son and heir to Richard Fitz-William, of Baggotrath, deceased, 20 December 1541[2]. He had a warrant from the Council of England 30 April 1551, to have a lease in reversion for 21 years, of the dissolved House of Holmpatrick, in the county of Dublin; which county he represented, with his father-in-law, in the Parliament of 1559, and in 1561, was Sheriff thereof; being also appointed Constable of Wicklow, in 1566, 8 Q. Elizabeth, and by a large commission, Seneschal or Chief Ruler of the Marshes of Dublin, the barony of Rathdowne, and over the Sept of the Archibolds, and all persons, of what degree or quality soever, within his jurisdiction; with a power to summon all the forces under his government at pleasure, and to take such order for the prosecuting of rebels and punishing malefactors, either in their lands, bodies or goods, as he should think fit; being also entrusted with full power to hear and determine

[1] Decree 10 May 1625.   [2] Rot. 33 Henry VIII. a. p. f.

determine all causes whatsoever, growing and arising between any the said inhabitants, or any other within the said marshes: And 15 Elizabeth, being again constituted Sheriff of the county of Dublin, a power was granted him to execute martial-law therein, upon all malefactors.

On 21 February 1578, he was nominated a Commissioner, for the making of limits and bounds of certain territories, appointed to be made shire-ground, and named the county of Wicklow, with the division thereof into six baronies.—In 1584, he made a settlement of his estate of Thorn-Castle, otherwise Meryon, which he held by Knight's-service, to the use of his eldest son Richard Fitz-William, for life, remainder to the sons of the said Richard, viz. Thomas, William and Christopher, in tail-mail, and to every other son that the said Richard should beget by his wife Jane Preston, or any other wife; remainder to his own second son Nicholas, and his heirs male; remainder to his third son Thomas, and his heirs male; remainder to William, eldest son of his late late brother Michael [1]. 10 October 1592, he gave to his well beloved son and heir Richard, all his corn in Holmpatrick, Skerries, Meryon, Boterstone, Simon's-Court and elsewhere, as well sown as unsown, or which thereafter should be sown, and all other his goods and chattels, which were not comprized in a former gift, made to his said son, to hold to such use, as by the said former gift and his last will was limited, and for further declaration of his said will, did thereby declare and notify, that his full mind, will, and bequest was, that his daughter Dame Catharine Fitz-Williams, Lady Gormanston, should have his full crop of corn, growing upon the demesnes of his farm-house of Holmpatrick, at the time of his death to her own use, and if the same was not then fully sown, then his will was, that all the fallow and birche, of that his demesne should be sown with such corn, as he then should have in his haggard or granaries there, and that she should have the same to her own use. And to his said son Richard, he left all such debts, rents, and duties, as should be due unto him, both out of all his lands and tithes, as otherwise, at the time of his death, to his own use; in consideration whereof, and of other things, he had left a portion and sum of money with his sons Nicholas and Thomas.—His wife was Genet, daughter of Patrick Finglas, of of Weſtpalſton, Eſq. Chief Baron of the Exchequer, by his wife Iſabella, alias Elizabeth, daughter of Robert Golding, of Churchtown, Eſq. and departing this life (as by inquiſition) 9 November 1592, had three ſons and one daughter, viz.

(1) Sir Richard, his ſucceſſor.

(2) Nicholas, of Holmpatrick and Balldungan, in the county of Dublin, who married Mabel, daughter of Walter Nangle, of Kildalky, in Meath, Eſq. died 5 December 1635, and was buried with his anceſtors in the church of Donnybrooke, having iſſue two ſons and two daughters, Thomas; Nicholas or Patrick; Mary, married to Bartholomew Ruſſell, of Seaton, county of Dublin, Gent.; Jane; Elizabeth, to John, ſon of Sir Richard Bolton, Chief Baron of the Exchequer; Eleanor, to James Birmingham, of Ballogh, Eſq.*; and Margaret, to William Underwood, of Dublin, Merchant.

(3) Thomas, of Moylagh, who married Mary, daughter of Chriſtopher Segrave, of Dublin, Eſq. and had a ſon Thomas, who died without iſſue.

(1) Daughter, Catharine, married firſt to James Plunket, of Dunſoghly, Eſq ſon and heir to Sir John Plunket, Chief Juſtice of the King's-Bench, and ſecondly, to Chriſtopher, the fourth Viſcount Gormanſton, to whom ſhe was ſecond wife, and was buried 10 February, 1602¹,.

Sir Richard. Sir Richard Fitz-William, of Meryon, was of full age at his father's death and married. He was Conſtable of the Caſtle of Wicklow, Lord Warden of the marches of Leinſter, in the reign of Q. Elizabeth; and 24 September 1593, brought two archers on horſeback to the general hoſting at Tarah; but died 5 March 1595, and (as is proved

---

* He was eldeſt ſon of Richard Birmingham, who died 13 March 1638; and with his wife Eleanor, lies buried under the Eaſt window, in the North aile of the church of Luſk, having a large table monument over them, with his effigies upon his knees, in compleat armour, and on the North-Ledge,

For James Firmyngham of Ballogh Eſquire,
On the South Ledge,
And his wife Elinor Fitz-Williams 1637
and on the Weſt Ledge,
WÆ IHI Mercatori

¹ Ulſter.

FITZ-WILLIAM, Viscount FITZ-WILLIAM.

proved by inquisition *post mortem*) was seized of Baggotrath, Finstown, Kepock, Baye, Kiltiernan, Lasturnan, Rathellin, Dullick, Chaunterstowne, Kintale, and Kilclogher, in county of Louth.[1]. He left issue by Jane, daughter of ——— Preston, five sons and two daughters, viz. Sir Thomas, created Viscount Meryon; William, of Dundrum, who in 1614, married Mary, daughter of Mr. Smyth, and widow of Dr. Henry Usher, Archbishop of Armagh [*], but died 16 July 1616, without issue; Christopher died childless in 1649; Patrick, killed by Sir Robert Newcomen, unmarried; Richard, of *the Rock*, the youngest son, who married the daughter of Sir Thady Duffe, of Dublin, Knt. and sister to Richard Duffe, Esq.; Catharine, (wife to Henry Chevers, of Monktown, in the county of Dublin, Esq. second son of John Chevers, of Macetown, son of Sir Christopher, son of Sir William or Walter, of Macetown, son of Sir Nicholas, of Ballyhally, in the county of Wexford, and by him, who died in June 1640, had Walter, who married Alison, daughter of Nicholas, Viscount Netterville; Thomas; and Patrick, who died unmarried); and Mary, first married to Matthew Plunket, the fifth Lord of Louth; and secondly, to Gerald Aylmer. Esq.

Sir Thomas Fitz-William, who succeeded at Meryon, was 14 years of age, at the time of his father's decease, and 23 August 1608, was honoured with knighthood; he was Sheriff the ensuing year of the county of Dublin; had a grant 17 December 1610, of 1000 acres of land, in the barony of Orier and county of Armagh, at the rent of 8l. English; and by K. Charles I. was advanced to the dignities of Baron Fitz-William, of Thorn-Castle, and Viscount Fitz-William of Meryon, by letters patent[†], dated

Sir Thomas, 1 Viscount.

---

[*] By Primate Usher she had three daughters, Margery, Mary, and Elinor; to the eldest of whom the said William, as executor to the Primate, was to pay 150l. and to the two younger 100l. each. (Lodge.)

[†] The Preamble. Vere Regium est eos e muis inter Subditos suos, quos ob eis Virtutibus præcellentiores et Nobilitate Sanguini eminentiores invenerunt, eos ad Honorum Gradus præ cæteris ejusdem Orbis evehere, *et in* Honoribus rite disponendis hoc præstat maxime, ut in eisdem Locis, ubi et propria et Antecessorum suorum Merita elucesserint, optime merent, quasi in propria Sphera sua moventes, Nobilitatis titulis insignire. Hinc est quod nos Thomam Fitz-William de Merryona in Comitatu nostro Dublinensi, five in

[‡] Chancery Decree made at St. Mary's Abbey, 23 June 1619.

dated at Cornbury, 5 August 1629, with the annual creation fee of 13l. 6s. 8d payable out of the customs of the port of Dublin.—In the first Parliament after his creation, held in the castle of Dublin 14 July 1634, he took his seat in the House of Lords, and was again present (after the recess) 4 November following¹; 24 October 1641, the day after the breaking out of the rebellion, his Lordship repaired to Dublin, and waited on the L. J. with great professions of his loyalty to the King, and readiness to assist in suppressing it; but their Lordships declining to accept his offer (being a Roman Catholic*) he went into England, and, with his two sons, there served K. Charles I. who, in recompence thereof, granted him a privy-seal for an Earldom of that kingdom; in virtue whereof the patent was drawn, and bears date at Oxford 1 May 1645, 21 Car. I. but the great seal not being then in the power of that unfortunate Prince, the patent could not be legally perfected; and, after the restoration, the family having a great man to their enemy, they were obliged to drop their undoubted claim to that honour: for these his services he was outlawed in Ireland, which outlawry was reversed by K. Charles II.

23 August 1605, he married Margaret, eldest daughter of Oliver, the fourth Lord of Louth, by his first wife Frances, daughter of Sir Nicholas Bagenal, Knight Mareschal of Ireland, and his issue were four sons; Richard, (by some falsely named Thomas) who married Ellinor, daughter of ———— Stanihurst, widow of Sir Henry Pierce, of Shercock,

---

in Comitatu Civitatis nostræ Dublinensis Militem ex antiqua Familia ejusdem Cognominis in Anglia, sed per aliquot Sæcula jam retroacta, in Regno nostro Hiberniæ transplantatæ, oriundum respiciente, recoslentesque generosam Prosapiam suam et Sanguinis Nobilitatem, et Antecessorum suorum fidelissima Servitia et Obsequia Coronæ nostræ Angliæ; utpote qui tempore Pacis Officio Capitalis Custodi Pacis in dicto Comitatu Dublinensi, Custodi Castri de Wicklae in eodem Regno, ot Vicecomitis dicti Comitatus Dublinensis, et primi Vicecomitis ejusdem Comitatus, et aliis Muneribus summa cum fidelitate et diligentia fungebantur; et qui tempore Belli contra Hostes et Rebelles fortiter et fideliter sese gesserint. Denique Virtutes et Fortunas proprias prædicti Thomæ animadvertentes, Progenitorum suorum haud minores, et Honori nostro et Meritis suis consentaneum esse duximus, ut eum in Baronem et Vicecomitem illius Regni nostri Hiberniæ erigeremus. Sciatis igitur, &c.

* It appears from the list of claims in 1662, that his Lordship frequently received and entertained rebels at Merrion, who robbed many persons about Baggotrath of their sheep, &c.

Shercock, in the county of Cavan, and died before his father without issue; Oliver, the second Viscount; Christopher, who by Jane, daughter of ——— Brereton, of Malpas, in Cheshire, Esq. left a daughter Alicia; and William, who succeeded his brother Oliver, in the honours.

Oliver, the second Viscount Fitz-William, after his succession to the titles, stipulated with the French King, to take 3000 men from England and Ireland, into France for his service, which he performed, and commanded them there as Colonel; and by articles, concluded in that kingdom with the Queen of K. Charles I. he was made General of 10,000 foot and 3000 horse, to be sent out of Ireland, to serve his Majesty in England; but the defeat at Naseby, (where he fought for the King) put a stop to this proceeding. —He was also a Lieutenant-General under the Marquess of Ormond; acquired a compleat victory at Roscomon, and gained the province of Conaught to the King's service; for which and other signal services, K. Charles II. created him Earl of Tyrconnel by patent, dated 20 April 1663[*], or rather 1661, for we find him Earl of Tyrconnel, 29 July that year, and 9 July 1662, he took his seat by proxy, in the House of Peers[1].

Oliver, 2 Viscount.

He married first Dorothy, sister to his brother Christopher's wife; and secondly the Lady Eleanor Holles, eldest daughter

---

[*] His Lordship being declared *Nocent* by the act of settlement, upon the account of a seditious and rebellious letter sent by him in 1646, to the Supreme Council, that clause was rendered null and void by the act of explanation, and he was restored to his estate in such condition, as if no such decree had been made: And it was further enacted, that he should hold and enjoy to him and his heirs, the lands in Keppocke in the county of Dublin, with those of Hanlaston and Athronan, in Meath, mortgaged by his father and forfeited to the crown; and that his Majesty's patent under the great seal of England, bearing date at Westminster, 8 June 1664, containing his gracious pardon to him of all crimes, treasons, &c. committed before 29 December 1660, in relation to any war in England and Ireland, or under colour of any commission or instruction of the King or his father, or any person in authority under them, or both houses of Parliament; and a clause of restitution to his estate, should be confirmed. He passed patent accordingly 11 July 1666, for Ringsend, Meryon, &c. in the counties of Dublin, Meath, and Wicklow; and that year made a settlement thereof to the use of himself and his Countess Eleanor, for their respective lives, remainder to the heirs male of their bodies, remainder to his brother William, for life; remainder to Thomas, son and heir apparent of the said William, and the heirs male of his body, with other remainders over. (Lodge Collect.)

[1] Lords Jour. I. 274. 317.

daughter of John, the first Earl of Clare *; but departing this life without issue, his brother William succeeded to the titles of Baron and Viscount, the Earldom, limited to the heirs male of his body, becoming extinct; and he lies buried under a handsome tomb of black marble, in the chapel of the family's foundation in Donnybrooke-Church, with this inscription, over which are the arms of Fitz-William, and the coronet, but no crest or supporters:

> Here lyeth the Body of the Right Honourable
> And most Noble Lord Oliver, Earl of Tyrconnel,
> Lord Viscount Fitz-Williams of Mervonge,
> Baron of Thorn-Castle, who died at his
> House in Meryong April 11th 1667, and was
> Buried the 12th day of the same month.

William, 3 Viscount.
William, the third Viscount Fitz-William, was Lieutenant-Colonel of the 3000 men, which his brother took into France, and in the time of the civil war was Governor of Whitchurch, in Shropshire, and Lieutenant-General of that county.—He married the daughter of Thomas Luttrell, of Luttrellstown, and sister to Thomas Luttrell, of Ranaghan, in Westmeath, Esq. (who by his will, dated 4 July 1673, settled his estate of Ranaghan, and Callaghtowne, on his nephew Thomas, Lord Fitz-William) and dying before the year 1681, had issue the said Thomas, his only son, and five daughters.

(1) Mary, married in May 1685, to John Browne, of Clongoosewood, in the county of Kildare, Esq. son and heir to Thomas

---

* She survived him, and preferred a petition to K. Charles II. for an abatement of the quit-rents, imposed on the estate by the act of explanation; in which she sets forth, "That her Lord was ever faithful to the interests and "persons of his Majesty and his father, and had several times exposed his life "and fortune upon that account; but notwithstanding, upon a very great "mistake, it was his misfortune to pass for a Nocent in the Court of Claims, "and to have his estate adjudged forfeited: But, upon better information, his "Majesty being fully satisfied of his loyalty and integrity, was pleased to "take off that mark of delinquency, to restore him to the possession of his "estate, and to give order for taking off the quit-rents; but his Lordship "dying before he could enjoy the benefit of his Majesty's intentions, she "prayed for a discharge thereof." Which was not only granted 6 November 1667, but she had also a pension of 300l. a year for life, from his Majesty's bounty.—She is called Ellen in the grant of her prayer, and in the reversionary grant thereof to Adam Loftus and Samuel Kingdon, Esqrs. 30 May 1677, she is called Bridget. (Lodge and Rolls Office.)

FITZ-WILLIAM, Viscount FITZ-WILLIAM.

Thomas Browne, Esq. Counsellor at Law, and by him, who died in 1693, had three sons and two daughters, Stephen Fitz-William; Christopher, of Castle-Browne; Bruno, Counsellor at Law; Alice, married to Mr. John Taylor; and Anne, who died unmarried in 1737, and was buried at Maynham, with her brother Christopher.

Rose, to Christopher Mapas, of Winston, Esq. who (2) died 19 February 1718, and was buried at St. Audeon's, leaving by her, who deceased 1 March 1744, John Mapas, of Rochestown, in the county of Dublin, Esq.

Margaret, to James Crawley, Esq. whose daughter Isma, (3) married ——— Russel, Esq.

Catharine, to Nicholas, son of Robert Netterville, of (4) Crucerath, in Meath, Esq.

Dorothy, to Thomas Magher, of the Queen's County, (5) Esq.

Thomas, the fourth Viscount Fitz-William, was of the Privy-Council to K. James II. by whom he was appointed 17 June 1690, a Commissioner of the Treasury; commanded a regiment of horse in his army; 12 October 1695, he appeared in the House of Lords to take his seat, but bringing no writ of summons, his Lordship was not admitted, on the 19 he again appeared and took the oath of fidelity, but being again required to take the other oaths and make and sign the declaration his Lordship said he would consider of it and withdrew; and 2 December 1697, the Lord Viscount Massareene reported from the committee appointed to inspect the journals, &c. of that House, that the said Lord Fitz-William had been outlawed, but had reversed the same[1].—He married to his first wife Mary, daughter of Sir Philip Stapleton, of Wigill, in the county of York, Bart. by whom he had Richard, his heir; and a daughter married to her first cousin the said Stephen Fitz-William Browne, of Castle-Browne, in the county of Kildare, Esq. who died 23 July 1722.—His Lordship's second wife, was sister to George Pitt, of Stratfieldsea, in the county of Southampton, Esq. and by her he had a daughter Mary, married 11 March 1718, to George, Earl of Shrewsbury. He departed this life 20 February 1704, and was succeeded by his only son

Thomas, 4 Viscount.

Richard, the fifth Viscount, who 18 May 1710, conforming to the established religion, took his seat in the House

Richard, 5 Viscount.

[1] Lords Jour. I. 525. 550, and 673.

House of Peers the 25 of that month [1]; his Lordship was of the committee appointed 14 November 1715, to prepare an addrefs to congratulate K. George I. on his accefsion to the throne; 9 October 1714, he was called into the Privy-Council, as he was by K. George II. on his accefsion to the Crown; and in January 1726, he was elected to Parliament for the borough of Fowey, in Cornwall.—He married Frances, only daughter of Sir John Shelley, of Michael-Grove, in Suffex, Bart. (who died 25 April 1703, by his firft wife Mary, only daughter of George Nevil, Lord Abergavenny, who died 2 June 1666, and fifter to Lord George, who died without iffue 26 March 1695) and his Lordfhip deceafing at Thorpe, in Surry, 6 June 1743, left iffue by his faid wife, who died 11 December 1771, aged 99, three fons and two daughters, viz.

(1) Richard, his fuccefsor.

(2) William, baptized 11 September 1712, was appointed in July 1747, Ufher of the Black-Rod in Ireland, 4 December 1750, married the only daughter of Thomas Bouchier, Efq. and had an only child Julia, who died of a confumption at Abergavenny in July 1770 [2].

(3) John, baptized 28 March 1714, was made Page of Honour 17 November 1726, to his Royal Highnefs the Prince of Wales; was one of the Equerries to Prince William; was appointed 30 September 1731, a Cornet in the Horfe-Guards, Blue, and in November 1745, Captain of a troop in the fame regiment; being alfo in January 1746, made a Groom of the Bedchamber to his Royal Highnefs the Duke of Cumberland; in 1754, returned to Parliament for the borough of New Windfor; in 1755, made Colonel of the fecond regiment of foot; and 26 March 1765, a Lieutenant-General [3].—In October 1751, he married Barbara, daughter of Doctor Chandler, Bifhop of Durham, and widow of ——— Cavendifh, Efq. [4].

(1) Daughter Mary, appointed 27 April 1726, Maid of Honour to Caroline, Princefs of Wales, in which ftation fhe ferved her when Queen, was firft married 28 Auguft 1733, to Henry, Earl of Pembroke, by him, who died 9 January 1749, hath an only fon Henry, Earl of Pembroke, born 3 July 1734; fhe married fecondly in September 1751,

North

---

[1] Lords Jour. II. 349.   [2] Lodge.   [3] Idem and Gazette.   [4] Almon's Peerage.

FITZ-WILLIAM, Viscount FITZ-WILLIAM.

North Ludlow Bernard, Esq. Major of Dragoons, who died at Nenagh in November 1754, and she died 13 February 1769[1].

Frances, married 18 May 1732, to George, Lord Carbery. (2)

Richard, the sixth Viscount Fitz-William, baptized in St. Andrew's Parish, Dublin, 24 July 1711, was appointed 18 November 1733, Cornet in the Royal Regiment of Horse, commanded by his brother-in-law the Earl of Pembroke, and at his father's death was, in Germany, in his Majesty's service.—On 28 May 1744, being elected a Knight Companion of the Order of the Bath, he was installed 20 October following; and in April 1746, was made a Member of his Majesty's Privy-Council; he was Vice-Admiral of the province of Leinster, and Fellow of the Royal Society.—On 3 May 1744, his Lordship married Catharine, daughter of Sir Matthew Decker, of Richmond, in Surry, Bart. who died 18 March 1748, and had four sons, viz. *Richard, 6 Viscount,*

Richard, his heir. (1)

William, married 25 August 1782, to the only daughter and heir of John Eames, Esq. one of the Masters in the High Court of Chancery, in England. (2)

John, and (3)

Thomas[2], who in July 1780, married Agnes, daughter of ——— Macclesfield, Esq. (4)

His Lordship deceasing 25 May 1776, was interred in Donnybrook-Chapel[3], near Dublin, being succeeded in the honour by his eldest son

Richard, the seventh and present Viscount, born in August 1745. *Richard, 7 Viscount.*

TITLES.] Richard Fitz-William, Lord Viscount Fitz-William, of Meryon, now Merrion, and Baron Fitz-William, of Thorn-Castle, in the county of Dublin.

CREATION.] So created 5 August 1629, 5 Car. I.

ARMS.] Lozengy, Pearl and Ruby.

CREST.] In a ducal Coronet, Topaz, a double Plume of five Ostrich Feathers, Pearl.

SUPPORTERS.] Two Ostriches, Pearl, each holding in its Beak, a golden Horse-Shoe.

MOTTO.] DEO ADJUVANTE, NON TIMENDUM.

SEATS.]

---

[1] Lodge.   [2] Ulster.   [3] Idem.

SEATS.] Mount-Merrion, in the county of Dublin, 3 miles from the city; and Thorpe, in the county of Surry, 23 miles from London.

COCKAINE, VISCOUNT CULLEN.

14.

John.
Andreas.
William.

THE family of Cokyn, Cokeyn, Cockaine, for many ages was seated at Ashburne, in the county of Derby, whereof was John Cokeyn, the father of Andreas, whose son William, by Sarah, his wife, had a son of his own name, who taking to wife Alice, daughter of Hugh de Dalbury, left two sons, Roger, living in 1284; and John, living in 1276, who married Matildis (Maud) daughter of Robert Olderney, and had a son Andrew, who died, without issue in 1284, 12 Edward I. and a daughter Margery.

Roger.

William.

John.

John.
John.

Roger Cockeyn, of Ashburne, Esq. by Elizabeth, his wife had two sons and three daughters, William, Richard, Margaret, Elizabeth, and Sarah.—William, the elder son, lived at Ashburne, in 1299 (28 Edward I.) and married Sarah, daughter of Adam, the sister of Aldercinder, a Merchant of Ashburne, by whom he had John his heir; and Robert, who left issue William and Elizabeth.—John was living at Ashburne, 33 Edward I. 1305, and was father of John Cockayne, residing there 17 Edward II. who by Letitia, his wife, was father of another John, living 46 Edward III. a person of great distinction in that King's reign, in several of whose Parliaments he represented the county of Derby; and in the 22 year, with Adam de Houghton, the

county

COCKAINE, Viscount CULLEN.

county of Lancaster, being allowed their expences of 15l. 4s. for thirty days attendance.

He married Cecilia, daughter of —— Vernon, of the county of Derby, and had two sons, Edmund, his heir; and Sir John Cockaine, of Bury-Hatley, in the county of Bedford, which manor he purchased from Sir Edward Butler, and (as Fuller, in his Worthies of England, writes) founded a worshipful family at, and imparted his name to Cockaine-Hatley.—He was born at Ashburne, in the county of Derby;[1]—In 1394, was Recorder of London[2]; 15 November 1401 (2 Henry IV.) Chief Baron of the Exchequer, and 14 May 1405, made one of the Justices of Common-Pleas, by that King, with whom he sided in 1403, against Henry Percy Earl of Northumberland, Thomas Percy Earl of Worcester, Henry Percy surnamed *Hotspur*, and their adherents, who in July the year before, with the Earl of Dunbar, (who had deserted his countrymen) obtained a signal victory over the Scots at Halwedown-Hill, wherein Earl Douglas, their General, was wounded, and taken prisoner with many others; all whom the King demanding of the Earl of Northumberland, not only took them from him, but forbad him his presence; which treatment, together with his refusing to reimburse the expences he had been at, in his wardenship of the marches, raised so great a discontent, as to effect the ruin of himself and son : for hereupon flying into rebellion, he raised a considerable army in Northumberland and Scotland, with which he met and fought the King at Shrewsbury who obtained the victory over him, after a very sharp engagement; but Sir John Cockaine lost his life on Saturday, the eve of St. Mary Magdalen, having in the morning received the honour of Knighthood.

He lies buried in the North-Aile of the parish church of Ashburne, under a monument, with his effigies in his Judge's robes, thus inscribed :

Tumuli Alabastrini JOHANNIS COKAIN primo Capitalis Baronis de Scaccario, deinde unius Justiciariorum de Communi Banco sub Rege HENRICO IIII^{ti} accurata Effigies.

[1] Fuller's Worthies. [2] Maitland H. 1205.

COCKAINE, Viscount CULLEN.

He married Edith, sister to Reginald, Lord Grey, of Ruthen, by whom he had four sons and two daughters, Reginald; Henry; John, living 13 Henry VI.; Thomas, Chaplain to his uncle the Lord Grey; Elizabeth, married to Sir Philip Butler; and Cicely, to Edward, son of Nicholas Fitz-Symons, of Symonsid and of Almesse, in Hertfordshire.—Reginald, of Cockain-Hatley, the eldest son, was living in 1424, (2 Henry VI.) and married Beatrix, one of the four daughters and coheirs of John Walleys*, by Joan, daughter and heir to Sir Richard Turk, which John, in 1430, gave to them his manor of Woodcroft, in Bedfordshire, and by her he had John, his heir, John, called the younger; Philippa; and Margaret.—John, the elder son, married Elizabeth, eldest of the three daughters and coheirs of John Boyville, Esq. who died in 1468, in which year on 17 May, the manor of Little Packington, in Warwickshire, came by partition to her, and he deceasing 22 June 1490, left a daughter Beatrix, married to Sir Thomas Tyrrel; and Edmund Cockaine, his successor, sheriff of the counties of Bedford and Bucks, 8 Henry VII. who sold the last mentioned manor to Sir Robert Brudenell, of Dene, about the latter end of that King's reign, and died in 1515, leaving issue by Elizabeth Lock, his wife, four sons and one daughter, viz. William; Humphry, whose wife's name was Margaret; John; Edmund; and Anne; the eldest of whom died in 1527, having married to his first wife Dorothy, and to his second Catharine, daughter of John Savage, by which last he left issue two sons and three daughters, Chad; John, who left no issue; Frances, married to William Markham; Isabel, to Michael Fisher, of Clifton; and Margaret.—Chad, the elder son, married Elizabeth, daughter of Sir Walter Luke, Chief Baron of the Exchequer, and had four sons and as many daughters, viz. John; Nicholas; George; William; Rose, married to ——— Spencer, of Copley, in the county of Bedford; Margery; Judith, married to John Reynont, of Ashwell, in the county of Herts; and Frances. John, the eldest by Elizabeth, daughter of Thomas Stacey, had six sons, viz, Lodowic, John, Oliver, Nicholas, Lawrence, and Thomas. Lodowic, the

---

* Son of Sir William, Lord of Patchington, in Sussex, 1 Henry IV. who was son and heir to Sir John Walfisse, living 14 Edward III. the son of Sir Godfrey de Walliffe, the son of another Sir Godfrey. (Lodge).

the eldest was ancestor to Samuel Cockaine, of Cockaine-Hatley, Esq. a Captain in his Majesty's navy, who died in January 1745.

We now return to Edmund Cockaine, of Ashburne, Esq. eldest son of John, by Cecilia Vernon. He was living there in the reigns of Richard II. and Henry IV. and marrying Elizabeth, daughter of Sir Richard de Herthull, of Pooley, in Warwickshire, heir to her nephew William, who died in 1403, 3 Henry IV. had that estate, and by her, who after married John Franceis, of Ingleby, in the said county, he had Sir John Cockaine, who for some time resided at Pooley, where he made three several wills, the first in 6 Henry IV. the second in 13, and the third in the 14 Henry IV. each sealed with his army of three cocks, and the crest a cock's head. The occasion of his making the second will was, his being summoned to France in aid of the Duke of Orleans against the Duke of Burgundy; it bears date the Thursday next after the Feast of St. Barnabas, and therein it appears, that having enfeoffed Sir John Dabridgecourt, and others, in his manor of Badiley-Endsor, in Warwickshire, to raise a certain sum of money thereout, for payment of his debts, and towards a marriage-portion for his daughter Elyn; he directed, that then his feoffees should make an estate thereof unto John his son and heir, and the heirs of his body; and in case of his death without issue, it should be amortized to find as many Priests, singing to the world's end, for his soul and those of his wife, children, and all his ancestors, as the rent thereof would reasonably maintain; namely, in St. Marie Chapel at Polseworth, 5l. to one priest in St. Marie Chapel; near Ashburne, 7 marcs to another, and the remainder to be spent in wax, vigils and alms-deeds, on the eve and day of his *Obit*.

He lived many years after this voyage, was a Justice of Peace in the county of Warwick from 5 Henry V. to the end of that reign, and in 1418, a Commissioner of Array. In the 1. 7. and 13. years of King Henry VI. he was Sheriff of the counties of Nottingham and Derby‡; and 12 of that reign, Knight in Parliament for the latter county, and one of the King's Commissioners to make a return of the gentry thereof.—He generally bore the arms of his mother's family, she being a great heiress, which were

argent,

‡ Fuller's Worthies.

argent, two barrs, vert; and died in 1438 (16 Henry VI.) leaving iſſue by Iſabel, daughter of Sir Hugh Shirley, anceſtor to Earl Ferrers, four ſons and one daughter, viz. John, anceſtor to the family of Aſhburne; William, from whom the Lord Cullen derives; Roger; Reginald; and Ellen (or Alice) married to Sir Ralph Shirley, Knt.

Family of Aſhburne. John Cockaine, of Aſhburne, Eſq. married Anne, daughter of Sir Richard Vernon; died in 1505, 20 Henry VII. and had two ſons Thomas and Roger; the elder of whom lived at Pooley, and having ſome difference with Thomas Burdet, of Bramcote, in Warwickſhire, Eſq. his near neighbour, ſo irritated him with affronts, that he was killed by Burdet, in his paſſage to Poleſworth-Church, in his father's life-time; and having married Agnes, daughter of Robert Barlow, of Barlow, Eſq. left two ſons, Thomas, ſucceſſor to his grandfather, and Henry.—Which Thomas, attended K. Henry VIII. into France, and there purchaſed knighthood by his gallant behaviour at the ſieges of Therouenne and Tournay. In the 12 and 21 years of that King, he was Sheriff of the counties of Derby and Nottingham, and reſided chiefly at Pooley, which manor-houſe he rebuilt with brick, and in 1507, (22 Henry VII.) imparked the woods lying weſtwards thereof, where his grandſon Sir Thomas frequently reſided in Q. Elizabeth's time.—On 4 April 1537, (28 Henry VIII.) he made his will, directing his body to be buried in our Lady's choir in Aſhburne, (where his anceſtors lay interred) before the image of St. Modwen, and appointed his executors to cauſe a marble tomb to be made there for him; which was accordingly performed with this inſcription:

> Here cheſted in this tomb, and cloſed in this clay,
> Doth lye Sir Thomas Cockaine, Knt. and muſt till Judgment-day.
> This martial man ſo bold, and eke this warlike Wight
> At Tyrwin and at Turney Siege was dubb'd a worthy Knight.
> Three goodly houſes he did build, to his great praiſe and fame,
> With profits great and manifold belonging to the ſame:
> Three

COCKAINE, Viscount CULLEN.

Three parks he did impale, therein to chafe the deer,
The lofty lodge within this park he alfo builded here.
He did his houfe and name renew, and eke the fame re-
    ftore,
Which others had with negligence in time decayed be-
    fore.
This virtuous Knight had iffue male 3 fons of manly
    port,
And eke 3 daughters virtuous, and married in this fort;
The eldeft to her hufband had a Knight of worthy fame,
Sir William Baffet, Lord of Blore, he called was by
    name.
To Vincent Lowe of Denby Squyer the fecond married
    was,
The third to Robert Burdet Squyer, as fate did bring to
    pafs.
The bodie of this worthy Knight fhall never come to
    Hell,
But yet in tomb of marble ftone 'till Judgment day fhall
    dwell.

His wife was Barbara, daughter of John Fitz-Herbert, Efq. Remembrancer to K. Henry VII. and his iffue were Francis, his fucceffor; Thomas; Anthony, who died childlefs; Anne, married to Sir William Baffet, of Blore, in Staffordfhire, Knt. Jane, to Vincent Lowe; and Elizabeth, to Robert Burdet, of Newton-Burdet, Efq. Member of Parliament for the county of Warwick, 1 Edward VI. who dying 11 January following, was by her, great-grandfather of Sir Thomas Burdet, of Sekington and Bramcote, created a Baronet 25 February 1618.

Francis Cockaine, of Afhburne and Pooley, Efq. married Dorothy, only daughter and heir of Thomas Marrow, Efq. Serjeant at Law, in the reign of Henry VII. by his wife Ifabel, daughter of Nicholas Brome, of Badfley, Efq. and by her (who remarried with Sir Humphry Ferrers, and was buried in the chancel of Badfley-Clinton Church, Warwickfhire, under a large ftone, with a plain crofs thereon, but no infcription) he had three fons and two daughters, Thomas; Francis, who married the daughter and heir of ———— Browne, of Wiltfhire; William; Alice, who in 1544, (36 Henry VIII.) was the wife of Sir Edward Lyttelton

telton (seventh son of Sir Edward of Pillaton-Hall) Sheriff July of the county of Stafford 5 Eliz. by him, who died 19 1574, had eight sons and several daughters, and she lies buried with him in Penkrich-Church, under an altar tomb of white marble ; and Barbara (or Dorothy) was married to John Ferrers, of Tamworth-Castle, Esq.

Sir Thomas, who succeeded, in 1544, accompanied Edward, Earl of Hertford, in his expedition to Scotland, by sea, with a large fleet and well provided army, and was knighted by him at the taking of Leith and Edinburgh; after the plundering and burning of which places, he attended him by land into England. In 3 Edward VI. and 1 and 11 Elizabeth he was Sheriff of the counties of Nottingham and Derby, as he was 21 and 27, of the latter county.[1]— In 1539, he married Dorothy, daughter of the before-mentioned Sir Humphry Ferrers, and dying 15 November 1592, was buried with his ancestors at Ashburne, having had issue five sons and five daughters, viz. Francis, born in 1545, who 35 Elizabeth, was sheriff of Derbyshire, married Anne, daughter of Sir Valentine Knightley, of the county of Northampton, and died childless in 1596 ; Thomas, born in 1550, died young ; Edward, who became heir ; John, Thomas, Tabitha born in 1549, Florence, Jane, Maud, all died unmarried; and Dorothy, wife to Jermyn Poole, of Radburne, Esq.

Edward Cockaine, of Ashburne, Esq. born in 1554, was Sheriff of the county of Derby, 42 Elizabeth, married Jane, daughter of Nicholas Ashby, Esq. died in 1606, and left Thomas his heir; who by Anne, daughter of Sir John Stanhope, of Elvaston (ancestor to Charles, Earl of Harrington) was father of Sir Aston Cockaine, born 28 December 1608, who married Anne, daughter of Sir Gilbert Kniveton, of Mircaston, in Derbyshire, Bart. and being a Romanist, suffered much for his religion and the King's cause in the civil wars; and then pretended to be a Baronet, created, after the King had by violence been compelled to leave the Parliament, about 10 January 1641, yet not so deemed by the officers of arms, because no patent was either inrolled, or mentioned in the docquet books belonging to the Clerk of the Crown in Chancery, to justify it. He was esteemed by many an ingenious gentleman, a good poet, and a great lover of learning ; yet by others a perfect

buon

---

[1] Fuller's Worthies.

boon fellow, by which means he wasted all his estate, having sold his Lordship of Pooley, to Humfrey Jennings, Esq. (reserving an annuity for life) several years before his death, which happened at Derby in February 1683, and the 13 of that month he was buried in the Chancel of Polesworth-Church.

We now proceed with William, younger son of Sir John Cockaine and Isabel Shirley, Progenitor to the Lord Viscount Cullen.—He was the father of Thomas Cockaine, Esq. the father of Roger, of Baddesley, in the county of Warwick, the father of William Cockaine, of London, Citizen and Skinner, and also Merchant-Adventurer in the Muscovy, Spanish, Portugal and Eastland Companies, of which last he was Governor; he married twice, but by the first wife Elizabeth, daughter of Roger Medcalfe, of Wensgale had only issue; and deceasing in 1599, was buried in the church of St. Peter Le Poor, London, under a handsome monument at the East end of the Chancel, with this memorial:

William
Thomas
Roger
William

> Here lieth the Body of the Worshipful Mr.
> William Cockaine the Elder, Citizen and Skinner
> of London, who departed this Life the 18th.
> Day of November. 1599. Also here lieth the Body
> of Elizabeth Medcalfe his first wife, by whom
> He had 7 Sons and 4 daughters. All which
> Daughters departed this Life before any of them
> Accomplished the Age of ten Years. The 7 Sons
> Lived, and the youngest of them (at his Death)
> Was fully 28 Years of Age. Which said Elizabeth
> Departed this Life the 5th. day of April 1589.
> Here also lieth the Body of Catharine Wonton,
> His second Wife, who died the 19th of September
> 1596, by whom he had no Issue.

Sir William Cockaine, who succeeded his father, also a Citizen and Skinner of London, and in 1609 Sheriff of that city; elected soon after an Alderman; and in 1612, K. James having the plantation of Ulster much at heart, granted a considerable tract of land in that province to the city of London; who sent over about 300 artificers, to begin and forward the plantation thereof, and appointed Mr. Cockaine their first Director and Governor, who had lands

was Sir William

assigned

assigned him there, and under whose directions the city of Londonderry was established.—On 8 June 1616, the King honoured him with his presence at dinner, at his house in London, when he was pleased to make him a Knight; with whom he was in such esteem, that he was often heard by him in parliament, and at the Council Table, and consulted with him in most private affairs; and so well satisfied was that King with his comprehension of business; his manner of conceiving his intentions; digesting and uttering his purposes, that he used to say of him, *He never heard any man of his breeding, handle business more rationally, more pertinently, more elegantly, more persuasively.*—In 1619[1], he served the office of Lord Mayor of London, and that year purchased the manor of Elmsthorpe in the county of Leicester from Sir John Harrington: but in 1626, after two days sickness, he departed this life, in a most exemplary manner, and was buried 12 December in the Cathedral Church of St. Paul, when a sermon was preached by Dr. John Donne, Dean of that church, in which his character may be seen at large; and in the South Aile a Monument was set up, in memory of so good a Magistrate, and worthy a Citizen, with the following inscription:

M. S.
Gulielmus Cockainus, Eques Auratus
Civis et Senator Londinensis, sep:
:temque abhinc Annis Urbis præfec:
:tus: Antiquâ Cockainorum Derbi:
:ensium Familiâ oriundus. Qui Bo:
:no Publico vixit, et Damno Publico
Decessit, et Gaudio Publico Regem
Jacobum, ad Decorem hujus Domus
Dei, senescentis jam et corrugatæ, re:
:stituendum, solenniter huc venien:
:tem Consulatu suo, magnifice exce:
:pit; idcirco in Templo Publico, ad
Æternam Rei Memoriam,
   Hic situs est.
At vero et Famæ celebritas, quæ viget
in Ore Hominum, et Gloria Beatitu:
:dinis, quam migrando adeptus est,
Et Splendor Sobolis, quam numero:

:sam

[1] Maitland, II. 1196.

:fam genuit, atque nobilem reliquit,
Junctim efficiunt omnia, ne dicatur.
   Hic situs est.
Unâ cum illo, tot Homines mortui, quot
In illo defunctæ sunt virtutes; simul:
:que et Acies Ingenii et popularis Elo :
:quii suada, et morum gravitas, et
Probitas vitæ, et Candor Mentis, et
Animi Constantia, et Prudentia singu:
:laris, et veri Senatoris Insignia
   Hic sepulta sunt.
Jam tuum est, Lector, Felicitatis ad cul:
:men anhelare per ista vestigia Laudis,
et venerandi Imitatione Exempli, cu:
:rare, ne unquam virtutis sic Semina
Intereant, ut dicatur,
   Hic sepulta sunt.
Obiit 20 Octob. An. Dom. 1626.
   Et Ætatis suæ 66.

His wife was Mary, daughter of Richard Morris, of London, Esq. by whom he had two sons, Charles, created Viscount Cullen; William; and six daughters, viz.

Mary, married 22 April, 1620, to Charles Howard, the second Earl of Nottingham, to whom she was second wife, and had no issue. (1)

Anne, the second wife to Sir Hatton Fermor, of Easton-Neston, in Northamptonshire, Knt. and grandmother of William, created Lord Lempster, ancestor to George, Earl of Pomfret. (2)

Martha, second wife to John Ramsay, created 30 December 1620, Earl of Holdernesse, for preserving the life of K. James I. from the conspiracy of John Ruthen, Earl of Gowrie on 5 August 1600; but he dying without issue in February 1625, she became the first wife of Montagu Bertie, the second Earl of Lindsey, and died in July 1641, being grandmother of Robert, created Duke of Ancaster. (3)

Elizabeth, first married to Sir Richard Fanshaw, Knt. and Bart. (younger brother of Thomas, Viscount Fanshaw, of Dromore) Master of the Requests, Secretary of State, and Ambassador in Spain and Portugal; after whose death she (4)
            became

became second wife of Sir Thomas Rich, of Sunning, in Berkshire, created a Baronet 20 March 1660*.

(5) Abigail, the second wife of John Cary, Earl of Dover, and having an only daughter Mary, married to William Heveningham, of Heveningham, in Suffolk, Esq. that title became extinct.

(6) Jane died unmarried.

Charles, 1 Viscount.
Charles Cockaine, Esq. the elder son, was seated at Rushton, in Northamptonshire, of which county he was Sheriff in 1635 (11 Car I.) and advanced to the Peerage of Ireland by patent, dated 11 August 1642.—He married the Lady Mary O'Brien, second daughter and coheir to Henry, the fifth Earl of Thomond, and by her, who re-married with George Blount, Esq. had Bryan, his successor, and a daughter Elizabeth.

Bryan, 2 Viscount,
Bryan, the second Viscount, in 1662, gave to the Vicarage of Drenchworth, in Berkshire, as an augmentation, the annual stipend of 23l. 6s. 8d. being worth before only about twenty nobles a year; and marrying Elizabeth, daughter and heir to Sir Francis Trentham, of the county of Stafford, Knt. she brought him the rich Lordship of Rosceter, in that county, and Castle-Heveningham, in Essex; by her, who died 30 November 1713, æt. 50, his Lordship had three sons and two daughters, Charles, Trentham, George, Elizabeth and Mary.

Charles, 3 Viscount.
Charles, the eldest son, and third Viscount Cullen, was left a minor, and married Catharine, youngest of the five daughters of William, Lord Willoughby, of Parham, by his wife Anne, daughter of Sir William Cary, by whom he left

Charles, 4 Viscount.
Charles, the fourth Viscount, who marrying Anne, sister to Borlace Warren, of Stapleford, in the county of Nottingham, Esq. was father of

Charles, 5 Viscount.
Charles, the fifth and present Viscount, who was born the 2 of September 1710, and 4 May 1732, married his first cousin Anne, daughter of the said Borlace Warren, Esq. who was chosen 8 May 1734, Member of Parliament for Nottingham,

---

* They were of an uncommon charitable disposition and generous spirit. For besides his large charities whilst living, he left 16,000l. to the like uses; and she left some thousands in annual charities for ever to debtors in Ludgate and St. Peter Le Poor, and to clergymen's widows. He died 15 October 1667, æt. 66. and had one son Sir William, ancestor to the present Sir Thomas Rich, Bart.; and one daughter Mary, married to Sir Robert Gayer, Knight of the Bath.

tingham, (and died in May 1747) and by her Ladyship who died in London, in July 1754, had Charles, Borlace, and John, who died unmarried, and six daughters, of whom Anna-Maria, the only survivor, became the wife of Nathaniel Mapletoft, of Broughton, in Northamptonshire. —His Lordship married secondly, Sophia, daughter of John Baxter, Esq. by whom he has issue William, who married Barbara, youngest daughter of George Hill, of Rowell, in county of Northampton, Esq. his Majesty's Prime Serjeant at Law, and has issue [1].

TITLE.] Charles Cockaine, Lord Viscount Cullen, in the county of Donegall.

CREATION.] So created 11 August 1642, 17 Car. I.

ARMS.] Pearl, 3 Cocks, Ruby, crested and jelloped, Diamond, a Crescent upon a Crescent for difference.

CREST.] On a wreath, a Cock's Head erased, Ruby, crested and jelloped as those in the coat.

SUPPORTERS.] The Dexter, parte per Fess, Topaz and Pearl; a Lion, Guardant. The Sinister, an Ostrich, Pearl, holding in his Beak, an Horse Shoe, proper.

MOTTO.] VIRTUS IN ARDUIS.

SEAT.] Rushton, in the county of Northampton, 63 miles from London.

[1] Information of Lord Viscount Cullen.

END OF THE FOURTH VOLUME.

THE INDEX.

A

Acton, John 103
Aldworth, George 81
Allen, James 12
―――― Thomas 146
Altham, Lord 129
―――― Arthur 130, 134
―――― James 130
―――― Richard ib.
Anderson, Francis 82
―――― Henry 222
―――― John 82
Andrews, William 66
Annally, O'Farrell, Prince of 21
Anneslei, Richard de 99
Annesley, Arthur 121, 128
―――― Charles 126
―――― Francis 109
―――― George 108
―――― Hugh 104
―――― James 127
―――― John 101, 128
―――― Maurice 118

―――― Ralph 99
―――― Reginald 99
Annesley, Robert 108
―――― Thomas 104
Antrim, Earl of 185
Archbold, William 214
Archdeckne, Richard 60
Argyle, Duke of 247
Arran, Earl of 55
Arthur, Prince 80
Arundel, Earl of 15
Ashburnham, Lord 63
―――― William 83
Ashwell, John 100
Aston, Arthur 49
―――― Edward 221
Athenry, Lord 247
Aubrey, John 282
Aungier, Lord 27
―――― Francis 281
Auvuquerque, Lord 61
Aylmer, Andrew 40, 211
Aylward, John 18
Axtell, *Colonel* 67, 70

Vol. IV.   Z   Babington,

INDEX.

B

Babington, John	104	Betagh, Thomas	211
Bagenal, Dudley	70	Bingham, Henry	241
——— George	32	Bird, John	256
——— Walter	60, 70	Birmingham, Meiler de	157
Bagot, Edward	284	Blacket, William	26, 264
——— John	79	Blake, Francis	119
——— Walter-Wagstaffe	284	——— Henry	119
Bagshaw, John	198	——— Martin	175
Baker, John	120	——— Richard	167
Baltimore, Lord	199	Blanchville, Edmund	19, 39
Banastre, Robert	282	——— Gerald	29
Barlow, Robert	326	Blandeston, Laurence	218
Barnewall, Alexander	207	Blayney, Lord	119
——— Christopher	160	Blount, Richard	105, 106
——— Edward	154		107
——— John	202	Blundel, William	72
——— Peter	26	Bodkin, John	231
——— Thomas	143	Bodley, Laurence	164
Barrett, Richard	239	——— Thomas	164
Basset, William	327	Boteler, John	82
Bath, Lucas	143	Bourke, John	194, 228
——— Bartholomew	142	——— Miles	232
Bathe, John	208	——— Redmond	38, 168
Bayning, Viscount	84, 88	——— Richard	228
Bealing, Richard	67	——— Rickard Fitz-David	
——— Henry	67		232
Beaufort, Edmund	15	——— Ulick	184
Beaumont, Anthony	83	——— Walter	118
——— Richard	81	Boyle, Richard	109
Becket, Thomas	3	Boynton, Mathew	165
Bellers, John	72	Bowless, Thomas	231
Bellew, Lord	71, 42	Brabazon, Anthony	181
——— Christopher	175	Bradstreet, Samuel	75
——— John	195, 139	——— Simon	ib.
——— Patrick	195	Branthwaite, Richard	66
Bermingham, Edward	31	Bredalbane, Earl of	94
Beresford, John	225	Brereton, William	220
Bergavenny, Lord	14	Brett, William	292
Berkeley, Lord	26	Bridgewater, Duke of	97
Berwick, Duke of	63	Bristol, Earl of	86
Betagh, James	177	Broc, Richard del	100
		——— Robert del	100
		Brome, Nicholas	327
		Broughton, Christopher	129
		Browne,	

INDEX.

Browne, Dominick 139
——— Francis 81
——— Geoffry 139
——— Valentine 199
Bruce, Edward 6
——— Peter 252
Bryan, Francis 25
Buchan, Earl of 255
Buckingham, Duke of 130
——— Marquefs of 200
Bullen, Thomas 17
——— William ib.
Bulleyne, Thomas 16
Bullock, William 219
Burdett, Thomas 326
Burgo, Richard de 5
Burke, Bingham 119
——— Dominick ib.
——— Theobald 235, 244
Burnell, John 2
Burton, Samuel 217
Bufby, Edmond 105
Buffy, George 97
——— Buttevant, Vifcount 38, 163
BUTLER, VISC. MOUNT-GARRET 1
——— Herveius 2
——— Herveius Walter 3
——— Theobald 3, 5, 6
——— Richard 18
——— Edmund 6
——— James 7, 8, 9, 11, 14, 42, 43, 59
——— John 15
——— Thomas 16, 31
——— Pierce 19, 28, 35
——— Walter 28, 60
——— Philip 11
Byde, George 90
——— John ib.

Byde, Skinner 90
Byron, Lord 222
——— Robert 47
Byrne, Gerald 44

C

Cahier, Lord 21, 30, 41
Caldwell, Richard 262
Callow, Lord 169, 174
Cantilupe, Nicholas de 102
Carden, William 120
Carey, Thomas 212
Carew, Peter 32
——— Richard 106
Carpenter, Lord 304
Carrick, Earl of 6
Carrick-Mac-Griffyne, Earl of 7
Carter, Thomas 165
Carteret, George 124
Caftlehaven, Earl of 41
Caftleton, Earl of 271
Caftlemaine, Earl of 88
Cave, Henry 84
Cavenagh, Morgan Mac-Bryan 40
——— Bryan 42
——— Donnell Reogh Mac-Murrough 19
——— Murtogh 18
Cavendifh, Henry 75
Chamberlayne, Thomas 285
Chambre, Calcot 81
Chandos, John 103
——— Walter ib.
Chatham, Earl of 91
Chaworth, George 105
Chernocke, St. John 84
——— Pynfent 84
——— Villiers 84
Chefterfield, Earl of 57
Chetwode, Richard 221
Chevers, Walter 212

Z 2   Chevercourt,

INDEX.

Chevercourt, Jordande	100	——— Vincent	220
Chicheley, Thomas	125	Cornwall, John	108
Chichester, John	203	Cornwallis, Lord	56
Chiffinch, William	95	Costello, John Fitz-Edmond	
Cholmondeley, Robert	220		232
Clancarthy, Earl of	39	Cotton, George	222
Claneboy, Viscount	161	——— Rowland	222
Clanrickarde, Earl of	189,	Courtenay, Thomas	165
	291	Courtenay, Peter	121
Clarence, Duke of	11	Coward, William	126
Clarke, Richard	81	Creiff, Thomas	81
Clervaux, John	254	Crew, Lord	64
Clifford, Lord	202	Crofton, Edward	176
——— Coniers	230	——— George	ib.
Clifton, Gervaise	104	Cromwell, Oliver	193
Clovile, William	108	Crosbie, John	118
Clynch, Patrick	141	Cruise, John	203
COCKAINE, CULLEN, VIS-		Culpepper, Lord	157
COUNT	322	Curson, John	104
——— Bryan	332	Cusack, Christopher	143
——— Charles	ib.	——— Thomas	203
——— Edward	328		
——— Francis	327	**D**	
——— John	326		
——— Roger	329	Dagworth, Thomas	8
——— Thomas	328,	Dakin, John	219
	329	Dalton, Christopher	174
——— William	329	——— Walter	47
Cockeyn, Andreas	332	Daly, Denis	195
——— John	ib.	——— John	182
——— Roger	ib.	Dandre, Walter	251
Coke, William	48	D'Arcie, Lord	262
Colclough, Thomas	43	Darcy, John	8, 138
Collier, James	221	——— Nicholas	39
Comerford, John	46	Darell, John	279
Compton, Henry	83	Davis, George	183
——— Thomas	ib.	Dayrell, Paul	198
Coney, George	221	Decies, Lord of	21
——— Matthew	109	Delawar, Lord	282
Cooke, George	120	Delion, Henry	136
Coote, Charles	187	——— Lochan	135
Copley, Christopher	313	Delvin, Lord	41
Cork, Earl of	ib.	Denham, John	85
Corbet, Andrew	220	Denmark, Prince of	61

Denn,

INDEX.

Denn, Patrick	28	Dillon, William	181
De le Touche, Count	200	Doily, Robert	67
Derby, Earl of	128	Domvile, Gilbert	301
Desmond, E.	25, 32, 33, 43	Donegal, Earl of	57
D'Estaing, Count	199	Dongan, Viscount	191
Devenish, Edward	174	Donnellan, Lochlin	139
Devereux, John	27	Dorrington, Francis	276
———— Nicholas	24, 29	Dove, Robert	108
Devonshire, Duke of	59	Doyne, Robert	118
Digby, John	80	Dowell, Lucas	181
DILLON, (DILLON) VISCOUNT	135	———— Luke	182
		Drury, William	224
———— Archbishop	196	Duff, Thadeus	210
———— Arthur	196	Dunboyne, Lord	21, 41,
———— Bartholomew	19,	Dungannon, Viscount	40
	142, 143, 145	Dunn, Hugh O'Connor	183, 184
———— Christopher	160, 174, 184	Dunsany, Lord	203
———— Edmund	174, 181, 194	Dutton, John	220
		———— Richard	166
———— Garrett	194	Dwynham, John	282
———— George	187		
———— Gerald	169, 172, 181	**E**	
———— Henry	136, 137, 157	Egerton, Randal	223
		Elye, Prince of	9, 10
———— James	160, 172, 182, 184	Esmond, Earl of	27
		———— John	43
———— John	148, 181, 193, 194	———— Laurence	28, 43
		Essex, Earl of	96
———— Josias	177	Eustace, Maurice	28
———— Lucas	155	———— Rowland	26
———— Lucius	192	Everard, Richard	211
———— Maurice	140	Evers, Walter	292
———— Pierce	181		
———— Redmond	171	**F**	
———— Richard	170, 174, 175	Falconberg, Earl of	268
———— Robert	71, 137, 144, 161, 172, 184, 193	Falkland, Viscount	91, 92
		Fallon, John	210
———— Theobald	177, 190, 193, 194	Fanshaw, Thomas	276
		Farnaby, Charles	275
———— Thomas	137, 170, 182	Farrell, Brian	183
		Felton, Thomas	86

FERDINAND,

INDEX.

Ferdinando, King of Spain 80
Fermor, Laurence 280
——— Thomas ib.
Ferrall, Dennis 170
——— James 193, 210
Ferrers, John 56, 328
Ferreter, Dominick 294
Fettiplace, John 285
Fienes, Richard 84
Fingall, Earl of 41
Fitz Gerald, Edmund 45
——— Gerald 144
——— Gerald Fitz-John 21, 29, 90, 168
——— Maurice 21, 181
Fitzharding, Viscount 94
Fitz-Herbert, John 327
Fitz-James, Pierce-Butler 41
Fitz-Patrick, Andrew 67
——— John 40
Fitz-Ralph, Robert 102
Fitz-Roy, Charles 88, 89
——— George 89
Fitz-Warine, Fulk 5
Fitz-William, (Fitz-William, Viscount 306
——— Henry 308
——— John ib.
——— Philip ib.
——— Richard ib. 309, 311
——— Stephen 308
——— Thomas 309, 310
——— William 104, 307, 308
Fleming, George 19
——— John 68
Florence, Duke of 261
Flood, Frederick 133

Folliott, Lord 164
Forgusa, Andrew 255
Fortescue, James 147
Fowke, Thomas 93
Fowler, Francis-Levison 225
Frankland, Frederick 269
——— Thomas 199
French, John 157
Friscott, Don Francisco 209

G

Galmoy, Viscount of 48
Gammage, John 274
Gayer, Robert 127
Gennour, Richard 105
Geoghegan, Charles 144
Gerard, Lord 222
Glen, Gilbert de 78
Goddard, Austin Parke 142
Goldston, Thomas 16
Gore, Arthur 119
Gormanstown, Viscount 30
Gough, Edward 28
Gouldsmith, John 239
——— Francis ib.
Gouvernet, Count de la Tour du Pin 200
Gowran, Earl of 9, 56
Grace, Gerald 47
——— Oliver b. 74
——— William 49
Grandison, Lord 81
Greene, John 130
Gregor, Thomas 102
Grenvil, John 122
Grey, Lord 14
Griffin, Edward 84
Guiscard, Count 62
Gunning, Bryan 247
——— John ib.

H

Hales, John 68
Hall,

INDEX

Hall, John 106
Hallum, Robert de 220
Hamilton, Lord 93
————— George 40
Hankford, Richard 16
Harrington, Earl of 328
————— John 81
Harris, Ralph 198
Harrison, Richard 90
Haterington, Thomas de 103
Hatton, Fermor 331
Haversham, Lord 128
Hayward, Rowland 276
Herald, William 140
Herbert, John 105
————— Nicholas 89
Hereford, Thomas de 5
Hern, Frederick 96
Hervey, John 107
————— Sympkin 280
————— Thomas 107
Hexstall, William 220
Hewett, George 85
Hibbots, Thomas 209
Hoey, John ib.
Holderneſſe, Earl of 331
Hollywood, Robert 204
Horden, Lord of 251
Horne, John 105
Horſepoole, Simon 276
Howard, Lord 83
Hughes, Francis Anneſley 118
Huſſey, Thomas 211
Hyde, John 78
Hynde, George 174

I and J

Ikerrin, Viſcount 38
Iwareby, John 106
Jennings, Richard 194
Jephſon, Anthony 279

Jermyn, Alexander 264
Jerningham, William 198
Jerſey, Earl of 86
————— Lord 95
Jeſſon, William 85
Jocelyn, Thomas 78
JONES, VISCOUNT RANE-
   LAGH 300
————— Roger 184, 300,
                             301
————— Thomas 81, 300
————— John 123
Jordan, Waker 174
Judd, Andrew 274

K

Kelly, William 176
Kenmare, Lord 42
Kent, Earl of 79
Kildare, Earl of 6, 14, 21, 202
KILMOREY, (NEEDHAM)
   VISCOUNT 218
King, John 111, 185
Kingſland, Viſcount 214
Kirtling, Lord of 5
Kiteley, John 11
Knightley, Valentine 328
Kniveton, Gilbert ib.
Know, Francis 119

L

Lacy, John 222
Lally, Edmund 181
————— General 193
Lamborn, John 108
Lanſdown, Lord 94
Langdale, Lord 71
Langley, Roger 264
Lanier, John 265
Latimer, Lord 103
Latin, Patrick 170
           Lauderdale,

INDEX.

Lauderdale, Duke of	125	Mac-Carthy, Donogh Moyle	290
Lawless, Richard	61	Mac-Dermot, Terence	160
Lee, Family of	197	Mac-Donnell, Felix	177
Leech, Randolph	105	Mace, Philip de	100
Legge, Mr.	122	Mac-Egan, Owen	290
Leigh, Charles	129	Mac-Geoghegan, Bryan	109, 113
——— Francis	82		
——— Reginald	ib.	Mac-Mahon, Bernard	12
Lennard, Henry	107	——— Bryan	44
——— William	ib.	Mac-Shane, Dermoid	21
Lenox, Earl of	25	Macworth, John	104
Levinge, Richard	126	——— Thomas	ib.
Lichteburgh, Robert	307	Magawly, James	181
Ligondes, Chevalier de	225	Magrath, Meiler	28, 30
Lincoln, Earl of	101	Mahon, Nicholas	167
Litchfield, Earl of	84, 197	Malby, Nicholas	234
Longueville, Edward	302	Mallady, Patrick	160
Lovelace, William	105	Malone, Richard	176
Lucas, Lucas	185	Mandeville, James	43
——— Theobald	ib.	Mansel, Buffy	96
——— Thomas	ib.	Mansfield, Robert	12
Lumbard, John	10	Manwaring, John	220
Ludlow, Edmund	123	——— Randal	ib.
LUMLEY, (LUMLEY) VISCOUNT	250	Mapholder, Patrick	169
——— Liulph	ib.	Mapletoft, Nathaniel	333
——— Marmaduke	252	March, Earl of	12
——— Osbert	250	Markham, Robert	129
——— Ralph	252	Marlborough, Duke of	82
——— Robert	251	Marreis, John de	5
——— Roger ib.	262	Mason, Aland-John	91
——— Uchtred	250	Massareene, Viscount	195
——— William	251	Masterson, Richard	40
Luttrell, Thomas	36, 204	Mathew, George	43, 70
Luxemburgh, Marechal de	59	——— Theobald	30
Lynch, Henry	244	——— Toby	49
Lyster, John	175	Maynard, William	119
		MAYO, (BURKE) VISCOUNT	227
M		MAXIMILIAN, EMPEROR	16
		Meering, William	79
Mac-Carthy, Charles	48	Melure, Roger	218
——— Cormac	28	Mescines, Randolph	1
		Meyler,	

INDEX.

Meyler, Nicholas	29	Neville, Cosmas	199
Moigne, John	103	Newburgh, Thomas	119
Molyneux, Viscount	30	Newman, Dillon	147
——— Robert	77	Newport, Earl of	83
Monmouth, Duke of	61	Nithsdale, Earl of	84
Montacute, John	16	Norfolk, Duke of	17, 26
Montgomery, Thomas	305	Norris, John	106
Moor, John	193	Norton, Dudley	111
Moore, Lord	212	Nottingham, Peter	143
——— Garrett	192	Nugent, John	139
——— Michael	182		
——— William	289	**O**	
Mordaunt, Mr.	122		
More Mac-Carthy	172	O'Brien, Donald	31
——— O'Sullivan	33	——— Donogh	21
Morres, Hervey	49	——— William	144
Morris, William	122	O'Carroll, Carroll	28
Mortimer, Roger	7	——— John	27, 169, 193
Morton, Earl of	3, 4		
——— Mathew Ducie	268	——— Moelrony	17
MOUNT-GARRET, (BUTLER) VISCOUNT	1	——— Teige	10
		O'Cavanagh, Gerald	12
——— Lord	33, 41, 45	O'Connor, Bryan	47
		——— Hugh	192
Mountjoy, Lord	106	——— Hugh Oge	ib.
Murray, Walter	49	——— Teige Mac Dermot	183
		O'Donnel, Neylan	12
N		O'Dowde, Dominick	182
		O'Dwyer, John	28
Nangle, Robert	26	O'Farrell, Lord Callow	169, 174
Napea, Osep	261		
Needham, John	219	——— Connell	171
——— Robert	ib.	——— John	193
——— Thomas	220	——— Major General	167
——— William	219		
NETTERVILLE, (NETTERVILLE) VISCOUNT	208	——— Roger	160
		O'Ferrall, Prince of Annaly	137
——— Formal	203	Offeley, Thomas	210
——— Patrick	210	O'Flaherty, Bryan	232
——— Richard	ib.	——— Edmund	231
		——— Finola	ib.

VOL. IV.   A a   O'Flaherty,

INDEX.

O'Flaherty, John Bourke 246
———— Murrough 232
O'Flinn, Wodeney 4
O' Flynn, Columb 139
Ogle, Lord 259
———— Samuel 129
O'Gonagh, Mac-Brien 28
O'Hanlon, Patrick 109
O'Hanly, Dowaltagh Mac-Farry 183
O'Hara, Thady 216
———— Hiberies 298
O'Hedian, Richard 12
O'Kelly, Cornelius 139
———— Saba 231
———— William 139
O'Kennedy, Conor 298
O'Madden, 185
O'Maly, Owen 235
O'Molloy, William 160
O'More, Rory 21
———— Owny Mac-Rory 33
O'Mulrian, Connor 14
O'Neile, Charles 74
———— Daniel ib.
———— Owen 12
———— Phelim 293
———— Shane 25, 154
Onslow, Thomas 221
Orange, Prince of 59
O'Reily, Gildas 17
Ormond, Earl of 22, 27, 29, 39, 125
———— Marquis 187
O'Rourke, Con 183
O'Shaghnessey, Roger 210
Ossory, Earl of 59
Oughton, Adolphus 284
Oxenbridge, Edward 254

P

Pakeman, Simon 79
Park, James 81
Parker, Henry John 142
Parkyns, Isham 260
Parsons, William 162
Patrick, Mac-Gill 21
Paul, Jeffrey 118
Paulet, Amias 68
———— Philip . ib.
Pegge, Strelly 118
Pennington, John 92
Perkins, John 107
Perrot, John 117
Pershall, William 296
Petty, John 106
Pettyt, William 137, 169
Peyton, Thomas 122
Phaire, Robert 131
Phillips, John 117
Phineux, John 277
Pierpoint, John de 101
Piers, Henry 301
Pincheon, William 214
Pitt, George 319
———— Robert 91
———— Weston 210
Plantagenet, Richard 11
Plunkett, Alexander 19
———— Christopher 172
———— George 143
———— John 155, 206
———— Oliver 143
———— Patrick 168
———— Richard 157
———— Thomas 164, 184
Poer, Lord 21, 38
Pointz, John 39
Pole, Courtenay 215
Pope,

INDEX.

Pope, Thomas	198	Ruſſel, George		157
Porter, Endymion	83			
Portland, Earl of	83, 94, 214	**S**		
Powell, Robert	221	Saliſbury, Earl of		16
Prendergaſt, Thomas	28	Salkeld, Richard		15
Preſt, John	130	Samwell, Thomas		284
Preſton, Richard	38	Sancta Maria, Adam de		100
——— Robert	141			
Prowe, Robert	260	Sandys, Samuel		285
Pugil, Arnold	100	Sarsfield, Dominick		112
Puiſſars, Marqueſs	93	——— John		157
Purcell, Hugh	5	——— William		146
——— Philip	60, 68	Saunders, Arthur		119
——— Thomas	28	——— Richard		108
——— Toby	74	——— William		82
Purdon, Adam	301	Savage, John		219
		——— Philip		72
R		Saville, Thomas		84
		Say, Bryan		252
Radcliffe, George	44	——— Patrick		ib.
——— Robert	219	Sedley, Charles		127
Radiſh, John	218	Selby, James		ib.
RANELAGH, (JONES) VISCOUNT	300	Scriven, Richard		223
		Scrope, Stephen		10
Rayner, William	83	Scurlock, Barnabas		204
Reilly, Hugh	74	Shakerly, Peter		220
Ridge, John	184	Shaw, John		224
Rigdon, William	210	Shee, Edmund		40
Rimbrieck, Colman	135	——— Richard		40, 72
Roberts, Lord	52	——— Robert		60
Robinſon, James	85	Sheldon, *General*		196
——— John	ib.	——— Gilbert		53
Rocheſter, Earl of	63	——— Ralph		196
Rochford, Viſcount	20	——— Thomas		84
——— Robert	45	Shelley, Henry		264
Roper, Robert	140	——— John		320
Roſcommon, Earl of	46	Sherlock, John		28
Roſſe, Viſcount	216	Shirley, Hugh		326
Roſſiter, John	93	Shortall, Nicholas	18, 28
Roumarſh, Lord	100	——— Oliver	28, 30
Rupert, Prince	125	Shuckburgh, ———		264
Rupella, Philip de	6	Sidney, Robert		275

INDEX.

Simeons, George	70
Slane, Lord	19, 48
Slinsby, Francis	175
Smith, Edward	215
——— Erasmus	55
——— William	81
Smyth, Lionel	279
——— Philip	29
——— Thomas	274
Snape, Edmund	106
——— John	ib.
——— Richard	105
Somerset, Duke of	15
——————— Edward	164
Southhill, John	80
Southwell, Robert	57
Spencer, Thomas	66
Spendlowe, Peter	142
Springe, Thomas	118
Stafford, Richard	15
Stampe, John	106
Standish, Ralph	70
Stanly, James	71
Starkey, John	219
Steuart, Brigadier General	91
——— James	163
——— William	91
St. John, John	85
——————— Oliver	86
St. Laurence, Christopher	141
St. Leger, George	16
Stocdale, Thomas	111
Stourton, Lord	103
St. Quintin, Robert de	100
STRANGFORD, (SMYTHE) VISCOUNT	274
Stranguish, John	254
Suffolk, Earl of	86
Sussex, Earl of	84
Surrey, Earl of	19

T

TAAFFE, (TAAFFE) VISCOUNT	287
——— Lord	186, 294
——— George	144
——— John	288, 289
——— Lawrence	288
——— Nicholas	287, 288, 289, 298
——— Peter	288
——— Richard	287
——— Theobald	294
——— Thomas	288
Talbot, Lord	8, 103
——— Henry	176, 194
——— John	14, 182
——— Matthew	131
——— Richard	71, 160
——— Robert	71
Tencastle, John	219
Temple, Nugent	153
Thomond, Earl	21, 27, 31
Thompson, William	264
Thorp, John	160
Thurles, Viscount	24, 36
——— Lord	64
Thweng, Marmaduke de	251
Tobin, James	29
——— John	49
——— Thomas	29
Toole, John	134
Touraine, Duke of	15
Townshend, Lord	153
Trahern, Henry	7
Trentham, Francis	332
Tressenville, Ralph de	101
Trimblestown Lord	203
Tryon, Samuel	108
Tuite, Edward	173

Tuite,

INDEX.

Tuite, William	170	Walsh, Walter	28, 144
Tulleophelim, Lord	37	——— James	30
Tully, James	210	Wandesford, Mr.	44
Turner, John	106	Warburton, Peter	222
Tynte, Robert	30	Warren, Abel	67
Tyrconnel, Duke of	194, 204	——— Borlace	332
		——— Henry	118
Tyrone, Earl of	66, 216	Warwick, Earl of	15
Tyrrel, George	198	Washington, William	83
Tyrwhit, William	254	Waterhouse, Edward	81
Twisden, Philip	97	Wenman, (Wenman)	
		Viscount	280
U		——— Lord	86
		——— Henry	280
Upper-Offory, Lord	38	——— Richard	280, 281
		——— Thomas	ib.
V		Wentworth, Lord	44
		Westcot, Christopher	198
Valaines, Theobald de	3	Westmeath, Earl of	191
Valentia, Lord	112	Weston, Benjamin	84
Vassen, James Lewis le	93	Wharton, George	163
Vaux, Lord	70	Whitaker, William	304
Vavesor, Robert de	4	White, James	25
Venables, Thomas	220	——— Nicholas	9
Vernon, George Venables	97	Whitebrooke, John	276
		Wildgose, John	107
Villiers, Alexander	78	——— Annesley	ib.
——— Edward	92, 97	Willoughby, Lord	304
——— George	81, 85	——— Edmund	104
——— Geoffrey	79	Wilmot, Viscount	187
——— John	78, 79, 80	Wingar, John	81
——— Nicholas	78	Winnington, John	220
——— Paganus	76, 77	Wolverston, George	47
——— William	77, 78, 79, 81, 85	Woodhouse, Ernulph de	100
Vylers, Alexander de	78	Wotton, Henry	85
		Wright, Nathaniel	ib.
W		Wroughton, Seymour	284
		Wycombe, William	306
Wake, Lord	79	Wyers, James	204
Wale, Gerald	28		

Wykham,

INDEX.

Wykham, William Humphrey   286

Y

York, Duke of   11, 15

Young, Edward   199

Z

Zobel, *Colonel*   25

FINIS.

www.ingramcontent.com/pod-product-compliance
Lightning Source LLC
Chambersburg PA
CBHW020235240426
43672CB00006B/540